24 HRS AT
THE SOMME
1 JULY 1916

24 HRS AT
THE SOMME
1 JULY 1916

ROBERT KERSHAW

1 3 5 7 9 10 8 6 4 2

WH Allen, an imprint of Ebury Publishing,
20 Vauxhall Bridge Road,
London SW1V 2SA

WH Allen is part of the Penguin Random House group of companies
whose addresses can be found at global.penguinrandomhouse.com

Penguin
Random House
UK

First published by WH Allen in 2016

www.eburypublishing.co.uk

A CIP catalogue record for this book is available from the British Library

ISBN 9780753555477

Maps by Tim Mitchell
Typeset in India by Thomson Digital Pvt Ltd, Noida, Delhi
Printed and bound in Great Britain by Clays Ltd, St Ives PLC

Penguin Random House is committed to a sustainable future for our
business, our readers and our planet. This book is made from Forest
Stewardship Council® certified paper.

Contents

10. Blood-Red Sunset
9.30 pm to midnight

The Somme Time-Line

1914

28 JUNE   Assassination of Franz Ferdinand in Sarajevo.

28 JULY   Austria declares war on Serbia.

29 JULY   Russia mobilises.

3 AUGUST   German invasion of Belgium.

4 AUGUST   Britain enters the war.

SEPTEMBER   German advance halted at the Marne.

               German Army on the defensive in Somme area.

               Kitchener appeals for mass British volunteer army.

OCTOBER   First battle of Ypres, Western Front stabilised.

1915

6–8 DECEMBER   Chantilly Conference. Allies agree to launch co-ordinated offensives across battlefronts in the west, east and south.

19 DECEMBER   General Sir Douglas Haig takes over as Commander-in-Chief BEF from Field Marshal Sir John French.

29 DECEMBER   Haig attends conference to discuss Anglo-French offensive on the Somme.

1916

24 JANUARY	First Military Service (Conscription) Bill passed by British House of Commons.
21 FEBRUARY	The German offensive at Verdun begins.
12 MARCH	Allied Conference at Chantilly for coming summer offensive.
25 MAY	British conscription extended.
31 MAY	Naval battle of Jutland.
4 JUNE	Russian Brusilov offensive begins on the Eastern Front.
5 JUNE	Kitchener drowned during the sinking of HMS *Hampshire* en route to Russia to discuss joint strategy.
24 JUNE	Beginning of the preliminary bombardment for the Somme battle.
27 JUNE	Haig moves his headquarters forward to the Château Valvion, 12 miles from the front.
28 JUNE	H-Hour postponed for two days due to bad weather.
30 JUNE, MIDNIGHT	Relief of some German regiments in the Somme line under way. 158 British battalions march forward from village staging areas to the front line.
1 JULY 5.46 AM	Sunrise.
7.20 AM	Hawthorne mine explodes in front of Beaumont Hamel.
7.28 AM	Remainder of preliminary mines exploded.
7.30 AM	H-Hour.

8.30 AM	30,000 of 66,000 British infantry are casualties. The Schwaben Redoubt is captured. There is failure between Gommecourt and Beaumont Hamel and between Thiepval and Fricourt. Partial success near Mametz and Montauban.

9.30 AM — Only one third of objectives are taken, one third of the remainder achieve only small enclaves, the rest are repulsed.

The French attack to the south of the River Somme and achieve total surprise.

9.45 AM — Generalmajor von Soden orders the recapture of the Schwaben Redoubt, taken by the 36th Ulster Division.

11.15 AM — Orders issued for the recapture of the Schwaben Redoubt.

MIDDAY — The British have suffered 50,000 casualties and have been repelled along 80 per cent of the front. Comparative lull.

1 PM — There is success to the right of the line next to the French XX Corps, and Mametz and Montauban are captured.

2.30 PM — 50th Brigade attack repulsed at Fricourt.

2.45 PM — Last British attacks called off. Haig confers with Rawlinson, Commander Fourth Army.

3 PM — German three-pronged counter-attack underway against the Schwaben Redoubt. Losing impetus at 4 pm.

7 PM — Haig places VIII and X Corps under command of Lt.-Gen. Gough, forming new Fifth Army. Planned attacks cancelled.

9 PM	German artillery fire concentrated on the Schwaben Redoubt to support the final counter-attack to restore the Thiepval plateau.
10.03 PM	Sunset Last-ditch elements of the London Division quit Gommecourt and the 36th Ulster Division survivors depart the Schwaben Redoubt. British wounded and stragglers return to the British line.
10.30 PM.	The Germans recapture the Schwaben Redoubt.
MIDNIGHT	The German line is restored across 80 per cent of the front to Fricourt. The British have penetrated just over one mile to the right at Mametz and Montauban.
18 NOVEMBER	The end of the battle of the Somme.

1917

6 APRIL	The United States declares war on Germany.
OCTOBER–NOVEMBER	The Russian Revolution begins, ceasefire Eastern Front.

1918

MARCH	Final German offensive in the west, the Somme gains re-occupied.
APRIL–JULY	Successive German attacks.
JULY	Allied turning point.
NOVEMBER	Final Allied assaults.
9 NOVEMBER	The Kaiser abdicates.
11 NOVEMBER	German Armistice in the west.

Introduction

In 1916, when the war had been going on for 24 months, and even though the previous year had seen a complete victory for defence, the war continued to have popular support in Britain, as in Germany. The conflict was not going well for the Allies. Verdun in early 1916 was bleeding the French Army white. Kitchener's 'New Army', the 'Pals' battalions, recruited in the first flush of 1914 enthusiasm, was filling in the line along the Somme. They replaced skeletal regular and Territorial Army battalions, decimated by two years of Western Front stalemate. The plan was to overcome the impasse with combined Allied offensives from west, east and south, but the 'Big Push' had to be prematurely launched by the British to relieve the French crisis at Verdun. Kitchener's un-blooded recruits were prematurely hurled at the German Western Front through a storm of machine-gun and shell fire against intact barbed wire before they were ready. On 1 July 1916 more than half the size of the present-day British Army perished in the first 24 hours at the battle of the Somme.

This iconic day transformed the prevailing opinion in Britain that one 'Big Push' mounted with spirit, patriotism and guts would see the end of the war. It was a day when hope died. The British General Staff placed its faith in an optimistic concept that concentrated artillery fire would clear the way for Kitchener's untrained army to conduct a 'cake-walk' through the German lines.

24 Hours at the Somme describes that catastrophic day hour by hour through the differing perspectives of both sides. The British trench view is juxtaposed against that from the German parapet and dugout alongside the backdrop of their staff commands, who, ensconced in châteaux to the rear, could see nothing. Staffs on the Western Front were not soft-hearted. Planning and decisions were to decimate 75 British battalions, the equivalent of six divisions of infantry.

No single battle has had such a widespread emotional impact on the psyche of the British public. Two hours of the 24 decided the battle. By nightfall 57,470 men lay dead, or were wounded or missing, at a cost of just 6,000 German dead. They encapsulated the cream of British volunteer manhood. Relatives from these casualties would have numbered some six million, from a population of 43 million, so that 13 per cent of the island community was affected by one day's events. Entire districts and streets in major cities and rural village communities retired behind dark curtains having lost their menfolk that day. A documentary film was made and released even before the battle had finished four months later. It is estimated that within six weeks of its release 20 million people had viewed it at 1,500 cinemas across the country. Men were seen to fall on screen as they clambered out of their trenches on that July day, bringing home the horrors of war to the public for the first time. 'Oh my God, they're dead!' cried out one woman in the audience. Almost half the population queued to see *The Battle of the Somme,* a box-office success that has never been equalled. More British soldiers died on 1 July 1916 than were lost in the Crimean, Boer and Korean wars combined.

The day begins with optimism and expectation in the crowded British trenches. Nothing, they are convinced, could have survived the seven-day artillery concentration preceding the attack. But the Germans secure in their deep dugouts have survived. They are veterans.

I have to date avoided writing about the Great War. Two questions have posed an enigma. As a former serving soldier, it is immensely difficult to rationalise what motivates simple soldiers to advance to certain death in the face of intense machine-gun fire and battered by overwhelming artillery fire. They volunteered to do this, following impractical orders, even though the carnage of the leading waves was strewn about the ground before them. How could this happen?

The second conundrum is that senior officers, probably more intellectually gifted than you or I, sent them on their way. How could this be so?

24 Hours at the Somme charts this dreadful day through the eyes, ears and senses of the soldiers themselves, through eyewitness accounts, diaries, unit logs and a mass of supporting material exhaustively harvested from across Europe. Château generalship is juxtaposed with the trench parapet view.

It attempts to offer some answers by using the words of the soldiers themselves to explain what happened. The reader may judge.

The Chain of Command

ARMY
Commanded by a **General**.
Comprised about four corps, but precise numbers depended on the army's role.

CORPS
Commanded by a **Lieutenant-General.**
Usually comprised three or four divisions.

DIVISION
Commanded by a **Major-General.**
Usually comprised three brigades.

BRIGADE
Commanded by a **Brigadier-General.**
Four battalions.
German equivalent comprised two Regiments each of three battalions with a machine-gun (MG) company.

BATTALION
Commanded by a **Lieutenant-Colonel.**
Four companies. Normally about 900 to 1,000 men with MG platoon.
German equivalent 1,000 men with 90-man MG company.

COMPANY

Commanded by a **Major** or **Captain**.

Four platoons. About 200 to 250 men.

German equivalent about 230 men with MG platoon.

PLATOON

Commanded by a **Lieutenant.**

Four sections. About 40 men.

German equivalent 45 men.

SECTION/SQUAD

Commanded by a **Corporal** with 8 to 10 men.

British and German Ranks

Field Marshal	Generalfeldmarschall
General	Generaloberst
Lieutenant-General	General der Infanterie, Kavallerie etc
Major-General	Generalmajor
Brigadier-General	no German equivalent
Colonel	Oberst
Lieutenant-Colonel	Oberstleutnant
Major	Major
Captain	Hauptmann
	Rittmeister (cavalry)
Lieutenant	Oberleutnant
Second Lieutenant	Leutnant
Sergeant-Major	Stabsfeldwebel or Feldwebel (ac to unit)
Staff Sergeant	Vizefeldwebel
Sergeant	Feldwebel
Corporal	Unteroffizier/Gefreiter
Officer deputy (cadet)	Offizierstellvertreter
Artillery gunner	Kanonier
Light machine-gunner	Musketier
Rifleman	Schütze
Infantryman	Landsturmmann /Grenadier/ Füsilier
Driver	Fahrer

Some of the Voices from the Somme

THE BRITISH

Private Albert Andrews was with the 19th Manchesters opposite Montauban. His great-grandfather had charged with the Light Brigade at Balaclava. A former clerk, Albert was not taken in by the 'bull' of Kitchener's New Army. He would go over the top with a cigarette in his mouth.

Corporal George Ashurst, with the Lancashire Fusiliers, was aware of the ugly mood in the ranks when they were given a pep talk by their 29th Division Commander, General de Lisle. They were lined up and told not a single German would bar their progress to Beaumont Hamel after the massive artillery bombardment going on in the background. He and his men were not so sure; they had experienced catastrophe at Gallipoli the year before.

Captain Charles Carrington, with the 1/5th Royal Warwickshire Regiment, was manning the battalion command dugout overlooking Gommecourt Wood. As the acting adjutant, he was to report back to brigade what he saw once the attack started. He could not see anything.

Lieutenant Richard 'Rex' Cary, with the 9th London Rifles, was in fine fettle waiting for the attack on Serre. Next month he would be engaged to Doris Mummery from Leytonstone – her parents had just agreed.

Brigadier-General John Charteris was General Haig's over-optimistic intelligence chief. Despite the inexperience of the troops, he was quietly confident about the coming attack. A 14-hour day was the norm for General Staff officers.

Lieutenant-General Walter Congreve, commanding XIII Corps on the far right of the British line between Mametz and Montauban, next to the French XX Corps, was the only corps commander to achieve all his objectives this day.

Lieutenant-Colonel Frank Crozier, with the 9th Royal Irish, would attack the Schwaben Redoubt with the later waves of the reserve brigade of the 36th Ulster Division. He had taken the UVF oath of the Irish brotherhood, and, whatever the cost in casualties, they would take the 'Devil's Dwelling Place'.

War correspondent Phillip Gibbs had watched the artillery bombardment from the 'Grandstand', the high ground above Albert. He had been tipped off at midnight that the 'Big Push' would begin at 7.30 am. He was optimistic it would go well.

General Sir Douglas Haig, the British Commander-in-Chief, slept easily this night, secure in a devout belief that God was on their side. This was his first major operation as C-in-C, and he was about to oversee the largest British attack the British had ever mounted on the Western Front. Artillery would pave the way, and his Corps Commanders were confident they would get through.

Private 'Tommy' Higgins would attack with the 1/5th North Staffs at Gommecourt. He had been standing all night in knee-deep water, waiting for H-Hour. He was very impressed when an 18-inch gun fired and blew down all the old barn buildings nearby.

Lieutenant-General Aylmer Hunter-Weston, known as 'Hunter-Bunter', took the decision to blow the Hawthorne mine prematurely, ten minutes before H-Hour. It warned every German soldier in his sector that the attack was under way and proved the undoing of the VIII Corps.

Private Frank Lindley, with the Barnsley Pals (14th Yorks and Lancs), was unimpressed by assurances that the artillery bombardment would enable them to walk unscathed across no man's land. He knew that the Jerries knew they were coming. Before he went over the top, he strapped his entrenching tool over his private parts. They were told not to stop for the wounded.

Lieutenant Edward Liveing was about to go into action for the first time with the London Regiment at Gommecourt. He carried in his pocket the seventeenth century Cavalier prayer, sent by his father, which he continually repeated under his breath in the front line. 'Lord, I shall be very busy this day,' it read. 'I may forget Thee, but do not Thou forget me.' He was disconcerted to realise the German trenches up above looked directly down into their own.

Cinematographer Geoffrey Malins, officially embedded with the 29th Infantry Division, was poised opposite Beaumont Hamel to film the massive explosion of the Hawthorne Ridge Redoubt mine, charged with 40,600 lbs of ammonal. He would record some of the most iconic images of the Great War that day.

Major-General Ivor Maxse's 18th Division attacking between Mametz and Montauban was not relying on artillery alone to break through. Maxse employed every tactical and technical ruse, from mines to flame-throwers and explosive saps, to get his men across no man's land with as few casualties as possible.

'McCrae's Battalion' consisted of the core of Scotland's formidable Heart of Midlothian football team and supporters. 'Kick-off' for the attack into Mash Valley would be a whistle blow, which would send them over the top at 7.30 am.

Lieutenant-General Morland, the Commander of X Corps, observing from his tree-top command post, failed to reinforce the potentially decisive breakthrough by General Nugent's 36th Ulster Division.

Private Leo O'Neil was a 5 ft 4 in, 15-year-old boy soldier with the Newfoundland Regiment. He had left five sisters behind at home, and the army was now their primary provider. He would be in the second wave attacking 'Y' Ravine, one of the most formidable German strongpoints along the line. Being second wave increased the chances of survival.

Lieutenant-General Sir Henry 'Rawley' Rawlinson, the Commander of the British Fourth Army attacking on the Somme, was regarded as an over-ambitious 'cad' by his Sandhurst contemporaries. He was a capable if inexperienced army commander, who had compromised his plan at Haig's direction. Artillery firepower would either enable him to break through or 'bite and hold' the German line. He would then destroy the inevitable counter-attacks.

Brigadier-General Hubert Rees had recently taken over command of 94th Brigade, the left-flank unit attacking Serre. The plan for the approaching attack arrived in a 76-page document that made little sense. It catered for everything accept the unexpected.

Sergeant-Major Ernest Shepherd was a regular soldier with the 1ˢᵗ Dorsets opposite the Leipzig salient. He had been on leave in England the week before. Unaware of having been Mentioned in Dispatches, he thought his friends were congratulating him for simply being alive. Ever professional, he had already walked the route his men would follow through the communication trenches to reach the front line. He had high expectations of the 'Big Push'.

Sergeant Richard Tawney would attack with the 22ⁿᵈ Manchesters south of Montauban. He was a socialist economics lecturer who had turned down the chance of a commission. He and his men were already exhausted by the stop-go progress to reach the front line through the communication trenches in pitch darkness. The war, he believed, would herald meaningful social, economic and political change.

Captain Thomas Tweed commanded B Company of the 2ⁿᵈ Salford Pals opposite Thiepval. He realised his men would suffer more casualties on this day than ever before, it being their first deliberate conventional attack. Tweed had personally recruited many of the men around him in 1914 and had lived cheek by jowl with them ever since.

THE GERMANS

Generalleutnant von Auwärter commanded the 52ⁿᵈ Brigade, defending a critical sector that covered the vital approach to the Thiepval plateau and the Schwaben Redoubt. This was the division commander's *Schwerpunkt*, or main point of defence effort. Von Auwärter had been shelled out of his command post in the middle of co-ordinating a major relief in place for his 99th Infantry Regiment, and now the British attack was upon them as he was setting up his new command post.

Oberstleutnant Alfons Ritter von Bram, commanding Bavarian Infantry Regiment 8, was tasked by von Soden, the 26th Division commander, to co-ordinate measures for the three-pronged counter-attack to retake the Schwaben Redoubt. At no time was he in contact with all three attack groups, but he took the decision to attack with less, rather than gamble and wait for all to assemble. Ordered at 11.15 am, the attack did not get going until 3 pm. It was a risk.

Feldwebel Karl Eisler, with Reserve Artillery Regiment 29, was an artillery observer positioned on the Contalmaison castle tower. For days he had been watching hundreds of lorries moving forward behind the British front line. An attack was clearly coming and he was starting to feel vulnerable.

Oberleutnant Franz Gerhardinger was in reserve with the 2nd Battalion 16 Regiment south of Bapaume. He had watched the villages of Pozières and Contalmaison burn each night during the bombardment. Every observation balloon tethered in viewing distance had been shot down by marauding British aircraft. They were to be warned off about a British break-in near Montauban.

Leutnant Matthäus Gerster was dug in with 119 Regiment at Beaumont Hamel. He knew that after seven days of artillery fire their only hope of surviving the coming attack would be to get to the parapets before the British. The trigger was the firing of the Hawthorne mine.

Unteroffizier Friedrich Hinkel was with the 7th Company 99th Infantry Regiment defending the front line in front of the Schwaben Redoubt, opposite the 36th Ulster Division. He was a hardened veteran. 'Give it 'em hard, boys' was his Westphalian battle cry. Goaded by seven days of non-stop artillery fire, he and his men were determined to exact bitter revenge when the British attacked.

Unteroffizier Felix Kircher was a forward artillery observer with Artillery Regiment 26. He had watched the steady British build-up and been shelled out of his observation post on the church tower at Pozières. They had escaped by climbing down the bell ropes.

Walther Kleinfeldt was a 16-year-old artillery gunner, whose battery was dug in near Pozières. He was so young that his mother had had to sign his recruitment papers to go to the front. She also sent him a Contessa camera, which he had started to use during the British artillery bombardment. 'At least now I can say I have been in a war,' he wrote to her.

Vizefeldwebel Laasch commanded a reserve platoon with 110 Regiment, deeply dug in near La Boisselle in Mash Valley. He quickly realised that part of the line nearby was overrun by the British and he and his men would have to fill the gaps.

Unteroffizier Otto Lais from Baden was a machine-gun commander awaiting the British onslaught at Serre. He was a tough, resourceful, hard-bitten veteran and proud of his association with the elite machine-gun corps. He and his men were methodically proficient in spinning impenetrable webs of interlocking arcs of fire, through which no British infantryman would pass. He had already noticed that a new British Division had surfaced opposite their sector.

Generalmajor Maur was von Soden's artillery commander, a recently arrived veteran from the Eastern Front. He immediately regrouped the 26th Division's artillery assets into three distinct sub-groups. This enabled them to rapidly and flexibly concentrate and redirect fire, creating task organisations that would be familiar to present-day gunners.

Otto Maute was a wagon driver with Infantry Regiment 180 and carried munitions between Bapaume and the front line before Albert. This was his first battle. Being a private soldier meant nobody told him anything. He was pessimistic about the massive British build-up; if the enemy broke through, they would have to move.

Generalmajor Franz von Soden's 26th Division would be attacked by two and a half British corps on the first day. He had commanded his division in peacetime and was called from retirement to mobilise it in 1914. He was a consummate professional. His division had fought in the mobile battles of 1914 and he had spent nearly two years on the Somme preparing for just this attack.

Generalleutnant Hermann von Stein was convinced his XIV Corps was to be the focus of the coming British offensive after Verdun. His *Schwerpunkt* was in von Soden's 26th Reserve Division sector. General Erich von Falkenhayn, his superior, was not convinced the blow would fall north of the River Somme. The artillery bombardment had already forced von Stein to move his headquarters over four miles further back.

Stephan Westman was a German Army surgeon attached to the 119th Regiment near Beaumont Hamel, where he had set up a Field Dressing Station. He had recently returned from Berlin, where he had seen the poor economic conditions inflicted on the home front by the Allied blockade.

Hauptmann Herbert Ritter von Wurmb was a company commander with the Bavarian Reserve Infantry Regiment 8, positioned in depth in the German second line behind the Schwaben Redoubt and between Irles and Pys. He knew the Schwaben Redoubt was vital ground, which if lost would need to be recaptured immediately, and that he and his men would have to do it. He had been up all night with his fellow company commanders conducting a reconnaissance in the forward 99th Regiment trenches they were due to relieve that night. They were exhausted, and the British attack started just as they got back.

Prologue —•

The Grandstand

Self-imposed censorship was a strain for war correspond-ent Phillip Gibbs, standing in a beetroot field on the 'Grandstand' viewpoint overlooking the panorama of the spectacular night-time artillery bombardment. He felt he wanted to write the truth as he saw it. 'I stood with a few officers in the centre of a crescent sweeping round from Auchonvillers, Thiepval, La Boisselle and Fricourt to Bray, on the Somme.' The view to his front was spectacular, 'our fire for a time was most fierce', he recalled, 'so that sheets of flame waved to and fro as though fanned by a furious wind'. Occasionally the artillery fire might pause for as much as 30 seconds when 'darkness, very black and velvety, blotted out everything and restored the world to peace'. But not for long – 'then suddenly, at one point or another, the earth seemed to open furnace fires'.

The sky was virtually cloudless during this final hour before midnight, heralding a promising summer dawn for 1 July 1916. Glancing south, Gibbs spotted another of those 'violent shocks of light, and then a moment later another by Auchonvillers to the north'. Gibbs enthusiastically wanted to write about what he instinctively knew to be the 'Big Push'. 'For nearly a week now,' he remembered, 'we have been bom-barding the enemy's lines from the Yser to the Somme' – but 'we had to keep the secret, to close our lips tight, to write vague words lest the enemy should get a hint too soon.' The evidence crackling to his front was clear to see:

And once again the infernal fires began, flashing, flickering, running along a ridge with a swift tongue of flame, tossing burning feathers above rosy smoke-clouds, concentrating into one bonfire of bursting shells over Fricourt and Thiépval, upon which our batteries always concentrated.

Gibbs was staring at the centre of the British Fourth Army front, shortly due to launch an offensive across an 18-mile frontage configured roughly in the shape of a capital letter 'L'. From Serre in the north to Fricourt due south, the British line faced east. Gibbs overlooked the Fricourt salient, where the line changed direction to Maricourt further east, where the British would attack north, alongside the French. His Grandstand view was where the perpendicular side of the 'L' met the horizontal. Along virtually the whole front the Germans dominated the tactical high ground. The observers accompanying Gibbs watched intently as 'red lights ran up and down like little red dancing devils' where the ground rose steeply to Usna Hill by La Boisselle and to Château Thiepval above the wood.

Gibbs had been sending reports to the *Daily Telegraph* and *Daily Chronicle* virtually since the war began. He knew, 'when the guns spoke one morning last week with a louder voice than has yet been heard upon the front', that this was the likely opening of the new offensive. A mass of men and materiel had flowed in from the French ports for weeks now, 'new men of new divisions'. He sensed an atmosphere of pent-up emotion among the troops. 'There was a thrill in the air, a thrill from the pulse of men who knew the meaning of attack.'[1]

Corporal George Ashurst, with the 1st Lancashire Fusiliers, had spent the preceding week in the trenches of Beaumont Hamel, to the left of Gibbs's field of vision. He called it the 'Big Bang' and, like the correspondent, appreciated 'what a spectacle it was to stand quite upright in our front line at night-time'. This was a rare event indeed because of the risk of incoming German fire.

To see the sky illuminated with hundreds of large and small flashes like lightning dancing on the distant ridges, and listening to the continuous roar of big and little shells passing overhead.

He tried to discern the course of the shells arcing overhead and 'then to turn about and look towards Fritz's lines, to see a sight that made one feel pity even for an enemy'. Huge howitzer shells dug deeply, gouging out great fountains of earth from the German ridge line to his front, 'shaking the very ground under our feet four or five hundred yards away'. The explosions displaced tons of earth, leaving gaping holes 'in which a house could be placed'. The sound of an aeroplane overhead momentarily distracted them from the noise of the flying shells. Strangely illuminated, they could even pick out the tell-tale red, white and blue British roundels beneath its wings. It disappeared almost as quickly and was lost from sight.[2]

Pilot Cecil Arthur Lewis, flying overhead in a Morane Parasol with No. 3 Squadron Royal Flying Corps, recalled the terrible beauty of the scene when he flew this last patrol over the Somme front just as it grew dark. 'The whole of the ground beneath the darkening evening was just like a veil of sequins, which were flashing and flashing,' he recalled. 'Each one was a gun,' he appreciated, a dangerous environment, because his aircraft was 'continually bucketing and jumping, as if in a gale' as shells shrieked past. Not many servicemen could like correspondent Gibbs indulge in the view as a visual spectacle. Sergeant-Major Ernest Shepherd, a regular soldier, already seven years with the Dorset Regiment, was moving through the night towards the front-line salient via Aveluy Wood and Authuille, south of Thiepval. He had watched from Senlis Mill, which gave 'a good view of the bombardment' near his holding area, five days before. He knew the 'Big Push' was imminent. 'The whole country is light as day with the gun flashes,' he wrote in his diary, noting 'several fires at points in enemy lines'. Looking rearward he saw 'our lamps busily flashing messages behind us'.[3]

Despite the ferocity of the bombardment, Phillip Gibbs at his Grandstand vantage point above Albert felt 'it was all muffled'. Distance appeared to mute the violence being visited upon the shadowy ridge lines opposite. He remembers the night sky with a few low-lying clouds, with the air calm and moist, not stirred by the wind. 'Even our own batteries did not crash out with any startling thunder,' he thought, despite hearing 'the rush of big shells, like great birds in flight'. Most of the noise was distant rumbling, interrupted now and then by a 'dull heavy thunder-clap'. It all seemed so remote. Star shells were continually rising above the German lines, 'cutting out the black outline of the trees and broken roofs, and revealed heavy white smoke-clouds rolling over the enemy positions'. Yet all 'along this stretch of the battle front there was no sign of men'; all he could see close by was the beetroot crop and wheat gently waving beyond.

Gibbs was not the most popular correspondent at General Sir Douglas Haig's General Headquarters (GHQ) at Montreuil. His first contact with the British Commander-in-Chief had been the previous year after the battle of Loos, when Haig had commanded the First Army. Hostile to the press, he had drawn a line across his operational area, beyond which the media would have no access. Brigadier-General Charteris, Haig's intelligence chief, was also his press-minder and nervous about Gibbs's frank responses to imposed censorship. 'I understand fairly well what you gentlemen want,' Haig had insensitively pointed out, and it was not what the press wanted to hear:

> *You want to get hold of little stories of heroism, and so forth, and to write them up in a bright way to make good reading for Mary Ann in the kitchen, and the man in the street.*[4]

Haig was taken aback at the restrained passion of the response from the assembled press. He was reminded that men who had been sent to war from the Homeland and British Empire had a right to 'know what they were doing and how they were doing'. The correspondents wanted to 'mention more frequently the names of troops engaged – especially English troops – for the sake of the soldiers themselves, who were discouraged by this lack of recognition, and for the sake of the people behind them'. Charteris advised Haig to mellow and relax the censorship rules as far as possible. He took the advice. Casualty lists alone willed it.

As Gibbs watched the flashing 'points of flame' stabbing across the sky across the front visible from Thiepval to La Boisselle, he heard the steady tramp of marching feet for the first time. 'Shadow forms came up out of the dark tunnel below the trees,' he recalled, and some 'were singing some music-hall tune, with a lilt in it' as they marched towards the flashing and crackling vista of the front line opening before them. They were 'tall boys of a North Country regiment'. Gibbs had to admire their composure. Some whistled the 'Marseillaise' while others gossiped quietly as they walked past. They did not seem to be in dread of pending action, perhaps because this was their first time. 'A young officer walking at the head of his platoon called out a cheery good night to me.' They could just as easily have passed on a London street.

At midnight a staff officer gathered the press in a small room. The door was shut and the window closed before he whispered conspiratorially, 'The attack will be made this morning at 07.30.' There was absolute silence from the dozen or so officers who heard the words:

> *Men who were to be lookers-on and who would not have to leave a trench up there on the battlefields when the little hand of a wrist-watch said, 'It is now.'*

'Our hearts beat jumpily for just a moment,' Gibbs recalled. 'There would be no sleep for all those men crowded in the narrow trenches on the north of the Somme.' It was now 1 July 1916, he realised.

'God give them courage in the morning ...'[5]

The Attack Plan, 1 July 1916

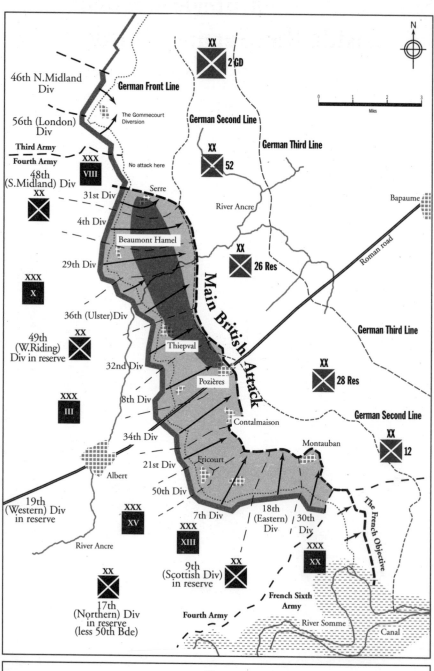

46th N.Midland Div

56th (London) Div

Third Army

Fourth Army

48th (S.Midland) Div

XXX VIII

XX

X

XXX X

49th (W.Riding) Div in reserve

XXX III

XV XXX

19th (Western) Div in reserve

River Ancre

17th (Northern) Div in reserve (less 50th Bde)

XX

German Front Line

The Gommecourt Diversion

No attack here

German Second Line

31st Div

4th Div

Beaumont Hamel

29th Div

36th (Ulster)Div

32nd Div

8th Div

34th Div

21st Div

Albert

50th Div

7th Div

XXX XIII

9th (Scottish Div) in reserve

Fourth Army

Serre

Thiepval

Pozières

Fricourt

XX 2 GD

XX 52

German Third Line

River Ancre

XX 26 Res

Main British Attack

XX 28 Res

German Third Line

Contalmaison

Montauban

XX 12

German Second Line

18th (Eastern) Div

30th Div

XXX XX

Bapaume

Roman road

The French Objective

French Sixth Army

River Somme

Canal

Key

British front line   British divisional boundaries   British Advance   Area of German *Schwerpunkt* (main defence effort)   Marsh

CHAPTER I

*Materielschlacht**:
Inside the German Bunkers

1 July 1916. Midnight to 4 am

* Battle of materiel attrition

00.10 am

Fritz

Dimly lit dugouts shook with the impact of near misses on the German ridge lines; chalk dust and loose spoil cascaded from the ceilings. Reverberating cracks scattered shrapnel against dugout entrances, fluttering groundsheet curtains as spent air from blasts wafted the pungent smell of cordite inside. Anxious faces glanced up from the murk 20 feet below. The momentary displacement of air dispersed the musty aroma of sour sweat and tallow, with which the German field-grey uniforms were waterproofed. 1915 had been the year when the spade had triumphed over the gun, and now men relatively safely ensconced in deep dugouts were realising the benefit. Infantryman Bernhard Lehnert remembered how cosy bunkers had been during the first winter of 1914, but 'nobody,' he reflected, 'could have thought then that we would be living in them for years'.[1]

Soldiers perspired freely in the evil-smelling underground chambers. Unteroffizier Otto Lais, a machine-gunner in 169 Regiment at Serre, near Puisieux on the northern tip of the Allied attack sector, recalled that 'the second, the third and fourth line trenches held deeper and deeper dugouts; that needed thirty, forty or fifty steps to get down'. Men lay on wired bed frames below or sat on long wooden benches, pensively watching as their hanging jackets and equipment swung from the ceiling rods with each artillery impact.[2]

'We were well pleased,' recalled Vizefeldwebel Laasch, with a reserve platoon occupying the Mittelweg Trench behind La Boisselle, 'that the deep dugouts constructed by us after such hard work, also protected us against the heavy calibre shells.' Card games provided a distraction, but 'scat' hands were slapped down with little enthusiasm. Men tried to sleep, but the incessant banging and howling impacts precluded this. It had been another dreadful day; dust from countless detonations 'swirled as high as towers', Laasch dolefully observed. 'Satan pulled out all the stops as the men in the forward destruction zone had the sunlight blotted out.' Tension was palpable, and soldiers were watchful, they knew an attack was coming. Phillip Gibbs on the Grandstand would have seen Laasch's position simply as a succession of flashes periodically crackling over the dark mass of the ruined village of La Boisselle, alongside the straight Roman road from Albert to Bapaume. 'Whoever went above as sentry could barely still recognise the position,' Laasch observed. 'Instead of well dug trenches, one saw shell hole after shell hole.' Despite this, the seven-day bombardment 'had brought us barely a casualty' but 'the remaining ruins of La Boisselle were ground to powder'.[3]

The artillery barrage had spluttered into life seven days ago on 24 June and escalated ever since. Leutnant FL Cassel ensconced in a deep dugout near Thiepval with Infantry Regiment 99, at the battered epicentre of the threatened front, had been warned shortly after midnight the attack would come that same day. Who could tell? Previous experience suggested it came on the third day, but the British still had not moved. As no food was getting through the battered communication trenches, they broke into the iron rations secured in the platoon commander's dugout. 'The bread of course was not exactly fresh,' Cassel remembered, 'and rumour had it that not all the meat rations could be found, but at least it gave something for the stomach.' Hunger was less an issue than thirst. Springs and pumps had been buried by displaced earth from the huge craters. Men were reduced to drinking from puddles. Twenty-year-old infantryman Hermann Baass remembers being lucky enough to have a small stream behind his position. That there was a body lying in it 'played absolutely no role whatever', he recalled, because 'we were constantly being inoculated'.[4]

It had been raining shells for 160 hours. At first it was shrapnel, cracking overhead with dry metallic reports, lashing overhead cover, but having no effect on men in dugouts. The 'heavies' opening up on the second day had been an entirely different proposition. These monster shells whistled in from a great height and bored deeply into the earth with a reverberating thud before setting off massive explosions. Huge blocks of chalk mixed with tons of earth were spat out into the sky, gouging 12-foot craters 15 feet across. Only solidly constructed and deep dugouts could withstand such blows and most were, having been systematically excavated over the previous 22 months. There was a five-metre danger circle. Even those landing outside could still bend earthen walls and snuff out trench candles with the pressure wave. A direct hit collapsed trenches, bulged out bunker walls and flung masses of spoil across dugout entrances. Everyone's inner dread was of being buried alive, clawing and scrabbling at the crushing weight of earth before suffocating or being overcome by gas and fumes.

Unteroffizier Braungart's machine-gun post dugout with the 2nd MG Company of Reserve Infantry Regiment 119 was hit by an 'air torpedo' two days before. They were dug in on the Hawthorne Ridge outside Beaumont Hamel. It took three hours for the trapped to dig their way out. Eighteen-year-old German soldier Herman Siebe recalled a like incident, 'something I'll never forget', when interviewed in the

1990s. His bunker was shaken up by a near miss, which pinned a comrade caught outside beneath masses of earth. 'Ooooh Mama, Mama,' he piteously wailed, 'I've been wounded.' They could hear him underneath and see one of his legs protruding from the soil. 'Perhaps we could pull him out,' Siebe and his comrades decided:

> We loosened him a little and then I pulled on his leg and it came off. I'll never forget that in my whole life. It only lasted for a few minutes before the whimpering stopped. When it was over it was very, very quiet.

Unteroffizier Baungart's gun crew was jinxed. Two days later it was buried again. 'MG Schütze Kottler,' he reported, 'who was on guard, is buried under the rubble' of the second exit 'and cannot be saved as the entire wall threatens to give way'. The dugout containing the number 2 machine-gun had also to be evacuated because it too was threatened with collapse. The gun was left inside; they were covering a key sector from the Hawthorne Ridge and the dugout might have to be re-occupied. Meanwhile, 75 feet below them sat a lone British soldier on watch with a candle, guarding a chamber packed with 40,600 lbs of ammonal. The German machine-gunners had no idea. It was set to explode in six hours' time.[5]

Leutnant Rupp in the same regiment was bombed out twice in the same sector. Thirty minutes of frantic digging was needed to release the buried Vizefeldwebel Mögle on the second day of the bombardment. Speed of reaction was crucial, as reserve Leutnant Walter Schulze recalled in a similar, later incident on the Somme, with the 76th Regiment:

> Terrified shouts were still coming from the mounds of earth. They had recognised [my voice]. 'Dig, Walter, dig! Walter, help

us quickly, for God's sake, help us! Quicker, Walter, quicker! We are suffocating!' they shouted desperately from the mound. My blood ran cold at the fearful shouts. It was just horrible.

Schulze and his comrades dug as carefully and quickly as they could. 'Yes! There was a helmet, a head!' One of the missing, Liefering, was uncovered as far as his chest; 'his face was as white as a sheet from the horrible shock and fear from the event,' Schulze remembered. Another man, Wartemann, was still buried, calling faintly as he expired. But they could find no trace and soon 'all is quiet from the mound, as quiet as a grave'. It was now a question of retrieving his corpse. Eventually they found a hand, thankfully still attached, then hair and at last a head. 'What a horrible sight!' Schulze recalled:

I had known this man for the entire time I had been in the field, but I could not recognise him. We cleaned his face, but it was swollen. His lips were blue and his eyes were wild and staring madly. His nose was fat and bloody, but at least his torso was free.

After dragging him out they instinctively tried artificial respiration and miraculously his chest began to heave. When his eyes appeared at last to focus 'he recognised me', Schulze remembered, and said 'Walter, is that you? What's happened?' They told him he had been buried, and with that a spark of life returned, because 'he suddenly went mad and we could hardly restrain him'.[6]

Near misses were frightening. Leutnant Cassel at Beaumont Hamel recalled the seemingly remorseless sequence of events that occurred when Allied gunners began to register on their dugouts. The 'dull boom of a heavy gun' was followed by the 'awesome whizz and swish of a rising heavy missile', which would land nearby. The systematic process of 'walking' shells onto targets as guns methodically registered on objectives initiated a cringing unease as the sinister exploding footprints approached. Tension could drive men to hysteria. Cassel recalled one such strike:

The earth was quaking and white dirt falling through the boards, I saw the beams above bend and slowly descend by about 10 cm. My heart seemed to stop, now comes the end ...

He froze, awaiting the inevitable massive detonation, 'but the catastrophe did not come'. Emotionally spent, he relaxed back on his bed overcoming 'momentary paralysis' before abruptly jumping up and running outside. Better to 'die in the open air than be crushed between the boards', he decided. Just outside was a crater several metres wide, which had been gouged out by a 21 cm dud. 'Had it exploded,' he reflected, 'whoever was in the dugout would not have seen daylight – not before the Day of Resurrection.'[7]

Passing time inside dimly lit and claustrophobic dugouts, intimidated by successions of shrieking, howling near misses and impacts, was testing the resilience of the German XIV Reserve Corps. They sheltered beneath this firestorm that stretched from Gommecourt in the north 18 miles across the Ancre and Somme rivers to the French sector beyond Maricourt further east. Schütze Eversmann, with Infantry Regiment 143, scribbled down diary impressions inside the *Wunderwerk*, or marvel, a massive bulwark within the Leipzig Redoubt, south of Thiepval. 'When will they attack?' he asked himself on day two, 'tomorrow or the day after? Who knows?' By early morning of the fifth day the British had still not made a move. 'There must be an end sometime to this horrible bombardment,' he despaired. Subsequent diary entries became more despondent, even alarmist:

Haven't we had enough of this frightful horror? Five days and five nights now this hell has lasted. One's head is like a madman's, the tongue sticks to the roof of the mouth. Almost nothing to eat and nothing to drink. No sleep. All contact with the outer world cut off.

'Even the rats became hysterical,' observed newly arrived medical officer Stephan Westman, attached to Infantry Regiment 119. Men snapped out of their shell-induced apathy to flail at them with spades as they ran up the dugout walls. 'They sought refuge in our flimsy shelters,' he recalled, fleeing the storm of steel outside.

By the early morning hours of the seventh day, 1 July, the British guns had fired 1,508,652 shells into the German lines. 'All around there was a howling, snarling and hissing,' recalled Leutnant Matthäus Gerster, also with the 119th north of the Ancre. 'With a sharp ringing sound, the death dealing shells burst, spewing their leaden fragments against our line.' The deluge of shells was as remorseless as it was incessant:

Large calibre shells droned through the air like giant bumblebees, crashing, smashing and boring down into the earth. Occasionally small calibre high explosive shells broke the pattern.[8]

It was worse for German units facing the French, at the end of the 'L' horizontal of the front, near the River Somme. The French on the right were about to attack with five, compared to 13 British, divisions, but they had four times more artillery per mile of front and it was heavier. The Mametz area had more recently come under control of the German 28th Division following a rationalisation of the front line, with a likely Allied offensive pending. Infantry Regiment 109 had been assigned its new sector just eight days before the opening of the British bombardment. On arrival they found too few deep dugouts to house trench garrisons, most of which were situated in the first line and very few in the second or third lines. Feverish digging started to rectify the shortfalls and was now being done under heavy fire. Men sheltering in the older shallow dugouts found they were vulnerable to medium and heavy calibre shells. Casualties rose: 12 men were killed and 32 wounded in the first six days of the bombardment. Forward companies with the 1st Battalion lost one third of their strengths. Discussions at corps and division level decided some form of relief ought to be attempted. One of the 109 Regiment's companies had been reduced to 149 men, and it was agreed two companies from Infantry Regiment 23 should attempt a changeover.[9]

Such a relief at night under intermittent shell fire could be unsettling for morale and was an administrative command nightmare to organise and set up at short notice. Anticipating a likely enemy attack, 109 Regiment HQ received an unexpected order shortly after midnight to set up a relief operation, which had to be executed before dawn. The move appeared unnecessarily risky; the men in the trenches were confident enough to receive an attack without a changeover and their morale was intact. Two 23 Regiment companies had already set off from the rear between Mametz and Montauban. Approach communication trenches along the *Matratzenweg*, *Siegelgraben* and *Kabelgraben* had been reduced to ditches by the bombardment and became choked with men, struggling forward laden with heavy equipment. Large sections of trench were either blocked with debris or simply levelled by earth thrown up by exploding shells.

The first men did not arrive at their designated trenches until 2 am, with daylight barely three and a half hours away.

The exchange was taking too long and the 23 Regiment companies were ordered to stop midway by 109 Regiment headquarters. The risk of approaching twilight was too great. The message came too late to warn the lead platoon under Leutnant Preuss, whose men continued to struggle on in the darkness and smoke obscuration to reach 12th/109 Company in sector 'e' just north of Carnoy. Without realising it, Preuss and his men were crawling towards the jaws of an impending British attack. Relief casualties had not been excessive, but this whole sector of the line before Mametz was now thoroughly unsettled. Was there to be a relief operation tonight or not, men asked. Expectations were cruelly dashed. Most of the 23 Regiment reinforcements had only got as far as Montauban.

To be hit and wounded during such a complex move in darkness could be catastrophic for individual soldiers. 'I should say,' explained surgeon Stephan Westman, that recovering casualties from the forward line was 'one of the most difficult tasks of the medical officer'. Courage was needed to venture out and pick up a wounded man, when everyone was crouching in his hole. They had 'to lay them carefully on a ground sheet or often an improvised stretcher, and then carry them step by step through the deadly rain of shells or across minefields'. Doing it at night was even worse, throwing themselves flat if a Very light went up, and 'they were easily mistaken for patrols and fired on'. A man hit during a night relief was completely dependent on his comrades. German soldier Gerd Rehder described the feeling of utter helplessness this could induce:

He lay before me and was still breathing. I think his name was Pingel. I must say it got on my nerves. The man wouldn't die. I thought he wanted to die. Whenever he held his breath, blood flowed out of his nose. He must have been completely broken up inside. I thought how pitiful it is in war, when you can't help.

Recovery by stretcher was as laborious as it was dangerous. Westman recalled they 'had to crawl through barbed wire entanglements, creep on their bellies through shell holes, filled with mud and water' and then drag the casualty on a groundsheet, 'provided they could find him'. The process might last days. All this was done under intermittent shell fire, like the relief operation crawling towards sector 'e' below Mametz. Westman saw one stretcher party hit by a shell:

Over the spot where the two men had been, hung a cloud of black smoke. We could not see the men; and we ran out to try and discover what had happened to them. At first all we found were several pieces of the stretcher, then one man, with one foot dangling out of his trousers without its boot, and blood spouting out.

There was no trace of the second man:

Until suddenly one of my orderlies saw half a naked torso spiked to one of the tree stumps. Apparently the blast of the explosion had cut him in two and had hurled one half so high up that it was impossible to take it down. More shells were landing in our vicinity, and so we had to leave the torso to rot away, the torso of a man who had gone out to help his fellow creatures.[10]

Leaving the security of a trench, even at night, was not an act to be undertaken lightly. Shortly after midnight reserve Leutnant Stahlhofer, with the 2nd Company from the 8th Bavarian Infantry Regiment, volunteered to deliver an order to their 4th Company, garrisoning the Schwaben Redoubt. This veritable fortress, roughly triangular in shape, dominated the high ground overlooking the Ancre valley between Thiepval and the village of St Pierre Divion. Its 500-metre frontage provided depth to the first line of trenches below, with overhead fire options out to the flanks and above the trenches facing the British-occupied Thiepval Wood. The position, begun in early 1915, was built around two parallel trenches. The forward *Kampfgraben*, or battle trench, had 20 traverses with nine deep dugouts, while the *Wohngraben*, or accommodation trench, backed it up with 15 traverses and eight dugouts. The system included an aid post and company and battalion command posts. The dugouts, which had two or three entrances, were garrisoned by the 11th Company Infantry Regiment 99, more recently reinforced by a second company, the 4th, from Reserve Bavarian Infantry Regiment 8. There was a searchlight position and signalling station on the redoubt, covered also by three heavy machine-guns and four *Musketen*, or light automatic weapon battle positions.

The strength of the Schwaben Redoubt reflected its importance. Hauptmann Herbert von Wurmb, who commanded reserve elements from the 8th Bavarian Infantry Regiment, was on standby between Irles and Pys, just behind the German artillery massed behind the third line. He knew he would have to counter-attack immediately, should this high point on the German line be breached in any way. Generalmajor Franz Ludwig von Soden, commanding the 26th Reserve Division, holding the key sector north of the Albert–Bapaume road, regarded the Schwaben Redoubt as his *Schwerpunkt*, or main point of defence effort, to which Infantry Regiment 99 holding it was designated. His XIV Corps commander Generalleutnant von Stein also saw von Soden's sector on the Thiepval plateau as his *Schwerpunkt*, securing the vital high ground in the coming attack. Von Wurmb was clear about the decisive importance of taking back the position, should it be lost. 'Not only would the whole position of the 26th Reserve Division on the southern bank [of the River Ancre] have been extraordinarily endangered, but also the entire viability of the divisional artillery on the northern bank.' It was the key position along the Somme front, because standing on the redoubt suddenly brought all the German artillery batteries to the rear, hidden by the slope, into full view. Beaumont Hamel and the rear artillery positions would then become vulnerable to observed British fire, as also St Pierre Divion, overlooked in the Ancre valley below.[11]

Shortly after midnight, Leutnant Stahlhofer, one of the few who knew the way to the redoubt in darkness, set off with two men, one of whom had accompanied him before. They experienced the same problems in miniature as the companies attempting the night relief in the Mametz sector further south. 'We ran as if possessed, threw ourselves along' to avoid shellfire, 'then hurried again'. It took over an hour clambering between shell holes during a cold night, but 'we were sweating a lot', he recalled. They slowly traversed the gully from the northern section of the second line to the crest of the Schwaben ridge. 'The flash of exploding shells blinded us,' remembered Stahlhofer, who resorted to forced jokes to raise spirits, 'but nobody laughed'. The first of July was his birthday and he began to feel an exuberance, under intense shell fire, which 'animated me oddly'. Finally they reached what probably had been a trench, which randomly curved to the right, and found a dugout entrance. 'There were traces of men, but the smell indicated that they were not socially acceptable,' he wryly observed, so they moved on. They passed the medical bunker calling for Hauptmann Schorer, the commander, only to be told 'still somewhat further'. He eventually relayed his order in a dugout 'completely filled with men'. Many were his friends, who regarded their sudden appearance with amazement. Having survived the maelstrom outside, they were regarded 'as if we were like beings from another world'.

Stahlhofer received backslapping all round for his 23rd birthday, greeting friends Leutnant Traub and Vizefeldwebel Weinmann, and petting Weinmann's dog Fipps. Schorer, the redoubt commander, told him to return without delay. 'It will be broad daylight before the order is executed,' he said, 'and then it will be impossible for you to return.' Stahlhofer's birthday turned out to be his lucky day. Traub and the rest of 4th Company would be dead or prisoners within hours. Weinmann was to disappear without trace. As Stahlhofer left the doomed garrison he was well satisfied he had completed his audacious administrative mission and not without considerable risk. On the way back he paused 'to observe the trajectory of German projectiles, how they flew over us in a graceful arc like glowing meteors'. By 3.30 am he was safely back in his trench, where he was presented with an 'official order: sit here and drink a couple of draught beers and then go to sleep'. '*Zum Befehl*,' he responded, clicking his heels – 'as ordered'. In fact, 'Sleep was worth a great deal more than beer.'[12]

2 pm to 4 pm

The Trench Pigs

The 'trench pigs', as the resilient veterans with the German 26th Reserve Division called themselves, continued to maintain discipline. Most of them had two years' conscripted peacetime military service under their belts and two years' active service since 1914. Their opponents, Kitchener's New Army, had just 20 months' basic training with at first scant resources and equipment. They were a newly formed fledgeling volunteer army. Furthermore the Germans had fought large-scale conventional battles, including mobile and positional engagements, whereas the British had mainly engaged in trench raids. German soldiers were stoic, disciplined and used to being told what to do in a highly organised and militaristic society. Wearing a uniform conferred social status. This was encapsulated by the final symbolic act by German conscripts on leaving barracks when conscripted service ended before 1914. On departure they all roared out a last 'Hurrah for the Kaiser!'[13]

German reserve divisions like the 26th had emotional as well as veteran bonds. They had been conscripted between the ages of 17 and 45 from a resurgent population, which since the 1871 unification of Germany had risen from 39.8 to 67.8 million, a rise of just under 60 per cent. Many of the men serving with the 26th Division had fathers and sons who served in the same parent regiments. As children they flocked to watch the Kaiser's army on local manoeuvres. Everyone was familiar with uniform types and played at soldiers with each other. Nineteen-year-old German soldier Hermann Kottmeier recalled that everyone who had a uniform put it on:

The children were proud of their father, the school pupils were proud of their teachers. Our Director was a small figure, but he was a captain with a Prussian Guard battalion and had a wonderful helmet. We were very proud of him.

Karl Thiel was advised very early on to 'go now into the military'. There were rewards; 'if you volunteered willingly, you could be a Civil Servant within a year,' he explained, which was a prestigious profession, conferring security and status. He joined the artillery. Another 19-year-old, Fritz Siemers, explained that on starting an apprenticeship you were not considered mature or even credible unless you had been a soldier. An interview would often begin with the question 'Where have you served?' or 'Were you a soldier?' If not there would be comments like 'What was wrong? A man like an oak tree and never a soldier?'[14]

Service in a reserve division like the 26th transcended the political divide. German soldier Kurt Schröder was a Social Democrat with an overbearing father who used to insist he sing the Socialist 'Internationale' at home. Socialists caught up in the nationalist fervour of 1914 were prepared to compromise their principles and Schröder joined up. Another reluctant recruit was Albert Benecke, who said to his doctor at the medical examination: 'I don't think you need to take me. I am too young and small and have no desire to go to war.'

The doctor thought otherwise. 'My son, your chest is wide enough to take both a bullet and an Iron Cross' and passed him as fit. 'Thanks very much,' Benecke replied, and later would wryly remark, during his 1990s interview, 'I did get an Iron Cross.'

Youth for such youngsters ended at the local railway station, when they boarded the troop transport horseboxes with symbolic flower posies stuck in their belts and on spiked helmets. Hermann Grieselmann's father, who had served in the same regiment, was there to see him off. He pointed out it was not the custom to festoon rifle barrels with flowers. 'One is the Hero, the most important person in the family when you marched away,' Hermann remembered. 'At the first signal from the horn, you were off.' The men serving in the trenches on the Somme were confident they would see off the coming Allied attack.[15]

Veterans respected and feared the power of artillery, fully appreciating the weight and quantity of Allied fire that had been levelled against them during the early morning hours of 1 July. Leutnant Ernst Jünger of Fusilier Regiment 73 had the habit, when 'walking along the trench, of keeping one eye aloft, and the other on the entrance to the nearest dugout'. Recognising the different types of incoming shells was the first step of a steep learning curve, which included how best to take cover. Realisation soon dawned that whatever a soldier might do, there was always the rogue shell that would shriek in unannounced and take their lives. Jünger admitted, 'One cannot but associate every single sound of flying steel with the idea of death, and so I huddle in my hole in the ground with my hand in front of my face, imagining all the possible variants of being hit.' Like all trench pigs, he appreciated the need to retain 'a bit of that subliminal feeling of optimism, "it'll be all right", that you feel during a game, say, which, while it may be quite unfounded, still has a soothing effect on you'. Schütze Erich Maria Remarque, who later famously wrote about his experiences of the front, rationalised that 'chance is hovering over us', which resulted in indifference. 'If there is a shot, all I can do is duck; I don't know for sure and I can't influence where it is going to come down.' The only recourse was to live each dreadful day as it came.

Willi Marquardt, an 18-year-old German soldier, remembered cowering and ducking to earth on one occasion as a shell howled overhead. 'We thought this was the end,' he recalled, but 'the old soldiers who had already been at the front before could detect that the shriek was not for us and would continue far overhead.' So the old soldiers laughed, and 'we thought, Ja, it's not so bad'. Certain shells were known to have a man's name on it, an inescapable characteristic of war on the Western Front.[16]

There were, however, grounds for optimism. German soldiers had been here since September 1914, when the first trench line was scooped out and had been improving them ever since. Deep solid trenches were constructed, with short bays and zigzags, eight to twelve feet deep. Strong wicker-work and wooden revetments prevented them from bulging and collapsing under pressure. Tiny fortlets were constructed from concrete and located at 50-yard intervals, where they blended into the front-line fire trenches and were invisible five yards to the front. Foot-long machine-gun slits enabled long traverses with complete protection for the gunner. Four-foot-high entrance shafts slanted 45° from trench to dugouts 20 feet below ground. Inside were strongly propped living quarters, panelled with wood, with benches and bunks. Other shafts provided alternative escape avenues in the event of a collapse, and connected living areas to each other, adding to emotional and moral cohesion.

Regiments provided tactical instruction, gleaned from experience, as battlefield notes to help men cope with sustained bombardments. A section commander or senior ranking soldier was put in charge of every dugout. Dugouts were tunnelled together to aid defensive counter-measures, provide access for leaders to maintain morale and provide emergency exits. It was recognised that dugouts should be lit with candles, with spares provided, for practical and morale reasons. An 'iron ration' reserve was maintained and protected from rats. Even wine and cognac were made available in medical bunkers, and each dugout was instructed to provide an emergency latrine bucket with a lid.[17]

Defensive positions had been systematically upgraded with concrete since the beginning of the year to improve protection. Instinct, confirmed by meticulous observation, suggested that the Somme was likely to be the next place for an Allied offensive. Nothing was left to chance. Trenches had already begun to snake out across the ridge lines that dominated likely British approaches in early 1915, connecting the fortified villages that formed the bastions along this sector of the line. German soldiers were familiar with every contour of the ground, having looked at it for two long years. Soldier Max Heinz recalled:

> *Again and again we looked upon the same scene. We knew every house and every tree; at every turn of the way we knew just how far we were from our goal ... We knew exactly what portions of the road came under enemy fire and we would pass them hastily, mechanically falling back into the ordinary marching tempo as soon as the bad spots were passed.*[18]

Not only did the Germans know the ground, they controlled the tactical heights. They could see well into the rear of the British lines, whereas all the British could see at the base of these amorphous ridge lines were re-entrants and blocked ravines. The concentric shape of the German trench network enabled them to utilise the height advantage so that the second and third lines could fire unimpeded over the heads of the first.

Unteroffizier Felix Kircher, with Reserve Field Artillery Regiment 26, had a near perfect view from his Observation Post (OP) atop the church tower of Pozières, 'straight opposite Albert on the highest point of the region'. From above 'we could see columns of English infantry marching off to their trenches, hundreds of guns firing and aeroplanes taking off and landing'. Like the famous Madonna with Child hanging precariously from the spire at Albert, the Pozières tower attracted British attention. The first shell smashed the altar below and the next tore away the staircase, marooning the German observers up in the tower. 'In mortal fear', Kircher and his observation team beat a hasty retreat and 'threw down the bell ropes and glided to the earth in the greatest hurry'. Within minutes the tower collapsed beneath a welter of shells accompanied by the sonorous clanging of falling church bells. Kirchner and his team were lucky.[19]

Sheltering inside subterranean hideouts, veterans depended on each other to maintain morale. *Kriegsneurose*, or 'war nervousness', i.e. shell shock, was more apparent to seasoned trench pigs than headquarters staff. The prevailing belief in the rear was that their men were impervious to pressure, particularly when the honour of the country was at stake. Mental breakdown was not something that happened to patriotic Germans who believed in their future national destiny. Front-line soldiers saw it differently. They were wise to the tell-tale distress signs: the man who constantly ground his teeth, haunted wild eyes and the clenching and unclenching of fists. English poet Wilfred Owen called them 'men whose minds the Dead have ravished'. In the claustrophobic confines of bunkers under artillery bombardment, with an attack pending, such men were a danger not only to themselves, but to others. It was small wonder that, blind to what was happening above and intimidated by the shrieking sounds of impending death or mutilation, soldiers were at their mental limits. Gerd Rehder, a 19-year-old soldier, recalled one of their men going mad. 'He was an NCO, and they tied him to a bed,' he recalled. But he carried on 'raving and would certainly have gone over to the enemy'. He watched as he was taken away.[20] Men winced at the possibility of death at any minute, while the deranged longed for it.

Sleep was out of the question. 'We were tired and slept as much as we could,' remembered Leutnant Cassel with 99 Regiment, but 'the noise of the barrage was too monotonous and so prevented sleep for over-tired people.' They had to stay alert because an attack might come at any moment:

There was only one harassing question – could one rely on the sentries? They stood on the top steps of the dugout and had to watch lest the fire was changed to the rear, and had to look in quieter moments across the ramparts to see whether the enemy was coming across, all day long, all night long. And not all these men are heroes, so from time to time one had to go up to see whether the sentries did their duty.

It was a lonely vigil. 'Behind our trench we had a mirror mounted on a post, so that we could see over no man's land,' recalled Wilhelm Lange, a soldier in Cassel's unit. 'The ground was shaking as though the end of the world was coming and the mirror was quivering, but it never broke.' Another soldier remembered, 'We went on taking turns in the hole, although those who went outside knew it was their turn to die, most likely.' As the bombardment interminably continued, day by day, nearly all of them were wounded, 'so that we lay in blood'.[21]

This was *Materialschlacht,* a battle of materiel attrition. 'How little human hands could do against the work of the machinery of destruction!' observed Leutnant Matthäus Gerster with Reserve Infantry Regiment 119.

Where the front line trench once ran, shreds of corrugated iron, splinters of timber shuttering, empty food tins, smashed weapons and the kit and equipment of the dead and wounded lay everywhere …

Noise, pressure waves and the shriek and whine of shells accompanied by the crack and blast of near impacts sent shivers up the spine. Trepidation came with any tell-tale bulge in a dugout wall – the fear of being buried alive. The screams and shouts that came from nearby trenches could be alarming. In time a listless resignation developed that they would not see their loved ones again or, worse still, they might suffer an anonymous death. Not caring was the first sign of shell shock. 'The feeling of powerlessness against this storm of steel depressed even the strongest,' admitted Leutnant Gerster. 'Better dead than a cripple,' declared one soldier. 'It was awful when a leg or arm was ripped off,' he recalled. 'Better dead, all's done, and then you don't feel anything any more.'

Dread came less from being struck by a bullet because this left a body, which meant an identity. The greater fear was to be dismembered or transformed to an anonymous pulp. Annihilation was not dying. Constant exposure to shell fire produced hysteria, a form of shock to the nervous system that effected sensory functions, known as shell shock. Outward symptoms were excessive fatigue, headaches and the loss of appetite, which came from prolonged physical and mental strain. Heart palpitations led to giddiness and fainting. A suspiciously silent or stuttering soldier, with a face looking tortured and drawn with fatigue, was the first clue. Emotional strain manifested itself by chronic frowning, wrinkling foreheads, trembling, twitching and sometimes partial paralysis of the body. German soldier Hans Ratschky, then only 18, remembered his whole body starting to shake after a gas alarm. 'At first I did not know what it was, after I realised it was "cannon fever". Everyone got cannon fever,' he explained, 'one here, one there.' He only felt it once, except later when the lid from his cooking utensil was shot off. Although there were scores of others lying about with the dead, he couldn't bring himself to pick up and use one of theirs. 'You certainly can't do that,' he maintained.[22]

Leutnant Gerster described Dantesque scenes in his bunker during the bombardment south of Beaumont Hamel:

Tired and indifferent to everything, the troops sat it out on wooden benches or lay on the hard metal beds, staring into the darkness when the tallow lights were extinguished by the over-pressure of the explosions. Nobody had washed for days. Black stubble stood out on the pale haggard faces, while the eyes of some flashed strangely as though they had looked beyond the portals of the other side. Some trembled when the sound of death roared around the underground protected places. Whose heart was not in his mouth at times during this appalling storm of steel?

Shell shock could be unsettling inside a claustrophobic bunker under intense shell fire. Johannes Götzmann watched 'a young man, as old as me' begin to go insane. He stuffed all the pages from his army pay book and identity papers into the end of his rifle barrel. 'What are you up to?' his friends asked. 'I have had enough,' he declared, 'I'm not doing any more, I want to go home.' With that 'he started to whimper and wanted to see his mother again'. Götzmann recalled it had an awful impact on the others, because he was one of them, their age, and in the same close-knit group. They left him alone and he was sent home.[23]

Nevertheless, they endured. The Somme had been a quiet sector for two years, apart from French attacks on Serre in 1915. Thiepval village, blanketed with mushrooming impacts of artillery fire, had been a favourite watering hole for French tourists before the war. They would dally on the tactically imposing ridge line to survey the refreshing Somme valley views. The seignieurial village was famous for its patisserie. As boring as the trench improvement programme had been, the soldiers of the 28th Reserve Division were astute enough to appreciate their lot could be a great deal worse if they were at Verdun. Even though the level in the courage bank was running low, the majority held themselves together, sustained by comrades, religious faith and memories of home. The older and more mature men were at an advantage, with wives, families and sweethearts at home, with a stake in life, holding jobs and property. 'Oh, sweetheart, we are still so young,' wrote one girl to her soldier:

> ... *life has so much to offer us yet. Let us hope that life will be better in the future than now. The two days we were together were real 'rosy days', weren't they?*

By 1916 there was a gulf between front and home. 'At home I found my bed too soft and I could not sleep,' remembered medical officer Stephan Westman. 'Those who were married told me that the first two or three days were like heaven, but then all kinds of friction arose' because relationships drifted:

> *The wife had, so the husband suspected, found a lover, perhaps a highly paid munitions worker, and he poor devil, had to be content with his penny three farthings pay, with which he could not buy even a glass of beer.*

Soldiers earned 22 pfennigs in peace and 33 in war; corporals got 50 pfennigs, literally pennies.

Soldiers knew that the Allied blockade stranglehold had created dismal economic conditions back home for families. 'You write that things are not too good for you,' wrote one wife. 'We are no better off. The people here have nothing to laugh about, for everything is so expensive.'

One soldier, Ernst, promised his girl, 'Dear, I shall marry you when I get my leave again, for sure; you must not mistrust me.' She probably did, because Ernst was killed on patrol during the final build-up of military activity during late June, before the letter was posted. The British found it in his pocket.[24]

'We had to prepare ourselves – perhaps for our departure from this life,' recalled Gefreiter Adolf Griesbaum with Reserve Infantry Regiment 111. He had attended confession in a small village church near La Boisselle before the bombardment started. 'There was no question of having to confess, but we were allowed to!' He was glad he had, because it left his 'heart strong and composed', qualities he had drawn on when he had to free himself after being buried alive by a large shell. Feldwebel Schumacher in the same unit claimed 'I know that there was prayer in the trenches and the dugouts' because 'many a time I came across a man on sentry, his rosary in his hand and his thoughts directed to the strict fulfilment of his duties'. Idealised principles like these belong to an age less cynically and materially driven than our own, but they sustained these men. One German veteran NCO offered 20-year-old Hermann Baass his own peculiar brand of theological advice. 'Praying is no use,' he explained, 'better to think about how we are going to get out of this. Once we are out, *then* pray and thank God.'[25]

Despite the persistence and destructive power of the seven-day English artillery bombardment, it had its limitations. British guns had an average aiming error of 25 yards but had to strike to within 16 feet to achieve the collapse of a trench or dugout. Up to a third may have been duds. German soldier Joseph Dornhof received a mouthful of mud from a near miss, but was undismayed. 'Dud!' he exclaimed, 'I felt like I was newly born.' In essence, the explosive content of British shells was insufficient to reduce the core of the German defence. They were the wrong type of projectile and the mass exodus of factory and munitions workers into Kitchener's armies in August 1914 meant that they were also poorly manufactured. Of one and a half million shells fired, a million were 18 lb shrapnel shells, scattering ball bearings from the air to scythe through the German wire. The rest were 'heavies' that needed substantial shell casings to cope with the enormous stresses of firing, which meant more iron than explosive. A 1,400 lb shell from a 15-inch howitzer contained only 200 lbs of high explosive. In short, the 12,000 tons of shells fired at the German line delivered only about 900 tons of explosive. Although the massive artillery effort was the heaviest weight of fire ever delivered by a British army, in real terms this was only about 30 tons of high explosive per square mile of front. Impressive, but not enough.[26]

Musketier W Stöckle, with Reserve Infantry Regiment 111 near Fricourt, recalled that humour did survive under pressure. One story was about a resourceful soldier who had to pander to his lieutenant's insatiable search for original war souvenirs. The officer identified a piece of shrapnel that would make an ideal ashtray and Fritz was dispatched to pick it up under fire. Old soldiers in the Kaiser's army knew better than to question orders but, as a former shopkeeper, the soldier drew on his aptitude for staying on the right side of awkward customers. He politely pointed out to his officer that the British would be sending over 'even more ashtrays' before evening and 'wouldn't the Herr Leutnant like to hold on a little?' – because then he would have access to 'a much larger selection'.[27]

There was no doubting the intimidating effect of the artillery bombardment to the south of the line, where the highly competent French heavies were systematically pulverising strongpoints. Gas attack was a different hazard, creating far more anxiety than the norm, way out of proportion to the number of shells fired. Practical advice leaflets had been issued to German soldiers earlier in 1916 telling them how to cope with gas attack. 'Do not fear' was the primary instruction, spelled out in capitals, and using the familiar 'du' form of speech, like a friendly NCO offering advice. Soldiers were told to shoot into the gas cloud, where the enemy was expected to emerge. Masks had to fit tightly, and spades and grenades had to be close at hand for the inevitable close-quarter fighting that would follow. All this was relevant and practical advice. Avoid dugouts, they were warned, where gas was prone to linger, and do not fall back. Stay in the trench and hold the position rather than be vulnerable in the open. When the gas attack was over they should re-clean their personal weapons, remain in position and watch the enemy trenches.[28]

Both sides feared the insidious menace of chemical attack, its creeping presence highlighted by urgent warning gongs and metallic rattling along the front. The characteristic dull thud of gas shells attracted more attention than the dry crack of high-explosive rounds. 'Whenever in the maze of ruins there was a human soul, the long drawn-out cry went up,' remembered Leutnant Ernst Jünger, with Fusilier Regiment 73, 'Gas attack! Gas attack! Gas! Gas! *Gaaas!*' Coats and tarpaulins were futilely flapped around dugout entrances to disperse vapours, but to little avail. Steely self-control, as leaflets encouraged, was the best antidote. Jünger recalled 'a sweetish smell in the air', the distinctive odour of phosgene.

Rubberised canvas masks were jerked out of containers and quickly donned in a mad flurry of activity. Early models had elastic cloth attachments on each side until improved 'Y' straps were introduced, holding them more firmly in place. 'The first few minutes with the mask tell you whether you will live or die,' wrote Erich Maria Remarque. 'Is it air-tight?' If not, soldiers would begin 'choking for days on end as they spew up their burned-out lungs, bit by bit'. The awfulness of gas was its unseen creeping progress, 'snaking over the ground and sinking into all the hollows'. It lingered around the bottom of shell holes. Angled eyepieces on facemasks misted over and distorted targets, making it difficult to shoot properly, while cumbersome breathing canisters protruding at chin level tended to catch on the rifle stock. Achieving a tight fit beneath the German *Pickelhaube* helmet, now minus its spike, was also tricky; so too with the new coal-scuttle design which replaced it and which at 4½ lbs was universally regarded as being too heavy.

Gas attack could be the final emotional straw, tipping soldiers beyond mental equilibrium. Scant sympathy existed at German staff level, where shell shock was regarded as a violation of military discipline and an indication of weak will. German neurologist Professor Gaup had been warning since 1915 that affected men were hardly malingering. He concluded that soldiers:

> ... *have enthusiasm and the best of intentions but these cease to inspire them when the horrors and terrors come. Their inner strength rapidly decreases and it only requires an acute storm to break upon the nervous system for their self-control to vanish completely.*

The Imperial Army's solution was the brutal application of electric shock treatment. Dr Fritz Kaufman, a psychiatrist at the German psychiatric hospital at Ludwigshafen, advocated high-dosage electric shocks. 'The powerful impression of pain,' he wrote, 'suppresses all negative mental desires.' Patients would be coerced into normality.

The German soldier, like his Allied counterparts, coped with gas. Four days into the bombardment men of the German Second Army observed 'the enemy's gas tactics, which are being aided by the prevailing west winds, releasing constantly repeated small clouds of gas, is aimed also at gradual attrition'. The veterans endured as Second Army concluded 'because of technical mistakes, the enemy has so far achieved little through the use of gas'. German soldier Paul Weiher was convinced rural 'village sons' had far greater powers of resistance and endurance than urban 'townies'. 'At the front,' he observed, 'there were those who did not have the same nerves as the village lads.' He noticed there were those 'who sank a little', not completely, 'but were so nervous that you could see it'. Not all were such 'mother's sons', but he could tell.[29]

4 pm

In the Line. 'Lord God! Just Let Them Come!'

The further back from the front line they were, the more nervous German soldiers became. They were unable to observe forward. Oberleutnant Franz Gerhardinger's 16 Regiment in reserve south of Bapaume sensed an attack was imminent. At night Gerhardinger had watched the villages of Pozières and Contalmaison burn. During the early hours of the morning 'nobody knew whether the enemy infantry attack had already started, and the forward line had been overrun'. Otto Maute, a wagon driver with Infantry Regiment 180, drove munitions forward from Bapaume and the front line. This was his first battle. He saw many of the trenches had been flattened and had not slept for days, amid the roar of the artillery bombardment. He felt homesick, writing to his family about Sunday walks before the war. Being a private soldier he had no idea what was happening beyond the ridge lines to his front, 'but you could not rule out the possibility,' he pessimistically wrote, 'that the English might break through our front, and we will have to move.'

'Enemy air observation was extraordinarily active,' Gerhardinger observed. Five days before several German observation balloons had been shot down nearby. Three to four enemy aircraft suddenly swooped through the clouds and circled the balloons, shooting incendiary rockets 'which left black smoke trails behind them'. Shortly 'a small thin veil of smoke appeared, which quickly thickened and in no time light flames shot upwards from the balloon sleeves'. They imploded and collapsed, sinking burning to the ground. The aircraft carried on circling, 'machine-gunning the observers who had jumped with parachutes'. Then as quickly as they appeared they sped off, flying low-level back to their own lines over Longueval. Otto Lais, with 169 Regiment further north, had seen the last German balloons shot down between the Ancre and Somme rivers just two days before. 'The highest alarm level began sounding in our hearts,' he recalled; the British would soon be upon them.

The coming attack would be no surprise. Artillery Feldwebel Karl Eisler, with Artillery Regiment 29 covering the Fricourt and Montauban area, had detected British 'unrest' since early May. From an observation post looking out from the Contalmaison castle tower they picked out 'huge lorry convoys moving every day, without interruption, between Bray-sur-Somme and the town of Albert and back'. There were 'often as many as 100 lorries, one after the other' and 'huge artillery columns, which sometimes took more than three hours to pass a given point'. Otto Lais at Serre appreciated even before the bombardment began that 'soon it would begin'. All the indicators suggested 'Tommy wants to get into the German trenches'. Patrol clashes increased, and 'the dead belonged to the 31st British Division,' Lais recalled, 'yet another fresh English unit in the line'. Air activity proliferated, and new, well-camouflaged 'Russian saps' or concealed trenches began to snake out to the German line. To deal with the threat, a Bavarian mining company was introduced into their sector, and Lais remembered 'there seemed hardly a day without muffled detonations being heard and fountains of earth being thrown up'. Then on 24 June 'a hell broke out all over us', when the barrage begun.[30]

Karl Eisler on the Contalmaison tower remembered that 'whistles and howls and thundering, snarling cracks permeated the air'. He had to 'bellow into his field telephone because he could not hear himself speak'. His tower soon attracted attention, and 'several direct hits shook the building, throwing up red brick dust, which blotted out everything'. Walther Kleinfeldt, a 16-year-old gunner sheltering near the Pozières church, was soon obscured from Eisler's sight, covered in clouds of smoke and dust. Kleinfeldt was so young his mother had to personally sign his service papers, when he was taken. She had sent him a camera, which he used avidly to take pictures around the gun position, with his comrades wearing gas masks. At the height of the bombardment he ducked out of his dugout to take a risky picture of the church, just as a shell struck it. He remembered the remarkable image well, because it was also the first day someone in his artillery battery was killed. 'I'm still in rude health, but quite run down by the excitement and stress,' he wrote to his mother, enclosing a picture of his gun and crew. 'At least now I can say I have been in a war.' Eisler remembered that in the early hours of 1 July 'nothing changed, they were immersed in smoke, gas and dust'.[31]

Unteroffizier Friedrich Hinkel was manning the forward line with the 7th Company of Infantry Regiment 99, facing Thiepval Wood, just below the Schwaben Redoubt. To his left, just beyond the *Markt Graben* trench was the village cemetery, a stark reminder of their tenuous mortality amid the thunderous bombardment. 'Seven long days there was ceaseless artillery fire, which rose ever more frequently to the intensity of drumfire,' he recalled. Their positions were being hammered; trenches and rearward communication links were all but impassable. Gas attacks had wafted across from the British lines two days before. 'The torture and the fatigue' by early morning, 'not to mention the strain on our nerves, were indescribable', and yet still the English did not come.

There was, however, some good news with the arrival of company and battalion commanders from Bavarian Infantry Regiment 8. They were systematically combing the front-line trenches between St Pierre Divion and Thiepval as part of their forward reconnaissance for a relief operation of sectors C1 to C4 planned for the following night. Hinkel and the men from 7th Company began to look forward to some rest. There would be no sleep, however, for the roving commanders that night; much administrative planning and orders would be required to co-ordinate the exchange between the 99th Regiment men and the Bavarians in the second and third lines to the rear. Many veterans were uneasy that this should be attempted in the teeth of an anticipated attack, but the British had still not made a move and there was acceptance that their experienced division commander von Soden – well known to them all – knew what he was about.[32]

Diary accounts vividly illustrate the tensions that many of the soldiers of the 26th and 28th Reserve Divisions were enduring. 'Every one of us has become years older in these five days,' wrote one soldier. 'We hardly know ourselves. Bechtel said that he has lost 10 pounds in these five days.' Unteroffizier Felix Kircher, with Reserve Artillery Regiment 26 near Pozières, remembered the difficulty of transporting precious water forward. The carriers:

> ... had to carry them three to five kilometres and had to jump from shell hole to shell hole. If they arrived at all it was well past midnight and they only had about a tenth left in the kettles.

'Luckily, it rained yesterday,' wrote one soldier in his diary, 'and the water in the shell holes, mixed with the yellow shell sulphur, tasted as good as a bottle of beer.' The cumulative effect of the thudding impacts was wearing them down physically and mentally. 'The villages are burning almost day and night; terrible to see,' wrote a soldier near Fricourt and Mametz. 'You can imagine the misfortune – there were many tears, the people were crying, very hard for them and especially little children.'

Witnessing these poignant domestic scenes inevitably turned thoughts to home. 'Dear Wife, we are in a beastly hole,' one captured letter revealed. 'The English have been shooting day and night since Saturday the 24th.' They were frequently gassed and 'we have no rest day and night'. Movement to and from the front-line trenches was virtually impossible. 'If the "push" had not come, we were to have been relieved on the 28th, now we will have to stick it out,' the disappointed soldier wrote. 'The strain on my nerves is terrible,' revealed another despairing diary, 'I cannot write any more of what I have gone through.'[33]

Forty-eight hours before there had been a sudden dampening of the artillery fire in front of Serre. 'Now, outside, everyone out,' the 2nd Battalion Infantry Regiment 169 was ordered. Otto Lais and his comrades raced up the dugout steps where 'already the shadows of attacking Englishmen were dancing out of the early morning grey fog'. It was a company size trench raid. The British were repulsed amid shouts of 'the bloody Fritzes are still in there!' Lais and his men had long lost count of the warnings and intercepts already passed down from higher headquarters.[34]

'Latrine rumours' about pending attacks proliferated. In early May, Second Army headquarters had warned all units about a French Army captain masquerading in uniform as a

German Army Oberleutnant. The report reads like a 1930s John Buchan spy novel. There was a full description of a suspect who had a peculiar index finger on his left hand while his right leg was 2 cm shorter than his left because of an old wound. Any suspicions were 'to be immediately reported to division'. German soldiers were easily convinced the enemy had a network of spies at their disposal. Gerhard Bahrmann for example heard English soldiers shouting across 'You sauerkraut eaters!' from the other side of no man's land. As it happened, sauerkraut was indeed that day's ration. 'I thought,' he recalled, 'had they smelled that today we were getting sauerkraut?' Shortly before midnight Grenadier Emil Kury, a machine-gunner in front of Mametz, was quietly informed in the field kitchen to 'tell your comrades the English will attack tomorrow morning'. It would take him seven laborious hours to get back to his trench, moving from shell hole to shell hole with the rations. 'When I got back I couldn't find my dugout because the ground was so torn up.' But by then everyone knew in any case.[35]

Veterans could 'sense' an impending attack. German soldier Hans Seidelmann reckoned 'because of the short distance from trench to trench, attacks lasted – until one correctly identified it – no longer than five minutes'. Speed of response was therefore crucial. Every conceivable measure, from the siting of dugouts to placing mirrors at the head of dugout steps to reflect an image of the enemy's trenches, was employed to aid this rapid reaction. The victor was the one who won the race to the opposing parapet. 'You didn't get attacks in the middle of the night,' Seidelmann calculated, 'most took place in the early morning twilight, or during the same twilight evening hour.' Full light was the time for eating and refilling water bottles, 'and when one could get to sleep'.

The key indicator for the approaching attack was provided by a Moritz listening device intercept from the southern point of the village of La Boisselle. It could detect signals transmissions. 56th Reserve Brigade notified its 28th Division headquarters about the fragmentary British message it picked up:

... the infantry must hold on obstinately to every yard of ground that is gained. Behind is excellent artillery ...

It was a fragmentary report, but enough to send important messages through the honeycombed ridge-line positions of the 26th and 28th Reserve Divisions overlooking the British line. The message fragment was heard at 22.17 hours. Surviving documentary evidence from division and regimental logs suggest it was widely distributed all along the German front line before dawn. It likely came from a British Fourth Army transmission to its corps and the IV Brigade of the Royal Flying Corps. This unnecessary but morale enhancing sign-off was to cost thousands of lives:

In wishing all ranks good luck the Army Commander desires to impress on all infantry units the supreme importance of helping one another and holding on tight to every yard of ground gained. The accurate and sustained fire of the artillery during the bombardment should greatly assist the task of the infantry.[36]

Some of the content was garbled during intercept and translation but the implication after the sustained bombardment was crystal clear. Every German soldier in the line could anticipate an early morning attack. 'There was just one single heart-felt prayer on our lips,' recalled Friedrich Hinkel sitting in his dugout beneath the Schwaben Redoubt:

Oh God, free us from this ordeal; give us release through battle, grant us victory; Lord God! Just let them come!

CHAPTER 2

Boulevard Street to Culver Street: The British Trenches

Midnight to 4.30 am

Midnight to 1 am

'Lord, I shall be very busy this day ...' The March-Out

The British had been on the move all night. The summer weather, which had been fine until now, changed when the bombardment began on 24 June; it became overcast, temperatures dropped and it rained every day. During the evening of 30 June conditions improved and the wind died down as more than 100,000 British soldiers began moving out of their village billets towards the front line in the gathering dusk. Many appreciated this might be their final sunset. Lieutenant Noel Hodgson, with the 9th Battalion the Devonshire Regiment, 'knew quite well' according to his padre, Ernest Crosse, 'that the chances were that he would be killed'. He was not unduly pessimistic, but like many of his peers, chose not to discuss it, because as the padre suggested, 'there are times when a man's thoughts are best left to himself'. Hodgson occupied a delightful billet in the Bois des Tailles three miles behind the line. Nightingales were heard here, and the atmospheric sunsets that Hodgson had enjoyed from his hillside school near Durham Cathedral were reflected in the same sky. He was inspired to write an especially poignant poem about them, found after his death, part of which reads:

> *Ere the sun swings his noonday sword*
> *Must say goodbye to all of this*

By all delights that I shall miss
Help me to die, O Lord.

Hodgson, moving forward with his men this night, had just hours to live.[1]

One hundred and fifty-eight British battalions would be heavily involved in the morning attack, numbering up to 66,000 in the first waves alone. Marching across gentle chalk-land in the evening twilight and traversing small valley streams with shadowy woodland, while winding their way along country roads, evocatively reminded them of home. Unlike the drab squalor of Flanders and the industrial landscapes of Lens and Loos, these surroundings were familiar. 'The land we were traversing recalled the downs of Hampshire,' thought Lieutenant GF Ellenberger, with the 9th King's Own Yorkshire Light Infantry, with 'its chalky slopes undulating and covered with coarse grass'. It was still 'abroad' because of the roadside crucifixes, gaunt churches and ugly single-storey farmhouse villages, set in seemingly defensive squares. 'It might be Kent if it wasn't Picardy,' remembered Captain Charles Carrington of the Royal Warwickshire Regiment. 'Poppies, cornflowers, deep green lanes, wide rolling downs, all the same except that France has long bluer distances and wider expanses of open country.'

Private William Holbrook, with the 4th Royal Fusiliers, remembered passing a paper boy with a bundle of newspapers under his arm shouting: '*Le Journal*: Germany buggered up!' From north to south, from Gommecourt and Serre to Fricourt, and east to Maricourt, British soldiers marched to the sound of guns across a 16 to 18-mile front.[2]

Since the spring, Charles Carrington recalled in an interview, 'we began to learn the great battle was coming'. He had been in the line since the previous December and knew 'a great push' was coming, which 'was to be the great moment of our lives'. Shelling increased, 'it began to get much more dangerous' and 'not nearly so much fun'. More and more guns appeared in the line, regiments 'crowded up more close together', and 'the war then assumed a different shape'. He called it 'the great test' and the sheer scale of the movement towards the front line was game changing. 'I don't think it was ever the same again afterwards, as it had been in these almost romantic days,' he reflected. The war was taking on an impersonal mass industrial character.[3]

'In a little courtyard on the evening of June 30th, I called the old platoon to attention for the last time,' remembered Lieutenant Edward Liveing, with the 12th Battalion the London Regiment near Hébuterne opposite Gommecourt, north of the line. He solemnly shook hands with the officers to be left in reserve and marched off. There was a pause as the London Scottish filed by. 'The men lit up their pipes and cigarettes and shouted jokes to the men of the other regiment as they passed.' Liveing contemplated the sunset, 'wondering a little if this was the last time that I should see it'. Many of his men would not. 'A great zest in the splendour of life swept over me,' he admitted, 'as I sat there in the glow of that setting sun.' He was reminded of the seventeenth-century Cavalier prayer by Sir Jacob Astley, which his father had enclosed on a card in his last letter:

Lord, I shall be very busy this day.
I may forget Thee, but do not Thou forget me.

The verse offered comfort during this 'calm before the storm' which 'sat brooding over everything'.[4]

Cinematographer Lieutenant Geoffrey Malins preferred to tie his bulky Moy and Bastie ciné camera to his shoulders.

This freed his arms when moving, enabling him to take cover more easily. Malins was based at General Headquarters (GHQ) at Montreuil and had realised from the prevailing atmosphere that something big was about to happen. With him was another movie cameraman John 'Mac' McDowell and stills photographer Ernest Brooks. Their combined efforts were to be edited and produced for a later documentary entitled *The Battle of the Somme*. Malins had already filmed masses of assembled troops waiting to move forward, amid an atmospheric backdrop of smoke from hundreds of camp fires and dust from the moving columns. There was always a smile and wave for a photographer. Ciné cameras were a novelty, and helmets were immediately waved aloft at the exciting prospect of maybe being seen by relatives in one of the moving picture theatres at home.

Malins and McDowell captured scenes of this last move to the front. The Moy and Bastie camera was cranked by hand, which powered a chain over a series of cogs, exposing standard 35 mm film at 16 frames per second. One crank revolution was eight frames, so a rate of two revolutions a second was required. These captured the ghostly columns heading for the front on film that can still be viewed today. Marching soldiers pull handcarts loaded with additional stores. Motorcycle dispatch riders dart in and out of the columns, with baskets of carrier pigeons on their backs. Excited and panting dogs run barking, in and out of the ranks, reflecting the same excitement evident on the faces of those who realise they are being filmed. Ten days before, Major Charles Ward-Jackson the Camp Commandant to VII Corps at Pas, had written to his wife Queenie describing just the sort of the scenes Malins filmed:

Everywhere there are troops; under every bank there are horses; Field Ambulance Hospitals are everywhere; huge howitzers on railway-trucks lurk stealthily in orchards; telegraph and telephone wires on flimsy stakes like hop-poles cross each other in every direction and make a sort of Aerial entanglement overhead.

Malins was there for £1 a day, granted the rank of honorary lieutenant and provided transport and free lodging. He had previously worked for Gaumont Graphic at the front in Belgium. They had given him a little money, a camera and several cans of film. In October 1915 the War Office appointed him an 'official kinematographer' in recognition of some short action films he had made. His was physically demanding and dangerous work. Cameras were unwieldy instruments, tripod-mounted and heavy, with hand-cranked motors that tended to jam. Once set up, the apparatus could be mistaken for a machine-gun and often attracted fire. Malins was lucky to be in the trenches at all. Lord Kitchener and the then Commander of the First Army, Sir Douglas Haig, loathed the press. Cinema, however, was seen as entertainment for the masses, so Malins was given his chance. Authorities brought up before the advent of moving pictures did not take them too seriously, unlike newspapers, which were read in the influential London clubs. Malins was allowed in the front line with the 29th Division opposite Beaumont Hamel on 1 July 1916. He was destined to capture some of the most iconic images of the war that day.

The troops followed four main routes moving north, northwest and east to occupy their attack positions. Route signs and guides were all in place and traffic control was efficient. Bridges had been painted with white lines to show up in the dim light, and tapes laid along dark paths. The whole Allied front appeared to be on the move this night. 'We were all agog with expectancy, all quietly excited and strung to a pitch,' wrote Captain Charles May of the 22nd Manchesters in his diary. 'But unhesitatingly I record that our only anxiety is that we will do our job well.' Morale and spirits were high. 'This is the greatest thing the battalion or any of us have ever been in,' May recorded. 'To the right one could discern the dim outlines of platoons moving up steadily at equal distances like ourselves,' remembered Edward Liveing, with the London Regiment. 'One could just catch the distant noise of spade clinking on rifle.'[5]

The men, as the films of Malins and McDowell show, were very heavily laden. Private Frank Lindley, remembers being in marching order without packs as the 14th Yorks and Lancs marched towards Serre. He had a bandolier of rifle ammunition slung across his shoulder, pouches full of 'ammo' and a Mills bomb in each pocket. A field telephone with big batteries was also suspended from his shoulder, which 'weighed a ton'. In addition 'I had a coil of signal wire as well, and my gun', which meant 'I hadn't a feeling for anything'. Harry Hall with the 13th Regiment remembered, 'We'd got bags of bombs, entrenching tools, full kit including blanket, gas masks, picks, shovels and rifles and God knows what.' They couldn't see much, and what they could was viewed through a veil of sweat.[6]

Tactical manoeuvring or any form of responsive movement with such loads was impractical. The best that could be achieved was a steady plodding pace. Constant halts added to the burden. Soldiers bent over to alleviate the load, because if they sat down they would need assistance to get back up. Sergeant Ernest Bryan, with the 17th King's Liverpool Regiment opposite Montauban, later got the chance to demonstrate the impracticality of the weights they carried. He suggested to his brigadier that his brigade major might wish to try it out.

I got two privates, Lewis gunners, to put everything on him –
bombs in the pockets, sandbags, spade, kit, rations, extra
ammunition round the neck – all of it.

'How do you feel, sir?' the wilting officer was asked. 'It's
a hell of a weight,' he concurred. 'You haven't started yet!'
Bryan insisted, placing a rifle in the brigade major's hand
and a 46 lb pannier in the other. 'There's a farm field at the
back of here that's just being ploughed,' he pointed out. 'Try
walking 100 yards and see how you feel,' Bryan said, 'and
that's a playground to what we'll all have to go over on the
Somme.' The brigadier, taken aback, ventured, 'You feel very
strongly about this,' to which Bryan responded, 'Wouldn't
you, sir? Wouldn't anybody?' Loads were heavy, but as the
artillery was clearly pulverising the Germans, the assumption
was that the infantry would simply walk across no man's land
in waves.

All infantry battalions were similarly burdened. Battle kit
without packs weighed around 40 lbs. The rifle and bayonet
was 11 lbs, and 220 rounds of ammunition about 13 lbs, and
the water bottle was the same. Often the harness would awk-
wardly pitch the load too far forward. John Veitch, struggling
into Bécourt Wood with the 16th Royal Scots, remembered
that 70 extra rounds in bandoliers and two bombs tended
to pull soldiers over, if they stumbled, and 'it took a bit of
getting used to'. 'It was about a 12-hour job moving up and
we were all tired out,' remembered Private Charlie Swales,
with the 14th Yorks and Lancs. 'Instead of going to attack we
ought to have been going to bed!'[7]

As they approached the artillery positions, the awesome
noise and flickering images provided a distraction from their
numbing fatigue. Intelligence officer John Masefield (not
the poet of the same name, who also served on the Western

Front but in a hospital) remembered the artillery was broadly located by the roads, to aid re-supply. 'The trees and banks by the wayside were used to hide the batteries, which roared all day and all night.' As Lieutenant Edward Liveing rounded the outskirts of Sailly-au-Bois to the north, 'the batteries soon let us know of their presence … Red flashes broke out in the gathering darkness followed by quick reports.' He followed the rushing noise of the shells and 'saw yellow-red flashes licking upon the horizon, wherever our shells were finding their mark'. Passing by the village of Hébuterne was the sort of domestic distraction that reminded them of home and their uncertain lease of life:

> *I experienced that unpleasant sensation of wondering whether I should be lying out – this time tomorrow – stiff and cold in that land beyond the trees, where the red shrapnel burst and star shells flickered.*

What would be the impact on those they loved at home? His men shared the same bleak considerations. 'I don't think that I am far wrong when I say those thoughts were occurring to every man in the silent platoon behind me.'

There was a pause as they came up against the congestion at the entrance of the communication trenches up ahead. 'Look at that fire in Sailly, sir!' one of his men, shortly to die, exclaimed. 'I turned round and saw a great yellow flare illuminating the sky in the direction of Sailly, the fiery end of some barn or farm building, where a high explosive had found its billet.'[8]

The huge army of 158 British infantry battalions moving forward had three distinct characteristics: 43 were regular battalions, 27 were Territorial, while the vast majority, numbering 88, were Kitchener's New Army, men who had not seen action before. All were volunteers, the cream of British manhood. In August 1914 there had been only 247,000 regular officers and men, with 268,000 in the Territorials. When topped up with the Special Reserve, militia and other volunteers, Britain's fighting strength on land was 733,000, against Germany's 700,000 strong peacetime army, which swelled to 3.8 million on mobilisation. Britain had never competed with mass conscripted continental armies before, but by July 1916 she was fielding the largest army that had ever taken the field.[9]

The regular divisions holding the line since 1914 were regular in name only; most of the 'Old Contemptibles' were either dead or wounded and had been replaced by new recruits. Sergeant-Major Ernest Shepherd, a regular soldier in the 1st Dorsets opposite Thiepval, had been moving forward for over four hours that night. On forming up before marching off the commanding officer had addressed the battalion. 'No prisoners for the Dorsets,' he announced. He suspected that two of his officers had been 'murdered by the Huns' during recent trench raids. As they entered the familiar maze of approach routes to the front line, 'a most terrible gunfire was going on,' Shepherd recalled, 'gun flashes quite blinding and noise deafening'.

Shepherd's battalion followed the Pioneer Road to the Authuille Road and arrived at the communication trenches preparatory for the attack at one o'clock in the morning. 'Place was already nearly crammed,' he noted in his diary, 'only four dugouts for company, ⅔ of us slept outside, enemy sending heavy shell and shrapnel all round us.' Shepherd had been in the line since January 1915 and knew what to expect; he was the consummate professional and had already walked and checked out these trench systems prior to their arrival. He knew the 'Big Push' as it was called was about to be launched. 'We have a terribly tough time ahead,' he wrote in his diary, 'but I am quite confident that we shall gain our objective and make things hum.'

Just nine days earlier he had been on leave, staying first with his sister Ethel in Brixton, before taking a refreshing break by the sea at Lyme Regis, his home town. Back to familiar surroundings, he found the gap between front and home unbridgeable. 'Various persons I met kept congratulating me,' he wrote. 'At first I thought it was for being alive,' he ironically reflected, 'later I found that I was "Mentioned in Dispatches" by Sir Douglas Haig.' Not a particularly happy event for Shepherd, because his close friend listed in the same dispatch had only recently been killed, and the publicity brought it all back. 'I assured everyone I met that I did not feel even a little flattered at being "Mentioned",' especially as many others from the Army Service Corps, Ordinance, Veterinary Corps and Military Police were included, 'who, I am ready to stake my life on it, have never yet seen a front line trench.' Shepherd felt accosted 'at every few yards by ladies old and maidens fair of my acquaintance'. Veterans on leave need emotional space and tend to shy away from intimate human contact, which they find claustrophobic. He was there to forget the war but 'all solemnly assured me that I was looking well' despite having been 'reported in papers killed, blown to pieces, killed from gas poisoning, wounded etc., at least six times'. Questions and enquiries about the war never ceased. By the afternoon of his idyll at Lyme Regis by the sea, 'I came to the conclusion that much more of this and I should be a nervous wreck.' Back in the line he swiftly readjusted to the familiar sights and smells of the front. A near miss from a heavy shell exploded a dugout store nearby containing flares, petrol and Bangalore torpedoes;

it killed ten people and two others burned to death. 'At 06.30,' he wrote, 'our artillery were bombarding intensely, a most awful din.'[10]

The veterans had been bled white over nearly two years of war. Mabel Lethbridge, a 17-year-old munitions worker, remembered what it was like when her father and brothers came back to London on leave. 'I noticed a strange lack of ability to communicate with us,' she remembered. There was tension:

> They couldn't tell us what it was really like. They would perhaps make a joke, but you'd feel it sounded hollow, as there was nothing to laugh about. They were restless at home, they didn't want to stay, they wanted to get back to the front. They always expressed a desire to finish it.

They sat with ghosts in their kitchens and living rooms.[11]

Heavy casualties had also blurred much of the distinction between regular and Territorial Army (TA). TA battalions had a regular captain adjutant, regimental sergeant-major and a small cadre of regular senior NCOs leading part-time soldiers. They were civilians, who drilled one night a week and soldiered at weekends. Regulars looked down on the 'Saturday night soldiers', while the TA invariably insisted they were more proficient than they actually were. Both could not do without the other. These battalions were sent to France early on and generally attached to a regular brigade for six months, before being collated into TA divisions. Major Philip Neame, VC, serving with the 56th Division, came to regard them as 'absolutely first class'. Many of the London Division TA soldiers had been clerks and white-collar workers and in Neame's view 'the personnel, taken on the whole, were more intelligent than the average regular soldier'.[12]

Lieutenant Richard 'Rex' Cary with the 9th London Rifles had set off from Hébuterne toward Gommecourt at about 9 pm the night before. His flurry of letters and postcards in June reveal just how regular and efficient the British field post was between home and front. Mail catered for physical and emotional needs. Cary, a new and proudly gazetted TA officer the previous November, enjoyed the good life. 'Don't forget,' he reminded his mother when she was about to send a parcel in early June, 'that I should like the contents of the very best quality.' Two weeks later he had specific requests: 'In about four days time, will you send me another cake, a tin of Golden Syrup and about a pound box of chocolates and a tin of biscuits.' Bizarrely, when he returned to the trenches in late June he asked for 'my white silk pyjamas – only the one suit'. He was enjoying the magazines his mother dispatched; 'if you send them every month it will suit me fine'.

Cary's letters were not fixated on the coming battle; front realities would upset those at home. He was more animated about his forthcoming engagement to Doris Mummery from Leytonstone. 'Of course as regards class they are above us,' he wrote, 'but I don't think that will worry Doris much.' It had probably caused a little anxiety, but the previous month her parents had assented. 'You will be glad to know,' he wrote to his mother, 'I am going to settle down at last. For I can assure you there is only one girl for me now and that is Doris.' So as Richard moved up to the front line he was in fine fettle. 'The fellows here are quite decent,' he wrote, and Gommecourt he was convinced would be carried. The 48-hour postponement of the attack was a reminder of mortality, but even during the reprieve he wrote:

Just a few lines to let you know I am quite safe. If you do not hear some time from me, do not worry, read papers about Gommecourt.

He was censoring his own letters, and even just before the bombardment began he exuded optimism. 'By the way, peace is going to be declared by the end of August,' he assured his mother. 'You see if this does not come true as Fritz cannot last much longer.' He intended to be engaged in August.

Like much of Kitchener's New Army, Rex Cary was untouched by the cynicism that came with interminable trench warfare. This would be his first set-piece battle. Even during the preliminary bombardment he assured his mother: 'am still in the pink and getting on fine here'. He was ecstatic about his pending engagement to Doris, pleased his mother had already visited her and that the consent from her parents had been forthcoming, so that 'on my first leave the event will come off'. As he strode forward at the head of his platoon towards the increasing din of battle, the future remained inviting; it was the other people that died. 'Of course,' he persuaded his mother 'we shall not be married until I have made good after the war but anyway I feel awfully proud in knowing I am going to be engaged to the best little girl on earth.' What could possibly go wrong?[13]

Just over half the battalions winding their way forward were Kitchener's New Army. Kitchener with his piercing eyes and accusing finger had called out from the famous poster, *'Britons! Join Your Country's Army!'* The appeal was directly to the face, at whichever angle a man stood. The nation-wide appeal had brought in half a million recruits by the end of 1914, five times the intended target. Simple patriotism and the desire to stand up against the German foe 'for King and Country' was the initial spark. Many men were also motivated by a zest for adventure or simply the chance to escape from the tedium of the office, the hard graft of the workshop floor, isolated farmyards or the drab coal mines of the Midlands and North. One Irish agricultural labourer enthused, 'It's the finest life in the whole wide world.' Kitchener's Army meant 'mate, drink, lodgin' and washin' all in one'. As he pointed out:

Wasn't I working hard for ten long years for a farmer there beyant in Kerry, and never once in all that time did the ould boy say to me, 'Stand at aise'.[14]

Katie Morter, a factory worker, lost her husband to the music hall star Vesta Tilly, glamorously draped with a Union Jack over her evening gown. She was recruiting at the Palace Theatre Manchester. If she had known, 'I wouldn't have gone of course,' Katie recalled. 'We don't want to lose you,' Tilly sang, 'but we think you ought to go', as she placed her hand on the shoulder of Katie's newly married husband, Percy. 'I was terribly upset and I said I didn't want him to be a soldier, because I didn't want to lose him.' Her husband characteristically said, 'There has to be men to go and fight for the women, otherwise where should we be?' Katie Morter, who did not make friends easily, was heartbroken to lose her companion:

We was very happily married, very happy, because we were very much in love. He thought the world of me and I thought the world of him, and then it came to be that the war started.

Percy was waiting, like thousands of others on the Somme. 'Kitty', his affectionate name for his wife, was pregnant. He only ever had six days' leave after joining, two of which were taken up by travel. Katie missed his final departure by tram, but he had confided to a friend, 'I don't think I shall ever come back again.' He occupied the centre of her very small universe in a Manchester local community. 'I would wonder what he was doing,' she recalled, 'and if he was thinking about me.'[15]

More than fifty cities and towns in Britain formed 'Pals Battalions', with the counties of Lancashire, Yorkshire, Northumberland and Durham raising the most. Larger cities formed several battalions, such as Manchester with 15, Hull with four and Liverpool, Birmingham and Glasgow with three. Many medium-size towns had two, and these formed the bulk of the unblooded battalions moving into their assault positions along the front line. Attitudes between battalion types differed. Regulars were prepared to accept discipline unquestioningly as a matter of course. The Territorials and New Army men were acutely aware of their recent civilian origins and were generally more intelligent, perceptive and questioning.

Private Albert Andrews, 23, had been a clerk when he joined the 19th Manchester Pals in September 1914. His father worked on the railways, whereas his grandfather had survived the Charge of the Light Brigade in the Crimean War. Albert was marching towards a similarly perilous undertaking. Like most New Army men, Albert could see through the mindless authority the army wielded to mould its infantry recruits. A fastidious newly arrived officer was rejecting his efforts at shaving with a blunt razor. When his sergeant told him off, pointing out, 'This is three times, Andrews, for not shaving,' he was having none of it. 'I don't care if it is 43,' he replied, 'we are going over the top on Saturday anyway!' For him 'show soldiering' had no interest.[16]

Unlike the German Army conscripts they would shortly face, this British Army consisted entirely of volunteers, a microcosm of the society from which they were drawn.

It is my intention that this unit will be characterised by such a spirit of simple excellence that the rest of Lord Kitchener's Army will be judged by our standard.

This was part of the address made by Sir George McCrae in the Edinburgh Ulster Hall on 27 November 1914, as he formed up the 'Heart of Midlothian' or 'McCrae's Battalion' of the 16th Royal Scots, now marching toward the communication trenches. The battalion had formed around a nucleus of 16 professional footballers who had joined from a particularly inspirational Heart of Midlothian football team that had been comfortably leading the First Division in November 1914. Some 500 Hearts supporters and ticket holders joined, as well as 150 followers of Hibernian and other professional footballers from Raith Rovers, Falkirk and Dunfermline. They were shamed into signing up by a public debate over the morality of continuing to play professional football when young soldiers were dying at the front. The 'Footballer's battalion' had left Edinburgh in the spring of 1915. Their paternal manager John McCartney watched them go, later claiming, 'The finest men I ever knew had gone.' Many of the battalion's soldiers, like Henry Wattie, Duncan Currie, Ernest Ellis and James Boyd, had been predicted to be footballing greats.[17] Now they were advancing through the night with their heavy loads towards their assembly area in Bécourt Wood. In six hours' time they would attack around La Boisselle. There were disturbing reports that the wire in front of them was 'knocked about' but looked worryingly intact.

Men from the 36th Ulster Division were filing into the communication trenches in Thiepval Wood, in readiness for their attack on the high ground overlooking the Ancre valley. On top of it was the parallelogram-shaped Schwaben Redoubt, with four lines of German trenches in between. Its formidable appearance had earned it the nicknames 'Devil's Dwelling' and 'Hell's Corner'. The ground before it rose 250 feet over 1,000 yards. An observant artillery officer had counted 16 rows of wire protecting its front, with an average of five rows screening its second line. The Irishmen had resolved that although 'some of them would "get the beck" – the call from death' in taking it, the redoubt *would* fall.

The Ulster Division belonged to a deeply bonded group recruited from the oath-bound members of the pre-war Ulster Volunteer Force (UVF) in 1914. These men subscribed to a form of tribal, warlike, 'it was the fight that was the thing' mentality more akin to ancient Ireland than the industrial age. Some commented: 'Were not soldiers who died in action to be envied, rather than pitied, by those who found themselves alive when the war was over?'

During the crisis in the months leading up to the outbreak of the European war, the Protestants of Northern Ireland had fiercely contested any attempt to impose Home Rule. The UVF was a quasi-paramilitary organisation set up by Dublin barrister and MP Sir Edward Carson in early 1913. Local volunteers participated in 'Sunday afternoon strolls', which were ten-mile route marches, carrying rifles. Afterwards they conducted manoeuvres, dressed in bush hats with Boer War pattern bandoliers and leather belts. They were not unlike the TA, and the success of the iconic Larne gun running incident in April 1914 convinced them, God was on their side. Despite the prickly Home Rule issue they supported the British call to arms – some reluctantly. Carson insisted the prefix 'Ulster' be included in the title of the division, when the force was handed over on 18 September 1914. The Ulster Division shared the same closely bonded aura promoted by the Pals battalions on the UK mainland, adding the resolve, aggression and basic training skills that two years in the UVF had conferred. Most had signed the Ulster Covenant, an oath binding them to the collective survival of Protestant Ulster as well as the British Empire, which they agreed to fight for. Tense months of pre-war drilling, marching and populist public gatherings had instilled a pent-up belligerence that could now be harnessed. These men were physically fit and served in platoons and companies like extended families. Many NCOs were the relatives and friends of the soldiers they commanded.

The training for Kitchener's New Army was short of adequate. 'In our battalion we did very little training with the barbed wire,' recalled RH Stewart, serving with the Ulster Division:

> *They put a few rows before the trenches we dug and we crawled about under and over them, but all we got was cuts and scratches.*[18]

Basic training focused on breaking a new recruit's will so that he would automatically follow orders, and the emphasis was on drill and unending fatigues. At the outbreak of war, the rapid departure of the British Expeditionary Force left few serving soldiers behind to train the New Army. All that was left were retired NCOs and officers, many of whom had not been in the army since the Boer War. Drill and tactics were outmoded. Training was left to those forming the new battalions, and they concentrated on practice skirmishing, outpost duty, drill and physical training with regular route marches of 15 to 25 miles with full packs. Rifles were outdated and training ammunition was insufficient and inferior. Poor quality American ammunition was used, as one disgruntled 16th Ulster Rifles soldier complained: 'Men who could shoot the eye out of a blackbird at 50 yards using a UVF rifle now found themselves missing the targets.' The paucity of training instructors debased training in every arm and at every level. Many soldiers were not issued up-to-date rifles until the week before departure to France. The winner of one rapid-fire rifle competition succeeded in firing 12 rounds a minute into a target 200 yards away. Pre-war recruits could shoot 15 rounds into targets at 300 yards, and first-class shots and marksmen could achieve 30.[19]

New Army battalions arriving in France shortly before the winter of 1915 spent the cold months training for and conducting trench raids within static positional warfare. They were not taught how to attack. During this period, the close-knit Pals battalions suffered their first losses. 'A chap called Holt, whose family kept a butcher's shop on the corner of Barton Lane and Boardman Street, was killed by a sniper,' Private Frank Holding in the 2nd Barnsley Pals recalled. This was the first Eccles Pal in B Company to die. 'There were notices all over the trenches telling you to keep your head down – he didn't.'[20]

Battalions broadly only conducted three activities before this attack: holding the line, labouring around the dumps and training on defence works. Weapons skills had to be developed in between. This was hardly preparation for an offensive. The odd hour of instruction, interspersed with a high proportion of heavy labour fatigues and an occasional outburst of platoon to company size trench raids – and with little sleep – was no preparation for a deliberate attack. Months of progressive training is needed for a soldier to develop the sort of 'feel' for his weapon that enables him instinctively, day or night and however critical the moment, to correctly align his sight and squeeze off accurate shots under control. 'Training was more or less by word of mouth,' recalled Private Frank Lindley with the Barnsley Pals.

We'd been training to go in one man covering another, but on the first of July we went across in waves. They told us to walk.

Kitchener's new and untested army was fit, intelligent, aggressive and patriotic, but its combat effectiveness was unknown and its initiative blunted by mindless defence fatigues. Corporal Don Murray, with the 8th King's Own Yorkshire Light Infantry, remembers being taken back 'about 10 kilometres, right away from the fighting. There, they had the whole country flagged out, a precise replica of the German lines with little flags.'

When the two VII Corps divisions started practising with their obvious mock-up of the Gommecourt defences, a German aircraft suddenly flew overhead. It was regarded as a bad omen. Rehearsals were simply about orientation and illustrating the outline plan. They practised for days. Staff officer Major Charles Ward-Jackson thought them 'a splendid idea'. 'We had a mocked-up battlefield,' remembered Private Tom Bracey, with the 9th Royal Fusiliers:

The trouble was that we were all concentrating on one point. All these men attacking one trench. But when we came to the actual attack, you couldn't do that. There was barbed wire and artillery fire, and it wasn't like the practices.[21]

Concentration invited death. The reality in assaulting trenches is that only small, evenly spread groups arrive.

The 2nd Salford Pals Battalion was presented with a 40-page dossier of orders for its attack on Thiepval. The attack plan read like a railway timetable, with nine separate artillery lifts dictating a pace of advance so complex that a table was included. Such detail was pedantic and dismaying, likewise the 24 inches space per man provided for in the trenches dug for their assembly in Authuille Wood. Direction verged on the bizarre. 'The top three buttons and hooks of the tunic will be left undone,' they were instructed, 'so as to facilitate the adjustment of helmets.' No detail was being left to chance, but every experienced soldier knew that rarely does a plan survive the crossing of the start line in a deliberate attack.[22]

The 25 officers and 776 men of the Newfoundland Regiment with the veteran 29th Division had left the village of Louvencourt four hours before. The Newfoundland men came from Britain's oldest self-governing Dominion. They were fiercely loyal to the crown, maintaining their non-Canadian status. Its young men had dropped out of school and quit jobs to be part of this enterprise. Among them was 24-year-old Private James Howard, who had a dark hair and complexion and came from a well-to-do family. His father had been a sea captain. James trained to be a printer but dropped all that in 1914 and had already seen action with the 29th Division at Suvla Bay, Gallipoli. By contrast, the older Linus Coombs, at 25, was the new boy. He had arrived in France just two months before, enough time to make friends. A slight figure at 5 ft 7 ins tall, his small 39-inch chest was supporting a 70-pound load. Many were carrying equipment weighing up to a third of their body weight.

Even smaller, at 5 ft 4 ins, was 15-year-old boy soldier Leo O'Neil. His mother had died in childbirth and his father had drowned two years before. He had five sisters and was the only provider left, trapping the odd rabbit on the Southside Hills near their home. When Leo told his sisters he had joined up 'all hell broke loose'. May, the eldest, threatened to go to the War Department and reveal his true age. 'May, it's like this,' he had said. 'If I fight I'll get paid and it will help you out, if I stay here with you we may all starve this winter.' Nothing more was said. The young Leo O'Neil doubtless struggled with his pack, but he had already grown two inches since joining two years before.

The Newfoundlanders had re-checked their gas masks, 'the google-eyed booger with the tit', earlier in June, preparatory for the attack. 'Going through a gas filled chamber with our gas masks on' was a challenge for Coombs; 'after a half hour of it,' he admitted, 'you'd sell your soul for a breath of fresh air.' Masks were hot, and made it difficult to speak clearly or shoot straight. Morale in these purposeful columns trudging through the night was still high, however. 'It is surprising to see how happy and light-hearted everyone is,' wrote Lieutenant Owen Steele in his diary, 'yet this is undoubtedly the last day for a good many.' Steele himself had barely six days left to live and this was to be his last entry.

Three days earlier the Newfoundland men had celebrated their final Holy Communion in the village church at Louvencourt. They enjoyed a special relationship with the villagers, having been billeted there 34 days. Used to practising thrift in their own harsh climate, the Newfoundlanders were shocked at having to trample down acres of knee-high crops around the village during training rehearsals. So it was an open secret there would be a battle. Howard and Coombs likely joined this final service alongside Private Leopold Morey, who remembered:

There were over 300 of us in the churchyard. There were quite a lot of graves of Frenchmen from 18 to 21, killed in August 1914. One of the girls cried quite openly in the church. I expect we reminded them of their own sons and brothers and husbands and loved ones that had been killed.[23]

While the Gallipoli veterans knew what to expect, newcomers were blissfully ignorant. There was a temporary hold-up at Tipperary Avenue, but soon the Newfoundland soldiers were filing into their destination: the deep dugouts in

St John's Road. They were directly opposite 'Y' Ravine, one of the most formidable German obstacle belts, just south of the Hawthorne Ridge. They were in the third wave, so had a better chance of survival.

Many veterans recalled such final communions and church services. Cameraman 'Mac' McDowell filmed the 24th Manchesters being addressed by a wind-swept padre, cassock blowing in the breeze, at the Bois des Tailles near Albert, before they set off. 'We were told that Christ gave up his life for others,' Albert Andrews of the 19th Manchesters remembered hearing during their 15-minute service. 'We were about to go forward and some of us would be called upon to make that great sacrifice.' To men of the 7th Bedfords their padre was 'a grand chap,' Second Lieutenant Tom Adlam reckoned. 'He don't ask if you're a Roman Catholic, Church of England, or a Hottentot. He just takes you and buries you.' Relationships could be volatile. Sergeant Frederick Goodman, a field ambulance medic, recalled that when the last rites were administered, 'those clergy fellows did not have their feet on the ground'. 'A man who is passing out doesn't want religion pushed at him too hard,' he explained, because 'he's not in a fit state to give it careful consideration.' If the padre insisted, the outcome could become fraught. 'The man would sometimes tell the padre to go away – not with the best of language – and it was pretty awful.'[24]

Pep talks, particularly those extolling sacrifice, were not always well received. General Beauvoir de Lisle addressed his 29th Division soldiers in a hollow square on the eve of the attack, filmed by cameraman Geoffrey Malins. The 2nd Royal Fusiliers and 1st Lancashire Fusiliers listened as the general talked up the size of the Allied push, the enemy's dubious plight and the need to uphold the traditions of Gallipoli. 'The faces of the men shone with a new light,' the patriotic Malins claimed as the men were marched off, heads back and chests out, their souls reflecting 'their inflexible determination to win'. Malins's driver David Laing saw it differently. 'One thing that amused and amazed me was the pep talks given by the brigade generals to the troops just before the big day of the Somme battles,' he recalled. The backdrop to this speech was two heavy batteries of artillery, banging off shells nearby, providing an audible reminder of what to expect:

> *They got the battalions to line up on a three-sides square, with the general addressing them on the enormous amount of troops and guns we had, and that Jerry's lines would be knocked into pulp. The British troops would then go over the top and walk right on to Berlin.*

Listening to this was 21-year-old George Ashurst, with the Lancashire Fusiliers. George came from a humble background; his father was a quarryman, who spent half the family's income in the village pub. George was an 'old' soldier, having been mobilised as a special reserve into the regular army, and had experienced the 1914 Christmas truce. De Lisle claimed 'the coming great advance … might mean the end of the war'. George and his comrades were told that if all the guns, deafening them during the speech, 'were placed side by side – that is wheel to wheel – they would stretch from the English Channel to the Alps'. Ashurst and his comrades were sceptical when they heard that 'not a German soldier would be left to bar our progress'. Fresh from the debacle at Gallipoli, Ashurst knew both Turks and the Germans. 'I wonder if while he was talking,' he recalled:

... he heard the ugly murmurings in the ranks or noticed our officers turning round and in an undertone order silence and issue threats.

If the General had picked up on this undercurrent of opinion, 'he would have thought they were not so enthusiastic about the big push'.[25]

1 am to 4.30 am

'Stumbling in the dark'. The Trenches

At about 1 am many of the battalions marching up to the line were passing the artillery gun lines. These tended to be just off the roads, for which they were dependent for re-supply. 'The guns were now roaring worse than ever,' recalled Private Albert Andrews coming up from Bray. 'To speak to anyone you had to get close to their ear and shout at the top of your voice.' Corporal Henry Ogle of the 7th Royal Warwickshires recalled seeing 15-inch howitzers in action for the first time:

These monster 15-inch howitzers were ponderous masses of machinery and castings, with levers, hand wheels, recoil devices and a crane for hoisting the big shells into a sort of shoe or shovel and thence into the breech.

The awesome sound of the huge shells emerging from the muzzle and climbing into the sky made a big impression:

I felt as if in a tube of sound. It was a sound made up of giant unlubricated screwing as the shell spiralled away, of rushing wind as the air closed in like thunder behind it, of screaming and whining as fragments of copper driving band cut the air in its wake.

From far away in the distance, some seven or eight kilometres, 'might be heard a mere hrrumph!' Staff officer Major Charles Ward-Jackson saw one detonate and 'a huge patch of ground about as big as Betty's rose garden seemed to rise bodily in the air in a great column of smoke higher than poplar trees.' There were 1,537 guns and howitzers, with one field gun to every 20 yards of front and a heavy gun every 58 yards, banging away with seemingly inexhaustible supplies of ammunition. Private Tommy Higgins, with the 1/5th North Staffs, was equally impressed by the 18-inch naval gun at Humbercamps. 'The first time they fired it,' he recalled, 'the wind blew some old barns down like a pack of cards.'

Captain Charles May, with the 22nd Manchester Regiment opposite Montauban, saw 'the face of the earth is changed up there'. Seven days of bombardment had impressed his men, one of whom exclaimed, 'Fritz you're for it!' It led May to think, 'The greatest battle in the world is on the eve of breaking. Please God it may terminate successfully for us.'[26]

Not all were convinced. Rifleman Percy Jones, approaching Gommecourt from the north with the Queen's Westminster Rifles, thought, 'The fact is that this attack is based entirely on the supposition that there will be no Germans left alive to oppose us.' The plan appeared sound, 'but if the Germans obstinately refuse to die' they could be in trouble. Jones kept his opinion to himself. Knowing the Germans facing them occupied 40-foot dugouts, 'I do not see how the stiffest bombardment is going to kill them all off … nor do I see how the whole of the enemy artillery is going to be silenced.' They could not even see it from their side of the high ground.

His division, the 56th London, was due to link with the 46th Division to the east of Gommecourt as a major diversion to the north of the line. If they failed to meet, they would have open flanks left in the air.[27]

Methodical artillery preparation on the Western Front to date had generally caused more problems for the attacker than the defender. They gave the game away, tore up the ground, created obstacles for assaulting troops in return for minimal impact on barbed wire, and made it impossible to move artillery further up to support gains. On balance it created more problems than solutions. German machine-gunners tended to simply occupy fresh shell holes. Artillery was supposed to break up defence integrity in five ways: killing or mentally breaking defenders, destroying defence positions, nullifying counter-battery fire, keeping defenders' heads down and neutralising reinforcements. The British had still to achieve three of these objectives after seven days' bombardment and were only partially successful in the other two. The Germans were weathering the storm better than anyone on the Allied side had appreciated.

'It was a tiresome job getting up to the trenches,' remembered Sergeant Richard Tawney, who was with Captain Charlie May in the 22nd Manchesters. 'I don't know anything more exasperating than walking one to two miles with a stoppage every ten or twenty yards.'

The constant stop-start was physically and mentally debilitating, 'especially when you're one of a long string of tired men and have a rifle and other traps hitched onto you'. If the march-out from the village billets had not been enough, entering the maze of communication trenches for the 158 battalions moving up was even worse. It was about 1 am.

Getting into position appeared to many to involve more effort than actual fighting.

They made us spend nearly two hours in getting through trenches that we'd known for five months as well as their native populations of rats — fat old stagers to whom men meant grub — and had been accustomed to man in 40 minutes.

The first indication of arrival, despite the pitch darkness, was the pervasive stench. 'The smells in those trenches were terrible,' recalled Second Lieutenant WJ Brockman, with the 15th Lancashire Fusiliers. It was a blend of stagnant mud, latrine buckets, chloride of lime, half-buried corpses and rotting sandbags. 'It's stayed with me all my life,' he claimed, 'excreta, urine and cordite from exploding shells.' The sickly-sweet cloying smell that seemed to permeate clothing and remain in the mouth was the pungent smell of death. As they entered, they were picked up by guides. 'The trenches to the uninitiated were a maze,' explained Sergeant Charles Quinnell with the 9th Fusiliers.

Before you entered you got the order 'Load'. You put nine in your magazine, one up the spout, and put your safety catch on, prepared to use your rifle immediately without having to load.

Tawney's company had to quickly close up. As each company was due to attack in two lines, both had to be packed into the same fire trench. British trenches had just two lines: the fire and support trench. The Germans defending often had five. British soldiers never envisaged defending. They occupied intermediate positions, poised to take ground, not hold it. Intelligence officer John Masefield described the British side of the line as 'improvised … by amateurs with few resources, as best they could, in a time of need and danger'. The German side did not give this hurried, scraped-together impression. They were deeply and more permanently ensconced, and were staying.

'It was what the lads called a "box-up",' Tawney explained. Nobody liked it because they were totally immobile and vulnerable to incoming fire. The only way to get about to pass on orders and check the line was to push and shove, 'to see that everyone was in his right place and understood what he was to do'. Here and there clouds of nervously exhaled cigarette smoke sweetened the aroma of stale sweat rising from the damp uniforms of packed soldiery. Drifting back from across no man's land were the characteristic smells of the bombardment, cordite and lyddite, tinged with the sweeter aroma of dispersed phosgene gas.[28]

'Men going into the lines saw little of where they were going,' recalled Masefield. 'It was accompanied by a little "sinking of the heart" as they entered the gash of the communication trench, following the load on the back of the man in front.' To many it seemed as if they were entering a narrow country lane, winding between high banks. There was nothing to see except the black walls of the trench sides, perhaps broken by the gleam of reflected lights from the bombardment, momentarily reflecting on water underfoot, as they sloshed through stagnant pools. The gloom was broken here and there by lanterns and flashing torchlights at the junctions where several trenches crossed. Soon the trench became narrower and more tortuous. One Ulster Division soldier described how his battalion 'was now a floundering, staggering, overloaded and perspiring closely packed mass of men, walking in couples or in single file and treading on each other's heels'.

This was it: the trenches. 'When I got up to the front line, I was frightened out of my life. I saw a mangled body blown to bits on a sack. I was scared stiff,' recalled Private Albert Day, with the 4th Gloucesters. 'You go stumbling along in the dark, cursing, falling and slipping into holes and tripping over wires,' remembered Captain Charles Carrington, with the Royal Warwickshire Regiment. As the battalions poured into the trenches there were inevitable traffic problems. 'Because there are several parties going along the trenches, they have to be controlled through a labyrinth of trenches, up trenches and down trenches,' explained Carrington. 'You can have a traffic jam in old, bad trenches as bad as a London traffic jam.' Everything, rifles and machine-gun ammunition, awkward trench mortar projectiles, had to be carried by hand by over-tired soldiers; food, drinking water, heavy equipment and, worst of all, coils of barbed wire:

> *Barbed wire is the most damnable stuff to handle. It was made up in coils that weighed half a hundredweight that we carried on a stick over two men's shoulders. You were very likely to cut your hands to ribbons before you got it there.*

Communication trenches and duckboard tracks were often simply not there, having been destroyed or damaged by artillery. 'So going along a trench,' Carrington continued, 'meant stumbling along a dark wet ditch with an irregular floor and a right angled turn every few yards so that you can't see where you are going ... to manoeuvre these cursed things round a corner was something so fatiguing it can hardly be described.'[29]

Edward Liveing recalled moving through a maze of trenches with the London Regiment, edging towards Gommecourt. 'We clattered along the brick-floored trench' of Boulevard Street, turned right into Cross Street then into Woman Street. They moved around the grisly evidence of incoming shell strikes en route. At one stage, in order to avoid blocked sections of trench, Liveing and his men clambered over the top into no man's land. His company commander approached him at about 1 am and 'putting his hand on my shoulder in his characteristic fashion, informed me in a whisper that the attack was to start at 7.30 am'.

Private Tommy Higgins was approaching the Gommecourt salient from the opposite north side, moving down the road from Foncquevillers with the 1/5th North Staffs. Tommy had joined in 1915, even though he had been a munitions worker, a protected occupation. 'I caught the fever for it,' he admitted, 'and enlisted in the infantry. He was well used to hardship, as an orphan baby who had been abandoned on a doorstep and ended up in the workhouse. The previous week he had narrowly escaped death in no man's land, being pinned down by German fire as part of a digging detail. 'Bullets had come like streams of water from hose pipes,' he fearfully remembered. His company commander had taken his name on the eve of the attack, because he had not managed to get all the mud off his uniform after lying prostrate in no man's land for hours during the last crisis. 'Not bad,' he commented, after what he had just been through. Now he was as dirty as ever, 'up to the knees in water' waiting as part of the second wave in a rearward trench, 'and here we stood and waited for daylight'. Spirits were already beginning to flag:

When they came to serve our platoon with rum, they found out someone had pinched it. So we got none. We stood there in the water with our teeth chattering with cold.

They longed for dawn.

Men had tried to sleep on arrival, but bruising and aches and pains from carrying the heavy loads, combined with a damp chill, prevented it. Combat harnesses had to come off to provide at least a layer over the cold chalky ground. Many simply stood still, gazing at nothing, packed tightly into closely packed trenches, prey to wandering morbid thoughts and tension. 'The only thing I can compare it with is like waiting for someone to die,' one Ulster soldier remembered:

You know it's coming and you wish to God it was over and done with. You smoked fag after fag, took sips of water, oiled the rifle, did everything over and over again. Even above the shelling you could hear small noises like a man sucking in air between his teeth and this got on your nerves more than the shelling.

Star shells periodically lit up the trench like day. 'The men, all of them, looked an odd colour, and tired and drawn, like people done out,' the soldier recalled. Nerves were stretched to breaking point. 'There was one fellow who took off and put on his tin hat until another man shouted at him for Christ's sake to stop it.'[30]

Men's lives were still being plucked at random by German counter-battery fire, which was unsettling after being assured that the opposition had been annihilated. Men felt especially vulnerable in trenches crowded for the assault. Corporal Harry Fellows, with the 12th Northumberland Fusiliers, recalled that when shell strikes erupted either side of their trench one of the newly arrived soldiers was suddenly buried:

All we could see of him were his legs kicking. I got hold of one leg, my mate got hold of the other, and we pulled as hard as we could but we couldn't move him.

Time was running out, they tried to scrape away the earth, but eventually his legs stopped moving. He was dead by the time they got him out. He was a new soldier, and they found he had fastened his helmet strap around his neck instead of over his chin. Fellows was horrified to realise 'the helmet had trapped in the earth, and in pulling his legs we'd pulled his neck out'. 'My God, we've strangled him,' declared his mate, 'we've murdered him.' They did not even know his name.[31]

Most men had penned their final letters over the previous two days. Some were still scribbling at the bottom of trenches. 'This is the most difficult letter I have ever sat down to write,' wrote Second Lieutenant Frank Potter, in command of a trench mortar battery. 'We are going into an attack tomorrow and I shall leave this to be posted if I don't come back.' His battery was firing at enemy targets to the north of the line opposite Serre.

> Of death I haven't any fear. I have no premonition of anything happening to me, I have every faith that I shall come out safely, but the chances are against one in a big attack and it is well to be prepared.

Frank Potter accepted he might die if necessary for his country, but saw the significance of the act to his parents. He owed them the debt of a wonderful home life and recognised 'the enormity of your sacrifice in giving your son to our country' should he not come home. 'I hope Eddie and Dick never have to face the horrors of war,' he added 'and that they will grow up to be better sons than perhaps I have been.' Front-line letters mostly reflected soldiers' anxious concern for those left at home rather than their own physical safety. 'Let Ruth have any of my belongings she may want, and I know that you will do anything in the world you can for her.' He signed off with his 'fondest love to all at home'. Frank would be shot in the head shortly after his battalion went over the top.[32]

Two types of letter were written: those that were posted straightaway and others, like Frank Potter's, that were intended to be forwarded on in the event of death. Second Lieutenant Eric Heaton wrote both. He was standing in his communication trench with the 16th Middlesex Regiment directly behind Geoffrey Malins's vantage point opposite the Hawthorne Ridge. His first was a cheery letter sent to his parents thanking them for a parcel, discussing the weather and how the padre had organised a boxing contest. 'Well, let us hope the Bosch is done for this time,' he emphatically concluded, 'he will get it strong on all sides!' They were about to 'move soon now I believe – may it be to victory'. This was the type of letter all soldiers wrote home, short, cheerful, full of mundane facts; nothing to worry the parents, full of love and significantly re-engaging with the only link they had to domestic normality. Soldiers were generally less effusive than officers and more down to earth. 'That morning we turned out our pockets,' recalled Private Jarrie Jarman, with the 7th Queen's further south of the line, 'dumping postcards of naked French girls to ensure they weren't sent home with any of our personal effects should we be killed.' They apprehensively looked on as the trench ladders were placed against the parapets.

Eric Heaton's second letter, written in the same dugout 48 hours before, was not posted. He gave it to the company quartermaster sergeant with instructions that it be passed to his friend Captain Wegg, if he did not survive the attack. 'My darling Mother and Father,' he wrote with neat precise handwriting:

Tomorrow we go to the attack in the greatest battle the British Army has ever fought. I cannot quite express my feelings on this night and I cannot tell if it is God's will that I shall come through – but if I fall in battle then I have no regrets save for my loved ones I leave behind.

There are no crossings out, the letter is neatly composed; Eric Heaton knew exactly what he wanted to say. 'No one had such parents as you have been to me,' he emphasised. He wrote about his love for his men, that 'my great aim had been to win their respect' and 'that when the time comes I shall not fail them'. He did not; within the hour he was to be shot in the knee and bleed to death in no man's land.[33]

There was little to do but wait for the tell-tale emergence of light in the sky to the east, over the German positions. Joseph Murray, a seaman with the Royal Naval Division, later described the characteristic aimless waiting:

> We stood there packed like sardines, unable to even stand up in comfort. Men were fast asleep on their feet, others just stood staring at the clouds in the sky. The laddie next to me checked his rifle and ammunition, over and over again, but apparently still not satisfied. Others just stood and stared, silent as a grave, looking forward.

'There were ways in which you could maintain self-control,' remembered Captain Charles Carrington, with the Royal Warwickshire Regiment. The number of incoming German shells was becoming particularly alarming, despite the week-long bombardment. 'If you hum a little tune to yourself, you feel that you could quietly get through this tune, before the next explosion, to give you a sort of curious sensation of safety.' Drumming fingers on knees and other irrational exercises helped. Rifleman Percy Jones opposite Gommecourt realised 'you cannot have an omelet without breaking eggs' – lives were going to be lost:

> Who will go? Who can say? I have only one wish: that nothing may happen to Billy Green. He is only eighteen, he is always

cheerful, he can always make others cheerful, and that is the sort of man we want in the trenches.

Survival was very often dependent upon the men that were to lead them over the top; their experience and expertise could determine whether they would live or die. Officers were generally well regarded and trusted, but for the majority, this would be their first big battle. Sergeant Wilfred Hunt was unconvinced – 'the quality of the officers was *shocking*,' he claimed. He was about to attack towards Mametz with the 9th Devons. 'The one we got collapsed when we got to where the guns were opening up. He just collapsed and we never saw him any more,' he commented disdainfully. 'They weren't taught to think,' declared Corporal Harry Fellows with the 12th Northumberland Fusiliers, blaming their public school backgrounds, 'only to lead.' Officers, like the men, were human, good and bad. 'My chaps were Lancashire labourers,' remembered Second Lieutenant WJ Brockman, with the Lancashire Fusiliers, 'and the class distinction was much greater then, than it is now, and they *preferred* to be led by what they described as the "officer classes".' Society was hierarchical and accepted as such; it was appropriate to be led by their 'betters'. Relationships forged in the crucible of the trenches were to engender mutual respect and would contribute to a softening of such class distinctions after the war. At this early stage of the war, leaders and the led were measuring each other up.

At 4.30 am Lieutenant Edward Liveing made the final checks on his platoon, before the attack on Gommecourt. Standing still for a moment, he noticed 'there was just a suspicion of whiteness creeping into the sky beyond the rising ground opposite'. Half the trees that had previously stood in Gommecourt Wood had now gone, he realised. Looking intently into the growing twilight revealed 'that I was gazing right into a line of chalky German trenches, and consequently that the enemy in those trenches could look straight into this trench'.[34]

It was an unsettling thought.

CHAPTER 3

Château Generals* —•

Midnight to 4.30 am

---

* See The Chain of Command, p. xvii

Midnight to 4.30 am

'With God's Help'. The British

Montreuil-sur-Mer was a very prim and dull seaside resort, according to one of the British staff officers working at GHQ (General Staff Headquarters). General Sir Douglas Haig's headquarters was established in the barracks of the École Militaire. Even at midnight isolated officers still consulted the general situation map, in one of the pleasant rooms near the officers' mess. This was a world apart from the filth, tensions and stench of the crowded front-line trenches. Haig was in his forward headquarters at the Château Val Vion at Beauquesne, two miles nearer the line from GHQ, and 12 miles from Albert. General Rawlinson commanding Fourth Army was on a par with Haig, 12 miles behind the front.

After dinner at Montreuil, the established routine was to check the map before settling down to a couple more hours' work before sleep. There has always been a traditional gulf between the front and rear. 'They swanked about in red tabs and cars,' Staff Captain Frank Fox mockingly observed, encapsulating the typical regimental field officer's view, 'and to keep up a show of work, issued all kinds of fool orders which nobody in the trenches had any time to read.' They served generals who in photographs look comfortable and well breakfasted, dressed in impeccably tailored uniforms, breeched, booted and spurred. Memoirs and diaries, however, testify to cripplingly long days. Brigadier-General John

Charteris, whose intelligence staff updated the daily situation map, reckoned 'there are few, if any, officers who do not do a fourteen hour day, and who are not to be found at work far into the night'. Frank Fox claimed to 'have seen a staff officer faint at table from sheer pressure of work' and observed 'dozens of men come fresh from regimental work, wilt away under the fierce pressure of work at GHQ'.[1]

Staff work had been relentless in the build-up to the eve of the 'Big Push'. Advance headquarters had moved forward two days ago. 'Up to now things have gone quite well,' Charteris recorded in his diary. They had staffed the assembly of the largest British Army that had ever gone to war. Huge stocks of guns, ammunition, food and fodder for horses had been dumped as near the front as possible. Wells had been dug for scarce water and miles of pipeline laid. Extra roads, railways and additional railway sidings had been constructed. The logistic system was stretched to virtual breaking point. Additional medical facilities and prisoner of war cages had been prepared, and improved communications laid. Every requirement to facilitate the efficient march-up of over a hundred infantry battalions, including guides, had broadly been met. It was an unprecedented logistic and administrative effort, competently staffed and executed by the various formation headquarters.

'The attack is to go in tomorrow at 7.30 am,' Sir Douglas Haig had written to his wife the previous evening. 'I feel that everything possible for us to do to achieve success has been done.' The role of GHQ was now essentially to monitor staff efforts at corps and division level; their work was over. The canny staff officers at Montreuil, 14 miles behind the front, were sleeping in their beds as the infantry battalions were winding their way through the communication trenches during the early hours of 1 July; there would be much to do in the morning. Fourth Army headquarters was 12 miles behind the front, Rawlinson's five corps commanders were about eight miles back. Division headquarters were close behind the artillery gun line, their brigade HQs forward of it. Eighteen British divisions were poised to attack, of which 14 would go over the top in the first line. 'The casualty list will be big,' Brigadier Charteris predicted. 'Wars cannot be won without casualties,' he confided to his diary, likely echoing the fears of the waiting infantry 12 miles away. 'I hope people at home realise this. We are *winning*.'[2]

The problem with headquarters was that the further back they were, the more optimistic the predictions. Getting the mass of troops into the forward trenches had been administratively achieved; but there was a psychological and physical divide between front and rear. Communications between the two were inadequate. Very few British staff officers regularly visited the front. 'In the early stages of the war some of the "smart set" considered it rather the thing to get over to the battlefields,' Captain Frank Fox commented, 'and make a week-end sensation of a glimpse of the Calvary of Civilisation.' Unlike German General Staff officers, who were the 'eyes and ears' of the senior command, very few British staff officers regularly ventured forward. Charteris wrote animatedly about his trip to the front 48 hours before. 'It is impossible to describe the scene,' he wrote, dwelling more on spectacle than hard analysis:

> We have been bombarding for five days, and the Germans replying. The whole area is torn with shells, trees stripped to skeletons, villages just heaps of ruins.

The noise 'is terrific' and observation balloons 'hang in the sky like great gorged leeches of the air'. Little of consequence attracted his unpractised front-line eye; 'one could see no sign of life' on the German side apart from the odd gun flash. He could see movement in the British trenches and another column moving up. He presciently remarked, 'One cannot see the rise and fall of the ground which means so much tomorrow.' His observations exemplified the gulf that existed between army and corps and the divisions and brigades below them. The brigades and divisions had intently observed this ground, only displayed on maps at Corps and Army HQs, and did not like what they saw. Charteris visited one 'more than satisfied' corps commander, who 'was convinced of a very great success'.[3]

The psychological and physical remove was exacerbated by the lack of reliable communications between front and rear. It was easier for Haig's HQ to get a message from London than from the front line just 12 miles away. Telephone links between the 'spider's web of wires' at the Montreuil telephone exchange was good down to corps level and acceptable to division. Forward of division, wires were often cut by shell fire, leaving just dispatch riders, runners or pigeons to reach battalion headquarters. Once a battalion went over the top, surface-laid telephone wires were soon severed by shell fire or signals teams would be knocked out, leaving only runners and semaphore to communicate, always intermittently. Small wonder therefore that war correspondent Phillip Gibbs felt able to comment, 'Nine out of ten in the ranks did not even know the name of their Army General or of the Corps Commander.' They were glossed over as 'one of those sturdy men in his "brass hat" with his ruddy face and white moustache'. If anything went wrong with the attack in the morning, it would be difficult to identify and fix problems.

Douglas Haig slept easily that night, devoutly secure in the knowledge that God was on his side. 'Whether or not we are successful lies in the power above,' he wrote to his wife. *'I do feel* that in my plans I have been helped by a power that is not my own,' he confided. 'So I am easy in my mind and ready to do my best what ever happens tomorrow.'[4]

There had been no military imperative to attack on the Somme; it was a political decision. It was the junction where the British and French came together on the Western Front. The German defence found 1915 to be a victory: the efficacy of barbed wire, the machine-gun and artillery. The conflict was not going well for the Allies. At Chantilly on 29 December, General Joffre of France had proposed a massive Franco-British combined offensive on a 60-mile front. This was to be in concert with Allied offensives in Russia and on the Austro-Italian front. However, a pre-emptive German offensive at Verdun in early 1916 was bleeding the French Army white, so the 'Big Push' had to be prematurely launched by the British to relieve the French crisis at Verdun.

Convoluted negotiations between the two, and the distant objectives identified, revealed the extent to which politics was driving this military operation. Frontages were scaled back. It was agreed that 26 British divisions would attack alongside 14 French. A divergence of view led to a diversion of the attack axis once the offensive got under way. Having broken the line, the British planned to move north, to outflank the key high ground blocking their advance, while the French would continue east. Fourteen British divisions were to attack six German on this first day. Haig was confident a breakthrough might well be achieved, but since 1914 no Allied attack had yet breached the German line.

Lieutenant-General Sir Henry Rawlinson's Fourth Army was spearheading this attack with five corps. 'Rawley', to his friends, was an experienced, intelligent and efficient general.

He owed his career, indeed political survival, to Haig. The lanky, balding and mustachioed Rawley was also known as 'the cad' to his less charitable Sandhurst contemporaries, who regarded him as overly ambitious and self-important. Rawlinson conducted a thorough and methodical reconnaissance of the Somme front, stretching from the village of Hébuterne to the north, on the flank of Allenby's Third Army, to Mametz and Montauban along the line of the River Somme to the south and east. The main problem along the northern perpendicular line of the pronounced 'L' shaped front was the series of spurs and re-entrants the British would have to penetrate to gain access to the plateau fortified by the Germans. Along the horizontal west to east line north of the Somme the front was characterised by broad, very open and gentler valley features and more woods. The Germans, with 18 months in which to plan, had chosen their ground well. Gains made in 1914 were readily sacrificed to readjust the line so as to take advantage of every conceivable terrain height advantage. Rawlinson was faced with a trench system 18 miles wide, up to three integrated lines deep, expertly stringing nine fortified villages and additional redoubts into a formidable defence necklace, covering virtually any approach.

The dominating German feature was the high plateau stretching from Serre in the north to just above the straight Roman road from Albert to Bapaume to the south. Capturing the central feature from the Ancre valley high ground at Thiepval to Pozières and the continuation of the ridge to High Wood and Longueval to Ginchy in the south would be potentially decisive. Not only would it nullify the German flanks at either end, it would carry away key segments of the first and second line positions.

Rawlinson faced the intellectual dilemma of how to do it. Experience suggested two options: what the Germans had done at Verdun, all out successive assaults, or capture the vital ground in two stages? Should the effort be preceded by a short concentration of artillery or a long drawn-out bombardment? Rawlinson was understandably nervous when he briefed Haig on his plan. He offered Haig a 'bite and hold' strategy, which was to gain entry into the first line after a sustained bombardment, then hold off the counter-attacks, before moving his artillery forward to take out the second line. At best, his army, about to embark upon the biggest British attack to date, could take limited parts of the first enemy line. If they failed to break in, he could point out to Haig that he would attract large numbers of enemy counter-attacks, which could be worn down and destroyed.

Douglas Haig was a difficult and remote figure and made his subordinates feel nervous. The command philosophy at the time was to promote an exclusive aura. One of his soldiers, Ted Rimmer, later claimed:

> *He was a good looking chap. He looks every inch a soldier, every inch a commander. He was a capable man.*[5]

Although Haig subscribed to the more modern notion of giving an objective and letting subordinates execute it, he tended to interfere. He was not a good oral communicator, however, and his nervous subordinates, Rawlinson included, often missed the point and failed to detect a clear objective. Haig sought a more ambitious attack after a short hurricane bombardment – he wanted a breakthrough, with his cavalry able to exploit it in open country beyond. Five successive private discussions followed between the end of April and the beginning of May 1916, resulting in a compromise plan.

Both men were wrestling with the operational problem, unsolved since 1914, of how to achieve a breach in the German line sufficiently wide to be exploited in depth. It would not take long for the enemy to mass a defensive force from railheads behind the line, before an attack on the Western Front could exploit initial gains on foot. Haig saw that only cavalry might do this. The commander wanted the second line overwhelmed by the impetus of the first attack following a hurricane surprise bombardment. Rawlinson wanted to effect his breakthrough by concentrated artillery fire, but his front was too wide and British artillery technologically not up to the task. The second line was out of artillery range and observation. There were insufficient high-explosive shells for Rawlinson's purpose. Ideally the aim would be to engage in small fights along the front, holding back the main effort out of sight until the right moment. But in the technological and tactical conditions of 1916, the main force was needed to actually break through. There was no time or space to manoeuvre. The agreed Fourth Army objectives were to seize and consolidate the key high ground of the Pozières Ridge from the River Ancre to Montauban, secure the northern flank by taking the high ground at Serre, then push on to the second German line.

The onus was now on the corps commanders to deliver these objectives. Three corps were to assault the northern perpendicular line dominated by spurs and re-entrants of the 'L' shaped front, from Serre to the Albert–Bapaume road. A feint attack by two divisions of the Third Army would secure Gommecourt on their left. Two more corps would attack over the gentler and more wooded terrain running west to east from the Fricourt salient. The British effort would be across 18 miles of front. Another French corps would attack to the right of this line at the same time. Two more French corps would attack south of the River Somme two hours later, across a further eight miles of front.

Rawlinson, the Fourth Army commander, had been a division commander in 1914, most of the corps commanders had been leading brigades two years before, while many of the division commanders were battalion commanders on the outbreak of war. The rapid expansion of the British Army had meant senior officers had risen too far, too fast. By necessity they had been selected from a very narrow field, and none of them had experience of trench warfare at battalion command level or below, where this battle would be fought. The Russo-Japanese war of 1905 had been the last recent modern operation shaping attitudes. Successive Japanese bayonet attacks, by troops trained by the Germans, in the teeth of modern Russian firepower suggested that the 'offensive spirit' would dominate the attack–defence tactical conundrum. Haig's chief of staff General Launcelot Kiggell had concluded as a brigadier at a 1910 staff conference that 'the late war in Manchuria' demonstrated that 'victory is actually won by the bayonet, or by the fear of it'. Kiggell was working and planning in Haig's shadow and was committed to the plan of attack, convinced the indomitable British infantryman would, despite casualties, win through. It was instinctively felt that faint-heartedness in the attack would make battles longer and indecisive. The armies in 1914 had gone to war in Europe anticipating horrific casualties from new modern weapon technology, but their officers were still convinced flesh and blood would impose its will over modern firepower.[6]

Rawlinson commented during his reconnaissance for the plan of attack that 'it is capital country in which to undertake an offensive when we get a sufficiency of artillery'; observation was excellent. When his 'bite and hold' strategy was worn down to 'rush and hope' by Haig's penetrating criticism, Rawlinson gambled on a sustained artillery effort. 'A long bombardment gives the enemy no chance to sleep,' he explained, as strong points were pulverised one by one:

> Food and ammunition are difficult to bring up, and the enemy is kept in a constant state of doubt as to when the infantry assault will take place. His troops in the front line must be relieved every 48 hours, or they will break under the strain, and it will be our business to regulate our fire so as to inflict heavy losses, even at night, on any relieving detachments he may endeavour to bring forward.

This pre-supposed that the average German soldier had less spirit than his British counterpart. However, in 1916 British artillery was still more suited to infantry support, rather than defence suppression and counter-battery fire. The primary artillery piece, the 18-pounder, introduced two years earlier, was designed to shoot shrapnel at close range, over the heads of infantry in the open. Even the larger 60-pounders were mainly loaded with shrapnel. Technology was one pace ahead of tactics; it is rarely decisive in battle in any case, unless one side has the technical monopoly. Command and control shortcomings were to bedevil Rawlinson's aspirations. British artillery lacked sufficient communications equipment and the requisite staff organisation to manage and co-ordinate such a large-scale artillery effort. The Germans were better organised and had heavier guns.

Corps commanders were instructed to take the objectives assigned to them, and few if any had the experience or hard-headed resolve to question the mission, even if underwhelmed by the plan. Essentially the artillery was the main effort. All the infantry had to do was quickly advance across no man's land and occupy the neutralised German trenches. Rawlinson after pressure from Haig was not prepared to countenance any creative suggestions from his own staff. 'All criticisms by subordinates,' Fourth Army declared, 'of orders received from superior authority will, in the end, recoil on the heads of the critics.' Make it work, the corps were directed, and division headquarters were likewise informed.

Corps attack plans resulted in many divisions simply opting for wide-front 'wave' infantry assaults. Heavy loads precluded anything other than a plodding walk towards the enemy. Some attack plans, such as the Third Army two-division feint, sought to pinch off the Gommecourt salient by aiming to penetrate the line and link up behind the fortified village objective. Major-General Ivor Maxse, whose 18th Division was attacking between Mametz and Montauban, recognised the need to get his men as close to the German line as possible, utilising Russian saps. They were trained to advance in smaller groups, under a primitive 'rolling barrage' plan, accepting that the week-long bombardment was unlikely to finish off the opposition. Most of the wide frontage division advances were less creative. Battalions were given specific objectives, but in reality they sought to advance to capture a linear goal. Soldiers were told to advance and capture the trenches, generally on the higher ground opposite. There was no uniform tactical approach at corps level. Divisions made their own decisions how best to traverse no man's land. General Hunter-Weston specifically warned his VIII Corps commands about advancing at the double for long distances, because the men would be exhausted by their heavy loads. Some X Corps battalions in the Ancre valley and with the X Corps opposite Fricourt would attempt to take positions at a rush, while both the divisions of III Corps around La Boisselle would go at the walk. There was not a lot of experience to call upon.

Château generalship was conducted from a multitude of large buildings and often included stately homes, for perfectly good reasons. Headquarters required office space, living quarters and stabling. Substantial houses of various types soon came to accommodate entire brigade or division headquarters or parts of corps and army commands. The same was to occur in the Second World War but attract less opprobrium. Despite the pressure and long days at GHQ, it was a good living. Walking the ramparts at Montreuil's École Militaire to reach the officers' club was the chief recreation for its staff officers, who could play tennis in the courts. Staff Captain Frank Fox described the place as being 'like a college in which every one was a "swotter"'. Even with the coming offensive 'the club kept up a good cellar'. During the evening, as the assault battalions were marching out from their village billets, staff officers could have checked out the situation map before turning in, having enjoyed a good dinner at tables replete with napkins, tablecloths and menus. Up to the end of the war, Fox recalled:

> *When good wine was almost unprocurable in London or Paris except at exorbitant prices, the officers' club at Montreuil could sell vintage claret or burgundy at 9 francs a bottle, a decent wine at 5 francs a bottle and champagne at 15 francs a bottle.*

Once a week there was a fixed guest night with a band, but not on the eve of the Somme. Lighting a cigar before 8.20 was contrary to etiquette and junior officers were promptly checked. When one general officer insisted at 8 pm, the mess sergeant-major ostentatiously set up a ladder against the mess clock and moved it forward 20 minutes. War correspondent

Phillip Gibbs remembered that 'rivalries, intrigues, perjuries and treacheries like those of a medieval court' were a feature of GHQ. After dinner, the staff would be back at work, where they 'kept their lights burning, and smoked more cigarettes, and rang each other up on the telephone with futile questions'.

Regimental officers posted to GHQ found working at staff was a mixed blessing. They might live, and maybe in relative comfort, but in 1916 Lieutenant Alan Hanbury-Sparrow told his mother:

> *I am feeling most frightfully homesick for my regiment and bitterly repent the day when my selfishness urged me to go onto the staff ... My conscience pricks me most horribly as I know I am far more useful with them than here.*[7]

'A young staff officer, in his red tabs, with a jaunty manner was like a red rag to a bull among battalion officers,' explained Phillip Gibbs. They personified:

> *... the supreme folly of 'the staff' which made men attack impossible positions, sent down conflicting orders, issued a litter of documents – called by an ugly name – containing impractible instructions as to the torment of the adjutants and to the scorn of the troops.*

'If bread is the staff of life, what is the life of the staff?' officers in the line would ask. 'One long loaf', of course, was the popularly recognised jocular response.[8]

Major Charles Ward-Jackson was billeted in the unscathed town of Pas, the VII Corps headquarters, and was the Camp Commandant. The 46-year-old Territorial Army officer was wealthy and rooted in the sporting traditions of the Victorian and Edwardian landed gentry. He had two batmen to attend to his needs, and those of his mare Dinah, and had a staff car to transport him on duty and social calls. His wife Queenie had joined him for a short leave in Paris the month before. Life was good.

Like many staff officers he had a grudging admiration for the Germans. Three days earlier he had observed the deadly efficiency with which the Boche had dropped a preventative barrage of fire across their front-line trenches, at the first hint of a feint during the Allied bombardment. 'One never finds a flaw in their staff work or their Army management and intelligence department,' he observed. 'We are hoping, at VII Corps headquarters, that before we have done with this bombardment there will not be quite as much kick left in them as there is now.' He wrote to his wife: 'If there is one thing in the world to prevent a General winning battles, it is to be afraid of casualties … That is the awful part of war,' he admitted; 'troops must hold on, or must attack, more indeed in this war than all others, more's the pity.' There would be a cost.[9]

GHQ and corps headquarters had passed on the onus for success for this deliberate attack after midnight to their subordinate headquarters. The division and brigade level headquarter locations represented the coal-face between aspiration and reality. Corps headquarters numbered about 23 officers and staff by 1916. Division headquarters was much smaller. 'The battles fought with a division were personal affairs,' recalled staff officer Colonel Walter Nicolson, because these were the commanders directing men over the top. 'The fighting, whether success or failure, meant heavy losses in friends.' It was the point where personal interest transitioned to the general bigger corps picture. The division sacrificed men to achieve corps objectives, which might be of an impersonal 'timetable' nature, like space for roads, logistic dumps and railways to further wider army objectives. 'They hated us,' Nicolson explained, referring to the interface between his corps and the divisions:

We were all business and no soul; just a damned nuisance to everyone ... We knew none of the divisional staffs and they knew none of us; a disastrous state of affairs. There was no human touch between the corps and the division.

Rawlinson's field army headquarters generated 10,000 telegrams, 20,000 telephone calls and 5,000 daily messages to the corps and divisions. Skeletal staffs at division, unlike corps, were hard pressed to simply respond to the deluge of paper, never mind develop their own attack plans. Haig's chief of staff General Kiggell issued a 57-page attack order, with 32 subsidiary sections to corps. Brigade staffs were even smaller, with just three red-tabbed officers: the commander, the brigade major and a staff captain. With such minuscule staffs, controlling four battalions inside the 24-hour battle scenarios about to unfold, on an unprecedented scale, was virtually unachievable. Brigadier-General Hubert Rees took over the 94th Brigade at short notice on the eve of the battle. His brigade brief dealing with the attack on Serre ran to 76 pages of close type. The plan made little sense. 'Our advance up the slope to the village,' he recalled, 'was in full view from the north, from the German salient of Gommecourt.' Not only that, 'the time allowed for the capture of each objective was too short'. Nobody was interested in reservations. 'I was looked upon as something of a heretic' by the corps staff, Rees explained, 'for saying that everything had been arranged, except for the unexpected, which usually occurs in war.'[10]

Battalion commanders were the only command agency able to deal with the unexpected, but they were very much at the bottom of the chain for this deliberately planned attack. They had neither flexibility nor authority to use initiative. A last-minute decision by the 101st Brigade to hold back their battalion commanders from going over the top with the first wave battalions in Sausage Valley to the south of La Boisselle was a telling indictment of this command ethos. Success was dependent on a mutual respect for the emotional link between leaders and led. The measure may well have been in cynical expectation of likely casualties. Brigade headquarters was the last level of flexible initiative, but they were in thrall to division. Battalion commanders had no recourse except to advance in waves, for which the men had been drilled, totally dependent upon their own artillery's ability to neutralise German defences. There was only a tiny number of officers at battalion headquarters to call upon to aid control other than the four company commanders.

Infantry battalions would attack in about eight waves, 400 yards across and 900 yards deep, taking nine minutes on average to pass a given point. Command was by whistle and voice, not much of an improvement since Waterloo. The first four waves were fighting platoons, the fifth a mop-up force, with the support weapons being carried up in the sixth wave, just ahead of the headquarters. The final seventh and eighth waves were 'carriers', bringing up defence stores and reserve ammunition to hold off counter-attacks and continue the advance. There was no manoeuvre or concentration of force beyond an echeloned advance. Rearward preparatory training had been about general orientation and illustrating the plan, by rehearsing movement. No man's land remained a mystery that few had the inclination or time to analyse or tactically assess. The direction of advance was often simply the high ground ahead, but seven days of artillery bombardment had transformed it. One ruined village with sparse trees around it on a gentle slope was much the same as any other in drab no man's land, particularly as it was being devastatingly re-modelled as they watched. Scattered white chalk quickly transforms a landscape. Ominously, most immediate reports and sightings were indicating that the wire ahead was disturbingly intact. They were about to cross a network of fire they had considered for barely two months, against German defences some two years in the making.

Only brigade headquarters could get the battalions out of trouble, or to exploit any breaches, because the battalions would have expended maximum effort to even achieve entry. Brigade in turn was dependent upon division headquarters to provide reinforcements. The storm cloud over the heads of soldiers was the seeming anonymity of corps headquarters directing the enterprise. Captain Charles Carrington of the Warwickshire Regiment explained:

> Heaven knows, we grumbled and joked about brigade and division, but within reason. Knowing them, we made allowance. Corps we did not know and since battles in France were mostly disastrous, the Corps Commander was rarely popular.

Sir Douglas Haig had visited all his corps commanders over the previous 48 hours. 'The men are in splendid spirits,' he confided to his diary before midnight. 'The wire has never been so well cut, nor the artillery preparations so thorough. I have seen personally all the Corps Commanders and one and all are all full of confidence.'[11]

There was no way of outflanking the German line. They would have to go through, and artillery would pave the way.

'It Requires Everyone to be Firm'. German Châteaux

On 12 April 1916 the German XIV Corps commander Generalleutnant Hermann von Stein had already announced to his staff that 'the overall situation suggests that in April or May an English attack will come'. He reckoned it would be north of the River Somme. The vital importance of the high plateau there meant its loss would seriously compromise the defensive stance of General Fritz von Below's Second Army. As a consequence the sector held by Generalmajor Franz Ludwig von Soden's 26th Reserve Division became the corps and army *Schwerpunkt*, or main point of defence effort.

For two days von Below had been badgering General Erich von Falkenhayn, the German Supreme Commander, for reinforcements. During the evening report covering the British bombardment that day, he ominously noted that 'the enemy activity opposite the XIV Reserve Corps (north of the Somme) and the XVII Army Corps (south of the Somme) resembles, ever more closely, the tactics of wearing down and attrition'. But von Falkenhayn was not listening. He did not believe a decisive attack was pending and was focused on his own Calvary of attrition at Verdun. The Germans had lost 337,000 men against 362,000 Frenchmen. They were barely six kilometres from the town where 21 million German and 15 million French shells were churning over an area 30 kilometres wide by 10 deep. As a result von Below received only eight artillery batteries and four companies of infantry. He was granted permission to reinforce hard-hit defending units piecemeal from the 10th Bavarian Infantry Division. Essentially the Second Army was being told to manage with its own resources.[12]

Von Soden's 26th Reserve Division headquarters was established in the two-storey Château de Biefvillers, just outside the corps headquarters at Bapaume. He had set himself up some 10½ miles from the front, not much closer than the British norm. The impressive house, characteristically French with shuttered windows and balconies, was more functional then comfortable. Wooden platforms had been erected outside for the headquarters generators and telephone cables. Von Soden was an impressive man, thick-set with a distinguished moustache and prominent nose. He was the consummate professional, an inspirational leader, whose wizened wrinkles beneath his eyes gave assurance of a considerable reservoir of operational and tactical sense. Unlike his English counterparts, von Soden had commanded at regimental level for three years, brigade for four, and had retired from the Kaiser's peacetime Imperial Army in 1910, having commanded the same 26th Reserve Division as he did now. He mobilised it in 1914 and fought it through large-scale offensive and defensive battles for two more years.

'Now it requires everyone to be firm,' he announced 48 hours into the seven-day bombardment. He expected his men 'to courageously persist, to do your duty, to shun no sacrifice and no exertion, so that the enemy is denied victory'. After being blooded by two years of war, he instinctively knew how to address his soldiers, emphasising:

> We hold the bloody embattled ground and that no Englishman or Frenchman who penetrates into our lines might remain unpunished.[13]

Von Soden had selected his headquarter locations very carefully. 'The effort and work in the course of the last two years, that were made in the extension of our positions,' he announced, 'may already have to endure a powerful test in the next days.' The general had done little else over the previous 18 months except develop ways of breaking up this pending attack. Unlike much of the rest of the German Army, the 26th Reserve Division had been permitted to retain two brigade headquarters to cover the Serre to Ovillers sector. They covered the vital high ground north of the Somme with Headquarters 51 Brigade north and 52 Brigade south of the Ancre valley. Brigade command posts were one step nearer the front than division, and better able to co-ordinate the tactical defence of the two regiments under their command. Most other divisions had only one brigade headquarters. This was the command arena where the contact battle would be fought when the British finally advanced. Division headquarters were more remote from the action, mainly concerned with co-ordinating and marshalling reinforcements and other resources forward.

Having had so much time to develop this position, von Soden had ensured that all his battalion headquarters had dugouts in either the second or third trenches in the first (or front) line. Regimental headquarters were well forward, generally between the second and third trench lines, while brigade headquarters were either alongside or directly behind. Headquarters were small, consisting of the commander and maybe two officers with telephone operators and runners. Telephone lines were buried deep and backed up with light and siren signals. Every infantry sector had an artillery battery on call. These followed a simple, logical system of labelling each sector with a letter, subdivided further into numbered segments, like 'C2'. The whole front was divided up with 'H' sector in the far north, 'B' to the River Ancre, 'C' below it and 'P' east of the Fricourt salient. Calling for fire on a letter and corresponding number immediately enabled pre-registered artillery to be directed to a spot with no pre-liminary description. Calling for 'C4', for example, would immediately drop artillery fire onto the approaches directly opposite the Schwaben Redoubt.

British artillery outnumbered the German by a factor of three to one, but an innovative German artillery organisation did much to offset the odds. British artillery was assembled in a linear fashion along the 'L' shaped 18-mile front, off roads stretching from Hébuterne near Gommecourt to Maricourt, next to the French on the right. Just over 1,000 light guns, 18-pounders mainly and 4.5-inch howitzers, were assembled with 427 'heavies', 4.7 to 15-inch howitzers. The limited range of these guns, unlike modern artillery, meant their linear deployment made it difficult to concentrate large numbers of guns onto a specific point. It took a lot of shells fired from a limited number of guns to produce a shock impact, because they were in lines. Modern artillery practice seeks to concentrate, to deliver a higher intensity of fire for a shorter time. The Germans were to use such gun 'parks' instead of linear dispersion.

Von Soden was fortunate in that his newly arrived artillery commander, Generalmajor Maur, had spent much of 1915 and early 1916 in Russia, as the LXXIX Corps artillery commander. On arrival barely two weeks before the start of the Allied artillery bombardment, he re-grouped 26th Reserve Division's artillery into three sub-groups: 'Zollern', 'Cäser' and 'Berta'. This resembled a task organisation that would be familiar to modern gunners today. He had 24 field batteries, six of them howitzer, numbering 72 modern field guns and 24 howitzers. These guns were supplemented by a miscellany of Russian, Belgian and obsolescent German pieces to produce a sum total of 154 guns. Maur deployed his three groups in the low ground behind the Pozières Ridge, concealed inside gullies and re-entrants. In support were two similar artillery concentration areas, 'Adolf' and 'Beauregard', grouped north of the River Ancre.

Von Soden's front was about to be attacked by two and a half British corps. One of them, VIII Corps alone, had 28 batteries with 103 guns at its disposal. Combined with heavy mortars, von Soden's 154 guns were outgunned at a factor of about three to one. Nevertheless, Maur's innovative grouping enabled him to quickly bring down intense concentrations of fire all along the front – firing fewer rounds than the British, but maximising the number of guns in range. Banding artillery together reduced the amount of telephone cable needed to co-ordinate multiple batteries firing. Maur set up his headquarters at Grévillers, virtually next door to von Soden at Biefvillers, just outside Bapaume.[14]

German regimental headquarters replicated the British in terms of distance from the front, but von Soden had achieved greater co-ordination and control compared to his less experienced opponents opposite. Telephone lines were dug deep, had been 18 months in preparation and linked brigades to regiments, where the intense combat would occur. They were the decision stepping-stone to division headquarters, 10 miles behind.

There were two fundamental differences between the German and British commands. The first was physical and unavoidable for the British. Once their infantry went over the top, communications depended upon vulnerable surface-laid telephone wire, physical signals and runners. In practical terms their directing headquarters would be in the dark. German headquarter installations were dug deep with sub-surface wire, with greater durability once battle was joined. Of more significance was the psychological divide in terms of 'reading' the battle as it developed. Germany fought the

Papierkrieg or 'paper war' at staff, like the British, but they were less prescriptive than the British, who tended to control the plan at every index or sub-paragraph.

Prussian command in the tradition of Scharnhorst and Gneisenau followed a command ethos based on free, intelligent co-operation between a commander and his staff. Infantry officer Ernst Jünger may have resented the 'fat little staffer' who taught him practical and theoretical courses behind the lines, but he did teach him what to look for during excursions and inspection visits. 'We called him the pressure-cooker,' he recalled, but the man had pointed out they should view 'slightly askance everything that happened' during unit visits, 'an insight into the incredible work that goes on behind a line of fighting men'. The British sought to regiment command, whereas the Germans accepted confusion as the battlefield norm. The way to master it was to decentralise and lower decision thresholds, the nearer one got to the front.

There was, nevertheless, as Leutnant Hermann Kottmeier described, a realisation that 'there was a huge distance between the front soldier and the rear zone'. Shocking casualties promoted cynicism in both armies. 'The order "Attack!" or similar, always came from the rear,' Kottmeier complained:

> *They sat in very thick concrete reinforced bunkers, had great big discussions and telephoned out of the bunker, while we sat forward in the murk. They appreciated the situation from green tables, while we knew what was possible or impossible. It is impossible to attack when you have five metres of barbed wire in front of you.*

First the artillery have to remove it, 'but those behind us ordered that'.[15]

Unlike the British in 1916, the German General Staff provided the 'eyes and ears' of commanders at the front. It was rare for British staff officers to regularly venture forward. Prussian staff officer Hermann von Kuhl recalled that every headquarters officer with his First Army 'was assigned a section of the front' and 'was to visit the foremost line once a week and keep himself carefully informed of developments'. Each officer was given a questionnaire to remind them about the most important issues to be investigated: the state of the trenches, supply or clothing, for example. Such officers met with their personal friends with whom they would informally discuss issues, again cutting across normal reporting systems. The imperative to harness energy and decision-making at all levels was why German counter-attacks could be so devastatingly rapid. One *Oberste Heeresleitung*, or High Command directive, issued early in 1916 instructed:

It is strictly forbidden to delay local counter-attacks while permission of the next higher headquarters is requested.

'Waiting for an answer,' the directive pointed out, might mean 'so much time is lost that the shock would come too late'. As von Soden had emphasised just four days earlier, 'Do your duty, shun no sacrifice and no exertion.'[16]

All of von Soden's command dugouts during the early morning hours of 1 July, from the first line back to brigade, sensed that the storm was about to break. The crisis had already engulfed some of them. Leutnant Wilhelm Geiger, the adjutant of the 2nd Battalion Infantry Regiment III at La Boisselle, had just vacated his old chaise longue, 'rescued from Fricourt', where he was manning the telephone in the battalion command bunker. 'I was fit to drop with tiredness,' he recalled, 'and wanted to snatch some sleep before the deadly dance started up again.' He handed the telephone to 'good old Jansen', the communications trench officer, who had offered to relieve him. He moved to the end of the passageway and lay down with a sandbag for a pillow and his coat for a blanket 'when there was a terrible crash'. The lights went out and he raced back to the other end of the dugout amid the shouting, darkness and choking gas.

> There sat Jansen on my chair, bent forward, dead with a splinter in his head. His hand still held the pencil that he was using to write a letter to his wife. It was, I believe, their sixth wedding anniversary.

Moments before, he had been sitting in the same chair. 'It got him, not me, luck?' Battalion staffs were small: a captain, doctor, batman, adjutant, runners and some telephonists. Any losses had to be immediately replaced.[17]

Photographs taken outside von Soden's headquarters at Biefvillers show small groups of British prisoners being addressed by a German officer outside. Two escorts nonchalantly stand by, with rifles and bayonets fixed. Being led into the small château courtyard, surrounded by pleasant trees in park-like surrounds, was disorientating to men suddenly and often violently plucked from the wasteland of barbed wire and shell holes, following trench raids. They were questioned by German interrogators who quickly sought to take advantage of their unbalanced state. What they said was significant.

Twenty-two-year-old British territorial soldier Victor Wheat was badly wounded with a 5th North Staffordshire Regiment wiring party at Gommecourt, the night before the British bombardment began. Struck by machine-gun fire, he blundered into the German wire in his weakened and disorientated state and was captured. He was carried to Miraumont, the main 26th Division dressing station and immediately on to Biefvillers, where von Stein's corps intelligence officers joined the interrogation team. Wheat had lost a lot of blood and was virtually incapacitated by shock. This added to the veracity of the information that staff officer Hauptmann von Scholz got out of him. They learned an attack was imminent, within three days on Wednesday 24 June, and that it would be launched over a 30-mile front. Gommecourt was to be bypassed and encircled from north and south. Wheat disclosed he had rehearsed for this behind the lines at St Leger. Neither Wheat nor the Germans were to know that bad weather was to postpone the attack. Von Scholz commented that 'British confidence in the success of their attack appears slim'. Wheat had grumbled that 'their general had made a mess of the attack at Loos and that they were unhappy with their conditions,' the interrogator reported. 'All this was said willingly,' he added.

The 29th Division in front of Beaumont Hamel added to the intelligence harvest, which had the Germans standing by in expectation of the attack, two days before. A catastrophic prisoner snatch and trench raid mounted by the British the night before was scattered by artillery, mortar and small arms fire. Private Coones and a severely wounded Captain Barrow from the Newfoundland Regiment ended up at the Biefvillers courtyard before being passed on to the XIV Corps headquarters nearby at Bapaume. 'A general English offensive is expected' was the main point to be gleaned. The Newfoundlanders 'were very confident the English attack would succeed, but admitted people were disappointed the war had lasted so long'. All this confirmed earlier information.

Private Josef Lipmann from the 2nd Royal Fusiliers was also picked up, a significant acquisition, because he was a disgruntled deserter, who had dropped out of a patrol after it took casualties, and came over to the German line. Lipmann gave a lot of information: about his battalion's tactics, the colour codes of flares to summon British artillery; that gas and smoke would signal the assault; and that the attack would be on within ten minutes of the release of smoke. Lipmann, who was Russian born and a carpenter by trade, had been totally disillusioned by the debacle at Gallipoli, where he had spent nine months with the 29th Division. Hauptmann Henke, likely his interrogator, produced the subsequent Second Army report. Lipmann had apparently heard British officers state:

> *The war could last for ever, if a decisive result was not achieved here, through a general attack on the German line between Arras and Albert, in which the best divisions would take part.*

Lipmann actually expected the attack to succeed. When asked what would happen if it did not, he accepted 'we will come to terms'. All the prisoner reports were passed on in note form to numerous formations, with priority given to the reserve counter-attack units, behind the German third line.

Lipmann's information was nullified by the two-day extension of the British bombardment, caused by the bad weather. Analysis of numerous front-line 26th Division regiment post-action combat reports reveal the extent to which this information was widely disseminated. It went down as far as the individual machine-gun crews of the 2nd Machine Gun Company in the line on the Hawthorne Ridge next to Beaumont Hamel. When one of the Moritz listening posts near La Boisselle intercepted an English order from 34th Division shortly before midnight that an attack was about to be delivered in hours, there was no credibility issue. It was not doubted.[18]

By 4 am on 1 July, the seventh day of the bombardment, General von Soden's carefully crafted command organisation was starting to appear ragged. Two days earlier the smoke stack of the sugar factory at Courcelette came crashing down. The nearby artillery command post for the 'Cäser' group north of Pozières began to feel vulnerable and moved to a new command post on the western edge of the town. Generalleutnant von Auwärter, von Soden's highly experienced 52nd Brigade commander, was becoming increasingly concerned at the extent of British air activity. As many as 21 observation balloons were peering down on his sector between St Pierre Divion and Ovillers. Enemy aircraft were sweeping down to as low as 100 metres to bomb and machine-gun his forward trenches. It would only be a matter of time before they located his 153rd and 6th supporting artillery batteries to the rear. Eleven aircraft were circling overhead during the day.

Von Auwärter was busy co-ordinating the complex relief of his 99th Regiment that night. It had lost 16 officers and 456 soldier casualties during the seven-day bombardment. The 180th Regiment to their left had lost a further 8 officers and 285 men. Twelve hours ago four 28 cm shells had crashed into his Zollern Redoubt (*Feste Zollern*) command bunker, the heaviest impacts to date. His ordinance officer was struck in the head and eye by shrapnel and gassed. Von Auwärter had been plucked into the air when the bunker door burst open, which injured his shoulder. With the telephone system knocked out and all links to his two regiments cut, there was no option but to abandon the smoking bunker and move to Courcelette, harassed by incoming rounds the whole way. 'Oh, to pay them back, to take vengeance!'

Leutnant Matthäus Gerster railed. 'Let them just come and attack.' Many command dugouts were only recognisable as semi-collapsed holes from the outside, where trenches had been totally levelled. Stairwells within were buried beneath piles of earth, which meant a scramble up loose chalk to get out. 'Unbroken, but in a dangerous mood the defenders waited for the attackers,' Gerster recalled. 'They were going to be made to pay for the days of torture.'

Generalleutnant von Stein's XIV Headquarters at Bapaume received similar attention. German observers had long noticed the smoke signatures from behind the Albert railway station siding, where a massive railway gun was parked. 'Very quickly a new tone could be heard mixed in with the brass notes of the known heavy shells,' noticed Gerster, with the 119th Regiment nearby. He remembered 'it had a characteristic roaring sound as though a very heavy body was boring its way clumsily through the air'. 'This was "Grandmother" which 'as an iron greeting sent us shells of 380 mm diameter.' Each shell was 4 ft 7 ins high and weighed 17.7 hundredweight. By night-time these shells were howling into Bapaume. 'The pressure wave created by the shell and the violence of the explosion,' Gerster recalled from his forward trench, 'could be felt from a considerable distance.' Von Stein decided to vacate the headquarters. Von Soden remained nearby at Biefvillers, but XIV Corps moved another 4.3 miles east to Beugny.[19]

German headquarters at all levels were distracted by the effects of the British bombardment at the very moment they anticipated an attack. The Moritz intercept suggested this would be at first light.

Who could tell? There had been speculation for days.

CHAPTER 4

'Over the Top' —•
4.45 to 7.30 am

4.45 to 6.30 am

'The Larks Were Singing' ... Hours to Go

Royal Flying Corps aerodromes were bustling well before dawn. Aircraft due for early morning sorties were being checked over by fitters, riggers and armourers in the growing twilight. The smell of aviation fuel and exhaust was already apparent amid the shouts, engine noises and increasing activity as the aerodromes came to life. Pilots and observers scanned maps by torchlight, checked the latest reports and clambered into tiny open cockpits, briefly looking over the simple instrument and control systems. The first reconnaissance sorties were due over Bapaume along the Roman road from Albert at 5 am, 15 minutes after sunrise, single Morane biplanes escorted by three Martinsydes. Another formation of 12 Martinsydes was being readied for railway bombing and 16 BE2cs were about to take off with escorts. Goggles were lowered and scarves wrapped around necks as throttles were opened. Successive flights of these ungainly looking aircraft began to climb into the lightening sky. 'The dawn came with a great beauty,' remembered war correspondent Phillip Gibbs. 'There was a pale blue sky flecked with white wisps of cloud.'[1]

The arrival of more technologically advanced aircraft – FE2bs, DH2s, Nieuport Scouts and Sopwiths – had enabled the Royal Flying Corps (RFC) to seize air superiority in the skies over the Somme. Major Lanoe Hawker, who commanded 24 Squadron, the first DH2s to arrive at the front, followed a brutally simple tactical philosophy: '*Attack everything*'. The RFC was flying 185 aircraft over the Somme, alongside many French, against 129 German aircraft, which included just 19 Scouts. Their moral superiority was also marked. 'If a Hun sees a Dehav,' recalled Second Lieutenant Gwilym Lewis with 32 Squadron RFC, 'he runs for his life; they won't come near them.' This ascendency, however, had come at a physical and psychological cost. Defeat in the air without a parachute invariably meant death.

The previous mainstay of the RFC had been the BE2c, the type flown by Lieutenant Cecil Lewis on his arrival at the Western Front the year before, aged 17. He had 20 hours' flying experience. 'My God, it's murder,' his squadron leader had declared, 'sending you chaps out with nothing in your log book.' He flew with observers whose view was obscured by the four main struts on their biplane, 'in a little seat he could just get into'. When enemy aircraft attacked from the rear, which they generally did, the observer or gunner 'simply had to get up in his seat' to engage, where there were no supporting wires, 'and kneel on the seat, which was a cold draughty business at 8,000 feet even in the summer'. Even pilots of the newer FE2b aircraft found it best to circle round with other friendly aircraft, to protect the vulnerable tail from attack. With the FE2b, dangerous gymnastics were required of the observer or gunner, who actually had to stand on his seat to fire the second Lewis gun over the pilot across the top of the upper biplane wing. Captain Harold Wyllie, with 23 Squadron, remembered:

> *Perched as he was with only his feet and ankles actually within the cockpit, the observer was almost completely exposed and could easily fall out [with any evasive action] to his inevitable death in the days before parachutes.*

New pilots waking up at dawn this day would rarely have had a restful night's sleep. Among the sufferers was Second Lieutenant Harold Balfour, with 60 Squadron:

> *I can remember my bedroom companion in the farmhouse in which we were billeted felt as I did, and how each of us lay awake in the darkness, not telling the other that sleep would not come, listening to the incessant roar of the guns, and thinking of the dawn patrol next morning. At last we could bear it no longer, and calling out to each other admitted a mutual feeling of terror and foreboding. We lit the candles to hide the dark, and after that felt a bit better, and somehow got through that night as we had to get through the next day.[2]*

A beautiful summer's day started to emerge. War correspondent Phillip Gibbs was making his way up the track to the Grandstand position on the high ground overlooking Albert, where he had been the previous midnight. 'It was cold and over all the fields there was a floating mist, which rose up from the moist earth and lay heavily on the ridges, so that the horizon was obscured,' he remembered. 'I was wakened about 5 am for breakfast,' recalled Private Albert Andrews, with the 19th Manchesters south of Montauban, 'dry bread, cheese and a drink of water.' Others like the West Belfast Battalion in the line beneath the Schwaben Redoubt were better off. The company cooks had procured rashers of bacon, and they enjoyed fried bread and jam with strong sweet tea. There was even cold tea and lemon for their water bottles. Lieutenant Edward Liveing to the north opposite Serre was also awake, 'the sun infusing more warmth into the air' and the bombardment easing. 'There was the freshness and splendour of a summer morning over everything.' It was good to be alive. 'One man said, it felt more as if we were going to start off for a picnic than for a battle,' Liveing observed.

Sergeant Richard Tawney near Carnoy was also enjoying this 'glorious morning', appreciatively observing the sky transitioning to a deeper hue of blue. Private Albert Conn, with fellow soldiers with the 8th Devons near Mansell copse, remembered a small bird that used to sing from a stunted tree nearby and brighten their day. 'At the break of dawn we used to listen to it and wonder that amongst so much misery and death a bird could sing.' But a disgruntled corporal had shot it, muttering, 'What the hell have you got to sing about?' This had not been well received. 'A couple of the lads told him to fuck off out of it. We missed the bird.'[3]

'Each man prepared his own breakfast,' recalled Sergeant Charles Quinnell, with the 9th Royal Fusiliers south of Beaumont Hamel. It could be rather a ritual. Tea and sugar was on the boil over a pile of burning wood chips as tins of milk and jam were readied. Holes were punched in either side of the tins, 'because the rats would get to it'; they would then 'blow on one side and it would squirt out of the other', a form of trench etiquette. 'Primitive Methodists we were!' Quinnell explained. Rashers of bacon went into the mess tin lid, joined by bread or a piece of biscuit, 'and there you are with a breakfast'. Nothing was wasted, neither time nor resources. The corner of a towel was dipped into the little tea left, and wiped 'round your face and that was your morning ablution'. These quaint rituals bonded the domestic community at the bottom of the trench. 'There'd be a little tiny drop of tea still left,' explained Quinnell, 'and you put your shaving brush in that and you would lather your face … We had to shave in the front line,' he insisted, 'otherwise – especially the dark chaps – we'd look like brigands.' It was a way of passing the final tense hours.[4]

There was some uneasiness in the Ulster Division trenches about the late morning attack, RH Stewart remembered. 'As the light grew stronger we talked about why we were not ordered out at dawn' to take advantage of the half-light. Looking up they saw 'the bit of sky above us turned grey then blue'. They were to attack east, into the glare of the rising sun. Breakfast was not uniformly good in the Ulster battalions. Stewart's men were sharing tins of bully beef and biscuits, washed down with water. 'There was some of us that did not want to eat much' in any case, he recalled. 'They were a bit tight in the belly.'[5]

'The larks were singing high in the first glinting sunshine of the day above the haze,' Phillip Gibbs noticed as another type of bird, a Morane Parasol from 3 Squadron RFC, patrolled up above. Lieutenant Cecil Lewis had quickly covered the 15 miles from the rear to reach the front. From the air the front 'looked like one of those edges to a lace doily. You know, it's got a fairly hard edge and then there are all those little fillets running back in. You put two of those together side by side' and there were the two opposing front lines, with the communication trenches running off behind. 'All this went wending away right down from Thiepval, up in the north, right around the Somme,' he recalled, 'and it was really like two pieces of lace put together in that way.'

He was flying at that mid-point between the lines where shells were going up and falling. Quite often aircraft might be unsuspectingly snatched away by the passage of one of these monstrous shells. 'The aeroplane was flung up with a shell which had just gone underneath and missed you by two or three feet, or flung down when it had gone over the top.' On one occasion he had been transfixed by the sight of a wobbling heavy shell at the top of its trajectory and followed it all the way down to the ground. His two pieces of lace were now obscured by 'a sort of great, broad swathe of dirty looking cotton wool, laid over the ground'. The sight of the flickering, bubbling cauldron of fire below was awesome. 'So close were the shell bursts, and so continuous that it wasn't a puff here and a puff there, it was a continuous band.' He had to navigate entirely by reading his map over the moving ground as the river valleys began to emerge from more layers of white cotton wool.[6]

Down below, ranges of chalk hills and ridges were coming into sight, most of which overlooked the British Fourth Army line. At about 5.30 am British tunnellers opened up numerous 'Russian saps' to the surface. These were communication trenches, dug before, with the top 12 inches of soil left in place on the surface. The covered trenches were in effect linear 'Trojan Horses', pushed out into no man's land. They offered concealed tactical approaches for soldiers, trench mortars and machine-guns to reach out to the German lines while avoiding detection. Five tunnelling companies were mining on the British front, constructing nine Russian saps opposite Serre in the north, ten more on the 36th Ulster Division sector further south and at key points all along the German line.

Explosive mines had also been set, such as the 40,600 lb charge against the Hawthorne Ridge Redoubt opposite Beaumont Hamel and astride the Albert–Bapaume road opposite La Boisselle. There was a 40,000 lb charge laid at 'Y Sap' north of the road and a double charge of 36,000 and 24,000 lbs at 'Lochnagar' south of it. These 'over-charged' mines were tamped from within with sandbags to channel the blast upwards, forcing additional spoil into the air to create a defensible lip eight to ten feet high around the huge craters blasted into the German defences. Movie cameraman Geoffrey Malins was told about the Hawthorne H3 Tunnel, which snaked out from the British line, 1,050 feet long and 75 feet deep. Former coal miners had been recruited and drafted in to construct it, some aged over 45 and with decades of underground experience. Chalk faces were softened with water and the flint and chalk was prized out at bayonet point, each lump caught by hand to deaden the noise. A rush to occupy the crater would follow the shock effect of the detonation.

Five days earlier, ten innocuous-looking three- and five-ton lorries turned up at the 'Ludgate Circus' sector of the British line near Carnoy. Two hundred soldiers from the Devonshire Regiment started to unload the lorries and cart off hundreds of metal components forward through the communication trenches via 'Waterloo Junction'. Four Livens 'flame projectors' were assembled and laid in saps 3, 4, 5 and 14, which were dug to within 65 yards of the German trenches in the Mametz West sector near Mansell Copse. The 'Squirts' or 'Judgements', as they were called, were 56 feet long and 14 inches wide, requiring scores of engineers and hundreds of soldiers to carry, manhandle and assemble the 2.5 tons of portable component parts, all done under intermittent shell fire. The system was powered with pressurised gas which forced a monitoring head or 'squirt' up from the ground, which squirted burning fuel over 300 yards out into the German trenches. The nozzle sprayed 1,300 litres of burning viscous fuel, sufficient for three ten second blasts from a virtual fire-breathing dragon. Captain William Livens had designed and built this terrifying contraption, taking only 25 weeks from drawing board to trench. Dozens of saps had been driven out east of Mametz for infantry to exploit the shock to be derived from this device. Two of the four had already been disabled by German counter-battery fire, but two were still operable just to the west of the Carnoy–Montauban road. So secret had this activity been, that very few of the troops earmarked to use the saps had even heard of their existence as they anxiously awaited the termination of the preliminary bombardment. They had a lot of open ground to cover.

'5.45 am. It is a glorious morning and it is now broad daylight,' Captain Charles May, nearby with the 22nd Manchesters, found time to write, from the bottom of his trench. 'It seems a long time to wait and I think whatever happens, we shall all feel relieved once the line is launched.' He had confided in the adjutant, FJ Earles, his closest friend, the night before and asked him to look after his wife and child should anything happen to him. This was insurance rather than pessimism, and Earles promised. Captain Alfred 'Bill' Bland in the same trenches had already written his final letter to his wife three days before. 'Give my lads such a lot of hugs from me and thank them for their clear long letters, which are beautifully written and spelt. God bless *you*.' His letters were normally exuberant, so he also was not necessarily being morbid about his chances, but he had seen sufficient action to appreciate the risks. Like Charles May, he took the opportunity to send a final brief message to his wife, somehow, amid the final checks and instructions in the crowded trenches before going over the top. 'My darling,' he wrote, 'all my love for ever. Alfred.' He included a pressed flower, a forget-me-not.[7]

As Phillip Gibbs made his way up the track leading to the Grandstand area of high ground near Dernancourt overlooking Albert, 'the battle line came into view'. He was able to view a 'long sweep of country' covering seven miles from the 36th Ulster Division's sector north of the Thiepval road further right to the 18th Eastern Division on the Montauban Ridge. Above Bray he could see a cluster of 17 observation balloons looking towards the German trenches and 'their baskets, where the artillery observers sat, caught the rays of the sun'. No German balloons were looking back. As he watched:

> *The mist was shifting and dissolving. The tall tower of Albert Cathedral appeared suddenly through the veil, and the sun shone full for a few seconds on the Golden Virgin and the Babe, which she held downwards above all this tumult as a peace offering to men.*

In January 1915 a German shell had dislodged her, and she bizarrely hung over the square below, in the attitude of a frozen, headlong fall. It was a macabre landmark for the countless British soldiers that marched through the town; if she should fall, the myth ran, the war would end.

Away in the distance towards Pozières, the view was far from celestial; the bombardment was raging. 'High explosions were tossing up great vomits of black smoke and earth all along the ridges,' Gibbs recalled. Curly white shrapnel air bursts were cascading down onto the ground. Up above the scene was a flight of six aeroplanes, led by a single monoplane traversing the 'deeply blue' sky, heading for the enemy, 'and when the sun caught their wings they were as beautiful and delicate as butterflies'. They were bombers.

Other bombers required escorts back from missions across the lines. At five to six Major Lionel Rees and Lieutenant JC Simpson took off from their 32 Squadron base at Treizennes to patrol between La Bassée, Loos and Souchez. They flew the small but robust newly introduced DH2 biplane, whose 100 hp engine mounted behind the pilot's small cabin could generate 85 mph at 7,000 feet. They were anticipating meeting a swarm of returning bombers, and when ten planes hove into view, sought to join them. Simpson was the first to appreciate they were German Roland CII Walfisch, or whales, but was struck in the head by the concentrated fire from the two-seaters. His aircraft spiralled into the Loos Canal below. Rees was also surprised when one of the German aircraft broke out of the formation and attacked him.

Though a small and comical-looking fighter, the DH2 was strongly built and could absorb a lot of punishment. Rees peppered one of the Walfisch with 30 rounds from his forward-mounted Lewis gun until he saw 'a big cloud of blue haze came out of the nacelle [crew compartment] in front of the pilot'. Realising they were up against one of the newly introduced British aircraft types, the German formation started to unravel. Rees flew back in among the scattering formation and shot down two them before being struck in the thigh from a shot that came up from below. This momentarily paralysed his leg, causing him to break off the attack. When some feeling and pain returned after the shock of the impact, Rees flew amid a group of five German aircraft, shooting a full drum of his Lewis gun ammunition empty. In frustration he drew his pistol and fired at one of the German two-seaters until it fell from his grip inside his nacelle. The German pulled away and soon outpaced him. It was futile to continue, but the previously disciplined German formation was 'scattered in twos and threes all over the sky', their mission aborted.

Major Rees flew back to Treizennes, where he taxied across to the ground crew 'and calmly told the fellows to bring him a tender to take him to hospital'. 'Of course everyone knows the major is mad,' declared Second Lieutenant Gwilym Lewis in his squadron. Squadron leaders were supposed not to fly.

I don't think he was ever more happy in his life than attacking those Huns. He said he would have brought them all down one after the other if he could have used his leg.[8]

Minutes to Go

Many of the former Heart of Midlothian professional footballers in McCrae's 16th Royal Scots 'Footballers' Battalion
stuck together and were in the same trench. 'Most of the
Hearts men were together at the last,' remembered Private
Murdie McKay. 'Crosson was quiet, he and Wattie had
palled up with Jimmy Hazeldean, and the three of them
were now inseparable.' They were afraid; this was hardly
pre-match tension. 'Some of my particular pals looked very
pale,' recalled John McParlane in the battalion. 'These were
older men, you understand, like me with wives and bairns.'
The irrepressible humour of the British soldier was never far
beneath the surface, lightening the palpable tension. 'Jim,
I've forgotten my rifle,' confided Private Bob Moyes to 'wee
Jimmy' Brocks. McParlane heard Jimmy respond, quick as a
flash, 'Never mind, pal. Take mine, and I'll bide here until
you get back' … 'Quite dead pan it was,' McParlane commented. Platoon sergeants sought to offer reassurance. 'We
were about to go over the top, and I was shaking so much
I could barely speak,' admitted Private Jimmy McEvoy.
'Steady lads,' Sergeant Sandy Yule his platoon sergeant said as
he went past, 'and mind you're Royal Scots. Mind your pals
and they'll mind you.' McEvoy was grateful; he was 'a grand
figure to us younger men'. When he paused alongside he felt
completely reassured, 'thinking how lucky I was, for I knew
that nothing could touch him'.[9]

The ground they had to traverse to the right of La Boisselle
was completely open. Moreover they suspected the seven-day
artillery bombardment had not cut the wire. The 15th Royal
Scots alongside had identified the same problem. Sergeant
Charlie Anderson recalled the obvious concern because

'we had three runners from the 15th, all tearing down our trenches as if their breeches were afire'. The trench periscope was passed around 'and right enough, I could see great bands of the foul stuff about 400 yards in front of our line'. There were gaps, but the wire was largely intact.

Meanwhile cinematographer Lieutenant Geoffrey Malins was wending his way through the crowded trenches with his Moy and Bastie movie camera strapped to his back. One moment he was bouncing along like a cork amid the stream of khaki soldiers, labouring under heavy loads; the next, he was trying to swim against the torrent. The communication trenches leading up to the front line were crammed with soldiers looking for their allotted positions. Men taking the wrong turning were sent back, only to collide with those anxiously pushing up from behind. Soldiers lost their tempers and shouted and cursed while commanders stepped in to settle disputes.

Malins had already located the best place to be to film the troops 'going over the top', having been advised that a huge mine packed with seven tons of ammonal was about to be exploded beneath the Hawthorne Redoubt at 7.20 am. This seemingly impregnable German position dominated the British approach to Beaumont Hamel. Malins needed a guide to take him to 'Jacob's Ladder', the intended filming vantage point. To get there he had to wind his way through crowds of khaki-clad soldiers in a scene reminiscent of the London Underground at rush hour. The route read like an extract from a tube map. He pushed his way along 5th Avenue 'full of men taking down munitions' amid 'crumps' of German artillery. At Lanwick Street, his guide advised, 'we will turn back and go by way of White City', so-called because its trenches were cut out of a white chalk bank, 'then up King Street'.

Malins's films reveal a poignant affinity with the soldiers who provided his subject material. As the son of a Hastings hairdresser he came from the same humble background as they did. His father had been disowned by his parents for marrying the housemaid. Because of this faux pas, Honorary Lieutenant Malins was obsessed with issues of status and prestige for the rest of his life. His origins may well have enhanced the quality of his wartime filming. 'These men knew they were going "over the top",' he recalled:

> *They knew that many would not be alive tomorrow night, yet I never saw a sad face nor heard a word of complaint. My feeling watching these men in the glow of the [early morning] firelight [in the dugouts] was almost indescribable. I was filled with awe at their behaviour. I reverenced them more than I had ever done before; and I felt like going down on my knees and thanking God I was an Englishman.*[10]

Malins had been at King Street the day before to recce this chosen spot. While there he was able to film an evocative sequence of soldiers from the 1st Lancashire Fusiliers fixing bayonets and being ushered from the communication trench into the forward fire trench by their company commander Captain Edmond 'Pongo' Dawson. The officer's great-granddaughter Anne Dawson was to view the same scene captured on celluloid 97 years later at the National Army Museum in London. 'I knew that my grandfather had been injured at the Somme, but to actually physically see him was amazing,' she admitted. She watched the film with her daughters. 'When he looks toward the camera, the family resemblance is incredible: he has a jawline and an expression on his face, which look just like my father and my brother.' The impact of Malins's documentary film *The Battle of the Somme*, which was to be finished and released even before the battle was over, remains striking, even to this day. 'To see him so much younger and about to go into that horrible carnage was a very powerful experience,' Anne Dawson confided. 'It was very moving; the hairs on the back of my neck stood up and for a brief moment I was in that picture with him.' Malins recalled:

> The great moment was drawing near. I admit I was feeling a wee bit nervous. The mental and nervous excitement under such conditions was very great. Everyone was in a state of suppressed excitement.[11]

Eccles-born Captain Thomas Tweed, with B Company of the 2nd Salford Pals, regarded his silent men in the trenches before Thiepval. They were a close-knit unit, volunteers to a man. Tweed had personally recruited many of them in 1914, Irish navies who had built the Manchester Ship Canal and miners from the pits beneath Salford and Irlam. These were men who had bonded in slums and trying social conditions numbered among the worse in Britain, yet despite seething local discontent they had immediately answered the national call to arms. Tweed had been a member of the Police Specials and cracked some of their skulls during the Liverpool strikes and unrest of 1911. Since 1914 they had lived cheek by jowl, like the rest of Kitchener's New Army.

Four of their men had died and seven were wounded in a single 'wizz-bang' stonk as they had passed the partially burning village of Authuille and entered the communication trenches in Thiepval Wood. Tweed was well aware that the previous scale of winter trench warfare casualties would be like nothing compared to what they would face today. It was their first ever deliberate attack. Losses would be severe and socially catastrophic in such a small community as Salford. Tweed's orderly was former shop assistant Walter Fiddes, who was the best friend of former travelling salesman Lance-Corporal Thomas Mellor, just married. Corporal Stephen Sharples completed a trio who had known each other well, through their local Eccles church. Who would be left after they went over the top? The 2nd Salford Pals was in the second wave of the coming assault.[12]

At 6.30 am Malins had perilously passaged a Russian sap that had brought him out into a sunken lane, just before the German-occupied village of Beaumont Hamel. 'There lined up,' he recalled, 'crouching as close to the bank as possible, were some of our men', bayonets fixed, 'ready to spring forward'. It was an unmissable opportunity to film a group of men from the Lancashire Fusiliers, 60 minutes before going over the top. The ruined rooftops of Beaumont Hamel could be seen from the top of the sunken lane they occupied. The lane provided complete cover. They had no idea that the innocuous slope above, which they would have to climb, was completely registered by German machine-guns out of sight in defilade.

Malins cranked his camera and recorded some of the most evocative pictures of the war. Hardly any cameraman had captured the facial expressions of men about to go over the top. Nearly every man Malins filmed would be injured or killed. Meanwhile here they were, smoking, sitting, lying and attempting to relax with their equipment at their feet, regarding the cameraman with obvious curiosity. Malins was sparing in his own description. 'Some of them looked happy and gay, others sat with stern, set faces, realising the great task in front of them.' He found it difficult to appreciate they were actually sitting out in the middle of no man's land, between the two lines. 'It was practically inconceivable,' he recalled. 'The shell fire seemed just as bad as ever behind in the trenches, but here it was simply heavenly.' The trench mortar crews, distinguishable by arm bands, are not so tense, because they are not going over. The remainder look pensive, some wide-eyed, dragging on cigarettes as if it may be their last. Mortar men are cleaning shells, while some of the infantry are nervously fiddling with their rifles. Malins's appearance has bobbed a few heads and brought on a few bravado grins. A second lieutenant, who will not survive, has his back to the camera talking with a soldier. A modern forensic lip-reader has analysed the footage and revealed the soldier is talking with a broad Lancashire dialect, saying: 'I hope we are in the right place this time, because if not, I am going to bomb them and get out of here.'

Corporal George Ashurst with this unit was 'detailed off in charge of a party of eight bombers', he recalled, 'and we were supposed to be the Colonel's body guard'. He may well have been nearby. He was familiar with Malins, having been on camera the day before. As Malins's camera pans, he captures a face so tight with tension, that the smile resembles a grimace. Once finished, Malins had less than an hour to reach Jacob's Ladder, back along the Russian sap, to film the Hawthorne mine explosion.[13]

Captain Charles Carrington was the acting adjutant for his Warwickshire battalion. He was forward in the battalion command post overlooking the ground between Gommecourt and Serre to the north of the line. 'I can only say that I have never been so excited in my life,' he admitted. It was the final hour before the attack, spent receiving reports from the front companies that they were ready and testing their telephone lines back to the artillery. 'This was like a boy going to the play for the first time in his life,' he remembered. The curtain raiser was the final artillery bombardment:

The noise rose to a crescendo such as I'd never heard before, for which we for the first time used the word 'drumfire'; which is a great description of it. A noise which made all bombardments that we'd heard in the previous days seem like nothing at all.[14]

Lieutenant Edward Liveing, with the 12th Battalion The London Regiment, waiting in the trenches to the north, opposite Gommecourt, turned to his corporal at about 6.25 am and said, 'They'll just about start now.'

The words were not out of my mouth before the noise, which had increased a trifle during the last 20 minutes, suddenly swelled into a gigantic roar.

'We are the guns, and your masters! Saw ye our flashes?' poet Gilbert Frankau, an artillery officer, wrote. 'Fathers or lovers, we break them, we are the guns!' The final artillery barrage was physical in its intensity. Henry Holdstock, with the 6th Balloon Squadron, observing the impacts recalled:

You could feel the vibrations coming up through the earth, through your limbs, through your body ... It was shattering. The whole ground trembled, and you felt sorry for anyone within half a mile of wherever they were piling it. It must have been terrible for them.

Sergeant Richard Tawney, with the 22nd Manchesters below Mametz, recalled how in his trench they involuntarily ducked, with the air 'full of a vast and agonised passion, bursting now into shrill screams and pitiful whimpers, shuddering beneath terrible blows ...' They could not see the howling projectiles, but the very elements appeared to be 'writhing' over their heads. Watching soldiers were filled with awe and 'triumphant exultation'. Fritz was never going to survive this. 'Yet at the same time one was intent on the practical details, wiping the trench dirt off the bolt of one's rifle,' Tawney recalled.

Corporal George Ashurst, viewing the intensification of the bombardment in front of Beaumont Hamel, recalled, 'The noise was like a hundred trains over the top of your head, all at once.' The men in the trenches were jubilant. 'I thought it would shift Jerry,' Ashurst anticipated, 'he couldn't stand up to something like this.'[15]

In the Ulster Division trenches beneath the Schwaben Redoubt men knelt and prayed, while others made out their wills in pay books. Many sat staring at family photographs or trench walls, wondering what their loved ones would be doing at home at this hour in the morning. Bombardiers were busy opening grenade boxes and handing them around. It was their task to bomb the German trenches into sub-mission when they reached them. Young 'Soldier Boy' Billy McFadzean, with the 14th Royal Irish Rifles, had been quite the lad at school. His father was a JP, yet Billy had been rep-rimanded as many as 34 times in his second year at the Trade Preparatory School for misbehaviour. Before joining two years earlier he had been a linen firm apprentice and a keen rugby player. Nevertheless, as he cut the retaining cord around a box of grenades he took his eye off it and dropped it. As the box hit the floor two bombs spilt out, in the crowded trench, and they had shed their pins. McFazdean threw himself on top of them and was torn apart by two muffled, compacted impacts. Only one man received a serious wound, and it cost him a leg. As Billy's mutilated remains were taken away on a stretcher, fellow soldiers instinctively removed their helmets, despite shrapnel whizzing around.[16]

Lieutenant Edward Liveing kept muttering under his breath the comforting verse his father had given him, 'Lord, I shall be very busy this day …' as he waited to go over the top. 'The idea of after-life seemed ridiculous in the presence of such frightful destructive force,' he remembered. The clock inexorably ticked away. Private Albert Andrews, with the 19th Manchesters south of the line, was asked by his colonel if they knew what time zero hour was. 'No, sir,' he responded. 'Well, it is 07.30. Anyone got a watch?' he asked. It was just after six o'clock. 'Put your watches right and don't forget, be ready,' they were advised. Liveing constantly asked the time, as did thousands of others, all along the line, anxiously awaiting the signal to go. 'What was time?' he asked:

> I had another 20 minutes in which to live in comparative safety. What was the difference between 20 minutes and 20 years? Really and truly, what was the difference? I was living at present and that was enough.[17]

The tension was made worse by the simple fact there was so little to see. Boxed in to left and right, front and rear, soldiers carried so much equipment that the physical exertion required to take a look made it hardly worthwhile, so they quietly endured. Albert Andrews recalled the load he carried, starting with his rifle and bayonet, which had wire cutters attached. There was a shovel fastened to his back and a pack with two days' rations inside, an oil sheet, jacket and mess tin. Inside the smaller haversack was another day's iron rations, two Mills bombs, 150 rounds of ammunition, a bag of ten bombs and two extra canvas bandoliers containing 60 rounds, one slung over each shoulder. All this weighed up to 75 lbs, the weight of half a man. Climbing out of the trench unaided needed physical effort and thoughtful preparation.

Other Tommies carried an assortment of knuckle-dusters, lengths of chain and vicious-looking knives, as if they were heading out for a street brawl. Of the 143 battalions waiting to go over, 97 were new 'Kitchener' battalions. Despite endless preparation and rehearsals there was hardly an officer and man among them who really appreciated the difference between a trench raid – which had been the primary activity before – and a deliberate attack. Machine-gunners had dismantled their guns and would sling the pieces over the parapet as they climbed out. They had practised it all a thousand times before. Once on top they had to quickly reassemble the gun and then catch up and stay up with the advancing infantry before coming into action. The need to think through and overcome these functional problems was a welcome distraction from what they would face when they climbed out.

What actually lay over the top was a mystery. Most had never really viewed it, because in a fire trench all that was visible was the opposite wall. If they tried they might see an array of stakes tangled with wire and in the distance something dark, with similar stakes or piled chalk, in front of what must be the German line. Sergeant Charles Quinnel, with the 9th Battalion Royal Fusiliers, remembered looking through a trench telescope:

All you could see was the devastated land of no man's land and the German barbed wire, and you never saw a sign of life. It was one of the most desolate sights in the world.

Yet out there, within shouting range, were hundreds and hundreds of men. Intelligence officer John Masefield remembered that the limit of the trench soldier's world encompassed a patch of grass to his front and wire, and that might be all he would observe for months. Seldom did the enemy make an appearance.

They could see nothing, even at a loophole or periscope, but the greenish strip of ground, pitted with shell holes and fenced with wire, running up to the enemy line. There was little else for them to see, looking to the front, for miles and miles and miles, up hill and down dale.[18]

At ten minutes to go, officers moved along their trench checking the men's equipment. This made little practical difference, but did make the men *feel* prepared. Then the officer would check his own kit: revolver loaded, rifle with bayonet and one up the spout slung over his shoulder. Clock watching became obsessive. 'My Captain, a brave man and a good officer, came along and borrowed a spare watch off me,' recalled Sergeant Richard Tawney. 'It was the last time I saw him.' The officer was Captain 'Bill' Bland, who had included the pressed forget-me-not flower in his last letter to his wife.

The relentless countdown continued. Veterans recall platoons waiting 'very still', often completely mesmerised by the noise and spectacle of the bombardment ahead. Private Albert Andrews heard 'the orders came down: *Half an hour to go. Quarter of an hour to go*'. One officer confided to John Masefield: 'I made up my mind that I was going to be killed. I kept on saying to myself, "In half an hour you will be dead. In twenty-five minutes you will be dead ..."'

The man experienced conflicting emotions, regrets, thinking of all the people he would not see again. 'Sorrow' did not describe his feelings; 'it is an ache and anger and longing to be alive'. A whole range of emotions swept the anxious waiting ranks, re-jigging equipment loads and positioning ladders, preparatory to scrambling over the top. 'The only thing I can compare it with is like waiting for someone to die,' recalled RH Stewart, with the Ulster Division. 'You know it is coming and you wish to God it was over with.' Many of the unseasoned troops with the Kitchener battalions likened the pent-up excitement to being with a sports team prior to a vital match. 'We hadn't got the wind up, we'd never been over the top before,' recalled one soldier. 'We didn't know what it would be like; we looked forward to it actually.' The veterans of Loos, Arras and Gallipoli viewed it differently; they knew well what was coming. A soldier would feel a heightened sense of fellowship with the man standing next to him. Some simply ran the soil of the trench sides through their fingers, feeling it for the last time. 'You smoked fag after fag, took sips of water, oiled the rifle, did everything over and over again,' recalled Stewart. There was banter; a final tot of rum, prayers and thoughts of loved ones at home. Indeed, those living along the south coast of England could hear the grumbling bombardment now. Masefield's morose companion continued to assess his prospects. 'In about five minutes I shall be dead':

I envied people whom I had seen in billets two nights before. I thought they will be alive at dinner-time today, and tonight they'll be snug in bed, but where shall I be? My body will be out in no man's land.

The real debilitating anxiety felt by all ranks was to do with outwardly showing fear, which could rapidly become contagious. Lance-Corporal J Cousins with the 7th Bedfords simply recalled thinking: 'For God's sake, let us get going.'[19]

Twenty minutes before, the Lancashire Fusiliers in the sunken lane started to receive incoming 77 mm fire from the Germans, who had spotted them. With minutes still to go, 20 men had already gone down. 'Fritz's guns seemed to be coming to life now,' George Ashurst remembered, 'his shells were dropping over pretty merrily and machine-gun bullets whistled over our heads, just as if he knew as well as we did that the time was near.' These last ticking moments became unbearable, with 'the terrible strain causing some men to utter almost unnatural noises'.

Geoffrey Malins had arrived at Jacob's Ladder to film the exploding Hawthorne mine. 'Heavens! How the minutes dragged,' he remembered. 'My nerves were strung to a high pitch, my heart was thumping like a steam hammer.' He observed an officer standing nearby 'mopping perspiration from his brow, and clutching his stick, first in one hand then in the other – quite unconsciously I am sure'. The officer kept looking at his watch, watching the minutes tick by.

At 7.19 am Malins grasped his camera handle, set his teeth and focused on the apparently innocuous mound to his front. There was hardly anything to pick out, no shape to the redoubt, just a slight protrusion on the ridge line. After 30 seconds, 'I started turning the handle, two revolutions per second, no more, no less. I noticed how regular I was turning.'

He was exposing the scene beforehand, earnestly hoping he had selected the right spot, because he wanted to record the explosion from the moment it broke ground. 'Any second now,' he reflected, but still no explosion; 'it seemed to me as if I had been turning for hours.' Had it misfired?

I looked at my exposure dial. I had used over a thousand feet. The horrible thought flashed through my mind, that my film might run out before the mine blew. Would it go up before I had time to reload? The thought brought beads of perspiration to my forehead. The agony was awful; indescribable. My hand began to shake. Another 250 feet exposed. I had to keep on. Then it happened.

There was a small clump of bushes visible to the left foreground in his frame, giving scale and perspective. Malins captured the awesome eruption in its entirety:

The ground where I stood gave a mighty convulsion. It rocked and swayed. I gripped hold of my tripod to steady myself. Then, for all the world like a gigantic sponge, the earth rose in the air to the height of hundreds of feet. Higher and higher it rose, and with a horrible grinding roar the earth fell back upon itself, leaving in its place a mountain of smoke.

'We felt a queer dull thud and our trench fairly rocked,' George Ashurst remembered:

A great blue flame shot into the sky, carrying with it hundreds of tons of bricks and stone and great chunks of earth mingled with wood and wire and fragments of sandbags.

Young Albert McMillan, with the 16th Middlesex Regiment, was determined not to miss this sight and had stood on the fire step of his trench, peering at the ridge line just 500 yards away. He was taken aback at the huge column of earth that reared up, and just a little sobered. This was no lark. Within seconds the shock wave reached his trench, making it sway from side to side and pitching him back inside. He was winded on landing, with his kit scattered around him. 'You silly little bastard,' his platoon sergeant admonished, standing over him. The mine had been set 30 feet below the surface and spewed up hundreds of tons of spoil to a height of 600 feet, creating a crater measuring 220 feet across.[20]

The time was 7.20 am, ten minutes before H-Hour. In the stunning aftermath of the explosion, despite the sound of the Thiepval heights being bombarded to the right and the mutter of gunfire further left, an eerie silence descended. Many of the British guns were re-registering to take on the second line in depth. By a strange coincidence the German guns were silent too; birds began to sing and hover in the strange sunlight.

The highly contradictory chain of events that led to 'Hunter-Bunter's folly', the decision by the commander of VIII Corps, Lieutenant-General Hunter-Weston, to blow the Hawthorne mine ten minutes early, has never been satisfactorily resolved. Nobody knew how a 40,000 lb charge would behave, because no one had seen one blown. The 29th Division assaulting at this point planned on the 2nd Fusiliers rushing the crater before the main attack at 7.30, even though previous mine detonations strongly suggested the Germans would get to the lip of a crater first. Nobody knew how long it would take for the debris to fall, measured against the safety of attacking troops, but recent experience at St Eloi suggested it was seconds. The confusing compromise was a disaster. Heavy artillery was ordered to 'lift' onto the next target into the depth of the German position at 7.20. However, it was ordered not only to lift in situ, but along the whole of the VIII Corps front.

Private Frank Lindley, with the 14th Yorks and Lancs just to the north at Serre, remembered that 'we knew what time they were going to blow the whistles, half past seven'. What happened was unexpected. 'The birds were singing and the sun came up' and off to their right 'we saw it going sky high. It was one huge mass of soil going up' and 'it shook all along our line'. At which point their own guns mysteriously lifted. 'That mine shouldn't have gone up till we were on the top,' he believed. The result was 'we had the morning chorus before we got the "other"'. Lindley remembered occupying their sector of the line earlier and hearing a German voice shout, 'When are those Yorkshire bastards coming?' Well, now they were, but 'in the time between that mine going up and us going over, well the Jerries were out'. Frank Lindley adjusted his entrenching tool and strapped it low across his groin, so as to protect his manhood as he went over the top.[21]

Ten minutes before, across the Ancre valley to the right, General Nugent's 36th Ulster Division men had already been stealthily moving out into no man's land. Their objective was the 'Devil's Dwelling', the Schwaben Redoubt, which occupied the high ground dominating the Ancre valley and plateau beyond. Key ground for both sides. Eight Russian saps snaked out of Thiepval Wood to the sunken Thiepval road from which soldiers emerged, covered by smoke from the bombardment as well as trees set ablaze by German counter-battery fire. The second wave had moved out five minutes after the first, and the third wave was moving up even as the thunderclap of the Hawthorne mine reverberated across the Ancre valley. It provided an irresistible urge to get moving even though there were still ten minutes to go. Some of them even broke into a run, others rose to their feet and started to walk briskly uphill towards the first German line, seven to eight hundred yards ahead.

Lieutenant-Colonel Ambrose Ricardo, commanding the Tyrone Battalion, recalled the quick start. 'The Derry's, on our left, were so eager they started a few minutes before the ordered time, and the Tyrones were not going to be left behind.' The whole division mass erupted into forward momentum: two battalions to the left of the marshy River Ancre and ten to the right. Some of the men who had stowed away their traditional Orange sashes pulled them on. Captain Gaffkin with the West Belfast Volunteers waved an orange handkerchief around his head and shouted, 'Come on, boys, this is the first of July!', echoing the war cry spat out by the defenders of Derry against King James's besieging Jacobites in 1689. 'No surrender!' roared the men. This was tribal.

'They got going without delay – no fuss, no shouting, no running; everything orderly, solid and thorough,' Ricardo recalled, as subsequent waves moved up. 'Here and there a boy would wave his hand to me as I shouted "Good luck" to them from my megaphone.' These were men who had sworn the Ulster Covenant and channelled their pre-war belligerence against British Home Rule towards the collective survival of Protestant Ulster and the British Empire. The battle was aggressively personal. Many passed Ricardo carrying cumbersome loads. 'Fancy advancing against heavy fire carrying a heavy roll of barbed wire on your shoulders,' Ricardo commented. Many coils were dumped in the sunken lane as they crossed; they impeded momentum. They were off to a good start, one *Times* correspondent observed. 'When I saw the men emerge from the smoke and form up as if on parade, I could hardly believe my eyes.' 'Let her rip, ye divils!' shouted some Ulstermen in jocular defiance at the first machine-gun bursts. 'The Boche let her rip all right,' remarked an officer. Veterans recalled 'the hollow, crepitating *tap-t-t-tap*' of the machine-guns 'and the swish, swish, swish' of incoming rounds. It was an unnerving sound, audible amid the fiercest artillery fire.[22]

Lieutenant Cecil Lewis, flying over Fricourt with the first 3 Squadron air patrol, was transfixed by the 'fantastic sight' of the final hurricane bombardment below, 'and it was wild … You could hear the guns above the roar of the aircraft,' he recalled, 'like rain on a window pane.' After the Hawthorne mine there were two larger and seven smaller explosions along the front. The biggest he knew was going to be near the straight Roman road by La Boisselle. As he watched:

Suddenly the whole earth heaved and up from the ground came what looked like two enormous cypress trees. Great, dark, conical-shaped silhouettes which lifted the earth three, four, five thousand feet up.

These were the Lochnagar and Y Sap mines, blown two minutes before H-Hour. The pressure wave from the blast 'flung us right away backwards over on the one side away from the blast. And then a second later up came the second one.' The Lochnagar explosion, with 36,000 and 24,000 lb charges fired in tandem, created a crater 220 feet wide and 55 feet deep, with a 15 foot lip 450 feet around it; the Y Sap crater was 130 feet wide and 40 feet deep, also with a lip out to 450 feet around. The shock waves travelled large distances through the soil, announcing the assault had started and warning every German soldier, peering over the parapet, that more explosions might well follow.[23]

Lieutenant Ulick Burke, with the 2nd Devons opposite Pozières, recalled:

I shouted down the left and right of my sector, 'Five minutes to go!' Then four minutes, then three minutes, two minutes, half a minute, then 'Ten seconds … get ready … Over!'

Albert Andrews's officer opposite Montauban called 'three minutes to go'. 'I lit a cigarette,' Andrews recalled, 'and up the ladder I went.' Private Cyril Jose's platoon commander, climbing up nearby, encouraged them by yelling 'Remember Belgium, Remember the *Lusitania*!' The soldiers shouted back: 'Fuck Belgium and fuck the *Lusitania*!' There was little empathy for 'the Belgians [who] had not shown us much friendliness in Belgium', Jose recalled, 'and we hadn't much sympathy for over-rich, pleasure seeking Americans who had died a comparatively quick death.' His immediate companion Dai Watkins received one, his head shattered by shrapnel as they climbed out. The majority of the soldiers streaming over the side of the trenches were more like Private Reg Coldridge, who remembered, 'When I went over I didn't really think of anything. I just had to go. That was all.'[24]

H-Hour: the time to laboriously climb the boxes, ladders and pegs at the side of the trench. Along the 16-mile stretch between Gommecourt and Maricourt, 55,000 British and French soldiers in the first waves climbed out; behind them another 100,000 waited. They saw very little ahead, there were still some green grass strips amid the smoking shell holes and generally no enemy. Intelligence officer John Masefield remembered the innocuous jokes, as when a man slipped on the ladder and muttered, 'I'll miss the bloody train.' Another soldier recalled, 'I heard a *whut-whut-whut*, just like that, just alongside my ears.' They could not see the jets of smoke, hardly bigger than the puffs blown from a kettle on the boil, spurting out from the first machine-guns opening up. 'What did I think while I was going over? I thought my last hour had come,' recalled another soldier. 'They'd got a machine-gun every five yards, it sounded like.' There was a belief that the Hun sighted their machine-guns low, so if they did not crouch they would only get it in the legs. If they quickly cleared the parapet they would be all right.[25]

'You can hear the gunfire all the time,' recalled Harold 'Hal' Kerridge with the London Scottish, winding his way through the trenches with the second wave at Serre.

It gets louder and louder and you're in the communication trench and the communication trench goes to a reserve trench and the reserve trench goes to a front line trench. Obviously you're scared, everybody is scared, but you don't show it. At least you hope you don't. Nobody else seemed to show it, so I hope I didn't.

It seemed to be going wrong from the start. Captain 'Pongo' Dawson, filmed by Malins the day before, climbed up onto the trench parapet near Jacob's Ladder with his sergeant-major, Nelson. As they urged the men out they were raked by the first bursts of machine-gun fire and tumbled back into the trench. George Ashurst had to wait for ten minutes after the last of the debris from the Hawthorne blast slapped onto the ground. 'We set our teeth,' he remembered. 'We seemed to say to ourselves all in a moment, "*To hell with life*"' as B and D Companies of the Lancashire Fusiliers burst out of the sunken lane in extended order. 'Huge black shrapnel shells seemed to burst on top of us' and the German machine-gunners were on them in an instant. 'Shouts of pain and calls for help could be heard on all sides' as they stumbled up the incline towards ruined Beaumont Hamel. 'Mortally wounded men tried to grab our legs as we passed them.'[26]

Phillip Gibbs was up on the Grandstand overlooking Albert with a cluster of officers watching this epic scene, from Auchonvillers to Bray-sur-Somme, opening before them. It was difficult to pick out detail.

Now and then, when the smoke of shell fire drifted, I caught glimpses of green fields and flower patches beyond the trench lines, and church spires beyond the range of guns rising above clumps of trees in summer foliage.

In stark contrast to the scene ahead, just beyond the beetroot field he saw 'a French farmer, cutting his grass with a long scythe, in steady sweeping strokes'. Malins's fellow camera-man 'Mac' McDowell had also captured a similarly incongruous scene nearby, two days before. Two farm women in traditional dress hoed weeds amid ripe corn waving in the wind, a bizarre backdrop to the artillery bombardment.

Just before 7.30 Gibbs remembered 'all the officers about me kept looking at their wrist watches' like the men below in the trenches. The 15-inch 'Grandmother' railway gun was firing behind Albert with its single distinctive strokes. 'I could follow the journey of the shell by listening to its rush through space.' The artillery bombardment reached its climax.

> *It was like the 'rafale' of the French soixante-quinze, very rapid, with distant and separate strokes, but louder than the noise of field guns. They were our trench mortars at work along the whole length of the line before me.*

The final ten-minute barrage from concentrated mortars caused more damage to the German first line than the previous seven days of bombardment. Gibbs and the officers around him felt like morbid, guilty onlookers. 'An officer near me turned away, and there was a look of sharp pain in his eyes.' The men below were friends and people they knew. Smoke was obscuring the entire front line. 'The only men I could see were those in reserve' coming up from behind, 'winding along a road by some trees which led up to the attacking points'. Then at about a minute or so after 7.30 they could detect a muted 'rushing sound', the sound of rifles and machine-gun fire. It had started.

General Rawlinson could see nothing of this from his specially constructed observation platform set among the trees at Pont Noyelles. It was within easy reach of his headquarters at Querrieu, 12 miles behind the front. He had been there an hour, watching the final bombardment and the mines exploding in the far distance. Little could be seen across the mist-shrouded ridge lines before 7.30 am, which made for a much sanitised view of the battlefront. At H-Hour there were momentary flashes, jets of smoke and eight seconds later distant thunderclaps, little else.

Rawlinson 'spoke habitually of the enemy as "the Old Hun" or "Old Fritz" in an affectionate, contemptuous way', war correspondent Phillip Gibbs remembered, 'as a fellow who was trying his best but getting the worst of it every time'. Rawlinson was powerless to affect events in any meaningful way at this point. He had just committed the biggest British Army to date on its largest ever operation, a formidable responsibility. It was now in the hands of his corps and division commanders. To achieve what Haig was hoping for, his men had to break through 32 German battalions. He had committed 158 battalions. Military intelligence had predicted there were 65 German battalions standing by in reserve. If he was not through within the five days it would take them to collect, his overwhelming numerical superiority would be at an end.

'Like most of our generals, he had amazing, overweening optimism,' Gibbs explained. The compromise plan insisted upon by Haig would likely produce a compromise result, which would not be Rawlinson's fault. The artillery might create a breakthrough; if not, with his troops closed up on the German line, Rawlinson could still 'bite and hold'. The indomitable British soldier could be relied upon to do exactly as he was told. Rawlinson 'had always got the enemy "nearly beat"', Gibbs commented, 'with the jovial sense of striking another blow which could lead this time to stupendous results'.

Rawlinson watched the start and then returned to his headquarters at the Querrieu château nearby to await reports from his five corps commanders. He was due to meet with Haig after lunch.[27]

VII Corps (Third Army)
Attack on Gommecourt, 1 July 1916

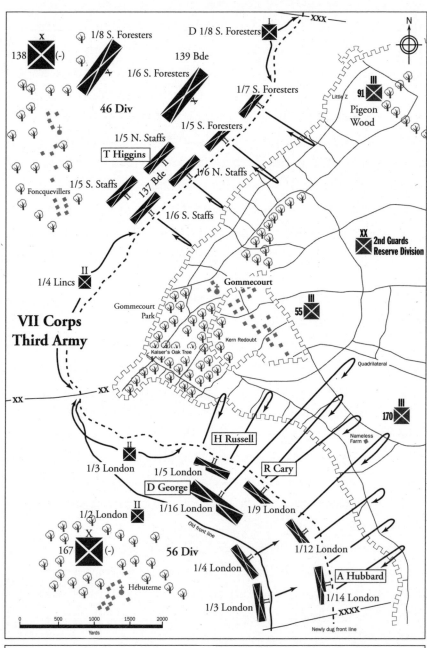

X 138 (-)

1/8 S. Foresters

139 Bde

1/6 S. Foresters

46 Div

1/5 N. Staffs

T Higgins

137 Bde

1/5 S. Staffs

Foncquevillers

1/6 S. Staffs

1/4 Lincs

VII Corps
Third Army

D 1/8 S. Foresters

1/7 S. Foresters

Little Z

III 91 Pigeon Wood

1/5 S. Foresters

1/6 N. Staffs

XX 2nd Guards Reserve Division

Gommecourt

Gommecourt Park

III 55

Kern Redoubt

Kaiser's Oak Tree

Quadrilateral

H Russell

III 170

Nameless Farm

1/3 London

1/5 London

R Cary

D George

1/16 London

1/9 London

1/2 London

X 167 (-)

56 Div

Hébuterne

Old front line

1/4 London

1/3 London

1/12 London

A Hubbard

1/14 London

Newly dug front line

0   500   1000   1500   2000
Yards

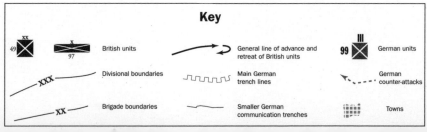

Key

XX 49 / X 97 — British units	General line of advance and retreat of British units	III 99 — German units
XXX — Divisional boundaries	Main German trench lines	German counter-attacks
XX — Brigade boundaries	Smaller German communication trenches	Towns

CHAPTER 5

The Race to the Parapet —•

7.15 to 9.30 am

7.15 to 7.45 am

Raus! Raus! Out! Out!

The final intensification of British artillery fire was still a shock after the deluge of fire over the previous seven days. Nervous tension permeated the German dugouts. Now the British would come. 'All hell seemed to have broken loose along the line,' remembered Leutnant Matthäus Gerster, with 119 Regiment at Beaumont Hamel. The bombardment ranged up and down the German line 'impact by impact, smoke column by smoke column … A monstrous line of geysers seemed to spring up as though the bowels of the earth were being torn apart,' he remembered. Sentries crouching near dugout entrances strained to detect any tell-tale lessening of fire, the precursor to an assault. 'It was impossible to distinguish one explosion from another,' Gerster observed. This was the key moment. Every German recognised there was one chance, one chance only, to live when the barrage lifted. They had to scramble out of the dugouts and get to the parapets first.[1]

The importance of observing the enemy's trenches, even under bombardment, by whatever means, had been drummed into the German soldiers by training and experience. They could not afford to be caught out. Observation slits had their backgrounds darkened to avoid any silhouette. They nervously fastened their equipment, preparatory for a sprint, checking and re-checking weapons. Wooden planks and chicken wire, erected to deflect grenade-throwing trench raiders, had long since been blown away. Every conceivable fighting option was considered. Would the angled trench bays that offered protection against shell or grenade explosions still be there, or collapsed by the shelling? Sharpened spades were thrust into their belts alongside stick grenades to deal with break-ins. They could be more lethal in the confined hurly-burly of a trench fight than the longer rifle and bayonet. Shoot into the smoke where the enemy was expected to emerge, they were taught. Boxes of grenades were dragged up from below and stockpiled near dugout entrances.

'My group was in position, ready to spring up,' remembered Unteroffizier Friedrich Hinkel, with 7 Company 99 Regiment near the Schwaben Redoubt. His men had their rifles slung, and were holding hand grenades, with a full water bottle and full bread bags at their belts. 'Everyone knew his place.' When the moment arrived they had to run and occupy the bend at the top of the path leading from their dugout by the crucifix, standing nearby. They were the link to 5 Company on their left. Hinkel had barely spent five minutes liaising with 'the little Leutnant of the right wing platoon when suddenly a shell splinter went through his head'. Sentries periodically dashed outside for a quick look across no man's land, checking for movement, before ducking back under cover. It was essential not to miss the crucial moment when fire switched to the rear, a lethal responsibility. Most of the forward units had already spotted the forward British trenches crammed full with troops. Hinkel had resourcefully positioned part of a framed mirror in his trench, 'a wonderful way to make observations of the enemy from the stairs of the smashed entrances to our dugouts'. The experienced Unteroffizier 'was not in the dark hole of the dugout'; both 'excitement' and the sudden intensification of artillery fire had drawn him virtually outside. The responsibility he felt for his eight-man Westphalian section made him reluctant to simply rely on a mirror. He was convinced something was about to happen.

He ran outside to the crucifix and took a quick look at Thiepval Wood below as the 'husch-husch' of successive explosive detonations flung chalk and pieces of wooden beams overhead to his rear. Hinkel shouted information for onward transmission to the underground section via 'my magnificent young farmer', a lad who ironically had stuttered all his life. 'We couldn't get caught out,' Hinkel recalled.[2]

Off to Hinkel's right, the first indication the men from the 9th Company 119 Regiment had that something was amiss was when the ground suddenly rushed up into their faces. Across the Ancre valley, 40,600 lbs of ammonal had detonated and removed the front lip of the Hawthorne Ridge. The energy released by this colossal explosion burst upwards and outwards at almost nine miles a second. Many of the 9th Company were dead before the pain registered. The supersonic blast wave, 'a terrific explosion', perforated ear drums, 'which for the moment drowned the thunder of artillery', claimed one German officer. 'Almost all of the 1st Platoon', with Leutnant Renz, 'and elements of the 2nd Platoon', under Leutnant Böhm, 'were crushed and buried in their dugouts by the explosion.' British movie cameraman Geoffrey Malins caught the whole episode on 23 seconds of film, from the bulge through to flowering detonation and collapsing debris. It left two huge palls of smoke hanging over a crater 40 feet deep and 130 feet across. British photographer Oswald Crawford, who captured the blast from the reserve trenches, recalled 'men and bits of planking' propelled through the air.[3]

The supersonic wall of air blew individuals caught on the surface 80 feet into the sky. Others, singed by the fireball, were brutally compressed by the near vacuum formed, suffering massive internal damage, if not dismembered by flying debris. Breitmeyer's 3rd Platoon dugouts imploded with the pressure and collapsed inwards, as did many of Böhm's. Three sections were killed outright, 24 men crushed or torn apart by the explosion. Buried wounded and uninjured survivors could measure life spans in minutes as they sought to dig themselves out before they succumbed to fumes or expended oxygen. Renz and some soldiers from the 1st Platoon were alive, but trapped beneath tons of spoil. They could hear fierce fighting raging above, which meant few people would be looking for them. They started to claw at the debris that blocked the entrance of their partially collapsed dugout. Steely self-control was required to suppress the claustrophobic urge to panic, as they struggled and dug on the very verge of sanity.

When the echo from the reverberating boom had died away, the guns at Beaumont Hamel appeared to fall silent. Sentries raced to investigate, everywhere German heads popped up over the edge of craters and partially collapsed parapets. The whole of the British VIII Corps's heavy artillery had lifted, along with half of the 18-pounder fire, onto the rear trenches. Ten minutes remained before the British would move. The hurricane of Stokes mortar fire that replaced the artillery lift gave immediate confirmation to the Germans, if any were needed, that the main infantry assault was on its way.

On the other side of the Ancre valley, Unteroffizier Friedrich Hinkel got moving. 'Raus! Raus! Out! Out!' he shrieked, calling his men up from the dugouts. 'Give it 'em hard!' they shouted, the Westphalian battle cry. Hinkel and his men were in an ugly mood, tired out, nerves stretched, and angered by the week-long bombardment. 'You made a good job of it, you British!' Hinkel remonstrated. 'Seven days and nights you hammered on our door!' Now it was their turn to inflict pain. In the rush for the parapet, three of Hinkel's men were swept away by 18-pounder shrapnel. Despite the risk, they stood and knelt, firing into 'the open gaps of the moving wall of smoky brew in front of us'. Hinkel took control, ordering '600 metres'; the enemy were still a long way off but closing. His men took deliberate aim, 'and now the enemy leaped and turned somersaults over there, the correct range the first time'. Target areas had been methodically registered over the past 18 months.

'It was a kind of relief to be able to come out,' recalled army surgeon Stephan Westman, 'even into air filled with smoke and the smell of cordite.' He watched as the soldiers poured out of their dugouts, clattering past laden with heavy weapons and equipment, glancing up 'with inflamed and sunken eyes'. They settled into their fire positions, 'their faces blackened by fire and their uniforms splashed with the blood of their wounded comrades'. It was the time for retribution and they would have it. Pre-registered German artillery began to shriek past, plastering the British parapets and wire gaps. 'Now your reception is going to match your turbulent longing to enter!' Hinkel declared with some relish. The VIII British Corps had assessed it was up against perhaps 55 guns on its sector, but now Generalmajor Maur's artillery concentrations at 'Adolf', 'Beauregard' and 'Berta' opened up with almost three times that amount.[4]

Unteroffizier Aicheler's machine-gun was blown backwards into the sap exit, where he and his crew had been poised waiting, when the Hawthorne mine blew. They were tossed inside in a jumble of Maxim gun, bodies and equipment. 'There were already about 20 British soldiers on this side of our entanglement,' he later reported, 'just 25 steps from the machine-gun.' The race for the parapets outside Beaumont Hamel, despite the ten minute warning, was fast becoming a close call. Aicheler managed to get the gun firing, but it jammed after ten shots. A nervous clearance got it going again but only for another ten round burst. British soldiers were throwing hand grenades and Aicheler yelled 'Back!' The crew ran around the next traverse and brought the gun back into action. This time it chattered away smoothly, cutting down the British soldiers in pursuit. Their action was protecting about 20 men from the 9th Company of 119 Regiment, 'apparently still very confused by the blast', Aicheler remembered. These men were not fighting, and recovering in the lee of a traverse until bullied into the fight by a Vizefeldwebel who shouted repeated commands. The mine blast had prevented the Germans from occupying their first trench. Aicheler was shooting down any British soldiers he saw attempting to get into it, and at 11 rounds per second the Maxim scythed six men in half. Four surviving British soldiers, overwhelmed at the horror, surrendered. With the immediate crisis over, Aicheler focused on methodically sweeping the crest of the Hawthorne Ridge as soon as any British soldiers appeared.

The men manning Unteroffizier Braungart's gun number 1 to the right had already been badly shaken up 48 hours before, when they were buried by the bombardment. Braungart now saw 'thick masses emerging from the British trenches' and quickly got his Maxim into action. 'The first wave had advanced so far,' he reported, 'that two officers, who were going ahead of the wave with drawn swords, had already arrived in front of our entanglement.' This wave, with its incongruous, almost Napoleonic leaders, was cut down even 'before the first belt was emptied'. Gun number 4, firing in defilade from the left, had also pinpointed a group led by men with swords. 'The enemy went for cover in shell craters and the trough' at the foot of the ridge, Braungart observed, and being 'crowded together' proved 'an easy mark'.

The German situation on the Hawthorne Ridge was in crisis, as men struggled to recover from the after-effects of the mine blast. Dazed men had perforated or ruptured ear drums and sought direction. Gun number 3 led by Unteroffizier Drobele had been much delayed gaining their position, because of accurately observed British 18-pounder fire. When they opened up, the third belt jammed and after being cleared the entire gun and crew were knocked off their feet by a succession of shells bursting directly in front of the gun, which 'gutted' an ammunition box lying nearby.[5]

Machine-gunners were regarded as an elite, and they had to be – the Spandau Maxim machine-gun was the linchpin of the German defence. It could fire 660 rounds a minute, which gave it an estimated value of 80 riflemen. In the deadly race for parapet supremacy it was faster to get a machine-gun into action than to position 80 men. It was stretchered forward by three men on an improvised metal 'sledge', one of whom carried a water container, while a fourth man carried ammunition. Unlike pre-registered artillery, firing from the rear, and directed by telephone or signal flares, machine-gunners could *see* what they were firing at, and quickly react. The irony was that it was King Edward VII who had persuaded his German relative to look at this weapon, developed in London in 1881 by Hiram Maxim. The Kaiser was impressed. In 1914 the British produced just under 400 Maxim guns, while German factories turned out their Spandau variant at 500 per month. Germany started the war with 5,500 Maxims, having channelled considerable money and creative tactical effort into its development.

'Who has had anything to do with machines?' the 17-year-old German soldier Paul Grünig was asked when he first joined up. 'That was the first time that I ever freely volunteered for anything,' he recalled. It was a sound move. 'I didn't go directly to the front, instead I was with a corporal behind the front, being trained on the machine-gun,' he explained – 'lucky again.' The British had seen the machine-gun as a force multiplier against less sophisticated opponents in colonial skirmishes to secure the Empire. The German Army appreciated its European potential, and in 1912 Hauptmann Friedrich von Merkatz had produced a practical training pamphlet, *New Methods of Machine Gunfire*. The groundwork had already been laid in a similar training aid written as far back as 1907. Experiments had been conducted long before the war on how best to deploy the weapon, after scientific evaluation of the ballistic performance of rounds in the air. The optimum deployment, it was found, was groups of machine-guns, shooting from the flanks or in defilade to create 'killing zones'. These were where the beaten cones of fire from several machine-guns intersected – geometric simplicity. Rather than targeting individuals, guns were located so that the enemy had to pass through a curtain of fire, like a 'death shield'. This was the lethal web that had been spun all the way along the Somme front, covering every conceivable approach. Designed to ensnare the unwary, defilade fire cloaked gun flash, invisible from the front. On the 4½-mile front sector, between St Pierre Divion and Ovillers, occupied by the German 52nd Reserve Brigade, there were 38 machine-guns. Each German regiment with three infantry battalions could count on 19 machine-guns firing in support, a force multiplier equivalent to an additional 1,520 riflemen, or an extra battalion and a half.[6]

Gun number 5, crewed by Unteroffizier Schwerdtle's men, was in action to the left of the Hawthorne crater even as the British infantry were going over the top. His gun layer Gefreiter Mack was mortally wounded in the head and his replacement Krausbeck was dead within 190 rounds, even as the dying Mack was being stretchered away. All the German machine-guns lining the Hawthorne Ridge were quickly in action, decimating British soldiers as they clambered out of their trenches. They also fired in defilade at the masses surging up towards the plateau to their left, shooting across St Pierre Divion and the other side of the Ancre valley. Some crews had been buried the night before, while gunner Baezner, manning gun number 9, had his skull torn open by a shell, but the Germans were ahead in the race to the parapet.

At 7.30 am, further south, just west of the Carnoy–Montauban road, two strange-looking tubular probes stealthily rose above the ground near the Mansell Copse, 60 yards from the German trenches. For those who had read science fiction, they resembled the Martian probe emerging from a crater that HG Wells had written about 18 years before in *The War of the Worlds*. This was just as devastating. The bizarre-looking weapons, which were only 14 inches wide, worked like a giant syringe. Compressed gas was forced into the 56-foot-long chamber containing fuel with a rush of air, blowing the liquid through the nozzle on the surface. As the fuel passed through the small fire initiator at the end, it burst into flame, and a curved shutter, like a finger pinching the end of a gardener's water hose, squirted the burning fluid. For ten interminable seconds a plume of red-orange flame was shot 300 feet in a fiery arc that splashed down on the German trenches.

Soldiers to left and right watched aghast at this curving plume of fire, playing over trenches from 87 to 94 yards away. Clouds of inky black smoke boiled into the air. Colonel

Charles Foulkes, directing the Special Brigade's flame-thrower or 'Squirt' operation, remembered the 'roar' as the infernal flame 'traversed slowly from side to side, while dense clouds of black smoke, flecked with flame, rose a hundred feet into the air'. Horrified onlookers had to cover their faces against the intense heat generated up to 200 yards away. Fire continued to burn for minutes after, where the molten arc touched the ground. All the victims saw was a huge fireball coming at them at breakneck speed, before their world was abruptly extinguished in searing heat.[7]

The Germans had accepted the flame-thrower into service in 1911 but had not used them until Ypres in 1915 and against the French at Verdun. The pragmatic and experienced German General Staff recognised early on that there was no defence against such a weapon, and tactical notes were issued to their troops offering practical tips. These were variants on getting out of the way and tackling the threat from the flanks. Flame was a terrifying weapon and troops were trained in fighting alongside flame-throwers. Soldiers were encouraged to believe the German weapon was far superior to the enemy's, from which they should tactically withdraw, but not too far. They had to re-occupy flamed trenches as soon as possible. 'Whoever is first at the parapet, remains the victor,' was the advice of one useful pamphlet. Calm down and aim one metre above the flame, German soldiers were instructed, and throw hand grenades. Remember, they were told, the trenches either side would hold, so strike from the flanks. Practice makes perfect, but as 19-year-old German soldier Fritz Siemens learned, initiation could be as terrifying as reality. As an assault pioneer he rehearsed a trench attack during training employing a live flame-thrower. 'All the infantry stood in a trench,' he explained, 'and we were behind the infantry line with our big flame-throwers.'

A siren howled and we set off the flame-throwers. Out came a scorching heat that went high over the trench. They could cover a ten, twelve metre wide area. Then the infantry should have got out, but nobody moved. They had all shit themselves. The officers saw it. Then there was trouble.[8]

Captain William Livens's 'Judgement' weapon, unleashed on the edge of no man's land south of Mametz, was a flame-thrower of unprecedented size and power. Although it was crewed by eight men, 250 were required to assemble it inside a sap. Three awesome ten second jets of flame were squirted at the German line, incinerating 40 German soldiers, before its 1,300 litres of fuel were spent. It is alleged that Livens, who developed the appliance with 'Z' Section at the Royal Engineer School at Chatham in England, hated Germans. His fiancée had gone down with the *Lusitania* the year before and he had vowed to kill as many Germans as he could, in revenge. The fuel had a viscous content that enabled it to burn a few minutes longer after it had slapped down. Surviving Germans fled down into their dugouts, where the searing heat sucked out the oxygen. 'No living things could possibly survive under this visitation,' claimed Colonel Charles Foulkes looking on. Those that did emerge found their trenches were full of British troops.

This German section of the line lost the race to the parapet. Private Robert Cude, a runner with the 7th East Kents, saw some of the shocked survivors later that morning. 'The burnt faces and hair of some of the Bosch bear excellent testimony to the effectiveness of our liquid fire,' he recalled, 'which was used considerably.'

There was no generally agreed policy for their use. Major-General Maxse with the 18th Eastern Division, to the right of the British line, was, unlike some inflexible division commanders, prepared to use any means to get his men closer to the German parapet with a better fighting chance. Robert Cude ironically alluded to the impact of flame. 'The Germans opposite us have come from Verdun for a rest, rather a good rest too I think!' But this dramatic impact covered yards not miles of front. GHQ had requested 22 Livens 'Flame Projectors', but only four were delivered in time and two of these were knocked out by German shell fire as they were being assembled. It was not enough.[9]

At 7.30 am 84 British infantry battalions clambered out of their trenches across a 16-to 18-mile front. The initial surge of 20,000 built up in waves minute by minute, until there were 66,000 troops attacking across no man's land within an hour. Some moved in rushes, the majority picked their way across in untidy waves. Whatever the tactics, devastating German shell fire soon turned the walking waves into crowds of soldiers, walking, running, advancing in rushes, all seeking to get to the opposite front line before the Germans. Distances varied from as little as 200 yards to nearly 2,000. From Gommecourt to Fricourt they attacked with the rising sun in their eyes. The early rays of a fine summer's day picked out light khaki as clear aiming points, against the sombre grey of no man's land. They presented an epic image never before seen in British history, her largest and finest army on the move en masse. Their appearance was greeted by a peculiar 'rushing' noise, like a distant train, as the level of small arms fire steadily rose. It was then punctuated by the cracking reports of artillery. Puffballs blossomed in the sky, propelling smoking trails of shrapnel downward, skeletal fingers pointing the way of death. The distinctive 'tat-tat-tat' of machine-gun fire mingled with the characteristic rapid cracking and thumping of their impacts, scything down whole sections of advancing infantry waves. Veteran accounts almost compete with each other in the selection of adjectives to describe these events and in particular the crescendo of noise that rose along the whole 18 miles of front. Leutnant Matthäus Gerster, defending with 119 Regiment north of the River Ancre, remembered 'shouts of command, cries for help, reports, dying shrieks' and 'cheers of joy' all mixed together to form a hideous din. In the German trenches he described 'heavy breathing, whimpering, begging, rifle shots, the rattle of machine-gun fire and the explosion of shells'. A wall of British infantry was approaching on a totally unexpected scale.

'The enemy wire was always deep, thick and securely staked,' British intelligence officer John Masefield recalled. It was generally erected to form 'a thick web about four feet high and from thirty to forty feet across'. The advance was breaking up and converging in places to seek gaps. Dismay soon registered because 'the enemy wire, not being galvanised, rusted to a black colour, and shows up black at a great distance'. Wire strands were 'thick as a sailor's marlin stuff', Masefield explained, with some 16 barbs to the foot. 'Trip-wire was as difficult to cross as the wire of the entanglements,' he recalled, and worse, because on approaching the German line it was hidden in the undergrowth. This low wire entanglement was secured with foot long spikes. 'The scheme was,' Masefield pointed out, 'that our men should catch their feet in the trip-wire, fall on the stakes, and be transfixed.'[10]

The minutes taken to cross no man's land were crucial. The clock ticked against survival in the open and moved remorselessly forward. Control was by shouted command and whistle, inaudible in the din. Ahead was a ravaged and confusing moonscape, where every ruined village and shattered wooded copse looked the same. The Germans had only to run metres, after scrambling up their crumbling dugout steps to reach the surface. The British had to traverse hundreds of yards across a landscape that had been churned up even more by multiple cratering into obstacles. The Germans were also well aware that in order to live, they had to be the first at the parapet.

The 'Kaiser's Oak'. Gommecourt

Gommecourt village to the far north of the line was a collection of red-brick buildings, standing in woodland, on gentle slopes. The attack against it was a deception, but not to the men from the 46th Division and 56th London Divisions, who aimed to pinch off this German salient, by enveloping it from north and south. The intention was to divert German reserves from being sent south, where Rawlinson's main Fourth Army blow would fall. The 2nd German Guard Division manned Gommecourt, acutely aware they stood on the most western point of German-occupied France, taken during the 'race to the sea' in October 1914. The so-called 'Kaiser's Oak', symbolising this, stood in the woods that screened the village from the British line. Gommecourt was a useful prize in its own right, because any high ground was at a premium. Its loss would compromise this sector of the German line. Lieutenant Edward Liveing knew the attack was to encircle what was almost generally considered the strongest German 'fortress' on the Western Front. General Haig had visited General Snow, the VII Corps commander, four days before, asking whether the Germans had swallowed the deception bait. 'They know we are coming all right,' he had responded.[11]

Edward Liveing, attacking from the south with the City of London Regiment, knew the Germans had watched their preparations. Since 4 am they had been under intermittent

German shelling. After the final British barrage three hours later it got worse, and they would have to advance through it. 'Crash' after 'crash' came raining down, he recalled, with 'the ping of shrapnel which flicked into the top of the trench'. He was with the third wave which went over 45 seconds after H-Hour. By this time 'the ladders had been smashed or used as stretchers long ago'. The race for the opposite parapet was on, but they moved off 'at the pre-arranged walk'. 'A continuous hissing noise all around' was an indication the German machine-gunners had found the range, even as he scrambled out of a part of the trench already battered down.[12]

Veterans often refer to the unreality of this moment, disorientated by noise, concussive impacts and gory, emotionally disturbing images. 'It was just a rain of bullets coming at you from right, left and centre,' explained Private Hal Kerridge with the London Scottish. 'It was terrifying really.' Private Henry Russell, with the 1/5th London Regiment, 'saw many of my colleagues drop down, but this somehow or other did not seem to worry me'. Daniel George, following on behind with the Queen's Westminster rifles, felt 'he was alone in a pelting storm of machine-gun bullets, shell fragments and clods of earth'. He seemed almost detached 'because the other men were like figures on a cinematograph screen – an old film that flickered violently'. The air around 'was full of black rain' and men he knew and recognised in an 'uninterested way' were falling down. 'Some of them stopped and fell down slowly,' he recalled. 'The fact that they had been killed did not penetrate his intelligence.' His friend Jewson disappeared in a fountain of earth; another, Bennison, was felled and scrambled up again. George's mind was anaesthetised by noise, smoke and dust. 'Men were dizzy and sick from the noise, which thrust between skull and brain', and which John Masefield claimed, 'beat out thought'. It produced alongside the terror 'an exultation, that one should hurry, and hurry and hurry, like the shrieking shells, into the pits of fire opening on the hills'. Daniel George felt the same imperative, 'unable to comprehend anything but the necessity for hurrying frantically on-on, on out of the storm'. The fact that his companions were being killed all around 'did not penetrate his intelligence'. Harry Russell continued to charge forward 'until I suddenly became aware that there were few of us in this first line of attack capable of going on'.

'One of the worse things of all, was heavy shell fire, you could hear the darn things coming,' remembered Hal Kerridge. 'But machine-gun bullets, no, all you hear is a continual clatter and you know all the time it's death flying around.'

Daniel George lowered his head as if in a snowstorm. 'His own turn might come at any moment,' he knew, as he bent even lower. 'If he was hit, let it not be in his face,' he willed, 'it would hurt to be shot in the face.' From all around came the shouts of 'Don't bunch! Don't bunch!' Suddenly the London Regiment soldiers burst into the German trenches. 'Dead Germans in silly attitudes, their faces the colour of dirty bone,' George recalled.

Dribbles of blood ... No stopping. On, on, stupidly, drunkenly – the five-mile race at school.

The sheer will-power and momentum of the attack enabled the forward waves to penetrate the forward German trenches. 'Barbed wire leaping and scratching like wild cats,' George remembered, jumping into a trench, with friends still collapsing around him, and he 'doubled up out of breath'. They were being shot at from behind, front and left, and were confronted with the immediate dilemma of every trench capture: the fire bays were the wrong way around. Fire steps were configured to face the direction of attack, the back was vertical and above head height. The only way to defend against a counter-attack was to scramble up the higher side. George was suddenly confronted by a grey uniformed figure filling his view. He snatched up a bomb and flung it full into the German's face. 'Christ that must have hurt,' he remembered thinking, but he had forgotten to pull the pin, and now the German was on his knees beseechingly looking up, his 'nose smashed and bloody'. George felt sorry for the man, who was helpless, had no weapon and was clearly badly wounded in the shoulder. He neither shot nor bayoneted him and left the fire bay, treading over heaped British and German bodies:

> *The air was thick with dust and things that sobbed and moaned and sang and whistled. Good God! He was piddling in his trousers.*[13]

Lieutenant Edward Liveing's first sight of no man's land, having gone over with the third wave, 'is almost indescribable'. The second line could just be distinguished ahead in the murky smoke, and as he watched, 'one man after another fell down in a seemingly natural manner, and the wave melted away'. The first wave were breaking into the German lines and wire, 'a mass of smoke the red of shrapnel bursting amid it'. His company commander was up ahead with them:

> *The Boche had met them on the parapet with bombs. The whole scene reminded me of battle pictures, at which in earlier years I had gazed with much amazement. Only this scene, though it did not seem more real, was infinitely more terrible. Everything stood still for a second, as a panorama painted with three colours – the white of the smoke, the red of the shrapnel and blood, the green of the grass.*

He was experiencing a form of out-of-body sensation, 'a dream, but I had all my wits about me'. They had been instructed to walk, but the urgency of their predicament and the impetuous élan of the soldiers resulted in a general forward rush. 'If I had felt nervous before, I did not feel so now,' Liveing recalled. They were completely caught up in the action. Liveing picked up to a fast walking pace and attempted to keep his platoon line together. Familiar faces dropped away, the carpet of bodies thickened and he became aware of 'a terrible groaning' rising up on all sides. Then Liveing arrived alone at the wire. His enduring memory was 'that a hare jumped up and rushed towards and past me through the dry yellow grass, its eyes bulging with fear'.[14]

The London Division on the south side of the salient stormed sections of German trench. Private Arthur Schuman, with the 1/5th London Regiment, remembers there was just one opening in the tangled wire, which still had to be negotiated with care. Men dropped all round the gap, which attracted fearsome fire. A man to his left collapsed clutching his stomach; another went down on his knees. 'The din was terrific, stifling any screams,' he recalled. 'Not many of us got through' what seemed an endless journey, after which 'a number of us fell into a German trench'. To his right was Sergeant Frank Hawkings, with the 9th Londons, and they were bracketed by a barrage on the edge of the German parapet, and then also inside the enemy trench. 'My next recollections are of a medley of Huns and Queen Victoria Rifles at close quarters with bomb and bayonet.' They reached the second and third trenches, but the increasing rate of German artillery fire was decimating subsequent waves, obliterated by a flurry of cracking detonations.

Lieutenant 'Rex' Cary's 9th London Rifles Battalion had attacked in close waves, barely two to four paces between platoons. Going at a stumbling walk and run, some had 400 yards of ground to cover. The German 2nd Company 55 Regiment soldiers facing them had not seen the attack coming through the black smoke. When they did, they were slowed down negotiating damaged dugout entrances. The effectiveness of the smoke-screen was dependent upon the southwesterly wind direction. Unlike north of the salient, only German angles on a north or northeast line were smothered by smoke. The broken ground and incoming fire had reduced regular waves of khaki to a mass of men who suddenly cascaded into the forward German line. It was a beach line of tumbled earth, splintered timber and scattered sandbags, but Cary's men were in. Within 30 minutes, vicious trench fighting had taken them as far forward as the third line. Behind them the German barrage shrieked down onto their departure trenches; 'not severe at first' according to the battalion after-action report, 'it increased in intensity later', blocking the passage of subsequent waves.[15]

'You know you've been hit, you don't know how badly, particularly if you can't see it,' explained Private Hal Kerridge, with the London Scottish:

> *If it's your arm or your leg you can see it, if it's in your back you can't see anything. So you just know you've been hit. The first thing you do instinctively – you're on the ground – and when you find your arms and legs work, a hundred and one things go through your mind, absolutely in a flash. You don't think about it at all, it's instinctive, it happens. You think, well, I've got to get out of this somehow, so you start trying to crawl back through the way you came.*

Leutnant Koch, in command of number 8 gun with Infantry Regiment 55, recalled two of his machine-gunners hauling their gun into a dugout and covering it with a ground sheet, when they were 'overrun in the first rush'. The intensity of the German counter-bombardment convinced them to hold on. They had every expectation of rolling back the British attack, at which point they would bring the gun back into action and shoot them up as they retired. The Germans kept their heads. Gun number 7 fought on even after its commander Gefreiter Niemayer was shot in the head and replaced by gunner Hennig. Koch coolly appraised their professional action. Hennig fought on, dispatching 'fleeing masses of British'. When their corpses were discovered, Koch appreciated the self-sacrifice of the gunners, who 'had fired with great calmness and excellent dispersion of fire' to the end. The German line was obstinately holding.[16]

'We had strict orders not to take prisoners, no matter if wounded,' admitted Private Arthur Hubbard with the London Scottish. He shot down 'three Germans that came out of their deep dugouts, bleeding badly, and put them out of their misery'. Once they were in the German trenches it was kill or be killed, and they had been butchered getting there. 'They cried for mercy, but I had my orders,' he confessed, and 'they had no feeling whatever for us poor chaps.' The incident was to plague Sergeant Hubbard for the rest of his life. In 1929 he committed suicide. The official inquest blamed shell shock, but Hubbard's family well remembered the extent to which these executions preyed on his mind in later years.[17]

Lieutenant Edward Liveing, alone at the wire, looked back and saw the fourth wave visibly disintegrating as it approached. They were leaderless, and he cupped his hands and shouted to come on up, but he was inaudible amid the noise of 'men shouting to one another and the wounded groaning above the explosions of shells and bombs and rattle of machine-guns'. A pile of wounded on the German parapet marked a gap in the German wire. This was the only visible opening, but then he felt 'I had been scalded in the left hip'. It was as if a shell 'had blown up in a waterlogged crump-hole and sprayed me with boiling water'. He went down with the 'curious warmth stealing down my left leg', which was gushing blood. 'So I lay, waiting with the thought that I might recover my strength.' The carnage and devastation around him convinced him to join the wounded, trying to crawl back. To stay 'was the greater possibility of death' and he instinctively appreciated there might be 'the possibility of life'. To reach it meant he had to get through cracking machine-gun bursts, thumping into the turf and 'throwing it four or five feet into the air'.

Private Henry Russell with the London Regiment realised 'that there were few of us in this first line of attack capable of going on'. The battlefield had started to empty. He was pinned down with Lieutenant Wallace, one of his officers, and they debated whether they should continue the suicidal attack. Wallace accepted it was his duty and raised himself 'and within seconds' Russell saw him 'dropped down riddled with bullets'. Russell, the private soldier, faced the same agonising conundrum. Duty and patriotism urged him up, inspired by Wallace's bravery. 'I felt I must do the same,' he decided:

> *Once the decision was made to stand up I had no further fear. I was not bothered at all even though I believed that I would be dead within seconds and would be rotting on the ground, food for the rats next day. I did not even feel appreciably the bullets going through and this was to me something extraordinary.*

Two bullets had immediately struck Russell.[18]

The 56th Division attack was withering away. Some reaped the dividend by storming the enemy's parapet first, but they were totally isolated from any further support by a storm of incoming German artillery fire. It was over, virtually within an hour, but resistance would splutter on for the entire day.

Across the salient to the north, the 46th Division arrived too late at the parapet and barely made an impression. Tommy Higgins, with the 1/5th North Staffs, was standing up to his knees in water at 7.30 am waiting behind the 6th North Staffs. Several waves had yet to go. It did not augur well when 'an awful shower of shells' descended on the 6th at H-Hour, so bad 'that hardly a man got to his lines … We then had orders to advance.'

It was not a breathless surge over the top, because they had to make their way to the forward parapet, impeded by bodies the whole way. 'The dead and dying lay in heaps at the bottom of the trench,' Higgins remembered, 'we had to climb over them as we went on.' Behind them, trenches were being blown flat by the deluge of incoming German shells. One of his officers, seeing him struggling and cursing with a roll of barbed wire he was carrying, offered to take his iron stakes. 'Mr Bowers from Caversham' was almost immediately killed, riddled with shrapnel from an air-burst, 'and I nearly fell on top of him'. They were fast losing men, Higgins recalled, 'falling in front and behind', and still they were struggling inside the departure trenches. 'We were walking on bodies all the way because with Fritz blowing the trenches about, they were so narrow.' Higgins jettisoned the cumbersome barbed wire and got to the forward trench, which had already been blown flat. 'At last we got to the jumping off place, with about half the number of men who started.' Colonel Burnett, the commanding officer, and Captain Fletcher commanding C Company waved them on, but were scythed down by shrapnel before they could even climb out of the trench.

'Fix bayonets,' they were commanded. Higgins was convinced that 'in about one hour over 600 men had been killed and wounded'. An officer yelled 'One, Two, Three' at the top of his voice and 'over we went with the best of luck … No one expected to come back again.' As Higgins scrambled up, 'the man next to me named Chorlton fell back with a bullet in his head'. A frantic rush began as they set off 'like mad men' to get across no man's land.

The line did not last for long. Men were falling like skittles, bowled over. Some would sink down in a heap, others would shout and throw their hands up and totter forward a pace or two then fall face downwards, never to rise again. The last one I saw was the officer Robinson firing his pistol like mad, then he went down.

As they approached the wire they found 'the 6th North was practically wiped out when we got to them', lying in clusters short of the parapet. Higgins spotted 'Fritz' tossing hand grenades over the top. 'There was a flash and I felt a fearful bang in my back' which flung him senseless into the wire. When he regained consciousness, he was choking with the fumes and dirt and hanging on the wire. He fearfully realised 'Fritz was riddling any poor devil he saw moving with bullets' and no more men were coming. 'If the Germans had made a counter-attack, they would have easily taken our lines then.' Higgins hung isolated on the wire. Any suggestion of movement brought bursts of machine-gun fire, which 'whizzed past just missing my head'. There was nothing he could do. 'I lay still after that with barbed wire sticking in me, I dare not move.' It was not even nine o'clock and the day seemed lost.[19]

The first German counter-attacks had started 15 minutes before.

VIII Corps Attack on Beaumont Hamel, 1 July 1916

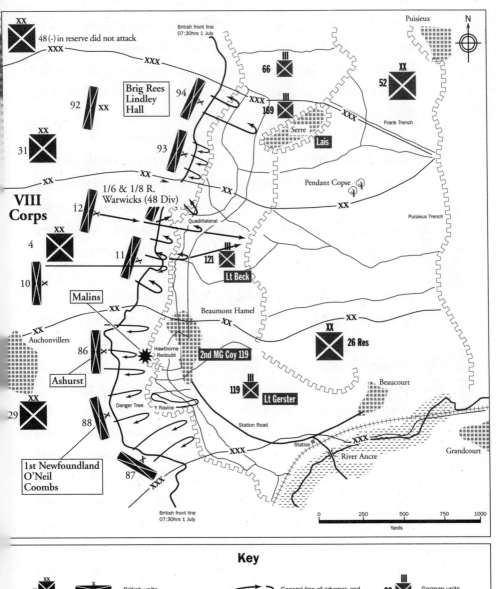

48 (-) in reserve did not attack

Brig Rees
Lindley
Hall

92

31

VIII
Corps

1/6 & 1/8 R.
Warwicks (48 Div)

Quadrilateral

4

11

10

Malins

Auchonvillers

86

Ashurst

29

88

1st Newfoundland
O'Neil
Coombs

87

British front line
07:30hrs 1 July

94

93

12

British front line
07:30hrs 1 July

66

169

Serre

Lais

Pendant Copse

121

Lt Beck

Beaumont Hamel

Hawthorne
Redoubt

2nd MG Coy 119

119

Lt Gerster

Danger Tree

Y Ravine

Station Road

Station

Puisieux

52

Frank Trench

Puisieux Trench

26 Res

Beaucourt

River Ancre

Grandcourt

| 0 | 250 | 500 | 750 | 1000 |

Yards

Key

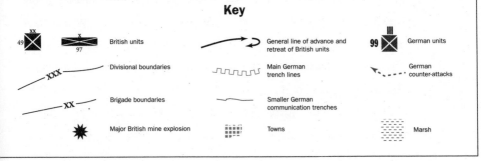

49	British units	97
	Divisional boundaries	
	Brigade boundaries	
	Major British mine explosion	

General line of advance and retreat of British units	
Main German trench lines	
Smaller German communication trenches	
Towns	

99	German units
	German counter-attacks
	Marsh

The 'Danger Tree'. North of the Ancre

Even before the Hawthorne mine exploded, Leutnant Beck with Infantry Regiment 121 was observing the 4th Division British line from his one-man concrete cupola behind the Heidenkopf Redoubt. As it grew light 'I could see that the British trenches were overflowing with masses of troops'. He had now to detect the decisive moment when British artillery fire switched to the rear. Meanwhile he watched as 'they stood there laughing and joking, some groups were having a quiet smoke, sitting on the parapet with all their equipment on'. When the earth was shaken violently by the mine exploding to his left, 'in no time flat the slope opposite resembled an ant heap'.[20]

Lieutenant-General Aylmer Hunter-Weston's 'folly' of launching his three divisions ten minutes after blowing the mine was a gift to the German defenders. The breadth of no man's land varied north to south from 200 to 500 yards. Many of the German defenders were at the parapet even before the assault got under way. The ruined fortress village of Beaumont Hamel was linked by trenches to the fortified village of Serre to the north and completely dominated the amphitheatre valley feature the three divisions had to cross. They were immediately confronted by tiers of well-observed fire from the German positions occupying the high spurs and ridge lines beyond. The 31st Division on the left, the northernmost point of the line, was the most exposed. It aimed to capture Serre and thereby anchor the VIII Corps flank, next to the less than two-mile gap between the main thrust and the feint. The 4th Division in the centre and 29th Division to the right were tasked with capturing the rising ground up to the German second line. Three German trench lines had to be crossed to achieve this, the second 500 yards beyond the front line and the third 1,000 yards. Hunter-Weston had nine brigades, which was 33,000 British troops, assaulting three German regiments numbering about 7,000 German defenders. The odds were over four to one in favour of the attackers.

The Germans were in an ugly mood. German unit after-action reports and veteran accounts consistently point out, with some relish, the extent to which the British had miscalculated the resilience and resolve of the German defence. German soldier Wilhelm Höpfner's company commander had lined his men up in a village square and shouted: 'We love together, we hate together, and we all have only one enemy!' At which point the whole company bellowed back '*England!*' in unison. 'We all hated the English,' Höpfner claimed, and especially so this July morning. The English, as Unteroffizier Otto Lais with the 2nd Machine Gun Company at Serre, with 169 Regiment remembered, had subjected them to a 'week long inner torment'. They poured into their battle positions. 'No longer,' he exultantly exclaimed, 'must we crouch in a flattened dugout like a mouse in a trap'. '*Raus, Raus, Sie Kommen!* Out. Out. They're coming!' was the cry. Their blood was up as they threw themselves into shell holes and craters, assembling their Maxims on the ubiquitous metal sledges and tugging and hauling boxes of ammunition across shell holes. The British were approaching in dense and crowded assault waves. 'The English infantry had their rifles hanging about their necks and over the shoulder,' Lais recalled, 'ready for the stroll to Bapaume, Cambrai, to the Rhine!' Red signal flares shot up to bring down registered defensive artillery fire.[21]

Musketier Karl Blenk with the 169th Regiment remembered that at first 'when the English started advancing we were very worried; they looked as though they must overrun our trenches'. After a while 'we were very surprised to see them walking, we had never seen that before'. The British came forward in their hundreds. It was an unreal scene. One of the officers in front was 'walking calmly, carrying a walking stick'. Blenk and his men started firing, loading and reloading. 'They went down in their hundreds, 'he recalled, 'you didn't have to aim, we just fired into them.' He was sure that 'if only they had run, they would have overwhelmed us'.[22]

Brigadier Hubert Rees had had his reservations about the 94th Brigade attack on Serre from the start, but had been encouraged when he observed the final bombardment raining down on the German trenches. He saw they 'changed shape and dissolved minute by minute'. For a brief moment 'I began to believe in the possibility of success', but when his troops moved forward the German counter-bombardment came crashing down, 'a perfect wall of explosive along the front trenches of my brigade and the 93rd'. His heart sank; 'it was the most frightful artillery display that I had seen'. Private Frank Raine, with the 18th Durham Light Infantry, was to his right. 'Up above,' he recalled, 'were these great big 5.9 inch shrapnel shells going off' and – 'Oh my God, the ground in front, it was just like heavy rain' – machine-gun bullets. He walked on, 'a terrific bang and a great cloud of black smoke above us' and something struck him on the hip, 'which I didn't take much notice of'. Fewer and fewer people were alongside him. 'I turned round and Broomhead had gone', but he grimly carried on until, to his dismay, 'I could not see a soul of any description – either in front of or behind me.' Raine suspected they must have 'tucked into shell holes', because nobody appeared to be in sight. 'I'm not going on there by myself!' he decided, and turned back.

'At the time the barrage became intense,' Brigadier Rees recalled, 'the last waves of the attack were crossing the trench I was in.' Rees was inspired by what he saw. 'I have never seen a finer display of individual and collective bravery than the advance of that brigade', torn to pieces before his eyes. Charlie Swales with the 14th Yorks and Lancs remembered the Military Police 'at the back of us' were 'seeing to it that you didn't miss your turn to go over'. Grim sights urged caution; he saw 'the top half of a man' as he jumped a trench – 'the other half was lying in the bottom'. It had to be one of the Sheffield City Battalion advancing ahead; 'they must have been wiped out by this time,' he deduced. Reginald Glenn in the 12th Yorks and Lancs, part of Rees's brigade, was also starting to feel very much alone, uneasily aware there were very few men ahead. 'The first line all lay down and I thought they'd had different orders', which puzzled him, because they had been told to keep walking, but they were dead, 'mown down like corn'. Nobody reached the German wire. 'We weren't getting any orders at all,' Glenn recalled, 'there was nobody to give any orders because the officers were shot down.' Rees peered through the murk watching as 'each line disappeared in the thick cloud of dust and smoke which rapidly blotted the whole area'. His brigade was withering away. 'I never saw a man waver from the exact line prescribed for him,' he described, and it was as depressing as it was inspiring, because 'I knew that no troops could hope to get through such a fire.'[23]

When a shell explodes, the area around the detonation becomes over-pressurised. The blast wave lasts a millisecond, wreaking havoc as it passes through the tissue and organs of the human body, leaving haemorrhaging and ruptures in its wake. The flash of the detonation singes and burns, while the blast wave propels metal shrapnel and debris through the air at anything from two to six miles a second. Bodies in the immediate vicinity of the blast are dismembered. The human body quivers like jelly when struck by the shock waves, which tear lung tissue and blood vessels. 'Shock lung', as it is called, produces the phenomenon of the apparently unmarked body. This is because the ability to breathe and move oxygen around the body is dislocated, the victim often drowns or suffocates in his own blood. The greater the distance from the explosion, the less the damage. Ear membranes are burst or damaged, sometimes causing a temporary blackout, headaches, nausea and permanent or temporary deafness. The body may only be bruised, because the soldier may only have been knocked off his feet or hit by flying objects. The only defence against shell fire is to take cover, below ground or behind a solid object, or get out of the way. Soldiers, in short, can only retreat or take cover if caught in an artillery barrage. This is the brutal reality of the 'perfect wall of explosive' Brigadier Rees described blocking the progress of his brigade before Serre. He heard garbled messages that some soldiers had actually penetrated the fortress village, but he could hardly believe it. Intense shell fire is a destructive, annihilating force, technologically indifferent to the impact upon bodies, minds and spirit.

Artillery barrages were decimating the Pals battalions along the whole breadth of the front. These were men who had waited in long queues at daybreak in the summer and autumn of 1914, fearful that recruiters might run out of enlistment forms. Men who had larked about and trained together, living cheek by jowl for nearly two years. Whole local communities were being swallowed up in these fearful artillery concentrations.

Private Frank Lindley went over the top with the Barnsley Pals. 'I was in the first wave on the extreme left,' he remembered. He scrambled up the fire step, 'almost touching' Second Lieutenant Hirst 'next to me', who went down. 'I think he got a machine-gun bullet in the head but I only took a fleeting glance … We had orders to keep moving' and 'not to bother with the wounded.' Once in no man's land, Lindley's trench-level perspective broadened when for the first time he realised the scale of the attack:

> *You could see both ways, you could see all the front laid out like a panorama; Gommecourt Wood and Serre all laid out and all these trenches of theirs riding up. We had to go up. They could shoot out of all their trenches but we were down below. It wasn't a steep rise, just undulating, but of course it seemed like a mountain that morning.*

'You could see the Germans at the top,' recalled Ossie Burgess, who was walking up with the same attack. 'As a matter of fact you could see how things were going, but things were going very badly at our place, very bad.' Clearly audible amid the crashing detonations of artillery fire was the insistent 'crack-crack-crack' of machine-gun fire, as Maxim rounds breaking the sound barrier sped through and over them at 2,953 feet per second.[24]

Unteroffizier Otto Lais's 2nd Company machine-gunners were over their initial exhilaration and had settled down to the professional business of systematically eliminating the maximum numbers of targets. Skilled gunners did not target individuals, they created a mesh of beaten fire zones in concert with other guns to right and left. One could engage almost the whole length of a wave in defilade, as distinct to only two or three men frontally, when muzzle flash might also compromise their location. The technique was to steadily 'tap' the gun on its mount along the extremity of one traverse to the other. The effect was to spray bullets like a garden hose, keeping a continual stream of bullets in the air, creating an insurmountable barrier. 'The machine-gunners, who lived a privileged life at quiet times and were envied for being able to avoid jobs such as carrying heavy mortar rounds forward, were earning their pay today,' remembered Otto Lais. The sound, 'the heavy, hard and regular Tack! Tack! of the machine guns', was distinctive amid the hurricane of noise. 'That one firing slower, this other with a faster rhythm,' Lais wrote; 'it was precision work of fine material and skill.' This steady and cool response provided reassurance and security for the accompanying infantry, shooting with rifles, and was devastating within the ranks of the advancing British infantry.[25]

'Most of our fellows were killed kneeling on the parapet,' recalled Private Arthur Pearson, with the 15th Royal Yorks. He ran up the incline of his flattened trench, 'under the hail of bullets which were whizzing over my head'. Just one of these rounds travelling at almost 3,000 feet per second caused massive damage on striking the human body. An entry wound may be small, but the subsonic energy following behind punches out large areas of tissue on exit, tearing and rupturing flesh. Bullets deflected by foliage or objects begin to tumble before entry or inside, if they hit bone, producing ugly wounds. Modern experiments using ballistic gel reveal just how much damage a tumbling bullet can cause, lacerating, churning and mincing flesh on its passage through the human body. The sharp crack of close overhead misses and the dull thump of visceral strikes on the human body were shocking and dismaying. Multiple hits with a machine-gun can dismember limbs or even cut a torso in half. Soldiers weathering such fire were given a brutal demonstration of the insignificance of flesh and will against impersonal high-velocity firepower. 'Our lads were going down in their waves, flop, flop, flop,' recalled Frank Lindley, exposed to this firepower and recognising the futility of what they were trying to do:

> *They were walking across. It was stupid, absolutely stupid. It was all right the Generals saying, 'You'll walk across,' even if we'd run across we'd still have been in the same fix because we couldn't have got through their wire.*

The Germans poured in the fire. 'Pass up the spare barrels!' shouted gun commanders. Otto Lais described the need to keep cool heads in a crisis:

> *Just keep calm, get the tangle sorted out and load! Speak loudly, slowly and clearly to yourself. 'Forward! – Down! – Back!'*

These were the immediate action drills, after sorting out a stoppage. Working parts forward, belt on, cock the mechanism, to get the working parts back.

> *The same again! Safety catch to the right! Fire! ... Tack! Tack! Tack! Tack!*

Constant automatic bursts of fire boiled the water coolant in the barrel sleeve, revealing positions with puffs of steam. One of Lais's guns boiled its water dry, there was no more and the British were fast coming up. One of the gunners rushed into a nearby crater and urinated into the water container, then 'a second pisses into it too – quick refill!' The gun was soon in action again. Many steam hoses were torn off or shot away and guns were becoming red hot. 'Skin hangs in ribbons from the fingers of the burned hands of gunners and gun commanders,' Lais noted. Unteroffizier Koch's machine-gun, shooting along the Mailly to Serre road, fired off 20,000 rounds that morning, 'cooking' the weapon.

Frank Lindley watched the remnants of the attack peter out on the German wire, which left soldiers 'hanging like rags'. It was an awful, gory finale to the failed assault:

> *Machine-gun bullets were knocking 'em round as if washing hung on the line. Legs and arms and everything were flying all over.*

Lindley's division left some 3,600 bodies and writhing wounded strewn about no man's land in front of Serre.[26]

Further south the 4th Division was attempting to scale the gentle slope of the Redan Ridge. The Heidenkopf Redoubt protruded so starkly from the German line that it was assumed to be booby-trapped, therefore better bypassed and attacked from the rear. Leutnant Beck, still observing for 121 Regiment from his one-man concrete cupola, thought the German artillery response too light for his liking. Even so, the enemy were 'so thickly massed that every shell found its mark'. Machine-gun fire exacted a fearsome toll, 'cutting down the enemy in waves, just like mowing machines'. He recalled that 'our somewhat primitive earth mortars' were proving lethal and that one strike flung bodies through the air in all directions, including 'a tall Scot' who 'came down on a steel post', left protruding when the barbed wire had been destroyed. The unfortunate victim 'was spitted straight under his lower jaw', in front of his cupola, which meant that for much of the remaining battle 'I was faced with the gruesome sight of a death's head staring at me'.

'We can see over the ridge now,' recalled Lieutenant William Colyer, when he crested the Redan Ridge with the 2nd Dublin Fusiliers. Colyer had been anxious going over the top, uncertain whether his men would be prepared to follow him in such fire. He put a lighted cigarette in his mouth, in order to look 'serene and cheerful'. The advance was an ordeal. 'I am wondering unpleasantly,' he later recalled, 'whether I shall be killed outright or whether I shall be wounded; and if the latter, which part of me will be hit.' His men followed but were steadily whittled away by casualties. The hot blast of a shell explosion convinced him 'this is a ghastly failure already'. Streaming with perspiration he laboured onward, resigned to death or injury. 'The anticipation of being hit has become so agonising that I can scarcely bear it … I almost wish to God I could be hit and have done with it.' With half his men seeming to disappear as soon as they enter the network of German trenches, the attack 'seems to be completely messed up'. The 4th Division only managed in places to carry any German front-line trenches. Nobody had ever explained what to do if it all went wrong. 'It's rather vague,' Colyer remembered. 'Where am I to go and what am I going to do when I get there?' The flagged rehearsals behind the lines had been boringly simple, but 'I certainly never anticipated the extraordinary situation I find myself in now.'

Colyer's dilemma became irrelevant when he was picked up and flung over by a violent shell blast. He was stripped of his senses and lapsed into a form of temporary shell shock. 'My whole nervous system seemed to be jangled up,' he remembered, 'and I ran like a hare down the trench.' He kept running until he hurtled into a British dugout. The officer and men within 'looked at me as if I had taken leave of my senses', which he had. He was confused and disorientated, but the officer seemed to understand his ramblings about a shell exploding nearby. He 'told me to come inside and rest awhile'. His demons would take longer to appease. The 4th Division was to suffer 5,752 casualties that day.[27]

At the Hawthorne Ridge, the front-line trenches were nearly 500 yards apart. 'Looking out from our front line at this point,' intelligence officer John Masefield recalled, 'our men saw the enemy wire almost as a skyline.' There was now a livid white scar, surrounded by snow-like chalk debris, in the side of the ridge. Two platoons of Z Company the 2nd Royal Fusiliers had run for the crater, with more soldiers manhandling four Stokes mortars and four Vickers machine-guns, a considerable load, following on behind. As the fire-fight broke out around the crater, bodies began to tumble into its smoking maw, hot from the explosion. 'Had this [rush] been timed for firing almost simultaneously,' one of the Fusilier officers later claimed, 'we should in the general confusion have been able to overrun the Redoubt with little or no opposition.' The first wave of the three companies that followed up met a storm of fire from the flanks and opposite crater lip.

The dazed Germans from the 9th Company Infantry Regiment 119 started to respond as best they could. The first British troops stormed the trenches of the 3rd Platoon left of the crater. Leutnant Breitmeyer and the company commander Oberleutnant Mühlbayer were feverishly trying to dig themselves out of the small hole that was all that was remained from four entrances. Before the sentry scrambling at the hole could enlarge it fully, he was bayoneted and fell back dead down the stairs. Vizefeldwebel Davidsohn, standing by him, shot the attacker in the face with a flare. Hand grenades and smoke bombs came tumbling through the hole amid shouted demands to surrender. The veteran survivors, who could hear the sounds of intense fighting raging outside, decided to fight on, taking their chances with the counter-attack that would surely soon come.

Unteroffizier Aicheler, with the 2nd Machine Gun Company, who had already beaten off the British intrusion into his trench, was ordered forward to the crater rim. He fired 500 rounds before experiencing yet another jam. Gunner Pfuhler was shot in the head as he tried to remedy the stoppage, but Aicheler and the crew fought on.[28]

The 500-yard British dash was completely in the open. Once they were on the forward slope of the ridge there was no dead ground, or cover from fire in front or to the flanks. Filming the desperate attack was cinematographer Geoffrey Malins, still perched on Jacob's Ladder opposite. Once the spoil from the massive explosion had landed, Malins panned his camera 'round to our own parapets'. He was in time to capture soldiers 'swarming over the top, and streaming along the skyline':

> What a picture it was! They went over as one man. I could see while I was exposing, that numbers were shot down before they reached the top of the parapet; others just the other side. They went across the ground in swarms, and marvel of marvels, still smoking cigarettes.

Many of the scenes that Malins later wrote about are clearly visible in the subsequently released documentary footage in *The Battle of the Somme*, released in 1916. Now on the UNESCO Memory of the World Register, it is a remarkably vivid piece of captured history. Malins appears to have filmed the two Z Company platoons rushing the crater prior to the main attack. Swarms of 30 or so men can be seen on the ridge skyline, heading directly for the crater. In the middle ground a group of six soldiers run from right to left before two of them fall, the rest changing direction, towards the camera. A modern survey retracing their footsteps, plotted from Malins's camera angle, shows the men were initially in dead ground, immune from small arms fire to their front. As they kept left to take advantage of this shelter, they are struck down by defilade fire, from the north side of the valley. Malins poignantly filmed one of the first moments of death to be recorded in a combat newsreel in history. He may well have run out of film at this point. A practised cameraman could remove and replace a spool in about a minute. When the camera begins running again, the edited sequence jumps to a larger body of men moving towards the German lines. These images, likely now of the main attack, appear authentic. The camera picks up officers and men observing from sandbagged positions in the foreground, as it pans across. There may be as many as a company's worth of men, the first wave eerily visible in the grainy footage of the skyline. Second and possibly third company waves can also be seen moving across the middle ground below the silhouette of the ridge.

Malins writes about the 'moment my spool ran out' during the attack. It may have been a long reel change, because he was anxious to ensure that 'the first priceless spool' of the awesome Hawthorne mine explosion was secure. What Malins cannot do is recreate the smells and din of battle. The film is a looking-glass view. 'The noise was terrific,' he claimed. Audiences today view this footage in a comfortable vacuum. German shells were bursting around him, and 'dirt was being flung in my face, cutting it like whipcord', he recalled. The lens had to be kept clean. He took four spools but had little idea what was happening except that 'fearful fighting was taking place in the German trenches' as the Fusiliers battled for the crater. He asked an officer for information and got the response 'Who knows?' Nobody had any idea. 'Everything over there is so mixed up', but they could see the cost. 'Look at our poor lads,' someone pointed out. 'I could see them,' Malins recalled, 'strewn all over the ground, swept down by the accursed machine-gun fire.'

When he got to his fourth reel, Malins was interrupted again. 'There was a grinding crash of a bursting shell,' he remembered, and when 'something struck my tripod, the whole thing, camera and all, was flung against me.' Shrapnel had sliced off six inches of stand from one side of the tripod. The camera appeared untouched.[29]

Most of the anxious men Malins had filmed in the sunken road an hour before were dead. 'In a few minutes the whole atmosphere of the place had taken on a fearful change,' remembered Lancashire Fusilier George Ashurst. Within minutes of 7.30 am the third and fourth waves of B and D Companies were virtually wiped out a few yards beyond the sunken road they had left. A Company lost all three platoon commanders and C Company its sergeant-major and company commander. Ashurst did not pause to help any wounded comrades because 'to stop at such a time was to be accused of cowardice'. Ashurst was behind the main group with the commanding officer's bombers and bodyguard. They had to pick their way through the grisly human debris left behind by the first echelon of the attack:

Men uttered terrible curses even as they lay dying from terrible wounds, and others sat at the bottom of the trench shaking and shouting, not wounded but unable to bear the noise, the smell and the horrible sights.

There had been no need to climb out of the front-line trench, as both it and the wire were battered flat. A mad dash was made to catch up with the lead elements as 'bullets made a horrible hissing noise all round me'. He ran over no man's land through the powder smoke towards the sunken lane, pathetically shielding his face with his tin hat. 'I could plainly hear the sickly thud as a bullet struck some comrade close by me,' and his whole stature was doubled over in cringing anticipation of a similar strike.

At 8.15 am he had to stop assisting one of his own wounded men, who had faintly appealed for a drink. 'I heard the colonel calling out for all fit men to line the bank of the road, waving his revolver menacingly as he did so.' They were going to do it again. The Stokes mortars opened fire as 75 men were collected in the sunken road under Lieutenant Caseby. The colonel ordered one of the signallers to get up on the bank and to wave for reinforcements. 'Without a moment's hesitation the signaller obeyed, but as he raised his flags to send the first letter the brave fellow dropped back in the road, riddled with bullets.' Ashurst would never forget that image for the rest of his life.

'Now, men,' the colonel ordered, 'as soon as I give the word over you go again' – it was a suicide mission. 'This time, don't stop,' he emphasised, 'until you reach that front line.' Whereupon he jumped out of the road, calling 'Come on!' at the top of his voice. The group of 75 was caught in the flank by machine-gun fire, ripping into them from defilade, as they crossed the crest line a few yards beyond the road. A repeat of what had happened before. Only two officers and ten men reached the German wire.[30]

'Come on, Tommy!' the exuberant Germans shouted. Some were even standing on the parapet to get a better shot at the British below. 'They were full of anger,' recalled Gottlob Mauss, with the 3rd Company Regiment 119. He saw his friend Vizefeldwebel Karl Losch shot off the parapet. Losch picked himself up and was shot down again, and then a third time. 'What happened was simply dreadful,' Mauss later wrote to Losch's family. The common concern for families back home was that their loved ones should be properly buried, anything rather than an anonymous 'missing in action'.

Mauss offered little comfort. 'Other ranks were all placed in one grave, where 60 to 70 men lie next to each other,' he wrote a month later. 'Herr Losch, your dear son is also there.' It was hardly reassuring to learn that 'even the company does not yet know the list of the men buried there accurately'.[31]

'Once more we sprang into that fusillade of bullets,' George Ashurst recalled. Inside minutes he felt he was the only survivor and took cover in a shell hole. The scene behind was one of total devastation. 'Hundreds of dead lay about and wounded men were trying to crawl back to safety.' The wounded appeared to try and rise, 'then fall in a heap and lie very still', he noticed. 'Surely Fritz wasn't killing these unfortunate men?' Ashurst indignantly thought. Shells were still ploughing up the ground 'blowing dead men into the air and putting others out of their agony'. He could not be certain if the others had reached the wire, or whether the figures ahead were English or German. To raise his head and look was to invite certain death. 'I asked God to help me,' he recalled.[32]

The 29th Division assault was going very badly; 86th Brigade had fought itself to virtual extinction within 30 minutes in front of the Hawthorne Redoubt, and the 87th to its right had fared equally badly. At 7.55 am the 86 support battalions across the front were unable to get through the forward trenches, clogged with dead and wounded. One soldier in the 1st Border Regiment, pinned down and showered by heavy clods of earth from shell bursts, heard a plaintive cry from a soldier nearby: 'Oh dear, we are done!' 'Can you pray?' he asked him, but 'the poor chap said he couldn't'. 'Well I will, and you just lie still.' There were only four of 22 officers left, and 575 of the battalion's 878 men were down.

If ever a man prayed hard, I did. I implored the Blessed Virgin Mary to save us, I prayed until I imagined I could see her.[33]

General de Lisle, the division commander, thought he had the answer to many a prayer when, acting on erroneous information, he decided to commit the two leading battalions of his reserve 88th Brigade. He wanted to maintain momentum. Reporting officers who were unable to see tended to interpret no news as good news. At 8.45 am the Newfoundland Battalion waiting in the St John's Road support trench had their objective modified. They were to advance alongside the 1st Essex Regiment to their right and 'occupy the enemy's first trench' in the area of the 'Y' Ravine and Station Road. This was perhaps the most impregnable sector of their sector front. The 1st Essex could not achieve the revised H-Hour, held up by communication trenches completely battered down and filled with dead and writhing wounded. One and a half hours into the attack, the urge felt by the 'Fighting Newfoundlanders' to prove themselves was to prove their undoing. They clambered out of the second line trench, avoiding the clogged communication trenches, and pressed forward in isolation over open ground to their front line, anxious to achieve the revised H-Hour. They moved two companies up, A and B leading across undulating ground, which offered some dead ground cover to the left. C Company laboured on behind the leading waves, carrying heavy equipment, with D Company to its right. The assault was very vulnerable to defilade fire from their right. It was a poor decision to proceed.

German machine-gunners on the Bercourt Ridge were quick to pick up the movement on the empty battlefield. Unteroffizier Seibold, with gun number 4 from the 2nd Machine Gun Company Regiment 119, spotted the sudden surge of British troops. He clicked his sight aperture to 500 and the belts began to clatter through. 'Observation revealed very good results,' he later reported. Schwerdtle's gun number 5 below him 'fires at the again attacking enemy' and 'after about 750 shots, our artillery begins', all within about a minute. Unteroffizier Zirris's gun number 6 joined in the intersecting fire after gunner Schindler 'noticed the enemy emerging from the trench and gave alarm'. Seibold's gun had already fired off 3,000 rounds earlier that morning in sustained bursts, and 'during the last shots, the automatic feeder had no longer functioned properly, so that the cartridges had sometimes to be fed manually'. The overheated gun was 'cooking off', in machine-gunner parlance, and the hot barrel had perceptibly bent. The crew banged it straight with a lead hammer, and amazingly the gun managed 'another 500 shots of sustained fire on individual groups that appeared'. The Newfoundland attack was steadily withering away beneath this sustained interlocking network of machine-gun fire.

Fifteen-year-old Leo O'Neil, who had lied about his age on joining, remembered the Canadians' plight: 'Bullets had come down like rain over them.' The fire was 'unrelenting, there was nowhere to escape it'. Artillery fire completely bracketed C and D Companies coming up in depth. Witnesses recalled that 'where two men had been advancing side by side, suddenly there was only one – and a few paces further on he too would pitch forward onto his face.' Subalterns found there were no more men to lead. 'Everyone there that day died,' O'Neil remembered. 'Boys from home, boys he got to know on the way over his own age, everyone died.' O'Neil thought he was dying too as he lost consciousness. His left leg was severed, part of his left hand shot away and his back 'opened up' by shrapnel.

Very few got beyond the skeletal remains of the so-called 'Danger Tree', about 50 yards beyond the British front-line trench. Its petrified remains have been preserved within a concrete plinth in the present-day Newfoundland Park, funded by the women of Newfoundland, preserving the ground where their men died. The lie of the land and the potential dead ground cover offered by the downward slope meant that many Newfoundlanders gravitated towards the illusory security of the Danger Tree. Most of the dead barely covered a hundred yards. 'The only visible sign that the men knew they were under this terrific fire,' wrote an observer, 'was that they all instinctively tucked their chins into an advanced shoulder as they had so often done when fighting their way home against a blizzard in some little outpost in far off Newfoundland.' Linus Coombs recalled, 'We got cut up pretty bad and I guess I was one of the lucky ones to have survived.' His right tibia was smashed and he was to lose a leg. 'Of about 750 that charged that morning, 68 answered the roll-call that evening,' he remembered; his companion James Howard was never found. When the leading man of a couple of soldiers carrying a 10-foot length of Trench bridge was hit, both went down. 'Without hesitation,' an eyewitness recalled, the survivor, 'gets up, hoists the bridge on his head and plods grimly forward until machine-gun bullets cut him down.'[34]

Unteroffizier Seibold, controlling gun number 4 on the Bercourt Ridge, after straightening the barrel, realised the attack was petering out, and began to husband fire. They fired off '500 rounds of precision shots against single men who were trying to retreat to their trenches'. Schwerdtle on gun number 5 had come to the same conclusion, 'there were only single enemy soldiers', so he left them to the infantry. Guns had now to be cleaned and greased and the coolant topped up. More attacks might yet come. The local German infantry commander told him not to engage single soldiers any longer, his infantry were almost out of ammunition. They were to remain 'ready for action in order to aim at worthwhile targets'. The time was 9.30 am.

General de Lisle was chastened by this heroic failure. He spoke later of the 'magnificent display of trained and disciplined valour' to the Prime Minister of Newfoundland. The Newfoundlanders had failed 'because dead men can advance no further'. Only 110 of 780 men remained unscathed, an alarming 70 per cent having fallen. De Lisle's 'Immortal' 29th Division discovered its earthly mortality that morning; 5,240 dead and wounded were strewn across its 2,000-yard front.

By 9.30 am virtually every British attack by the two corps north of the River Ancre had come to naught.

X Corps Attack on Thiepval, 1 July 1916

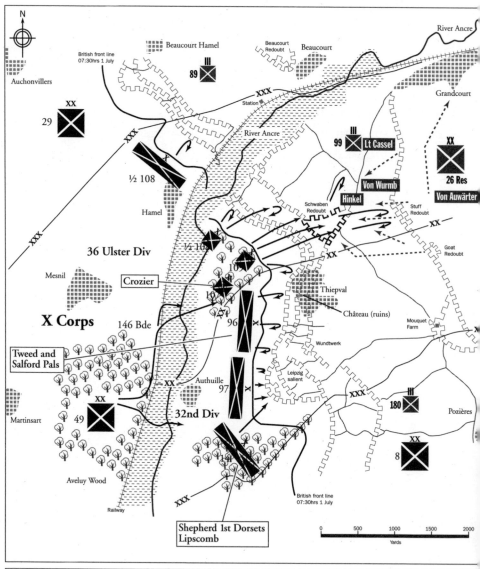

N

River Ancre

Auchonvillers

Beaucourt Hamel

Beaucourt Redoubt

Beaucourt

Grandcourt

British front line 07:30hrs 1 July

89 III

XXX

Station

29 XX

River Ancre

99 III **Lt Cassel**

26 Res XX

½ 108 X

Von Wurmb

Von Auwärter

Hamel

Hinkel

Schwaben Redoubt

Stuff Redoubt

36 Ulster Div

½ 10? XXX

10?

Goat Redoubt

Mesnil

Crozier

10?

10?

Thiepval

X Corps

96

Château (ruins)

Mouquet Farm

146 Bde

Wundtwerk

Tweed and Salford Pals

Leipzig salient

49 XX

Authuille

97

XX

32nd Div

180 III

Pozières

Martinsart

XXX

8 XX

10?

Aveluy Wood

British front line 07:30hrs 1 July

Railway

XXX

Shepherd 1st Dorsets Lipscomb

| 0 | 500 | 1000 | 1500 | 2000 |
Yards

Key

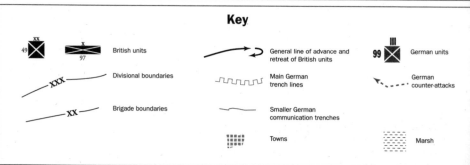

49 XX **97** X British units

99 III German units

XXX Divisional boundaries

General line of advance and retreat of British units

XX Brigade boundaries

Main German trench lines

German counter-attacks

Smaller German communication trenches

Towns

Marsh

CHAPTER 6

*Schwerpunkt**: Thiepval Plateau ——•

7.40 to 11 am

---

* Main point of defence effort

7.40 to 10 am

The 'Devil's Dwelling Place'. The Schwaben Redoubt

An untidy slurry of khaki-clad Ulstermen shouting 'No surrender, boys!' tipped into the front-line trench of the 9th and 10th Companies of 99 Regiment. The Germans were still emerging from their dugouts. Hugh Stewart, a Lewis gunner with the South Antrim Volunteers, had his chest respirator ripped apart by bullets as he hurtled through the shattered German wire. The Irish had got to the parapet first. Stewart snagged his boot on one of the thumb-long barbs, and in his panic to release it he tore off a chunk of boot, which left his big toe sticking out for the remainder of the battle. Sir Oliver Nugent's 36th Division had assaulted two brigades forward, two battalions attacking north of the Ancre, while the main thrust with ten battalions was heading for the 'Devil's Dwelling Place', the Schwaben Redoubt – the German *Schwerpunkt*, or main point of defence effort. Some 10,500 men were attacking 2,000 defenders. Even as the first German trench was stormed, heavy enemy machine-gun fire was opening up from Beaumont Hamel to the left and from Thiepval village to the right. Private Albert Bruce below on the sunken road shrank back at the sight of scores of figures tumbling over all around. So many bodies were flopping down so frequently up ahead that he lay down, as still as a corpse. Ahead lay oblivion. On his left one County Down volunteer saw his best friend caught by the British wire as he clambered out of his trench. As he struggled to free his clothing, his body shook convulsively as it was riddled by a burst of machine-gun fire.[1]

The Irishmen hurried; they had to be in the German third line trenches by 7.48 am to benefit from the lift in British artillery support. Dugouts in-between had to be swiftly bombed and cleared, and any surviving Germans heading for the parapet overcome in fierce hand-to-hand fighting. Private RH Stewart fought alongside 'as hard faced a crooked Sergeant as ever walked on two feet', already wounded when his young officer had been bowled over by a shell. Likely one of their own, because the rush of momentum was paying scant regard to the intricacies of six phases of artillery lifts.

With the first bomb he threw the door off a deep dugout, and the next two he flung inside. He must have killed every German in it. We left him sitting just below the parapet with a grenade in each hand ready for the next German that came along.

They did not stay long, but pushed on through the second and into the third German line. There was not enough time to thoroughly mop up the dugouts, which were left for subsequent waves. Germans began to snipe at the Ulstermen from behind. 'It was here,' in the third line, 'that the real fighting started,' remembered Stewart. 'I had never killed a man with a bayonet before and it sent cold shivers up and down my spine many's a night afterwards, just thinking about it.' It took about a quarter of an hour of exhausting fierce bayonet and grenade fighting 'to clear a hundred yards or so of trench'. By 8 am they were at the south face of the Schwaben Redoubt, just 30 minutes into the assault. The leading waves were bleeding manpower from German fire from forward, above, left and right.[2]

The 9th and 10th German Reserve Infantry Companies were overwhelmed by this demonic tribal onslaught before they could make a stand. No man's land was narrow in their sector, and the first Ulster wave had crawled to within 40–50 yards before rushing in. The boiling attack came in with such aggression that two machine-guns could only manage a few bursts before they were overrun. The Russian machine-gun higher up, in the Schwaben Redoubt, could not support because a direct artillery strike buried the gun with three quarters of the crew. The Fassbender platoon inside the redoubt found itself fighting an unexpected ground assault against an enemy who had already unexpectedly penetrated two trench lines below, as they were orientating themselves, having just emerged from their dugouts. Escaped German prisoners from Bavarian Regiment 8 came running through the communication trenches to escape the onslaught. They had no weapons and had lost watches, money and rings already looted by the Irish. A number were given weapons from the dead and wounded. The situation was very confused.

The Young Citizens 14th Royal Irish Rifles, following ten minutes behind the leading Inniskilling Battalion with 109 Brigade, had a fearful view of the awful punishment being meted out ahead of them. They were immediately ensnared in the web of intersecting machine-gun fire coming from Beaumont Hamel to their left and Thiepval to their right. The close territorial bonding of the former UVF meant they were viewing kith and kin, friends and neighbours dying before them. Private John Kennedy Hope, struggling with a 'donkey load' of barbed wire wrapped around a spade, saw one 9th Inniskilling man roll off the parapet to drop at his feet. It left him with an awful haunting memory:

His brain is oozing out of the side of his head and he is calling for his pal. An occasional cry of 'Billy Gray, Billy Gray, will you not come to me?'

Billy Gray could not. Hope recognised Gray as an officer's batman who was bleeding heavily with a fractured thigh nearby, who 'won't let anyone touch him'. 'They die together,' was Hope's poignant thought.

German artillery was regularly straddling Thiepval Wood, the assembly area and jumping-off point for the Irish. Burning trees added to the nightmarish panorama that troops following up could momentarily glimpse ahead. Many of the 11th Inniskillings lowered themselves in their trenches and intoned the Lord's Prayer, before a succession of whistle blasts sent them over the top. Beyond the smoke spewing up from the crackling and blazing trees was sunshine and a clear blue sky, 'as fair a morning as ever graced God's earth' said one soldier. 'The first wave went over the parapet in the regulated army fashion,' recalled RH Stewart, 'but the ones who went over late were more canny and did not jump over but sort of rolled over on their sides like.' Those caught by bursts of machine-gun fire fell back in, but the momentum was irresistible. 'The men were whistling Orange songs,' Stewart realised, 'and now and again you'd get a few words from "Dolly's Brae" or "The Sash".' Corpses were already piled high on the sunken road ahead.[3]

Fighting inside the Schwaben Redoubt and around the crucifix below it was savage. Wire entanglements had been shredded by artillery and the trenches were badly smashed up. Many of the garrison were trapped below in their dugouts. Leutnant Fassbender's platoon was trying to fight off elements from six battalions, who forced their way in from the front, left and rear. Leutnant Kottmeier later described how 'in the confusion of trenches, we set up a position' and that the typical experience was of fighting up and down communication trenches 'from the front up to us':

> *I watched the hand grenade fights in the saps. You have to picture it; there someone surfaces from a trench, a little further another. It's not possible to make out a clear line. The battle rages to and fro.*[4]

'The break-in point had been smartly chosen,' Hauptmann von Wurmb with Bavarian Regiment 8 later acknowledged. Much of the approach on the Ancre valley side of the slope was in dead ground to the deadly machine-gun fire from Thiepval, while the cam of the slope created blind spots from the German artillery observers on the plateau. Many of the men that Leutnant Stahlhofer had visited the previous midnight were dead. Vizefeldwebel Franz Wildman was torn apart by a hand grenade while fighting 'eye to eye' against the Ulstermen penetrating the north flank of the redoubt. Von Wurmb thought of Wildman's poor mother, who had apparently paid for his education. Weinmann and his dog Fipps disappeared without trace. Schorer's 4th Bavarian Company was completely overwhelmed alongside 99 Regiment's 11th Company in the bitter fighting.[5]

When Stewart broke into the redoubt, 'I had a bayonet in one hand and a revolver in the other'. His sergeant, who 'could clout a bomb further than any other man I knew', released them into a cross-trench at 20-second intervals. Being a farrier before the war, Stewart had developed strong wrists shoeing horses, so 'it was not a great hardship for me to fire one of them big heavy revolvers ... They had a kick like a mule, but if you hit a man with a bullet from one of them, he gave no more trouble.' Otherwise it was the bayonet up close. 'Give them it hot for the Shankill Road,' shouted an Inniskilling man, recruited from a company of street scrappers, who had come from the notorious Protestant Belfast district. Clearing the Schwaben Redoubt was 'a case of playing leapfrog with death', claimed one man; and was fought like 'a Belfast riot on the top of Mount Vesuvius', said another, using familiar local Ulster terminology. Gradual attrition was now taking a fearsome toll. 'We had been so eager that we had pressed too far forward,' explained a soldier, 'well in advance of our supporting troops.' Over-exposed, they were 'thus laying ourselves open to flank attacks'. By 8.30 am the reserve 107th Brigade was moving forward.[6]

Having achieved this inspiring break-in – up to the fourth line – the 36th Ulster Division was way ahead of its flanking formations and being severely lashed by fire from both flanks. It represented a narrow wedge, driven deeply into the German line. Suspecting they might be over-exposed, 36th Division asked X Corps at 8.32 am whether its 107th Brigade should be committed against the fifth line as planned? The corps response was to proceed, because they were aware new assaults were intended either side of the division, to protect its rapier-like insertion. Then confusingly, 45 minutes later, they were ordered to hold the reserve until the situation on the Ulster's flanks had improved. But it was already too late, 107 Brigade had begun its advance while commanders dithered. They were aware that there was fierce fighting at the fourth line.

On the northern shoulder of the break-in point, next to the River Ancre, the 1st Company of Bavarian Regiment 8 was holding, as also the village of St Pierre Divion. The two-battalion-strong Ulster attack north of the river had dissolved in a hail of fire. 'The bullets literally came like water from an immense hose with a perforated tap' was how one survivor described it. The 9th Fusiliers were whittled away from 15 officers and 600 men to less than a hundred, losing 532 men that day. 'You could see the bullets in the air and it looked like a fine shower of hail,' recalled another soldier; 'you know, the way hail looks as it's thinning out and the sun behind it.'

German machine-gunners on the Bercourt Ridge raked them from the left. Gunner Mainz next to the Station Road set his sights at 1500 and 'was able to effectively open fire on the enemy storming strongly against Regiment 99'. They also silenced a British machine-gun that had been trying to set up at the Ulster's break-in point. Gefreiter Fichner's gun joined in further along Station Road, reporting 'particularly effective fire'.[7]

Wilhelm Lange with Regiment 99 became so excited at the effect defensive fire was having that 'I scrambled up the back of the trench, took up my position with my rifle on a small rise and opened fire into the crowd of English soldiers coming across no-man's land.' He could see the Ulstermen had 'broke through on our left', but they were holding. He blazed away firing into 'so many of them, they were like trees in a wood'. Officers and NCOs tried to control their reckless soldiers, who were savouring the moment of revenge, after seven days of suffering. 'Come down!' an officer shouted at him, but Lange unable to contain his enthusiasm replied, 'But they're not shooting.' 'You fool,' the officer bellowed above the din, 'can't you hear the bullets whistling?'

Unteroffizier Friedrich Hinkel, with the 9th Company 99 Regiment, was on the other, south side of the Ulster break-in point. Feldwebel Günther, on the edge to Hinkel's right, was called upon to assist. 'Help! Throw them back with hand grenades.' It was a critical situation. Masses of Ulstermen were pushing through the gap where they had overrun the 9th and 10th Companies. 'The 7th Company was surrounded,' Hinkel appreciated; he could see British soldiers moving beyond their right rear. Remnants from the overrun companies and Bavarian soldiers came running down through the trenches, 'very downcast and giving all up for lost'. This had an intimidating effect on his own men, who began to doubt the outcome. 'Thank God! The 5th is at work in the attack with rifle and hand grenades, some of them in shirtsleeves', as they had been alerted at the very last moment. Battered-down communication trenches had delayed their arrival at their battle positions, but they were holding on the left. To his right, officer cadet Gelzenleichter was rallying his platoon, fighting wildly among his men – who, inspired, held their ground. He was cut down and killed.

'The situation of the English' directly ahead 'in no man's land was as if they were caught in a finely meshed net,' Hinkel observed. They were being mown down amid interlocking machine-gun arcs. 'The beginning of the tightly grouped, slow walking wall coming towards us was finished,' Hinkel saw, 'and soon came to a standstill.' Private Jim Maultsaid, charging forward with the Young Citizen Volunteers, remembered 'a wall of flame', hissing, burning metal, exploding shells and the cries and screams of men he knew so well. The horror of screams of pain from intimate companions was to haunt him for the rest of his life. They followed the tribal YCV pennant, with its distinctive Red Hand of Ulster and shamrock, tied to the barrel of someone's rifle up ahead, desperately pressing on. Friedrich Hinkel summoned his best shot, the 'young farmer' lad with the stutter, and told him 'to bring down the officer in front of the advancing line carrying a pennant on a stick'. Soon all the 7th Company marksmen focused in on this individual until he went down. 'Without their leader to rely upon, they became a mass,' Hinkel observed and 'came to a standstill'. Both shoulders around the Ulster break-in held. Such was the intensity of fire levelled at the gap that follow-on troops could only trickle manpower forward as though through a leaking sieve.[8]

Lieutenant-Colonel Frank Crozier with the 9th Royal Rifles was nervously waiting with the reserve 107th Brigade for the off, in 'that half hour [which] is the worst on record for thoughts and forebodings'. His battalion, sheltering in the lee of the steep Speyside, began singing tunelessly. They had escaped the worst of the punishing incoming German artillery fire, but knew what soon to expect. Off to their right it looked as though the 96th Brigade from the British 32nd Division was being taken apart. 'I see rows upon rows of British soldiers lying dead, dying or wounded in no man's land,' Crozier recalled. He watched the occasional officer urging on his men and here and there 'hands thrown up and then a body flops to the ground'. Obviously Thiepval village had not fallen and they had an open flank. 'I lose sight of the 10th Rifles [the battalion ahead] and the human corn stalks falling before the reaper.' As they approached the end of Thiepval Wood the 'plomb, plomb' of steady German shelling became increasingly apparent. 'It is goodbye, I think, as there is no way round.' From a wag behind came a shout of 'This way to eternity!' A few 'Blighty wounds' were inflicted on the edge of the shelling. 'Lucky bastard,' one of his pals says. 'You're well out of it, Jimmy. Good luck to you, give 'em our love, see you later.' The banter was a release.

At this point the shelling at the edge of the wood abruptly ceased. 'The next shell and I should have been absolutely synchronised,' Crozier remembered, but there was a lull. 'A miracle has happened,' he realised at the precise moment his men began to emerge from the wood. 'Now's the chance,' he appreciated and hurried his men across the sunken road before deploying them company by company. 'Men are falling here and there' but there was no artillery fire at the wood's edge. This respite lasted about five minutes, an indication that the Germans were bringing down predictive fire on unseen, but registered targets. Teutonic efficiency and timetable charts had prolonged the day for many of them. 107 Brigade was well on the move and Crozier's battalion were momentarily spared 'for a further few hours of strenuous life that day'. The shelling began again once they were clear of the wood. Crozier crossed no man's land at the cost of 50 dead and 70 wounded.[9]

Tommy Ervine, assaulting with the final waves of 107 Brigade, hurled grenades into German dugouts like cricket balls, shouting, 'Divide that amongst yez!' They were soon enveloped in a maelstrom of trench fighting:

Somebody shouts 'Go that way', so I did and sure enough somebody got me in the leg, so I made for him – a German and I got him, shot him in the face. Then I tried to walk back and I couldn't. I'd been shot. A big fella called Andy Robb pulled me back ... I'd have liked to get in among them Germans with my bayonet because they'd mowed us down like pieces of wood ... It was terrible ... it was cruel.

Hauptmann Schorer, the commander who had advised his messenger Leutnant Stahlhofer not to dally at the Schwaben after midnight, was taken prisoner. Over 60 of his men were taken out of the redoubt and herded across no man's land to the British lines. Crozier moving towards them saw 'an advancing crowd of field grey' and his men opened fire at 600 yards. 'Damned ...' shouted an officer, 'give them hell.' Men whose nerves had been stretched taut throughout the catastrophic advance simply blazed away. 'Cease fire, for

God's sake!' Crozier ordered, having observed who they were through binoculars. They were being escorted by wounded British, but the fire 'ripples on for a time'. Crozier got them back under control, but there were few regrets. 'After all they are only Germans,' one youngster remarked. Hauptmann Schorer never made it back to the British lines; he and many of his men were straddled by German artillery.[10]

As the momentum of the Ulster attack swept on to the fourth line and reached out for the fifth, the wounded left behind were abandoned to a miserable fate. Medics were often unable to reach them and many died alone. Private Hugh Adams recalled 'fellas crawling back that couldn't walk'. One put his rifle down and covered himself with a groundsheet, a pathetic effort to shut out the horrors all around. He was dead when Adams got to him. 'No one to touch them!' in their dying moment, he sadly recalled:

I used to think it was terrible to see young lives – the blood of life oozing out of them. Nobody there to lift their head – not one – nobody there to care – that was it!

Too often that was indeed 'it', even for those fortunate enough to be brought in and receive medical aid. 'One big fellow I seen from Donegal,' recalled a stretcher-bearer, outside a dressing station, 'had the steel helmet on OK but a piece of shrapnel the width of two fingers was right through into his skull.' Inevitably he was asked, 'D'you think, will I die with this?' – 'and I said, "No you'll not die," but I knew he hadn't an earthly.'[11]

The 32nd Division to the Ulster's right attacked Thiepval and the German line south with three brigades forward. Thiepval village with 93 houses was a great buttress on the western edge of the Pozières Ridge. The distraction of the

Ulster penetration enabled elements of the 1st Salford Pals, with 96 Brigade, to get through the German wire and trenches on the northern front of the village. Follow-on waves were decimated by artillery and machine-gun fire and pinned down. 'We dropped like ninepins,' Sergeant Bill Dutton recalled. 'One officer realised how futile the attack was and told us to stay there.' The few who entered the village were quickly cut off by Germans emerging from their dugouts behind them. 'You were shot down if you made any movement at all,' Dutton recalled, so nobody could support them. A fatal uncertainty, as to whether Thiepval was occupied by British or not, was to hinder the 32nd Division's efforts for the rest of the day. The 1st Salford adjutant had reported to division, more in hope than certainty, that his battalion had taken the German front line. Nobody could tell, because of the smoke. As a consequence, British artillery and trench mortar fire on Thiepval trickled to a standstill.

To the right of the Salford Pals, the 16th Northumberland Fusiliers were cut down in swathes and so depleted there were fears they could not even effectively man their own front line. Second Lieutenant Charles Marriot, moving up into the chaotic confines of the departure trenches with the final waves with C Company, recalled 'it was less of a trench than shell holes and hummocks'. They were under fire from active German machine-gunners, 'who weren't missing much that morning'. They had to negotiate a grisly landscape where 'hands, feet and shin bones were protruding from the raw earth stinking of high explosive'. It made an indelible impression. 'After all these years I still clearly see certain gruesome sights, burnt into the memory.' There was:

> ... a smallish soldier sitting in a shell hole, elbows on knees, a
> sandbag over his shoulders. I lifted it to see if he were alive, and

he had no head. Further on, a corporal lying doubled up and bloody; just in case anything could be done for him I bent down to raise him a little, and his head was only attached by a bit of skin.

Marriot found the front line 'was so blown up and gouged by high explosive that only bits of it remained'. His platoon could only deploy with difficulty, and reluctantly across such awful carnage, ghoulishly indicating what lay ahead. They found a badly wounded Northumberland Fusilier lieutenant 'shot through both knees, one wrist and one shoulder' as he had climbed over the parapet; the impact had flung him back inside. Marriot tried to bandage him up, later recalling that 'his courage was so superb I think I was weeping as I did so'. They were emotionally overwhelmed by the quantity of casualties around them and the awfulness of their wounds. 'I had to leave him,' he admitted, 'and never knew what happened to him.' Many others had been shot off the parapet they were about to cross. One sergeant he saw was 'drilled through the forehead, his brains spread out like hair over the back of his neck'. They braced themselves waiting for 'the hideous decision to go over the top'. Just before the whistles blew, a sweating runner arrived with a message from the CO. They were to stay put. 'My God, what a moment!' he recalled. He gazed over the edge of the trench, where 'the whole of no man's land, covered with bodies, was a sight I can never forget'.[12]

B and D Companies of the 2nd Salford Pals waiting with the second wave were likewise experiencing an anxious wait. They had watched the progress of the Ulstermen to their left and knew their comrades with the 1st Pals were in trouble pinned inside Thiepval. 'Above our heads an enemy machine-gun kept spitting away defiantly,' recalled Captain

Thomas Tweed with B Company. The clock was ticking and their time approaching; it was five to eight. The machine-gun, 'skilfully hidden behind a wood, in the ruins of a village which was to be taken by us', appeared to be holding out. It was obviously manned by 'very brave and capable soldiers' resourceful enough to survive the bombardment, who 'fired with a deadliness and accuracy which was amazing'. All the time 'we expected our troops to silence the gun', which fell silent just before they were due to go over the top:

> Then the Captain's voice, 'Fix bayonets', a few pregnant minutes and a further order, '5 and 6 over the top, and good luck boys'.

Tweed in later days was to document the shattering of his local Eccles community. 'Some like young Grindley were killed getting over, and rolled back into the trench', but the company pressed on 'ignoring the rain of death that whistled about them'. They ran from shell hole to shell hole and 'Pals of years association dropped, others fell riddled with bullets never to rise again.' The machine-gun had restarted. Corporal Stephen Sharples, a member of the local Eccles church, was cut down. Tweed's company, well over a hundred strong, was rapidly whittled down to little more than 40 men. Former shop assistant Walter Fiddes was dispatched back to battalion headquarters to get further instructions. As soon as he broke cover from an embankment he was shot down, and pulled into shelter. This was a personal loss to Tweed, who felt responsible for him because he was his orderly. The company was to be pinned down for two hours. As Tweed started to write yet another message, his notebook was snatched from his hand by a bullet. Later he wrote to Fiddes's family. Walter was hit again under shelter, which rendered him unconscious, after which they finally got the word to move back. 'A number of wounded were lying in the open,' Tweed recorded, 'and the enemy later in the afternoon riddled them with bullets.'[13]

Walter Fiddes lay in the open with hundreds of bodies as the broiling sun rose ever higher into the sky. The attacks made no impression on Thiepval, where, despite a few minor penetrations, the Germans weathered the crisis. British wounded left hanging on the wire were allegedly bayoneted. Machine-gun fire continued to lash the over-extended Ulster penetration to the German right.

'We had a terrible dose of machine-gun fire sweeping us through the wood,' recalled Sergeant-Major Ernest Shepherd, with the 1st Dorsets. They were trying to get through Authuille Wood south of Thiepval, and 'could not understand why'. He watched as the platoon ahead lost half its men killed 'and almost all the remainder wounded' as it crossed the 120-yard gap that led to their own front line. They had been delayed getting forward by two hours. With the time approaching 10 am it was assumed that the enemy machine-guns in their first and second lines would be out of action by now. 'I at once realised that some part of the attack had gone radically wrong.' He was not mistaken. The two German village bastions of St Pierre Divion and Thiepval, either side of the Ulster Division's deep penetration, were clearly holding. 'We were being enfiladed by batteries of enemy machine-guns,' Shepherd remembered. He scrambled into a communication trench with 'bullet holes through my clothing and equipment in several places and was hit in the left side'. He was lightly wounded and sheltered in a trench 'simply crammed with troops of all units in utter confusion'. His company was to lose 100 men that day. Pushing forward to obtain more information, he found many men who 'could only say they were the sole survivors of their battalion'.[14]

Nobody knew what was happening except it was not good. The 32nd Division had already suffered over 2,500 casualties. It would lose nearly 1,500 more.

Standing atop the Schwaben Redoubt, the German *Schwerpunkt* for the defence of the Thiepval plateau opens up a completely different vista of the battlefield. British observers could now see over the crest of the ridge and view the 'Berta' artillery concentration areas, south of Grandcourt, and other fire positions beyond. Shortly after 8 am British officers started to consult and orientate maps. Leutnant Scheurlen, commanding the 2nd Company of recruits with Infantry Regiment 180 opposite, spotted the tell-tale movement from the second main German position in depth beyond. German artillery observers at Grandcourt and others north of the Ancre could not be certain what they were looking at on the Schwaben position, obscured by smoke on the edge of the plateau. They had no idea a two-company-wide breach had been torn open in the German first line below. 52nd Infantry Brigade commanding forward had reported nothing of substance since its telephone wires had been cut in the firestorm of artillery that had clearly descended on the forward positions an hour before. German observers could not discern whether the movement was friend or foe. Surely they could not be enemy, after only 30 minutes of the attack?

'We moved the German dead out of our way,' recalled RH Stewart, by now moving beyond the Schwaben Redoubt towards the fourth German line. 'It was warm and clammy and we were sweating in the heat.' There was no water 'and we were very thirsty'. Empathy was in short supply. 'My friend was lying there beside me with his leg off – but conscious,' remembered Private Hugh Stewart, 'there was nothing I could do for him.' They trapped 'a bunch of Jerries' in an underground dugout and fired a trench mortar at point blank range 'down there' to get them out. 'We were blown off our feet, so goodness knows what it was like for the Jerries.' Another soldier crawled into a shell hole and found he was sharing it with a wounded German soldier. There was only a brief acknowledgement of mutual suffering. 'I pointed at my wound and he pointed at his legs.'[15]

The Ulster attack had transitioned from disciplined waves into small mobile groups, with men mixed together from six battalions, dashing forward in short rushes. A form of tribal aggression was carrying all before it. 'Would you like some Irish rebellion?' they taunted German soldiers. They were like Protestant 'beserkers', maddened by the loss of kith and kin around them. Every field-grey figure ahead was seen as a dangerous object to be destroyed, not an individual with human feelings. One soldier described the scene:

> *Vaguely I recollect that mad charge. A few swirlings here and there of grey clad figures with upraised hands yelling Kamerad. Heaps of wounded and dead.*

'How calm and peaceful it looked then,' recalled a soldier, referring to the pristine area they had just left and the contrast with the nightmarish landscape they were now crossing. 'How fresh, green, and invitingly cool looking at that long, blowing grass.' Now German artillery seemed to be digging up every square yard of the Ulster gap. 'Great jagged, gaping craters covered the blackish, smoking ground, furrowed and ploughed by every description of projectile and explosive.'

Blue skies above were being smudged with 'white puffy' shrapnel bursts, raining jagged steel splinters. By 9 am there was fierce fighting at the fourth line.[16]

'There was one soldier I'll never forget,' recalled RH Stewart, 'he fought like the devil':

> *He made himself a special weapon for fighting in the trenches. It was about half the length of a pick shaft and on one end he screwed in a pear-shaped lump of cast iron, on the other was a leather thong, which he kept tied about his waist. He used to parry a bayonet thrust with the rifle and then swing his lump of cast iron upwards. No matter where it hit a man it broke bones. He'd smash a man's wrist or hand, then when the rifle flew from the man's hands he'd shoot him.*

At the fourth line, Stewart recalled, 'we fought every second, there was no rest at all'. They were literally wading in blood, which seeped through the tongue of their boots and soaked their socks. By 10 am impetuous groups reached the fifth line ten minutes ahead of the timed British artillery lifts. Well aware by now that hesitation led to casualties, the Ulstermen pushed on, but were severely punished for it. Very few would ever return from this line, and many perished in the British bombardment.[17]

There was little apart from runners and the wounded that could advise the German rear what was happening forward. At about 8.35 am 52 Brigade Headquarters heard from its parent 26th Division that the Schwaben Redoubt might have been captured. Subsequent reports over the next 30 minutes claimed British troops appeared to be assembling and reorganising inside, but nobody could be certain. Once British soldiers appeared in front of the *Hansa Stellung* (Hansa Line) and started to dig in among the previously vacated positions of the 5th Battery Artillery Regiment 723, it was accepted that the Schwaben Redoubt had indeed been overrun. All that was barring their way into the forward German artillery positions was the company of recruits from Infantry Regiment 180, commanded by Leutnant Scheurlen, who had kept them at bay with rifle fire and a single machine-gun. With just one hour into the assault, Generalmajor von Soden's 26 Division *Schwerpunkt* was seriously compromised. Even as the outwardly unperturbed veteran general digested the alarming information given him over the telephone, he realised, with a sinking heart, that his superior, Generalleutnant von Stein, had to know. It was his *Schwerpunkt* also. Von Soden was formulating options even as he replaced the receiver. Speed of reaction was now of the essence.[18]

General Sir Oliver Nugent's 36th Ulster Division had made the deepest penetration so far that morning. Like the Germans, he was not completely aware of the situation, except there had been some success on his front.

'Look there, something *must* be wrong!' remembered one surviving Ulster soldier near the fifth line. Pointing to the left, he remarked to his comrades, 'Why, they're not advancing on *that* side at all.' The attacks by the 29th Division against Beaumont Hamel had been a catastrophic failure. 'Not a sign of life could be seen,' the soldier recalled. The 36th Division were becoming besieged inside the four lines they had taken. A head had been thrust into the German line, but the shoulders were not following. The soldier encapsulated their predicament: 'The Ulster Division were out to the Hun's first, second, third, fourth and even fifth line, with all the German guns pelting us from every side and at every angle'.[19]

They had already lost more than 4,000 men.

III Corps Attack on La Boisselle and Ovillers, 1 July 1916

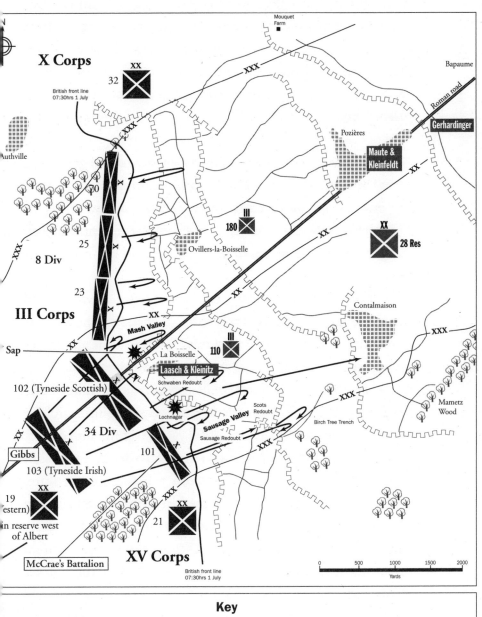

X Corps

32

British front line
07:30hrs 1 July

Authville

70

25

8 Div

23

III Corps

Mash Valley

Sap

102 (Tyneside Scottish)

34 Div

Gibbs

103 (Tyneside Irish)

19
(estern)

in reserve west
of Albert

McCrae's Battalion

XV Corps

101

21

British front line
07:30hrs 1 July

Mouquet
Farm

Bapaume

Roman road

Gerhardinger

Pozières

Maute &
Kleinfeldt

180

28 Res

Ovillers-la-Boisselle

Contalmaison

110

La Boisselle

Laasch & Kleinitz

Schwaben Redoubt

Lochnagar

Sausage Valley

Scots
Redoubt

Mametz
Wood

Sausage Redoubt

Birch Tree Trench

0   500   1000   1500   2000

Yards

Key

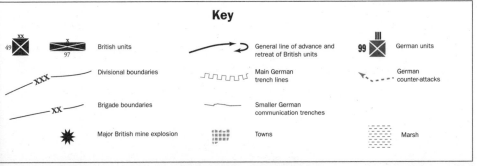

	British units
	General line of advance and retreat of British units
	German units
	Divisional boundaries
	Main German trench lines
	German counter-attacks
	Brigade boundaries
	Smaller German communication trenches
	Major British mine explosion
	Towns
	Marsh

49

97

99

7.28 to 11 am

Sausage and Mash

At 07.28 hours there had been a quiet 'sooch' along the front of the III Corps as two deep mines went off either side of the German fortified village of La Boisselle. Harry Baumber, with the 10th Lincolns, remembered, 'the trenches simply rocked like a boat':

> *We seemed to be very close to it and looked in awe as great pieces of earth as big as coal wagons were blasted skywards to hurtle and roll and then start to scream back all around us. A great geyser of mud, chalk and flame had risen and subsided before our gaze and man had created it.*

The Lochnagar mine with its 60,000 lbs of ammonal created the biggest detonation ever experienced on the Western Front, reaching almost 4,000 feet. With it went almost the whole of the 5th Company from German Infantry Regiment 110. During the eerie pause in the noise that followed it, Baumber heard 'several skylarks were singing – incredible!'[20]

III Corps attacked across 4,000 yards of front with 21,000 men against 5,000 defending Germans with Regiments 180 and 110. The depressions between the three spurs across which the German line ran created what was called 'Sausage Valley', to the right of the straight Roman road from Albert to Pozières. Predictably the broad valley on the north side of the road was nicknamed 'Mash Valley' by British soldiers. These wide-open spaces in no man's land could only be transited by the British if the flanking German defences targeted by the Y Sap and Lochnagar mines were neutralised. To attempt to advance otherwise would be suicidal. The Roman road steadily ascended to Pozières and formed a rough divide between two attacking divisions, the 8th left and the 34th right, with the 19th Division in reserve west of Albert. III Corps had the formidable task of capturing two fortified villages, six lines of trenches and to advance two miles in depth across its front. The 8th Division attacked with all three brigades in extended line at the village of Ovillers and either side. The 34th Division rose as one man over the top, two brigades forward and the in-depth 103 Brigade setting off 1.5 kilometres behind, from the Tara-Usna hillocks, a long perilous advance through Avoca Valley before reaching Sausage Valley beyond. The fortified village of La Boisselle, ground down by artillery, was to be rendered 'untenable' by a platoon of special bombing parties, supported by Lewis machine-guns and Stokes trench mortars. The main assault would simply bypass it.

Within ten minutes, 80 per cent of the assaulting troops were dead or wounded or simply disappeared in the welter of artillery and machine-gun fire that awaited them. The first soldiers to reach the parapet of the Sausage Redoubt to the right of the valley were immediately enveloped in slurry of flame from German flame-throwers.

'There's no need for these short rushes and getting down on your stomach,' Corporal James Tansley with the 9th Yorks and Lancs was told. 'Go over as if you were on parade.' Tansley was clear about the orders but admitted, 'Myself, I was a bit sceptical about it.' One officer remembered stepping over 'a dud shell every two or three yards over several acres of ground' as they moved through Sausage Valley – not very reassuring artillery support. Tansley was hit – 'down we went and my mate who was with me, he went down shot through the legs'. A bizarre discussion ensued, 'he had some qualms of conscience in him,' Tansley recalled, 'because he wasn't facing the enemy when he went down.' They had been hit by defilade machine-gun fire. 'I didn't realise anything like that myself, but he was an old regular soldier and it troubled him so much.' The issue was resolved when the next shot hit him in the mouth as they lay side by side. 'I didn't know when my moment might come,' Tansley admitted, 'I expected it any moment ... The best thing I could do was to lie low, keep quiet.' When another wave approached from behind, the fire became so intense that Tansley sought shelter in a shell hole. As he crawled towards it he realised 'it was chock-a-block full – dead, wounded, unwounded – I couldn't get in it!'

'Bullets were flying all over the place,' recalled Private Ernest Deighton nearby. 'It were Maxims they were firing and they were shooting across each other, with this hissing noise as they went past.' The advance had become completely enmeshed in a lethal web of intersecting machine-gun arcs. 'I thought I was a goner,' he remembered. 'I didn't think I'd get back. I didn't think I'd *ever* get back.'[21]

'Silently our machine-guns and the infantrymen waited until our opponents came closer,' recalled Oberleutnant Kienitz. His machine-gun company, supporting 110 Regiment, commanded the approaches across Sausage Valley. 'Then, when they were only a few metres from the trenches, the serried ranks of the enemy were sprayed with a hurricane of defensive fire.' So excited and determined were they to get to grips with their tormentors of seven days that Kienitz saw men 'standing exposed on the parapet' while 'some individuals hurled hand grenades at the enemy who had taken cover to the front'. They had been well forewarned. Feldwebel Karl Eisler with Artillery Regiment 29 had watched the steady build-up from the castle tower at Contalmaison. Forward infantry positions had told them the British trenches were completely full with infantry. Once it started 'there were urgent calls to shoot defensive barrages'. The II Abteilung (Battalion) of the 19th Bavarian

Field Regiment fired the first of 6,590 rounds it would fire that day, some 550 rounds from every gun.[22]

'When the English infantry began their mass attack with the huge explosion at 5th Company,' Vizefeldwebel Laasch with the 12th Company remembered, 'we immediately made ourselves ready to be deployed. Laasch was in reserve and had spotted that the English had penetrated the 111 Regiment line to his left. 'They were surging over the Mathy Trench through the Ovillers valley,' he recalled. 'Clusters of Englishmen' had penetrated a blind spot 'without being fired upon from anyone'. He pulled his men out of the dugouts and 'we fired partly standing upright, into the Englishmen at close range'. Their sudden intervention began to have a considerable impact and the over-excited Laasch constantly bellowed, 'Lads, fire, *fire!*' One of his irritated older reservists shouted back as he reloaded, 'Damn it, Herr Feldwebel, I *am* shooting!' 'How we knocked them down like rabbits,' Laasch recalled with some relish. As the Tommies fell back he realised there was no fire coming from the left of his position. 'Was everyone dead there, or prisoners?' he wondered. When he made his way along the Mittelweg Trench to find out, he was suddenly accosted by three British soldiers. He dropped a grenade at their feet and raced back to seek reinforcements.

When he returned to his position he found a severely injured Tommy and a dead British officer. Laasch noticed oddly that he had red hair and freckles. All around were dead and wounded German soldiers, with an abandoned machine-gun, surrounded by its lifeless crew members. They had obviously been overrun. He saw to his right that 180 Regiment was being assaulted by 'thick close-packed lines that gushed from the English trenches'. They were in defilade to their re-occupied trench, so 'I too fired belt after belt from our machine-gun into the flanks of the English'. They advanced in endless battalion waves. 'Never in the war did I see fire have such a destructive effect,' he recalled, as he fired directly into Mash Valley, where 'the bodies lay like a blanket'.[23]

There is a haunting photographic image of men from the 103rd Tyneside Irish Brigade after clearing their parapet, at 7.30 on 1 July, advancing in waves over the crest of the Tara-Usna ridge line. They have just over a mile to go. Soldiers are shrouded by an early morning sunlit mist and clearly heavily laden with large packs on their backs. They lean into the slight slope they are ascending. Rifles are generally held at the trail or sloped at the shoulder, with bayonets glinting in the sun. Only three of every ten men in the image would emerge unscathed. Losses were so severe that the 102nd Tyneside Scottish Brigade preceding them was temporarily withdrawn to be reorganised and reconstituted. The Tyneside Irish Brigade commander was struck down and his brigade practically ceased to exist, being renamed the 103rd Brigade.

As the Tyneside Irish advanced, the soldiers could clearly see the punishment being meted out ahead. Lieutenant WJ White was peppered with shrapnel down his left side when a shell blew up next to him. 'I was in insane agony,' he remembered, 'and took a handful of my morphia tablets and was just going to swallow them when one of my men knocked them out of my hand and said "Stop that, you daft bugger".' Captain Alan Hanbury-Sparrow, with the 2nd Royal Berks attacking to the left, remembered:

In no man's land were heaps of dead, with Germans almost standing up in their trenches, well over the top firing and sniping at those who had taken refuge in shell holes.[24]

As he waited to see what would happen next, 'another brigade was ordered to resume the attack'. Luckily for that brigade, the order was rescinded, but they would have gone.

What is remarkable, and remains a conundrum to those studying the events of that day, is what motivated men to continue to advance to certain death? Qualities such as patriotism, courage and self-sacrifice are more difficult to comprehend in a more cynical age today.

Five of every ten men struggling across no man's land that day were Kitchener's New Army men. Three were regulars and less than two of them were Territorial Army 'Saturday Night' soldiers. They were all volunteers and did what they were told because they believed in the chance pattern of destiny. They came from a rigid and more hierarchical society than our own, implicitly accepting and believing in the decisions of their 'betters' set above them. Most preferred their lives to be orderly and simple. They expected and were prepared to be told what to do. Inspired by love of country, they subscribed to a widespread conviction, reinforced by popularly received propaganda, that their basic human freedoms were being challenged by the Kaiser's militarism. They were saving mankind and indifferent to military science and the technical superiority of defence over attack. There was an aura about these men, the pick of their cities, towns and villages. Many had been prepared to queue all night to volunteer, anxious less they 'miss the boat'. Now the 'Big Push' was upon them, the culmination of 18 months' training and preparation. Surrounded by an arsenal of guns and masses of men, they felt they could end the war here on the Somme. How could they fail?

Spontaneous singing and cheering often accompanied the arrival of the 88 Kitchener New Army battalions. These fit and healthy soldiers anticipated they could end the trench stalemate and, like many of the regulars, believed themselves to be better than they actually were. They had been in the line during the previous winter and thought 'they were getting the hang of it'. Their greatest asset was spirit. New Pals battalions existed in a rarified atmosphere, the company was their city and the platoon their street.[25] They had been called 'Kitchener's ridiculous regiments' and the 'laughing stock of the armies of Europe'. They would prove their critics wrong. Their unique identity radiated a sturdy independence; they were modelled neither on the Territorials nor the Regulars. Officers had been pals in civilian life, who had cheered the same football teams and chased the same girls. Qualities like these encapsulate the poignancy of what happened on that fateful morning of 1 July. With 500 days in the making, many of the Pals battalions lasted mere hours in their destruction. It is these characteristics that provide some clue why so many sacrificed themselves, seemingly without hesitation on the Somme.

Tommy Oughton, with the Barnsley Pals at Serre, had gone over the top with mixed feelings, because 'we'd had no experience at all from a fighting point of view'. Ignorance was to some extent bliss. 'We were wondering what it would be like,' he remembered. That, matched with an unshakeable confidence in themselves, got them over the parapet. 'We had no idea that it would be like it turned out to be.' They had been in the line that winter, 'but we'd no idea of trench fighting at all', Oughton admitted, which 'was the biggest disadvantage we had'.

Spirit alone is still not sufficient explanation of why the attacks were pressed so suicidely. The shock of confronting impersonal modern firepower was insufficient in itself to check the advance. 'Five hundred yards, we didn't do too bad,' recalled Private Eric Haylock of the Suffolks, assaulting up the middle of Mash Valley with the 101st Brigade. 'We started at six foot apart – near enough – six foot apart.' At the start British artillery had kept German heads down for the first 100 yards. When the guns lifted onto the second line the Germans poured out of their dugouts and lashed them with machine-gun fire. 'Well after that they was going down like corn in a field.' With every step forward his line dissolved:

The last time I looked to see who was with me, there wasn't anybody within the length of a cricket pitch either side. And I thought to myself, well I'm not going to face this lot alone.

They were in this together, not alone, another factor spurring the advance. They were more afraid of going backwards than forwards, of being seen to let their pals down. The concept of comradeship was all-embracing; they were unselfish, friends had to be supported. Dying, however, did mean letting wives and families down. Captain Thomas Tweed's 2nd Salford Pals continued their suicidal advance on Thiepval because they knew the 1st Salford Pals ahead were in trouble. The men came from close-knit communities. Letting down the side would be heard about at once at home; they were all mates who knew each other; many were related, attended the same schools and churches, courted the same girls.

Eric Haylock's dilemma was soon resolved. 'I was just thinking about going down, when I feel this sting on me leg, and see all me trousers and equipment go up in the air.' Despite being virtually alone on the battlefield, he had an extraordinary commitment to duty.

I tried to go on, tell you the truth, I went four or five steps, and then I found I hadn't got any use in my leg. So I sort of went and

*sat down – there happened to be a tiny shell hole. I sat my behind
in that and put my knees up to protect my face.*

He sat there for the rest of the day, unable to move, with
bullets 'swishing over my head'. There was little else he could
do, so he covered his face with his helmet, 'to keep the bullets
off, or the sun'.[26]

The 'intoxication' of the attack was another factor providing impetus. Minds focused only on going forward. Doubters
kept up, unable to face the shame of staying in the trench,
where they might be picked up by the Military Police, or
they cowered in a shell hole forward. There was no collective wavering, no attempt by anybody to turn back. George
McCrae's 16th Royal Scots, the Heart of Midlothian football battalion, attacked to the right of Sausage Valley. Ahead
lay the grisly trail of the 15th Royal Scots preceding them.
Still they advanced. When Ernie Becker in the 16th was shot
through the cheek, his former postman pal Colin Campbell
paused to help. 'He never spoke,' Campbell later recalled,
'he simply looked and then I had to continue on my way.' A
Company crossed the first German line at 8 am, followed 15
minutes later by B Company. Former schoolmaster Captain
Peter Ross, the last surviving A Company officer, was caught
in the stomach by a machine-gun burst that virtually cut him
in half. In agonising pain, he begged someone to finish him
off, but nobody would do it, until two men were ordered.
One of the witnesses to this mercy killing committed suicide
himself 20 years later.

Losses in this tightly bonded footballing battalion were
intensely personal. 'To see a man I had looked up to and
thought a much better soldier than myself go under,' recalled
Lance-Sergeant Jerry Mowatt, 'made me think I could not be
far behind him':

It shook my faith in every certainty. Your officers, your pals, maybe even men you didn't care for much, all falling in front of you. Not a day goes by that I don't think of that bloody morning, and I always seem to settle on the awful moment when I saw [the CSM] go down. Right up to the last, there was a grave effort to maintain his dignity. Even on his knees, he looked to the direction of his men. 'Be brave, my boys,' he cried before he fell.

Jerry Mowatt looked back to check he was dead, and then carried on.[27]

Officers were often inexperienced. They were not veterans and were unable to reconsider options when the attack was clearly going wrong. Ordered to capture certain objectives, duty impelled them to expend all their strength and courage to continue the assault, even when it was demonstrably hopeless. Such dogged determination was another factor powering the momentum of attacks. Nobody had worked out what to do if they were faced with situations different from those they had laboriously worked out and rehearsed behind the lines in the days preceding the assault. The 15th Royal Scots penetrated the German third line ahead of the 16th, but the Germans coming out of dugouts behind them turned to oppose McCrae's Battalion following, with the Tyneside Irish catching up. The 15th were cut off. Artillery Colonel HW Hill, observing from the British line, thought the advance through Mash 'was an almost hopeless venture from the very commencement'. He could see the battalion visibly wilting and falling beneath the hail of fire. 'An attack on a valley from which good observation for defending machine-guns is obtainable for a distance of about 1,500 yards,' he calculated, 'should not be regarded as a reasonable military operation but as a serious criminal offence.'[28]

Inspiring acts of bravery added to the 'intoxication' of the attack, impelling waverers to clamber over the top into suicidal fire. The British press were later to revel in the 'Boy's Own' exploits of the 8th East Surreys, who kicked footballs into no man's land during the assault on Montauban. 'The Surreys Play the Game!' was the title of the iconic Caton Woodville pen and ink drawing published in the *Illustrated London News*. The *Daily Mail* reported:

> *A company of the East Surrey Regiment is reported to have dribbled four footballs, the gift of their Captain who fell in the fight, for a mile and a quarter into the enemy trenches.*

Captain Wilfred Neville had brought back two footballs from his last leave for the leading platoons of his company to 'kick-off' at H-Hour. One of the balls was inscribed: 'The Great European Cup – The Final – East Surreys v. Bavarians. Kick-off at Zero'. The other was more ominously labelled 'No REFEREE', envisaging few prisoners. The iconic tale captured popular imaginations back home.

The act was not just bravado. Wilfred Neville had approached his commanding officer Major Alfred Irwin suggesting, as Irwin recalled, that 'he and his men were all equally ignorant of what their conduct would be when they got into action'. Kicking the ball was deliberately intended as a distraction from the overwhelming tension of the coming assault. Irwin concurred: 'I think it did help them enormously,' he claimed, 'it took their minds off it, but they suffered terribly.' Neville, his second captain and sergeant-major were all killed. He was a much loved and popular commander and had rationally thought through the implications of the sacrifices that would be required of his men and that it would be difficult to get them over the top. One sergeant eyewitness later wrote to his sister describing how 'it is no disgrace to the men when I tell you they wavered':

The chaps had got 'the wind up' so he just lit a fag and talked to 'em – you know, the way he used to talk. Well he joked and laughed and smoked. Of course 'they' got him.

Neville was struck in the head just short of the German wire.[29]

The German counter-propaganda response was predictable. The English were obviously a race of idiots. Caton Woodville's iconic *Illustrated London News* depiction was reproduced in the German press and headlined: 'An English Absurdity: Football Play during Storm Attack'. German veterans repelling the East Surreys noticed nothing. The Germans were very practical in their response to human distress in battle. Courage is a bankable asset, and German field commanders acknowledged that it needed to be conserved. Although shell shock was still not a recognised medical condition at this stage of the war, German soldiers exhibiting such symptoms were sent home or elsewhere, rather than being executed or disciplined for cowardice. By 1918 the British were to shoot 346 soldiers, of which 266 were deserters; the Germans only admit to 48. The British were only beginning to come to terms with the realities of what happens when spirit is expended in the face of impersonal modern firepower.

Men often wrestled with the dilemma of how they would react when ordered to cross no man's land for the first time under withering fire. Inspiration did play a role. 'God is merciful,' declared Lieutenant Frank Crozier of the Ulster Division, 'he chloroforms us on these occasions.' Private Harry Russell had deliberately stood up in no man's land at Serre, certain he would be shot, after his platoon commander

Lieutenant Wallace had heroically insisted they continue to advance in the face of certain death. Wallace had been cut down. 'I had thought,' he later recalled, 'that a man who could stand up and knowingly face practically certain death in these circumstances must be very brave.' When it came to it, the 'intoxication' of the attack, like the merciful chloroform described by Crozier, did overcome all, so that 'I found that bravery hardly came into it … once the decision was made to stand up I had no further fear.' He did not even consciously feel the bullets punching through his body, which 'was to me something extraordinary':

> I am now convinced that when it comes to the last crunch nobody has any fear at all; it is not a question of bravery. In some extraordinary manner the chemistry of the body anaesthetises it in such a way that even when fully conscious fear does not enter into the matter.[30]

The anaesthetising effect of shock on the body once hit enabled men to carry on. Remarkably they often did. 'I got a bullet in me arm directly I was on parapet,' recalled one Liverpool soldier, 'and somehow it made me stumble like an' I fell … wonderful thick them bullets to be sure' – but he continued to press on until 'it was just past their first line I got this one in me hand'. Shattered nerve endings do require time before the pain registers with the brain:

> A bit sore like that was but not so very bad, but I got on all right till this third one got me here and I fell in a shell hole near by the second line.

This Liverpool soldier did not stop until he was hit three times. Soldiers in battle also have a blind faith that the other man will get it, never them. 'I hadn't gone ten yards before I felt a load fall from me,' recalled Sergeant Richard Tawney, attacking with the 22nd Manchester Regiment to the right with XV Corps. 'No one knows the rottenness in him till he cracks, and then it's too late,' he reflected. The fact that he was able to physically pick himself up and go forward under fire was a tangible relief. 'Imagine the joy of that discovery,' he recalled, superseded by the belief that all those about him were more vulnerable than he. 'I knew that I was in no danger. I knew I shouldn't be hit' – which was what sustained him, until he was.[31]

A practical problem, which impeded the leadership of officers and NCOs trying to sustain attacks, was the sheer din of battle. They were reliant upon hand signals, whistle and voice to keep soldiers moving forward. Tyneside Scottish bagpipes with 102 Brigade, advancing to the left of Sausage Valley at La Boisselle, started before they went over the top. Recent scientific surveys have suggested this may well have had an inspiring effect, encouraging exhausted and frightened men to do more. Clinical running trials record higher work outputs from trial participants exposed to pipe music. The unmistakable drone of the pipes is a 'driver' in terms of effect and unsettles the enemy. Tests show that high-pitched sounds energise, while droning music provides compulsion. Twenty-six pipers went into battle with the four battalions of the Tyneside Scottish crossing Avoca Valley into Sausage Valley, of which 20 were killed or wounded. The same survey, however, revealed that the audio mix of shell and machine-gun fire, cracking bullets, metallic ricochets and shouting and screaming would have prevented the pipes from being heard above the noise of battle. What likely provided compulsion was that the pipers were starkly visible. Scottish soldiers like the Pals battalions have a heightened sense of territorial belonging. Pipes would make them *feel* more Scottish, conferring compulsion in a scenario that would normally tax resolve. Observing unarmed pipers striding apparently unperturbed into a maelstrom of fire produced such an emotional response. The men's blood was up, they were inspired.[32]

Blood lust, in the ancient 'beserker' sense, also impelled these men forward. 'I were in the front row and the first one I saw were my chum Clem Cunnington,' recalled Private Ernest Deighton, attacking uphill at the north end of Mash Valley with the 8th King's Own Yorkshire Light Infantry:

> *I don't think we'd gone twenty yards when he got hit through the breast. Machine-gun bullets. He went down. I went down. We got it in the same burst. I got it through the shoulder. I hardly noticed it, at the time, I were so wild when I saw that Clem were finished.*

Deighton was incensed. 'We'd got orders,' he claimed, 'every man for himself and no prisoners!' It suited me after that, after I saw Clem lying there.' He hurled a Mills bomb into a trench 'full of Jerries', he recalled, shrieking, 'There you are! Bugger yourselves! Share that between you!' Savage hand-to-hand fighting erupted inside the trench, 'then I were off':

> *I went round one traverse and there was one – face to face. I couldn't fire one handed, but I could use the bayonet. It was him or me – and I went first! Jab! Just like that … Oh, I were wild! Seeing Clem like that.*

Deighton carried on making for the second line and was shot again, through the fingers 'as I were climbing out … on the same arm'. Wounded twice, he actually reached the second line, when 'I got another one'. This time 'it went through my tin hat and down straight through my foot. Well, that finished it!'[33]

McCrae's 16th Royal Scots then pushed beyond what became known as the Scots Redoubt and deep into the German line to the right of Sausage Valley. It was remarkable progress, bringing the forward elements to within 1,000 yards of the village of Contalmaison, just behind the second main German line. By 10 am Captain Lionel Coles was trying to penetrate the southern extremity of the village with 60 men. They had fortuitously found their way through a junction point of the defending German Regiments 110 and 111. About 30 men meanwhile from the Tyneside Irish had crossed no man's land and were making their way through the German communication trenches running into Bailiff Wood to the north of the fortified village. Neither group had any idea of the other's presence. Coles's group grew smaller and smaller as it fought its way forward. 'It was just cruel. We had no chance,' recalled Jim Miller:

You remember Jimmy Dods that we used to pal about with? I saw him fall beside me. We were going over when he was hit in the chest. I do not think he knew anything. That was when I got mine, only I was lucky for it was just my leg. I crawled into a shell hole with poor Jimmy just behind me, where I could see the bullets still tearing into him. It was just awful to see. I think it was deliberate on the part of the Hun, for they were potting the wounded all day long. Thank God he was dead by then.

Robert Stewart in the same group admitted, 'I was so unspeakably terrified by the sights I had seen' that 'I was quite praying to be wounded to get out of it'. When he saw his arm was bleeding he threw himself down with some relief, only to be confronted by the inspirational sight of 'one of our boys'. He was just a lance-corporal moving forward in the open, rallying his men, shouting 'Come on lads!' As Stewart remembered, 'I'm dashed if I didn't rise up and follow,' among several other wounded men. 'Anyway, I was spared any further trouble in this direction by a second bullet, which knocked me such a blow on the thigh that I crumpled up and fell away behind.'[34]

'The British, who advanced in hordes, managed to obtain a foothold in our lines,' recalled Leutnant Alfred Frick, with the 6th Battery of Field Artillery Regiment 28 nearby. The Scots had penetrated beyond their 3rd Battery and represented a serious threat; they had reached the artillery lines. Frick assessed they were only 500 metres from Contalmaison. Runners, telephonists and men from a construction company were hurriedly formed into a defence platoon, and an artillery piece was trundled up from the 3rd Battery (of Regiment 29) to lend direct support. 'This little united force succeeded in ejecting the bold intruders,' Frick reported.[35]

Corporal Kelly was the final surviving NCO from the small group that had broken into the village. There were nine of them left, two of whom were wounded. Kelly moved back down the road, seeking any British soldiers that might support them, but bumped into a group of German signallers. Kelly was the first to react, knocking over five men with rifle and bayonet before being shot in the chest. He fiercely pressed home his single-handed assault and killed two more, struggling with a third whom he eventually choked to death. He managed to get back to his group and lead them into the relative safety of the cratered fields in front of the village, where he passed out. He was still clutching one of the German signal flags tightly in his hand. At 11 am Captain

Lionel Coles was hit in the chest by a burst of machine-gun fire in a last attempt to cross the Quadrangle Trench at the southern extremity of Contalmaison. As he lay dying, his batman John Bird was killed trying to recover him. McCrae's Battalion had finally run out of impetus, 2,000 yards inside the German lines.

The Heart of Midlothian football team had led the Scottish league for 35 weeks out of 37 from 1914 into 1915, until 13 players and many of their fans had joined the 16th Royal Scots. The core of this battalion was now strewn across Sausage Valley into the streets of Contalmaison. The formation of the battalion likely prevented the best team in Hearts' history from becoming a side strong enough to dominate Scottish football for the rest of the decade, on a par with the mighty Rangers and Celtic. 'Don't let it be said that footballers are shirkers and cowards,' their manager John McCartney had proclaimed in the surge of patriotic publicity that came with the formation of the battalion. Now 576 of them had been cut down, 229 killed and 347 wounded. Three of their footballing greats had fallen. Henry Wattie and Duncan Currie were 23 years old. Currie, who had transferred to the team from the Kilwinning Rangers for two guineas, died after being shot in the shoulder. Ernest Ellis, the third, was downed by machine-gun fire just short of the German wire. Hearts were to lose a total of seven former players by 1918, five of them from McCrae's Battalion.[36]

The break-in to Contalmaison was the only serious penetration achieved by the III Corps attacks at Ovillers and La Boisselle. Sausage and Mash accounted for some of the most catastrophic losses of the day. The 34th Division lost 5,121 men, an average of 500 men in the 13 attacking battalions. The 8th Division further north was repulsed, losing 6,380 men.

North of Mash Valley, Corporal Don Murray, with the 8th King's Own Yorkshire Light Infantry, lost his officer Mr Morris, 'the officer with a lisp', straight away. Immediately after blowing his whistle and shouting 'Over!' he was shot 'straight between the eyes'. Like everyone else along the III Corps front sector they were told 'there was supposed to be no Germans at all in the front line', but as soon as the artillery had lifted, they had swarmed from their dugouts. Murray had reached the German wire, but:

> *It seemed to me eventually, I was the only man left. I couldn't see anybody at all. All I could see were men lying dead, men screaming, men on barbed wire with their bowels hanging down shrieking.*

It was eleven o'clock. 'I thought "What can I do?" I was alone in a hell of fire and smoke and stink.'[37]

XV Corps Attack on The Fricourt
Salient, 1 July 1916

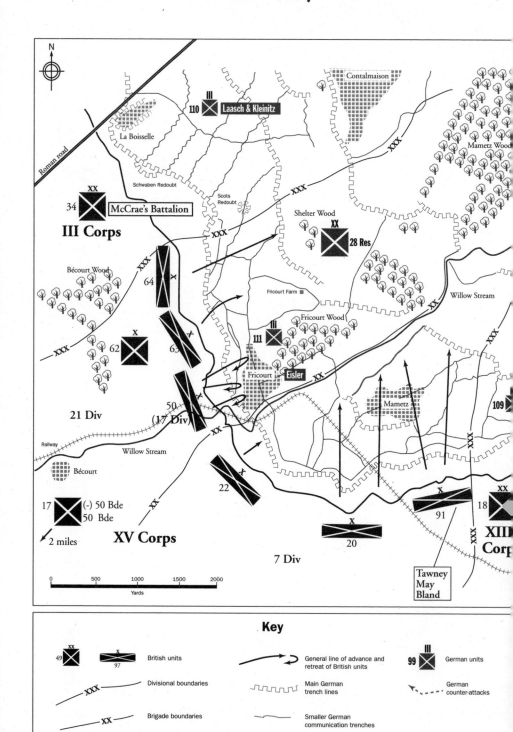

N

Contalmaison

110 **III** **Laasch & Kleinitz**

La Boisselle

Mametz Wood

Roman road

Schwaben Redoubt

Scots Redoubt

34 **XX** **McCrae's Battalion**

Shelter Wood

III Corps

28 Res **XX**

Bécourt Wood

64 **X**

Fricourt Farm

Willow Stream

62 **X**

65 **X**

Fricourt Wood

111 **III**

Fricourt **Eisler** **XX**

50 **X**
(17 Div)

Mametz

109 **XX**

21 Div

Railway

Willow Stream

Bécourt

22 **X**

17 **XX** (-) 50 Bde
50 Bde

91 **X**

18 **XX**

20 **X**

XV Corps

**XIII
Corps**

2 miles

7 Div

Tawney
May
Bland

| 0 | 500 | 1000 | 1500 | 2000 |

Yards

Key

49 **XX** 97 **X** British units

General line of advance and
retreat of British units

99 **III** German units

Divisional boundaries

Main German
trench lines

German
counter-attacks

Brigade boundaries

Smaller German
communication trenches

Major British mine explosion

Towns

Marsh

CHAPTER 7

Break-In —●

7.30 am to 1 pm

7.30 am to 1 pm

The Shrine. Fricourt to Mametz

The German-fortified village of Fricourt was where the 'L' shaped German line changed direction from north–south to west–east. This prominent salient was to be pinched off by the XV Corps attack, with 21st Division coming at it from the left of the protrusion and 7th Division from the right. Once the salient had been firmly grasped by the two-division pincer, 50 Brigade from the XV Corps 17th Division reserve would attack frontally. It was anticipated that the Germans in the salient would withdraw once outflanked, enabling the corps to link in with its neighbours, III Corps left and the XIII right. Although the elevated British line gave good observation into the village, nestled between two commanding spurs, it was hardly vulnerable. The German positions were well sited amid numerous salients and defensible flanks with a maze of defended trenches 1,200 yards in depth. British intelligence officer John Masefield thought 'the enemy had the stronger position', with much of it 'almost invisible and unguessable' except from air photographs above. 'One might have lived in those trenches' facing the salient 'for nearly two years without seeing any enemy except the rain and mud and lice.'[1]

The 21st Division assault from the left or west was aided by the detonation of the triple 'Tambour' mines, designed to create defensible craters and provide cover from observation and fire; but only two went off. The largest 30,000 lb charge was spoiled by water, while the 15,000 lb and 8,000 lb variants were too small. The attack was off to a poor start. Two companies of the 4th Battalion the Middlesex Regiment came under such heavy fire when they crawled out of their trenches five minutes before H-Hour, they had to get back in. The survivors, when they came back out for a second time at zero, could only form a single-line wave. Two lines of German trenches were penetrated in the first ten minutes, but the 10th West Yorkshires, attacking to neutralise German defilade fire from Fricourt, were virtually wiped out.

'To see a shell burst at men's feet and the effect it had on them as it destroyed and maimed them,' recalled Private JG Mortimer, fighting his first action, 'was a sickening sight.' He was with the 63rd Brigade, which with 64 Brigade penetrated as far as the Lonely Trench, beyond the right rear of the salient. 'The fact that it could happen to me I did not realise straight away, but when I did I trembled with fear.' He kept up with the others and controlled his trembling, resigning himself to the fact that 'what has to be, will be'. They captured three lines of trenches, but within four days his company was reduced to 20 men.[2]

'Couldn't have faced it unless afraid of funking before the men,' admitted Captain Rex Gee, attacking with the northernmost brigade of 21st Division. 'Scrambled from shell hole to shell hole, through the wire and craters and awful havoc.' He was confronted by 'terrible sights' with 'terrible slaughter by the Hun artillery and machine-guns' and 'snipers hurling bullets from every direction'. He admitted to 'dozens of close shaves' and being 'in a frightened stew throughout the whole advance'. At about 8 am he received a smashing blow to the head, which left him 'dazed for about an hour or so. The ricochet also left a huge dent in his steel helmet, which 'saved my life without a doubt'. He was then caught up in the pell-mell of trench fighting, shooting a 'Hun officer shooting into the backs of our men in front'. One German machine-gunner surrendered to passing troops and then 'mowed them down from behind'. He was absolutely incensed. 'I can vouch for this,' he claimed, 'such cases make you want to skin every Hun you see alive.' In order to maintain momentum, trenches were not being properly mopped up. They carried on through four German lines before consolidating:

> *Everything was horrible, ghastly and awful. May I never experience the same again. Saw scores of horribly wounded, horribly killed. Am being converted to conscientious objector. Words cannot express the horrors of it all.*[3]

The 21st Division had begun to isolate the Fricourt salient to the north, penetrating about a mile to a sunken road.

The 50th and 22nd Brigades were not due to go over the top until the afternoon, once both sides of the salient had been pinched off. For some unknown reason a company to the right of the Green Howards suddenly launched itself over the parapet. Being isolated they were immediately detected by Rudolf Stadelbacher and Otto Schüsele, with the German 111 Regiment machine-gun company, manning a Maxim in the gravel pit on Hill 110 near Fricourt. 'We saw the enemy assault out of all trenches,' they tersely reported, 'so we put down a hail of fire.' The 'two companies of British', they assessed, probably the Green Howards, 'who attempted to assault from the area of Fricourt Station, were quickly caught by our machine-gun and suffered dreadful casualties'.

'I got a message to say that A Company on the right hand had assaulted at 8.20,' remembered Lieutenant-Colonel Fife of the 7th Green Howards. 'I did not believe this but sent the adjutant to find out.' He could only assume, when told, 'that what was left of the company were lying out in front of our wire' and that Kent, the company commander, 'had gone mad'. It was a bad omen. The rest of the battalion was due to go over the top at 2.30 pm. Already 108 of the 140 men who had prematurely gone over were cut down within 20 yards of the British wire. It was a tragic mistake. There were no answers; the company commander was seriously wounded and the survivors were pinned down by heavy machine-gun and sniper fire. Kent did write from hospital three weeks later, 'still unaware of the terrible mistake he made in the attack on Fricourt'. He was highly thought of, and promoted, but was killed in May 1918. Nobody ever discovered for certain whether it was Kent who got it wrong.[4]

The 7th Division attacked to the right of the salient, aiming to capture Mametz, the fifth largest village in the area with 120 houses, and thereby isolate Fricourt from the southeast. In terrain terms, the section of German line running eastwards toward Mametz and Montauban, the base of the 'L' shape, was less formidable than the succession of mutually supporting spurs the attackers had faced in the north. This sector of the XIV German Corps line was manned by the 28th Division. Trenches and dugouts were less well constructed and fewer in number than von Soden's 26th Division sector further north. Casualties during the seven-day bombardment had prompted a number of last-minute reliefs in the line, which were to have a significant effect on the defending German 109th and 62nd Regiments. Two British corps were attacking from Fricourt to Montauban with 45,000 men against about 8,000 German defenders, odds of over five to one. Reinforcements from the 10th Bavarian Infantry Division were being plugged into the defences in a piecemeal fashion.

Hauptmann Klug had moved into the Prussian Infantry Regiment 62 sector 48 hours before, in the midst of the Allied artillery preparation. Although his company managed to get forward without significant casualties, he found the unit he was replacing was down to barely 30 men (from a normal strength of 170 to 200). He had inherited a parlous situation. The decimated company:

> … *had already given up the first and second trenches, inasmuch as it was still possible to speak of 'trenches'. Throughout the entire company area there were only three dugouts, which offered some guarantee of protection. In order to enter the company commander's dugout it was necessary to climb over the dead and unburied Prussian soldiers.*

The artillery bombardment in the south was having the anticipated nullifying effect on the German line, so badly predicted further north. German counter-battery fire had been much reduced, but machine-gun nests remained numerous and exacted a heavy toll.

Captain Duncan Martin was a company commander with the 9th Devons. During his last leave he had taken home a large-scale map of the German trenches in front of Mametz that his company was due to attack. Being artistically inclined, he had constructed a contoured plasticine model of the ground. The longer he studied it, the more he was convinced that his company would be in dire straits if the Germans had positioned a machine-gun position at the base of a small wayside shrine in Mametz. Once his company advanced over a small rise by a clump of trees at Mansell Copse, his men would be exposed to defilade fire from that shrine moving from right to left along the far side of the Carnoy–Fricourt valley. So impressed was his brigade commander with his contoured model that he ordered it displayed at his Grove Town HQ, the 'city of dumps' southeast of Méaulte. All officers were invited to view it. Martin even allegedly pointed out the danger of a machine-gun located at the base of the shrine. Martin led his company over the top from the support trench at H-Hour, because the front-line trench was badly chewed over by German shell fire. They topped the Mansell Copse rise and moved downhill and, sure enough, were riddled by machine-gun fire. There was a German crew at the shrine and they had survived the bombardment.

Martin advanced barely 15 yards according to a witness before 'he was shot above the right temple … He turned his head to the left, flung out his right arm and fell dead on his back.' The soldier eyewitness was convinced he was 'a secret service man', because of the much-publicised model. Despite such methodical preparation the casualties in the 9th Devons and A Company in particular were severe: 10 officers and 141 soldiers perished within minutes. Among them was Lieutenant Noel Hodgson, whose elegant and poignant last poem about the setting sun had implored, 'Help me to die, O Lord'. So many Devons fell at the front-line trench that it was utilised as a mass grave. Almost the first casualty recovered nearby was Captain Martin. 'The Devonshires held this trench,' the present-day inscription at the cemetery reads. 'The Devonshires hold it still.'[5]

Four Russian saps had been driven close to the German line in the 7th Division sector, and within 15 minutes a 700-yard advance was achieved. Casualties were heavy. 'Well, we crossed three lines that had once been trenches, and tumbled into the fourth, our first objective,' remembered Sergeant Richard Tawney, with the 22nd Manchesters. '"If it's all like this, it's a cake-walk," said a little man beside me', who was soon dead. Tawney was ill at ease because there was a badly wounded man shot through the stomach, lying on the parapet, and groaning for help. 'I hate touching wounded men – moral cowardice, I suppose,' he admitted. 'One hurts them so much and there's so little to be done.' He half-heartedly sought to help, eased his equipment, but couldn't lift him into the trench, which was too crowded, 'so I left him':

> *He grunted again angrily, and looked at me with hatred as well as pain in his eyes. It was horrible. It was as though he cursed me for being alive and strong when he was in torture.*

By 8 am the leading elements of the South Staffordshires were penetrating the outskirts of Mametz. They were held up by machine-gun fire to their right, which it was the task of Tawney's battalion to eradicate. Orders not to hold back to tend wounded were strict. 'It was time to make for our next objective,' Tawney recalled, 'and we scrambled out of the trench.'

At last they came across a tangible target. 'The Germans were brave men,' Tawney acknowledged; 'some of them actually knelt – one for a moment even stood – on top of their parapet to shoot' within a hundred yards. 'It was insane. It seemed one couldn't miss them.' Virtually every man he fired at dropped, 'except one, him, the boldest of the lot, I missed more than once'. When the Germans took cover, he observed 'in crossing no man's land we must have lost many more men than I realised then'. The carnage seeped into his consciousness. Before them 'lay a boy who had been my batman', who he had sacked for being slack and drunk. 'He might have been resting, except for a big ragged hole at the base of his skull where a bullet had come out.' His platoon commander was on his back nearby, with face and hands 'as white as marble'. 'His lungs were labouring like bellows worked by machinery. But his soul was gone.' Captain Charles May was dead. He had asked his close friend FJ Earles, the adjutant, to look after his wife and child if anything happened. Earles would one day marry her.

Tawney's company was fast running out of men. He moved to his left to make contact and elicit support from the neighbouring company:

> Of course it was idiotic. If our company had lost half or more of its strength, why should A Company have fared any better? But there! I suppose the idea of death in the mass takes alot of hammering into one before one grasps it.

He could not really comprehend that the air beneath the blue sky a mere foot or so above his hunched figure was so deadly. 'The weather was so fine and bright that the thought of death, if it had occurred to me, which it didn't, would have seemed absurd.' He rose up to wave to men away to the right to come over and reinforce them, at which point two bullets punched into his chest and abdomen.

> What I felt was that I had been hit by a tremendous iron hammer, swung by a giant of inconceivable strength, and then twisted with a sickening sort of wrench so that my head and back banged on the ground, and my feet struggled as though they didn't belong to me.

The air had been knocked out of him and for a moment he thought he had died. 'Pain, when I moved, was like a knife, and stopped me dead.' He was in shock. Now he was like all the other wounded men he had passed by and not helped. 'I could have cried,' he admitted, 'at their being so cruel … It's being cut off from human beings that's as bad as anything when one's copped it badly.' Then a youth wriggled up to him asking 'What's up, sergeant?' and 'I loved him.'[6]

Three more attacks were needed before Mametz was finally penetrated and the mopping up could begin. By midday the 1st South Staffords had established themselves to the north of the village ruins, but their flanks were still vulnerable.

Feldwebel Karl Eisler, with Reserve Artillery Regiment 29 firing in support of Fricourt and Mametz, knew they were losing the artillery battle. After observing the deluge of British artillery fire that descended on Height 110 at Fricourt, where they had their forward observers, 'We thought about our infantry in the trenches, how many would still be alive in a company?' Urgent calls for defensive fire came in, but 'our complete heavy batteries in Mametz Wood had been either put out of action by dense gas or direct hits'. They managed to fire for a full hour before 'direct hit after direct hit put our entire artillery out of action'. It was an unequal contest. 'The English artillery was like a virtual hurricane, whereas you could hardly hear our own guns at all.'[7]

The reduced number of German dugouts, thinned by the bombardment, compromised the distribution of troops able to man the front line, when the barrage stopped. By H-Hour at 7.30 am on 1 July at least two thirds of the dugouts in the 2nd Company Regiment 109 sector had been heavily damaged or destroyed. Unteroffizier Paul Scheytt with the regiment saw 'the English came walking as though they were on a parade ground or going to the theatre ... We felt they were mad, every man took careful aim to avoid wasting ammunition.' Resistance was patchy. Machine-gunner Emil Kury of 109 Regiment found himself rapidly outflanked. 'Our eldest soldier, a painter who came from Pforzheim with five children, was shot in the forehead and dropped without a word.' Before he appreciated how close the English actually were, Kury was shot in the chest, collapsing with blood spurting from the exit wound in his back. The British soldier 'shot three of us before I even had the chance to use my rifle,' he ruefully admitted. 'I would like to meet that English soldier, he was a good shot.' The lines in front of Mametz were buckling.

Karl Eisler, to the rear with Artillery Regiment 29, could hear the sounds of infantry combat seemingly coming from behind Fricourt. English soldiers had got to within 200 metres of their 3rd Battery. He came across the battery commander Hauptmann Fröhlich next to one of his shot-up guns, 'pale and bleary eyed'. There were no guns left in action, all had been hit. Eisler could see bitter fighting around Mametz and whole groups of 109 Regiment men being led away into captivity.[8]

'We took the first two lines' just to the east of Fricourt 'after a hard struggle', recalled Private Arthur Burke, with the 20th Manchesters, 'but taking the third was hell.' Capturing prisoners in the midst of hotly contested trench fighting was difficult. The anguish and pain of heavy casualties brought primal urges to the fore. Leutnant Ernst Jünger, with the German 73rd Fusilier Regiment, readily accepted that any 'defending force after driving his bullets into the attacking force at five paces distance' must take the consequences. Jünger, a hardened veteran, explained why:

A man cannot change his feelings again during the last rush with a veil of blood before his eyes. He does not want to take prisoners but to kill. He has no scruple left; only the spell of primeval instinct remains. It is not till blood has flowed that the mist gives way in his soul. [Once the position has been taken] he looks around him as though waking from the bondage of a dream. It is only then that he becomes capable of addressing himself to the next problem of tactics.

Arthur Burke was not taking prisoners as they mopped up dugouts. 'We threw bombs of every description down,' he remembered, 'smoke bombs especially and as the hounds came up, crawling half dead, we stuck the blighters.' After losing so many men, their blood was up. 'In one dugout,' Burke recalled, 'there were about 25 in there and we set the place on fire and we spared them no mercy, they don't deserve it.' Second Lieutenant YRN Probert, a forward artillery officer with the 2nd Gordons, remembered seeing one captain 'sitting in the front line eating his lunch with one hand and shooting snipers with the other as they came out to surrender'. Snipers were especially detested. 'I thought that rather rough, as some had their hands up,' Probert remonstrated, but the captain pointed out 'he had several jocks shot on their stretchers'. Burke explained that some snipers shot until the last moment, then 'they throw up their hands, *Merci Kamerad*!'

We gave them mercy, I don't think! We took far too many prisoners, they numbered about 1,000 and they didn't deserve being spared. What tales they told us, and they would give us anything for souvenirs to spare their lives.

Burke was not interested. 'The souvenir I treasure most is my life,' he insisted. Belts and spiked helmets were prized booty.

'I thought I might get one of those belts with *Gott Mit Uns* on it or perhaps one of those Prussian helmets,' remembered Private Albert Conn with the 8th Devons:

I did come across one bloke, but when I lifted his helmet, half the top of his nut was in it – it was full of brains like mincemeat. I'm not very squeamish, but I didn't fancy scraping that out.[9]

The first emotion on capture is shock followed by humiliation. This is also the optimum time to escape, but it tends to coincide with a dazed feeling of relief at being alive and an acute sense of vulnerability, that one's survival is at the whim of the captor. Watches and valuable possessions were quickly removed, an ageless consequence for those captured on the battlefield. When German soldier Gerhard Bahrmann was later captured, he had predicted that his first thought would be 'Good, now the shitty pressure is over.' But this was not the case. 'I did not say it, rather on the one side I felt dumb rage this had happened to me, on the other, a feeling of gratitude that they had not shot me.'

Shock and vulnerability were to the fore. Private J McCauley was part of a group who captured a German dugout south of Mametz. Inside, seven of the nine prisoners taken were already wounded; it was probably an aid post. 'One of the wounded was a huge man, and he lay on his back exposing a large hideous wound in the stomach.' His repeated shouts of *Kamerad!* (friend) and the intense pain he was suffering irritated one of his British captors. To McCauley's horror, he threatened the helpless figure. 'I saw him pick up an old sandbag that was soaking wet and covered with thick slimy mud', which he raised 'over his shoulder' and beat the helpless prisoner 'with all his strength over the gaping wound in the German's stomach':

Even that did not satisfy him. He jumped on top of the German and pressed the filthy sandbag into the open wound, and yelled, 'Take that, you square-headed swine.' The helpless German screamed like a madman.

The sickened McCauley could not stop him but remonstrated furiously. 'What the hell are you talking about?' was the response. 'I'd put a bullet through the swines as quickly as looking at them.' The veneer of civilisation was stretched thinly on the battlefield. McCauley stumbled out of the dugout to find a weeping German youngster at the foot of the steps. 'He held both his hands out to me in an appealing fashion, sobbing and murmuring.' McCauley never quite erased this nightmarish scene:

Years after the war, I still sit by the fireside and see in the flickering flames that poor German boy with his hands outstretched in tearful appeal.[10]

He never knew what happened to the boy.

By 1 pm the southern houses in Mametz village had been captured, as also the Danzig Alley trench, which extended beyond to the northeast. XV Corps had almost achieved its first objective and was over 2,000 yards into the German line. Fricourt was firmly held by the Germans, but dangerous penetrations were seeping into their line both left and right of the embattled salient. Success had come at a price not dissimilar to that inflicted on the British corps further north. The 21st Division had already lost nearly 4,000 men, while 7th Division casualties were approaching 3,000.

XIII Corps Attack on Montauban, 1 July 1916

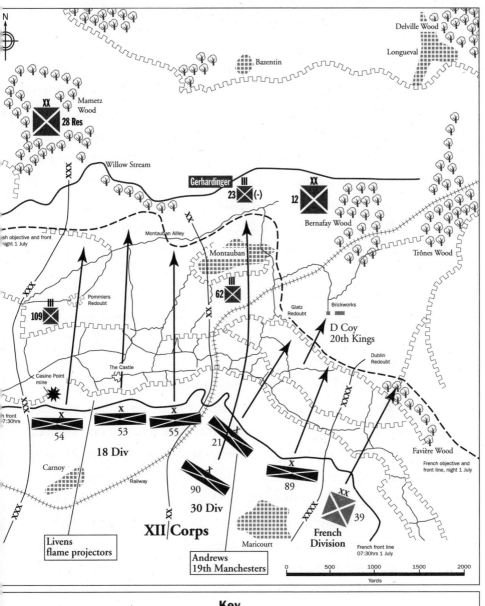

N

Delville Wood

Longueval

Bazentin

Mametz Wood

28 Res

Willow Stream

Gerhardinger III **23** (-)

12

Bernafay Wood

Montauban Alley

Montauban

Trônes Wood

Pommiers Redoubt

109

62

Glatz Redoubt

Brickworks

D Coy 20th Kings

Dublin Redoubt

The Castle

Casino Point mine

sh objective and front night 1 July

h front 7:30hrs

54   **53**   **55**

18 Div

Carnoy

Railway

90

30 Div

XII / Corps

21

89

39

French Division

Favière Wood

French objective and front line, night 1 July

French front line 07:30hrs 1 July

Maricourt

Livens flame projectors

Andrews 19th Manchesters

0   500   1000   1500   2000
Yards

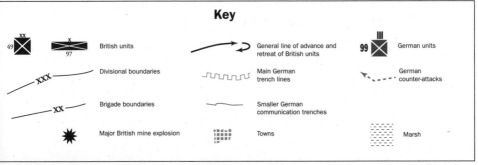

Key

49 / **97** British units	General line of advance and retreat of British units	**99** German units
Divisional boundaries	Main German trench lines	German counter-attacks
Brigade boundaries	Smaller German communication trenches	
Major British mine explosion	Towns	Marsh

Break-In. Mametz to Montauban

The southernmost sector of the British assault to the right of XV Corps was that carried out by Lieutenant-General William Congreve's XIII Corps. Here, unlike in the north, the Maricourt Ridge behind the British lines gave excellent observation of the German forward line, as well as cover for British artillery batteries on its reverse slopes. Augmented by French heavy batteries to their right, artillery superiority was quickly established over the Germans, whose counter-battery fire was largely neutralised early on 1 July.

XIII Corps attacked with two divisions forward. Major-General Ivor Maxse with the 18th Division left, and Major-General Shea with the 30th Division right, were far from the stereotype which led to the 'lions led by donkeys' label. Both had diligently used the time to prepare for the offensive. Maxse was particularly enlightened. The 18th Division actively encouraged the use of multiple weaponry from Russian saps; and troops were fully informed about tactics, supporting units, artillery and the ground. Maxse, unlike some of his conventionally staid contemporaries to the north, planned on the assumption the Germans would *not* be destroyed in the preliminary bombardment. A rudimentary 'creeping barrage' was devised to provide close support for troops to advance in small group rushes, under cover of supporting fire, an embryonic 'fire and movement' tactic. Russian saps were used extensively to get troops as far forward under cover as possible. Saps were also preceded by sap head mines to blow up identified enemy strong points. The huge Livens flame projector was employed in the centre of his sector, able to flame 75 yards of German trench. Push-pipe explosive charges created ready-made trenches, that were blown in the form of linear craters over 70 yards long, four deep and two wide. Dedicated mop-up teams were better trained and more methodically and extensively used than in the north.

The numerous saps and explosive charges were detonated at 7.27 am. Montauban was razed by a combination of British and heavier French artillery. The shallower German dugouts were collapsed, leaving the survivors traumatised, in perhaps the most intensive bombardment of an objective to date. At H-Hour, Stokes mortars and machine-guns opened fire from the freshly opened saps, augmented by the heavy 'Casino Point' mine and multiple charges blown from saps and bore-holes.

'Yes, we felt tense,' recalled Private Frank Bastable, waiting in reserve with the 7th West Kents, 'but this is what we'd waited for – for a year now.' It had been a misty morning start, 'but this soon cleared when the sun came right up – lovely day it was later on'. Private Jack Cousins preceded him in an earlier wave with the 7th Bedfords. 'It was a question of get stuck in, kill or be killed,' he remembered:

> It wasn't a question of wandering around the countryside looking for mushrooms. We had to get going. We were told, 'Don't advance on your own! Go together at the same pace! If machine-gun fire takes place, drop down flat to the ground!'

Despite initial successful rushes and pausing behind the creeping barrage, some deadly hold-ups were enforced by isolated and strongly fortified machine-gun posts. Some were forward, but most fired out from the intermediate line in depth. This created a haphazard advance, where units that pushed ahead were lashed by fire from the flanks. 'We were frightened and excited at the same time,' recalled Frank Bastable. 'That last barrage was terrible – just before zero, I'd never heard a noise like it.' They could see Montauban ahead on the ridge. Jack Cousins became 'disillusioned' when they found whole sections of barbed wire intact to their front, 'and the Germans firing at us from all angles … A lot of men were caught on the wire, and they were sitting ducks.'

Sergeant James Payne had also been in reserve with the 16th Manchesters. When the attack was about to start, he noticed a young lad alongside who looked as if 'he'd been out of school for six weeks'. Irritably, Payne asked, 'What are you doing here?' He was frustrated at having to take on the responsibility for one so young – the lad had arrived that day from England. 'Hang on to me,' he said. 'It was stupid – the boy couldn't hold a butty knife, never mind a bayonet.' He was shot down next to him. They came up against the surviving machine-gun nests, after fighting through a number of German trenches, and 'we were all knocked out'. Machine-guns had already filled all the nearby shell holes with dead, dying and blinded:

> *Tall men got it through the jaw, shorter men through the eyes. I was five foot ten and shot through the cheek. I was walking along, and a bullet blew all my teeth out. I fell forward and spat all my teeth out. I collapsed and, hours later, I came round. My left eye was closed. I couldn't talk. I could breathe, that was all.*

Frank Bastable had been fortified by a drop of rum, 'Dutch courage, I suppose', before going over the top. They too were pinned down by isolated machine-guns. 'You couldn't stand up,' he remembered, 'you had to crawl.' When his sergeant-major, Button, 'put his stick up for us to follow' he 'got killed almost straight away'. Progress forward was only by crawling. 'I remember it being hot, lying there and getting really thirsty.'[11]

Leutnant Preuss, caught up during the night in the chaotic reinforcement of 109 Regiment by his parent 23 Regiment, had reached sector 'e' north of Carnoy shortly before 7.30 am. By H-Hour most of the 23 Regiment reinforcements had got no further forward than Montauban. Preuss, however, was damned for his perseverance and diligence to duty because the forward 109 Regiment positions were overwhelmed in the first rapid rush. Nobody is certain what happened to Preuss; his 1st Company men were either killed or captured. The 4th Company, also relieving in place that night, reported 44 killed and 50 wounded that day; the rest were captured. Four days later nine men from 4th Company got back to the German line.[12]

Acting officer Josef Busl, with the 8th Bavarian Infantry Regiment, had barely been in the front line 24 hours. His platoon had moved into their relief positions a day ahead of Preuss only to find 'the trenches were partially levelled and the fire positions barely usable'. Only three or four dugouts could be put to use by his platoon of 62 men. Exhausted by the strenuous trek across craters and loose spoil excavated by seven days of bombardment, and harassed by artillery and shell fire the whole way, his men had no other option than to start clearing the position. During the night one of the few dugouts 'was crushed and eight men were lost'. Now, two and three quarters of an hour into the British attack, they were still holding on. By 10.15 am two thirds of his men were dead. The lack of dugouts and the battering the trenches had taken created substantial gaps in the German line, even before the attack started. The Bavarian Regiment companies had been inserted into a precarious and confusing situation. Soon Busl was severely wounded in the head and shoulder, and his platoon overrun.

'We were being fired on from the rear,' remembered Unteroffizier Gustav Lüttgens, with the 10th Company 109

Regiment. They thought they were being fired at by their own infantry, shooting over their heads from the rear. 'We jumped out of our trench,' he recalled, 'all waving and shouting *Higher! Higher!*' It was only when two or three men fell wounded that they 'realised it was the English who were behind us, so we jumped back into our trench'. They faced a dilemma:

> *We had a conference as to whether or not to surrender. One or two wanted to fight on, but there were many in our regiment who were over forty and, unlike the younger men, they had families and were the first to suggest surrendering. In the end the others were swayed.*

It was not always possible to surrender. 'We tied a handkerchief to a rifle and waved it and the English came and rounded us up,' Lüttgens recalled. 'We were very depressed' but convinced 'the English would not shoot us'. It was soon apparent from the looks on the faces of their English captors they were 'as pleased as we that it was all over'. The British immediately took away their watches. By 10 am the advance had reached the battle headquarters of the III Battalion Regiment 109 deep in the German line.[13]

Private Albert Andrews, with the 19th Manchesters, laboured across the loose earth of no man's land, hefting 60 lbs of equipment, with his rifle slung and smoking a cigarette. Delays caused by isolated machine-gun nests meant that 'about halfway across, the second wave catches up with the first', filling in some of the gaps from considerable casualties. As they approached the German trenches at the Glatz Redoubt his officer, Second Lieutenant Outram, called out, 'Up a bit on the left' before pitching forwards headlong. 'Dozens of Germans were running through us towards our lines with their hands up.' When he jumped into the German trench he was confronted by a German who 'was trembling and looked half mad with his hands above his head'. He was saying something he could not understand. 'Get out of the way, Andy. Leave him to me,' one of his mates shouted, 'I'll give him one to himself', meaning with a hand grenade. Although Andrews suddenly realised his bayonet was broken, his rifle was ready to fire with 'one up the chimney'. He did not shoot, though; he was as shocked as the German. 'He's an old man,' he recalled, 'he looked sixty.' Life and death had been a split second decision, taken at whim. 'This was the only German I ever let off,' Andrews admitted, 'and I have never regretted it because I believe he could have done me quite easily.' The next three they encountered in the trench did not survive. 'That's for my brother in the Dardanelles' and 'for my winter in the trenches', he remembered thinking. 'We walked up to them and one moved. My mate kicked him and pushed his bayonet into him. That finished him.'

Lieutenant-Colonel Frank Maxwell, commanding the 12th Middlesex 'Die Hards', had been unambiguous. '*Do* kill,' he instructed, '*don't* take prisoners unless wounded, and *don't* retire.' Heavy losses of course raised the emotional ante. 'I saw parties of Germans during the attack fire on our fellows until they were within a few yards of them,' recounted an 18th Division soldier, 'then as soon as they found out there was no hope for them they threw down their arms and rushed forward to shake our men by the hands.' Invariably they were shot. The same witness claimed that wounded Germans were shooting men in the back after being dressed by them. 'They are swine – take it from me,' he insisted, 'I saw these things happen with my own eyes'.[14]

Private Jack Cousins, attacking German dugouts with the 7th Bedfords west of Montauban, went down to investigate 'somebody moaning' after clearing one with a Mills bomb. 'I took a chance,' he remembered. Inside was a severely injured German 'with a great hole in his chest, blood pouring everywhere, pointing to his mouth'. It was not a good idea in medical treatment terms, but he knew what he wanted:

He wanted a drink. I gave him my water bottle. The water went into his mouth and came out of the holes. He was gone in a few seconds. It really upset me.

'I thought, "This is going to be easy!"' recalled Private AA Bell as he set off with the 17th Manchesters' second wave. 'Behind us was a battery. They were slinging it over, and the noise was terrible.' They were advancing on Montauban. 'Now!' an officer had shouted, looking at his watch as Private Albert Hurst went over the top with the same battalion. As the first wave had left there had been a wave of sound from rifle and machine-gun fire, but 'we couldn't see what was happening, and there was a very short interval between their attack and ours'. They laboured to clamber up the trench ladders; 'it was a struggle to get up with all the gear,' he remembered. Being the second carrier wave, 'we all had some extra load' in addition to full pack and rifle. Hurst had two bandoliers of rifle ammunition slung over his shoulders, two Mills bombs, a full size pick-axe and a water bucket in his hand filled to the top with Lewis gun ammunition. 'It would have been impossible to run,' he recalled, 'it was an effort just to walk at a normal pace.'[15]

'The fire got heavier as we went across no man's land,' Hurst remembered. By this time the first wave had captured the German front line and were taking fire from the second line. 'There was no cover,' he recalled. 'I was exposed, I was frightened and I got a bullet through my water bottle.' Men were going down, but he had little impression that people were falling around him, but 'of our platoon, perhaps a dozen out of fifty men were casualties'. Second Lieutenant Macardle remembered the 'slow walk' towards the village of Montauban. Men hit and crawling back from the first wave 'smiled ruefully or tried to keep back blood with leaking fingers ... We would call a cheery word or fix our eyes on Montauban – some were not good to see.'

Despite the ponderous loads, the 17th Manchesters got ahead of their support. 'We had done it all at the slowest walk,' Macardle explained, in artillery formation, 'but that walk had been quite unchecked.' So they lay down in no man's land under shell fire for 40 minutes, and 'waiting is hard'. They were due to rush the village at 9.56 am after more artillery preparation.

Bell came across some German soldiers with their hands up; it seemed the attack was going well.

I could hardly believe it. I shouted to them Par la! Par la! [This way!] and they went par la. That was lucky for me.

'Montauban village seemed to be flattened,' Albert Hurst recalled. 'The only thing left intact was a figure of Christ on the Cross, at the corner of the Péronne road,' he noticed. 'We took the village from a fleeing and terror stricken enemy,' remembered Second Lieutenant Macardle. All that there was to greet them was a lone fox; 'inside all was wreck and ruin, a monstrous garbage heap stinking of dead men and high explosive'. Down in the dugouts they pulled out 'cowering men in grey, living with old corpses'. The Germans made no effort to defend it at the end. The 30th Division had reached its first phase objective. At 12.34 pm D Company of the 20th King's pushed even further forward to capture the brickworks at La Briqueterie beyond. The German observation platforms on the chimney stacks had provided clear vision across the entire battlefield.[16]

When Sergeant James Payne with the 16th Manchesters recovered consciousness, after having his teeth shot out, he realised, 'There was nobody around. Just the dead.' He found and assisted a corporal shot in the foot and stumbled across a man whose left arm and leg had been blown off by a shell:

> *His left eye was hanging on his cheek, and he was calling out, Annie! I shot him. I had to. Put him out of his misery. It hurt me. It hurt me.*

Confronting such misery raised the emotional ante and dulled sensitivity. When Payne came across a captured German doctor, who would not treat his comrade's foot, he shot him. He then had to walk 15 miles to the rear before he found an ambulance. There were German prisoners on stretchers lying nearby. 'I tipped them off,' he recalled, and 'put the corporal on and put him in the ambulance and saw him off.'

XIII Corps 30th Division attained its first objective within 60 minutes of H-Hour. The 18th Division on its left was held up initially in the centre, but after two hours had captured the Pommiers Redoubt and was pushing beyond. At about ten o'clock the village of Montauban was taken by the 30th Division's reserve brigade, and the German line beyond the village and along the ridge towards Mametz was occupied between 11 am and midday. Frank Bastable, with the 7th West Kents, remembered, 'Well, we got through in the end and took our objective – I don't think many did that day, we were one of the few … I was lucky really.'[17]

Albert Andrews, held up by machine-gun fire outside the Glatz Redoubt, watched as artillery howled into Montauban and the 90th Brigade moved forward to capture it. 'The village went down like a box of bricks,' he observed. At midday he was checking out the captured German dugouts. 'There were cigars, tinned food and German helmets.' An officer caught them emerging from a dugout smoking cigars and wearing German helmets. 'Yes, you all look very nice,' he said, 'but get some fucking digging done!' It was hot sweaty work labouring in the midday heat. One of Albert's wounded mates, hit in the back, sought reassurance:

He would call out, 'Andy, give me a drink', then 'Andy, ease me', 'Andy, it does hurt. Why don't they move me and take this out of my back?' He then complained about it being hot and the sun in his eyes, so I put my khaki handkerchief over his face. I could hardly stand to see the agony written on his face.

They asked the captain if they might carry him back. 'No, we must not stir,' he said. 'It was sickening,' Andrews remembered; they had reached Montauban, but 'everywhere you looked there were dead and wounded'.

'I could see the French troops advancing on our right,' recalled Private Pat Kennedy, with the 18th Manchesters. 'It was a splendid sight to see them with their coloured uniforms and long bayonets.' He saw their artillery support was very effective and they seemed to know what they were doing. 'They advanced in short sharp rushes.' Kennedy watched them move by and off into the distance, and 'I thought, They're doing very well! Very well indeed!' The French XX Corps had attacked north of the Somme with the Sixth French Army under General Fayolle, alongside the British 30th Division. Despite stiff fighting they overran much of the German first line defences. South of the Somme the 1st French Colonial Corps and XXXV Corps had attained total artillery supremacy, having amassed about ten heavy batteries per kilometre of front. German batteries were literally wiped out and incapable of laying down effective defensive fire. Delaying the attack south of the Somme by two hours caught the Germans completely by surprise. They had assumed, after the bloodbath at Verdun, that the French had no offensive capability. Battle-wise French divisions were proving them wrong. They punched through the entire German first line trench system and established themselves within easy assaulting distance of the next. The German southern sector was teetering, in marked contrast to the catastrophic British setbacks experienced to the north.[18]

Private Albert Hurst moved to a position east of Montauban with the 17th Manchesters, facing Bernafay Wood. 'We were too exhausted from carrying so much gear to start digging trenches,' he remembered, so they simply lay down at the outskirts of an orchard. 'There was no noticeable firing from the German side,' but they anticipated counter-attacks. 'We had achieved our objectives, and as far as we were concerned, all the attacking battalions must have been similarly successful.' The biggest problem was a shortage of water, and 'I'd had a bullet through my bottle.' They chewed on grass to alleviate their thirst.

Lieutenant Kenneth Macardle watched as 'large parties' of German prisoners 'laughing and dancing like demented things full of mad joy went streaming back unguarded'. Many were broken men. They called out 'Mercy, Kamerad!' having thrown away equipment and arms 'and looked utterly demoralised in filthy stinking grey uniforms'. Montauban was left with 'dying Germans among the brick dust and rubble, horrible wounds and reeking corpses'. Henry Holdstock, back with the 6th Squadron Royal Naval Air Service, recalled the great excitement when the first prisoners came in. There were about 70 to 120 of them, 'very dejected, with pale yellow faces and German pill box hats'. XV Corps took over 1,600 prisoners and the 30th Division about 500. Holdstock noticed the interest their naval uniforms generated, the prisoners 'saying to themselves that not only were they fighting against the British Army but they were fighting against the Navy as well'.

German prisoner Gerhard Bahrmann described what it was like to be led through the British rear positions 'with gun after gun plastered about in batteries, and we didn't have any more'. This, he confessed, 'was the first time I had ever thought we would lose the war … that we held out for another two years, with soldiers not doubting or mutinying, was in fact amazing'. Holdstock thought the scene particularly poignant. There was a young British infantry officer with a German officer 'walking off almost hand in hand, with their little brood behind them, going back to captivity and safety' after only two hours of trying to kill each other. 'For me,' he admitted, 'it was very affecting to watch.'[19]

A gash was torn in the first German line about a mile deep and three and a half miles wide. It had swallowed up the villages of Mametz and Montauban. The view from the captured heights, for British soldiers long used to looking upwards at the German defences, was remarkable. Newly established XIII Corps outposts could look across Caterpillar Valley to see the southern slopes of the Ginchy–Pozières plateau. Longueval village with Delville Wood to its east was now visible, as well as part of Contalmaison. A whole new vista had opened up. It was at this point that Major General Shea, commanding the 30th Division to the right, next to the French, who had already advanced ahead, was ordered to delay any further advances.

Bernafay Wood ahead was patrolled and found to be empty. A real opportunity to exploit success was opening up.

German resistance on the XIII Corps front and before the 7th Division east of Fricourt appeared broken. The area was curiously quiet; battalions were reporting the enemy had cleared off. Some localities beyond the set objectives could probably be occupied with small loss. The French on the extreme right had taken thousands of prisoners. Albert Hurst of the 17th Manchesters remembered, 'We couldn't see any Germans or any defences, ahead of us in Bernafay Wood. It looked open.' Soldiers were told to consolidate where they were, however, because counter-attacks were anticipated.[20]

Oberleutnant Franz Gerhardinger's 16 Regiment, in reserve south of Bapaume, had heard the huge intensification of shell fire early that morning. Only a few shells had landed near them. His own second battalion was alerted and ordered to march south, through Beaulencourt to Flers northeast of Montauban, nearer the front. As they arrived the companies began to spread out in the high cornfields facing south, one company behind the other, towards Longueval. At 12 o'clock they received the order to move off. 'It was known,' he recalled, that the enemy appeared to have broken through our first line … My platoon received the order to attack through the gardens to the west of Longueval in a southerly direction.' The British had broken in rather than through, because Gerhardinger's battalion was launching its attack from the German second line. This trench system was dug along a ridge line extending from Bazentin-le-Grand to Longueval, north of the Willow Stream. The German soldiers knew the situation was precarious. Gerhardinger was reassured to realise, as he skirted the southwest edge of Longueval, that one of their companies was already established inside.

'What puzzled me most all day,' recalled German soldier Emil Goebelbecker with the 109th Regiment, 'was the lack of further forward movement by the British.' It seemed incomprehensible. 'The whole of our line had collapsed and it would have been a simple matter for them to have advanced much further than they did.' The line was held either by soldiers physically or mentally spent from fighting all morning or by men who had not fired a weapon in anger for over a year. For the first time in 18 months during this war, it appeared that a degree of movement was reoccurring at this sector on the Western Front.[21]

Emil Goebelbecker's incomprehension was also shared by some British soldiers. 'After we took Montauban, I thought that we would get reinforcements and exploit our success,' remembered Private Pat Kennedy, with the 18th Manchester Regiment:

We didn't know that the only success was where our division and the 18th Division gained their objectives. We thought the war would soon be over, and that our men were flushed with success. It was long afterwards that we found out that the battle had been a disaster except for us.[22]

The first hint came from the medics, who were talking about a complete catastrophe. Meanwhile, at one o'clock on 1 July, soldiers were optimistic that the faceless men at army and corps headquarters would take the right decisions from their châteaux. 'After we took Montauban,' recalled Pat Kennedy, 'I thought we would get reinforcements and exploit our success … But nothing happened.'

What were the men in the châteaux doing?

CHAPTER 8

'Silly Old Devils': Château Decisions

8.30 am to 5 pm

8.30 am to 3 pm

'The Invisible Battle'. British Headquarters

Command and control of the British infantry attacks on the morning of 1 July was conducted at battalion level. They relied on brigade headquarters to provide support if they got in trouble or to exploit a breach. Divisions supported their brigades by providing reinforcements of men and materiel, while corps headquarters at the top of the hierarchy decided priorities of support through the same. Success depended on the component elements speaking with each other. This was difficult in battle. The lowest level of decision-making was between battalion and brigade. Once the infantry had gone over the top, there was no reliable link between the battalion attacking waves and brigade command posts seeking to direct them.

'There they go!' announced Captain Charles Carrington, the acting adjutant with the 1/5th Warwickshire Battalion:

> And I looked over to the left and here were the London Scottish, who were on our left, running forward across the 300 or 400 yards of green grass between our village and Gommecourt wood.

This was at H-Hour, 7.30 am. Carrington had then to relay the progress of his battalion's attack to brigade headquarters. He faced the first problem encountered by all would-be decision makers along the line. 'They vanished into the smoke,' he recalled, 'and then there was nothing left but noise.' Stress and noise has an emotional impact, affecting credibility – do I believe what I can see? What is going on? 'After this,' Carrington observed, 'we saw nothing and we knew nothing and we lived in a world of noise, simply noise.'[1]

Carrington had previously tested telephone communications with brigade and the artillery, but the advancing companies had to leave theirs behind. The best they could do was to surface-lay telephone wire, pointless amid artillery fire, or send back runners – not a predictable or reliable outcome. Artillery officer Lieutenant Montague Cleeve remembered, 'We put [line] in the trenches for protection, but you can just imagine the confusion':

In some trenches there may have been up to 20 lines all mixed up. Occasionally I think they may have been coloured red, blue and yellow, or something like that, but not always. And whenever a shell burst in a trench, as thousands did, they bust all the lines and there'd be complete confusion, with mud and lines and debris everywhere.

The signallers then 'had a terrible job to find all the bits and pieces and to join them together again'. The Germans anticipating the attack had 'shelled the place to blazes, so nobody had any communications after that'.[2]

From the Grandstand above Albert, all that war correspondent Phillip Gibbs was aware of was the rushing sound of machine-gun and rifle fire coming through rolling smoke clouds. It was only 'when I saw the German rockets rising beyond the villages of Mametz and Montauban and our barrage lifting to a range beyond the first lines of German trenches' that he optimistically declared 'we had broken through!' The 'illusion' of victory was reinforced by the sight of 'crowds of prisoners', about 1,500, who 'had the look of a defeated army'. The same impression came from the lightly wounded returning, 'shouting and laughing as they came down behind the lines, wearing German caps and helmets'. Excited French civilians waved and cheered, 'Vive l'Angleterre!' Old men raised their hats and old women wept, which was success being communicated on the emotional rather than physical plane.

Signal flares were one method of reporting progress, but they could be misinterpreted. The signal for troops 'stopped at uncut wire' in the 4th Division sector between Serre and Beaumont Hamel was a single white flare, whereas success, 'objective gained', was three, one after the other. It was confusing and hard to tell the difference amid bursting shells and uncertain time lags. Lieutenant Cecil Lewis, flying the Somme front with 3 Squadron RFC early that morning, descended to 3,000 feet to see what was happening. They sounded a klaxon on the aircraft and the infantry were supposed to respond with red flares. 'They wouldn't light anything,' he recalled, 'because that drew the fire of the enemy to them at once.' His logbook records that not a single ground sheet denoting a battalion or brigade headquarters could be picked out. 'Only two flares were lit on the whole of two corps fronts.'[3]

Captain William Cardon-Roe was the battalion adjutant with the 1st Royal Irish Fusiliers who, like Charles Carrington, was responsible for feeding information back to brigade. He could only report what he saw, which was very little. The huge materiel build-up before the battle and the complete confidence displayed by all commanders had an insidious effect on reporting. Observers were anticipating and wished to report success, not a disaster. The Irish Fusiliers had established a company in the German Heidenkopf Redoubt, south of Serre. When, two hours and 20 minutes after H-Hour, the expected series of white rockets went up, indicating all was well and 'that the leading battalion of our brigade had arrived successfully on the third objective', Cardon-Roe's CO was delighted. He turned to him with an excited smile and told him to inform brigade. 'This is too good to be true,' he commented, and said, 'I will get these companies started.' As the adjutant enthusiastically descended the command post dugout steps to pass the message, he was called to the brigade major's line. 'Hullo – is that you, Cardon-Roe?' the metallic voice asked. The brigade major spoke to him hurriedly in urgent, staccato sentences:

Look here, have your people started yet? Well, then, hurry up and stop them. You are not to move until you get further orders. The whole show is hung up. We will let you know more when we hear something definite.

'What about the white lights?' Cardon-Roe stammered in response. 'Those ruddy white lights mean "Held up by machine-gun fire", the major insisted, 'and the damned things are going up everywhere.' Well over two and a half hours into the attack, recalled William Cardon-Roe, 'the whole rotten truth dawned on me.' This had the makings of a disaster. In reality British troops had pushed 500 yards through German communication trenches beyond the Heidenkopf, but nobody could tell whether they needed support or not. Communications along the whole front were failing.[4]

Brigadier Rees's advance 94th Brigade headquarters was in front of Observation Wood facing Serre. He had 15 staff in a steel-revetted shelter ten feet deep, with two exits, 500 yards behind the front line. His signallers were in a similar shelter nearby. He also was dependent on what he could see forward, and the verbal and written information that came back with runners. He had watched as each successive British wave had 'disappeared in the thick cloud of dust and smoke which rapidly blotted out the entire area'. But his entire brigade went through 'a perfect wall of explosives'. Nothing, he bitterly reflected, could have survived that:

> *I saw a few groups of our men through gaps in the smoke cloud, but I knew that no troops could hope to get through such a fire. My two staff officers, Piggot and Stirling, were considerably surprised when I stopped the advance of the rest of the machine-gun company and certain other small bodies now passing my headquarters.*

His brigade had ceased to exist as an effective fighting force in just 60 minutes.

At 9 am German defenders from 169 Regiment were already sending reinforcements to aid the embattled 121 Regiment to the south, secure in the belief that the attacks north of Serre had been effectively repulsed. Colonel Wiliford, who had lost his adjutant and two companies in these attacks, assured Rees, 'As far as I can make out, General, I have two companies left. If you want me to charge at their head,' he offered, 'I shall be delighted to do so.' By 9.30 am Rees was convinced further attacks would be pointless.

At 10.27, however, a string of optimistic reports came in from the 31st Division, his parent headquarters. These claimed that the 56th London Division, attacking on the other side of Serre from Hébuterne, 'have gone right through'. The 165th Artillery Brigade reported Serre had fallen and, 15 minutes after Rees watched his brigade wiped out, 'three or four hundred of our men advancing on the line Pendant Copse-Serre', which was his third objective. 'Messages now began to pour in,' Rees recalled, all erroneous. 'An aeroplane reported that my men were in Serre' and 'the corps and divisions urged me to support the attack with all the force at my disposal.' Further optimistic reports indicated considerable progress further south. Rees remained unconvinced.[5]

Even at trench level, the information was far from reliable. Artillery observation officer Lieutenant Adrian Consett Stephen remembered, 'I could see nothing', but 'reports and rumours came dancing down the wires':

'Our infantry have taken the front line without resistance.'
'Prisoners are coming in.'
'Enemy giving themselves up in hundreds.'
'Infantry have crossed the Serre Ridge.'
'Beaumont Hamel is ours.'
'More prisoners reported.'

When the smoke cleared at 11.30 am, however, 'I looked out upon the invisible battle'! So far as he could tell 'not a soldier could be seen, not a movement of any sort ... Could it be that we held those trenches?' he thought. 'Had we captured Serre?' He had no idea. The only change he detected was that the Germans were shelling their own trenches. Not until late that afternoon did he realise 'the infantry were cut to pieces, they came running back between the lines'.[6]

Much of the documentary evidence suggests division headquarters remained oblivious to the possibility of failure. They were located behind the artillery gun lines, whereas brigades could see further forward on the other side. 'It seemed to an outsider like myself,' recalled war correspondent Phillip Gibbs, 'that a number of separate battles were being fought without reference to each other in different parts of the field.' He might have been right. Rees's 94th Brigade was assured 'the 93rd Brigade on my right, reported that their left', in other words his brigade, 'had got on, whilst the 4th Division beyond them again claimed the first four lines of German trenches and were said to be bombing down our way'. None of this was correct.

When Rees saw the awesome artillery fire screening Serre 'had eased off now', he ordered two companies of the 13th Yorks and Lancs over the top, to support the reported progress:

> *As soon as this fresh attack was launched, down came the barrage again. One company was badly mauled, whilst the other wisely halted short of it.*

Phillip Gibbs rhetorically caricatured situations at higher headquarters as generals telephoned each other, divorced from front realities. 'All right, tell old So-and-So to have a go at Thiepval' or 'Today we will send such-and-such a division to capture Delville Wood'. In Gibbs's bleak view, 'Orders were drawn up on the basis of that decision, and passed down to brigades who read them as their sentence of death, and obeyed with or without protest.' Rees, convinced that his brigade had met with disaster on a grand scale, wisely declined all attempts by his division commander, Major-General O'Gowan, to send any more reinforcements over the top. Nevertheless, he was still being badgered at 10.50 am by yet another report received by division that 'several of our men have been seen in Serre'.[7]

By 8.30 am, just 60 minutes into the attack, out of the 66,000 men who went over the top in 84 battalions, some 30,000 were casualties. There was little to show for it. Anxious battalion commanders telephoned their brigade commanders hoping there had been a change of orders. They were reluctant to throw away their commands in fruitless attacks. Brigade commanders faced a dilemma. About one third of the attacks had taken their first objectives, another third had managed to attain tenuous small enclaves, while the remaining third were bloodily repulsed even before reaching the German line. The prevailing atmosphere in most brigade headquarters was grim. No knowledge was available from the flanks and there was no time to find out. Their only recourse was to ask division headquarters behind the gun lines for clarity and help. The response was invariably to stick to a plan that palpably was not working at trench level and follow orders.

Lieutenant-Colonel Magniac had watched his 1st Battalion the Lancashire Fusiliers go over the top at 7.30 am from the sunken lane at Beaumont Hamel and seen it bloodily repulsed. Two companies were reduced to about 60 men. Forty-five minutes later, 75 men attacked in the same place and only two officers and ten men reached the German wire. At 11.45 am the 86th Brigade commander, Brigadier Williams, ordered another attack. The battalion was down to its last 75 men, and Magniac was convinced by now that any further attempts to get beyond the sunken lane would certainly fail. Even so, the battle reserve of 25 men, led by Major Le M Utterson, tried to reach the survivors isolated at the German wire. They were shot to pieces and only the major and four others reached the vanguard. Brigadier Williams did not cancel the pending futile attack until 1.05 pm, by which time the survivors had been reflecting on life spans which could be measured in minutes.

Brigade commanders were given little alternative by divisions except to order their men forward. Major WC Wilson, serving inside the 70th Infantry Brigade headquarters at Authuille Wood, facing north of Ovillers-la-Boisselle, remembered the agonising dilemma his brigade commander faced:

Brigadier-General Gordon fully realised the gravity of the order he was giving when he ordered the 11th Sherwood Foresters to continue their forward movement. There was a tense silence in the dugout after he had given his decision and General Gordon was never quite the same again.

Seventeen officers and 420 men became casualties. Three hours later into the morning Major-General Hudson, the 8th Division commander, ordered him to attack again. Gordon's quiet reply on the telephone was 'You seem to forget, sir, that there is no 70th Brigade.'[8]

Piecemeal attacks continued until midday, by which time the numbers of attacking battalions was increased to 129, with 100,000 men. Divisions were under pressure from corps commanders seeking results, and fighting brigades with scant information. They insisted on sticking to the plan. Casualty figures by midday had risen to 50,000 killed and wounded and two thirds of the attacks could by now be judged complete failures. In Hamel village the atmosphere in the 36th Ulster Division command post became grimmer as temperatures rose alongside tempers. By mid morning, one witness observed, 'You could have cut the air with a knife.' Bad-tempered commands and complaints exhibited frayed nerves. The windows in the stone walled cottage had been sandbagged and the only ventilation was through the fireplace. Paraffin lamps added to the heat. Endless cups of tea and coffee were drunk as men came and went, speaking in hushed tones in the subdued atmosphere. Dugouts had become sticky and oppressive in the July temperatures. They felt cut off from the battle. The division had a firm grip on many German trenches, but were in turn under siege. The only certainty amid the confusing reports coming in was that there had been great loss of life.[9]

By midday the one third of attacks that had achieved results were becoming apparent in three locations, where significant penetrations or enclaves had been made. It was up to division commanders to reinforce the brigade successes and ask for further support from corps. The 56th London Division had quickly penetrated three German trench lines south of Gommecourt village. The 36th Ulster Division had made a rapier-like penetration onto the Thiepval plateau, overrunning the tactically vital Schwaben Redoubt in the process. The three divisions alongside the French in the south had achieved many of their first objectives. The Germans were reacting aggressively.

The failure of the 46th Division attacks north of Gommecourt had already enabled the Germans to redirect 13 companies against the 56th Division lodgement. With no reinforcements able to get through after 9 am, the situation in the lodgement was desperate by midday and hopeless by 2 pm. The first German counter-attacks had started coming in at 8.45 am. By comparison to this energetic response, 46th Division cancelled attacks at 12.15 pm, then at 1.15, and again three times that afternoon up to 3.15 pm. Major-General Montague Stuart-Wortley had lost five of six commanding officers early that morning and all six battalions had been bloodily repulsed. Pressured by his corps commander for a full effort, he was confronted by brigade commanders who said it simply could not be done. Stuart-Wortley eventually compromised, ordering a two-company-strong token attack – a death sentence for the units selected. Despite the direct orders from the corps commander that the division should attack, there was so much resistance from officers at different levels that in the end just one platoon attacked. Private GS Young, with the 1/6th North Staffs, described the reality of these dreadful predicaments at trench level, as the orders came down:

At about 3 o'clock a runner clambered along amongst the dead and wounded and said we were to attack again. At that moment I had found two others unwounded in my company and thought I was the only survivor in my platoon. Our clothes were torn and a mass of gluey mud, and our rifles caked and useless. We were attending to the wounded and the idea of cleaning our rifles for another attack never entered our heads. No officer had survived and we made jokes as to who would blow the whistle for the attack, if we could find one on a dead officer. Fortunately the attack was cancelled.[10]

A Sherwood Foresters platoon attacked, and every man except the platoon sergeant was hit. This was in apparent contrast to the 56th London Division on the other side of Gommecourt, who had advanced much further, albeit at greater cost. General Hull's London men had always regarded their commander as 'ruthless'. Accusations of stickiness hung in the air. The corps commander, Lieutenant-General Sir Thomas Snow, was unforgiving of anything less than full uncompromising effort. Stuart-Wortley would be sacked.

Lieutenant-General Sir Thomas Morland, commanding the X Corps, was incongruously perched on an observation platform built on a tree at Engelbelmer, three miles from the German front line. It was his command post, the nearest he felt he could be to the front without getting too involved in the division battle. A duplicate telephone cable ran to an exchange in the rear. He could actually see very little, and substantially less than the divisions and brigades ahead fighting his battle plan. He was aware that despite the successful advance of the 36th Ulster Division, the corps either side of him were making no progress.

Major-General Sir Edward Percival, commanding his reserve 49th Division, came up and recommended committing his reserve to the 36th Division penetration. He had personally spoken with its commander. Morland, however, was more intent on following the fortunes of 32nd Division's two abortive attacks on the fortified village of Thiepval. He considered it too early to change the plan. Percival felt that if he followed the line of the Ulster penetration he could take Thiepval from the north and rear. Morland insisted on sticking to the plan, ordering Percival to help 32nd Division mount a third fruitless assault. Percival's 49th Division had been earmarked as part of the 'army of pursuit', when the two forward divisions had secured their objectives. Under pressure from a changed situation, Morland preferred the certainty of sticking to the phased plan, rather than reacting to opportunity. By the time the extent of the Ulster penetration was realised, it was too late. 49th Division was delayed and dispersed by conflicting orders and unable to respond in time. Having achieved an epic advance, the Ulsters were going to be left to fend for themselves.

The biggest command divide lay between division and corps. If it was difficult for division headquarters to countenance failure, corps was not listening. The paucity of reliable information opened up the emotional gap, every bit as wide as the geographical distance. 'Today is a most important day,' VII Corps staff officer Major Charles Ward-Jackson wrote to his wife, 'I have to be up at the Château [Pas] on duty, transmitting messages from the front, altering maps and so on.' The experience 'was most thrilling', he recalled. 'I received all the messages from the different forces and took them round to the different officers so that I knew everything that happened.' Signaller Leonard Ounsworth, with a heavy artillery battery, remembered being addressed by an eccentric old officer, 'all spit and polish, parade and that sort of thing', back in England. 'You men fought with honour and glory in the field of battle in France and Flanders,' he announced, adopting a pseudo Napoleonic pose with a hand across his chest. 'Gad! How I wish I could have been with you.' Ounsworth and his companions were incredulous. 'We gaped open-mouthed at him, silly old devil.' Corps command was anonymous, and the hierarchical chain of authority did not encourage plain speaking.[11]

'I wonder if a corps commander eight miles behind the front line has any idea of what life is like in the front line?' asked Acting Captain Reginald Leetham, with the 2nd Battalion the Rifle Brigade. He was one of the lucky men whose attack was cancelled at the eleventh hour because of the fate of battalions that had preceded them. He watched three battalions 'being mowed down like grass' and was moved to write, 'They went into a greater hell and a worse valley of death than the gallant 600 the poem was written about.' He was bitter and appalled at what he saw. 'If we had heroes in previous wars, today we have them not in thousands but in half millions.' Corps commanders, generally intellectually gifted individuals, seemed as helpless as the men they were sending to their deaths. In the absence of reliable information, and like the junior officers caught by the totally unexpected in no man's land, they stuck to the plan.[12]

Lieutenant-General Hunter-Weston's VIII Corps headquarters occupied a very grand château at Marieux, about 11 miles from the front. It was a comfortable billet, where mail posted for London arrived the next day. VIII Corps reported to Rawlinson's Fourth Army headquarters after the bloody repulse of the first wave attacks at 7.46 am, and later at 8.07 that they were over the German line. The first setback was notified at 9 am, when it was reported that 29th Division was hung up in the German front trench, but 47 minutes later Rawlinson was assured that a fresh attack was being made in the same area and 'going well'. Late in the morning, at 11.19, Fourth Army was told the 4th Division had reached its second objective and 31st Division to its left was already consolidating east of Serre. Catastrophe was being reported as success.

There is a tendency within rigid hierarchical staff organisations for junior officers to be obsequious when dealing with their superiors. Plain speaking on the British General Staff was not a career enhancing characteristic. It is difficult to definitively prove from the surviving documentation that information was being filtered, but neither is it possible to offer rational explanations for the frequency and range of inaccurate or superfluous reports moving up the chain of command to Fourth Army. General Rawlinson was programmed to meet with Sir Douglas Haig, the C-in-C, after lunch. Was the Fourth Army staff guilty of preparing a wishful brief? Some 160 telegrams were to arrive during the course of the day from corps. Martin Middlebrook's analysis suggested, 'either the corps were reluctant to repeat the truth and were only sending back the more optimistic reports, or the staff officer responsible for keeping the Fourth Army's Diary was himself an incurable optimist'. What was happening was as emotional in its impact as it was physical, a very human response.[13]

At 8.46 am a report from III Corps stated, 'a wounded Captain from the 10th Lincolns reports: "Germans had had heavy casualties"'. It was further claimed the 'Lincolns have got over no man's land with very few casualties', when actually the Grimsby Chums Battalion lost nearly 500 men, with very few even reaching the German line at La Boisselle. XV Corps reported at 9 am, 'The 10th West Yorks are in the northern edge of Fricourt.' This was not true; nobody knew where they were at this moment except for a handful of survivors. Success was similarly misrepresented. Only at midday did Rawlinson learn that the 30th Division had succeeded along its entire line, capturing Montauban and consolidating. There had been a partial German collapse to the right of the line, with XIII Corps capturing virtually all its objectives and XV Corps, to its left, some.

That morning Sir Douglas Haig had attended a church service at Val Vion, his forward château headquarters set amid specially built huts at Beauquesne. After lunch he drove with his Chief of General Staff to confer with Rawlinson at his château at Querrieu. At 8 am, 30 minutes into the attack, the initial news had been good. 'By 9 am,' he wrote in his diary, 'I heard that our troops had in many places reached the one hour 20 minute line,' where he anticipated most units at that stage would be. On arrival at Querrieu, Haig received the same confusing and often contradictory information Rawlinson had been given. 'It is difficult to summarise all that was reported,' he recalled. Serre had been penetrated, then it had not; the Gommecourt attack was producing mixed results; 29th Division was held up. Haig was philosophical about the early reports of casualties. 'On a 16-mile front of attack varying fortune must be expected.' It was too early to call. Haig was a devout Christian, and sacrifice was part of his faith.

The meeting with Rawlinson was doubtless tense. This was the first major operation for both in their new appointments. They were presiding over the biggest British attack in history, with its largest army. Haig cultivated his remote image, which unsettled his subordinates, even more so because he was shy and not a good communicator. Feelings were vented in confidence through his diary. He was less than impressed with Hunter-Weston, the commander of VIII Corps, whom he branded along with 'the majority of officers' as 'amateurs in hard fighting'. He sniped in his diary, 'Some thought that they knew more than they did of this kind of warfare, because they had been at Gallipoli.' He considered the Germans far more formidable adversaries than the Turks. Haig cruelly commented on 'Hunter-Bunter's' calamitous performance. 'I am inclined to believe from further reports,' he wrote, 'that few of the VIII Corps left their trenches!' They lost 14,592 men that day and according to Haig 'achieved very little'. It was an unworthy indictment.[14]

Haig's hands-off style of leadership emphasised the need for responsibility and decision-making at lower level. Shyness and a lack of plain speaking fostered misunderstandings. Rawlinson likewise devolved too much to corps commanders. The army was not being fought as an army. Separate battles were indeed emerging along the 16-mile front with minimal intervention. The plan was starting to unravel and direction was needed.

Two decision points could be disentangled from the mass of contradictory information. Haig was informed 'our men are in the Schwaben Redoubt', almost certainly vital ground for the Germans and an entry point onto the tactically advantageous Thiepval plateau. Morland, the X Corps commander, had already decided not to exploit it, preferring to fragment his reserve supporting further fruitless frontal assaults against Thiepval village, when he had already turned the flank. Haig was also told 'we hold the Montauban–Mametz spur and village of those names'. This attracted his interest: a break-in if not a break-through. But he did not intervene; neither did the army commander Rawlinson. No discussion appeared to have ensued about vital ground or priorities.

When Congreve, the XIII Corps commander, telephoned through during the late afternoon for permission to carry on beyond his scheduled objectives, Rawlinson declined.

They were looking at open countryside seemingly devoid of German troops, with the French XX Corps prepared to advance further on their right. Congreve was told to consolidate. 'There is, is of course, no hope of getting the cavalry through today,' Rawlinson decided. By 3 pm they had received orders to turn around and retire.[15]

British patrols returning from Bernafay Wood reported it was empty apart from scattered German soldiers, who were taken prisoner. Haig ordered the 38th and 23rd Divisions in the GHQ Reserve to backfill the depleted Fourth Army reserve. XIII Corps had the 9th Division in reserve, but Rawlinson had planned that it should only be used for the next phase of the operation. It was late afternoon before the real significance of what had happened to the right of the line was appreciated. By the time Rawlinson received an accurate picture from the corps, there was nothing he could do.

Doing nothing was risk-free.

7.30 am to 5 pm

The Direct Order. German Headquarters

The German General Staff regarded confusion as a battlefield norm. Its task was to clarify, report facts and react. The German defensive battle at trench level was controlled and directed from battalion headquarters, generally in the third trench back from the front. Regimental headquarters controlled their three forward battalions from just behind. Brigade headquarters was often positioned at the front of the second main defensive line, about 1,500 to 2,000 metres from the front.

For the first hour, 52 Brigade headquarters, located at the *Feste Zollern* bunker east of Thiepval, was in difficulties. Shelled out by artillery the day before, it had had to pull back, in the middle of a major relief operation for 99 Regiment, to the western edge of Courcelette. The atmosphere in the alternative dugout was tense because Generalleutnant von Auwärter the brigade commander had no idea what was happening forward. Information came from runners and the steady stream of wounded. After the final bombardment, successive waves of noise from rifle and machine-gun fire indicted a major attack was under way. It was impossible to distinguish one explosion from another forward. All communications were severed, telephone lines were cut and only a few deep cables had remained intact. Few if any runners actually made it back. 'It is awful when shell splinters penetrate soft tissue body parts with such violence,' recalled German soldier Karl Bainier:

> Our two runners had received nothing less than a direct hit, one full in the chest, the other came apart at the trunk. The one hit in the trunk was instantly killed, the other still screaming. My Feldwebel [Sergeant] said, 'I'll fetch the medic.' It was already too late.[16]

Generalmajor von Soden's 26th Division was attacked by two and a half British corps that morning. Defence is less difficult than attack, and the veteran 26th Reserve Infantry Division had already fought through the massive mobile frontier battles in 1914. Little attention was therefore paid to the inevitably exaggerated reports from the wounded making their way to the rear. It was accepted they would paint a gloomy picture of events. 'To base decisions on these statements,' explained Leutnant Matthäus Gerster, with 52 Brigade, 'would have been to fly in the face of experience about the psychological state of the wounded in general.' The first clear message to arrive at 52 Brigade headquarters was at 8.35 am, a terse message from the 26th Division from its rear château headquarters at Biefvillers. 'It appears the British have penetrated the Schwaben Redoubt.'[17]

Various regimental battle logs chart the methodical destruction of the British infantry attacks to the north of the Albert–Bapaume road. 'Rifle and machine-gun fire can be heard,' reported 99 Regiment at 7.39 am, prompting them to fire three red signal flares to bring down defensive artillery fire. The 36th Ulster Division break-in is described through clipped messages, coming from forward battalions and passed back via regiment to brigade. Observation reports from flanking units soon indicated a large attack was under way. At 7.39 am, 99 Regiment headquarters reported, 'Trench fighting is being observed in the second and third trenches of Thiepval South.' A whole series of reports at 8.17, 8.19, 8.41 and 8.42 are concerned with repeated calls for support and assistance. By 10.55 am, 99 Regiment was reporting, 'The enemy is attacking in dense masses throughout the entire front.' Most telephone lines were down, so the reports were being brought by runners.[18]

Common to all these tersely written situation reports was that whatever the crisis level, accurate factual data was being passed horizontally and vertically along the chain of command. They are in contrast to sketchy and haphazard British reporting at the same level. However, communication in defence is easier and more reliable than in attack. Headquarters are physically more accessible, whereas they are left behind once troops go over the top. Not only was the German information prolific, the chain of command was trained and prepared to act decisively upon it.

The 119th Regiment, north of the River Ancre, was able to report it was bringing in artillery within six minutes 'that lay very well' on the first three infantry waves, inflicting 'extreme, bloody losses' that reduced 'the enemy to confusion, soon making them crawl back'. By 10 am the situation here in 'Beaumont North' was restored; all the momentarily occupied trenches were taken back. At one o'clock 'it was quiet'. The quality of cool veteran reporting along the German line enabled commanders to make rapid appreciations, establish priorities, take timely decisions and act.

Von Soden's 26th Division headquarters at Biefvillers was small and well informed by the forward brigade and regimental headquarters, to which he delegated sufficient flexibility to exercise initiative. Infantry division headquarters were subdivided within four sections with 11 staff officers in all. The Ia General Staff officer handled operations, assisted by his Ordinanze G3 Officer; the rest of the staff dealt with personnel, intelligence and logistics. Most officers, unlike the newly formed British Fourth Army, were used to working with each other and had done so probably even before mobilisation in 1914.

Within 50 minutes of the attack, von Soden heard from 119 Regiment that the Schwaben Redoubt had been taken and the Thiepval plateau penetrated. Both the division and corps defensive *Schwerpunkt* at this sector of the front had fallen. Von Soden now had the unenviable task of letting his superior, Generalleutnant von Stein at XIV Corps, know that already 60 minutes into the attack he had lost his vital ground. He sent his orderly officer Rittmeister Jobst to Beugny to orientate the corps commander and request reinforcements from the reserve. His unsympathetic corps commander left him in no doubt that he was to restore the situation with the forces at his disposal. He was on his own.[19]

Ten minutes after 52 Brigade headquarters heard the Schwaben Redoubt had fallen, it received a second message from division HQ at 9.45 am:

The Division Commander has ordered that the Feste Schwaben [Schwaben Redoubt] is to be recaptured at all costs. To this end the arrival of the 2nd Battalion Bavarian Reserve Infantry Regiment [ordered earlier towards the front, once the British attack had started] is not to be awaited. Instead the attack is to be launched immediately using forces drawn from the second defensive position.[20]

Von Soden was acting decisively with a veteran's eye for what was likely achievable. Unlike the British division commanders, he was not being closely monitored by corps. This was the rudimentary form of the later more refined *Auftragstaktik,* or mission orientated tactics, with which the German General Staff were schooled and familiar. It was about commanders setting a mission, with sufficient resources to achieve it. *How* the mission was executed was up to the commander; a far cry from the permissions that had to be sought, on the other side of the wire, for any deviation from the set plan. Von Soden appreciated that if the British were allowed time to reorganise on the Schwaben, and just short of his artillery line, the cost of recapturing it later would be even more bloody. This had to be balanced by the fact that an over-hasty or insufficiently prepared counter-attack might well fail.

Despite the frictions encountered on the ground, intermittent telephone communications, and a developing crisis with forward regiments calling for urgent support, the staffing mechanism functioned. Generalleutnant von Auwärter, commanding 52 Brigade, formed three counter-attack groups from Bavarian Regiment 8, located or working near the second German defensive line to his rear. They would direct three converging attacks against the Ulster penetration, coming from the northeast, east and southeast. Major

Prager led Gruppe 1, the first group, which received its orders at 9.50 am. He was on the right flank with four infantry companies, two machine-gun companies and additional sniper groups. Gruppe 2 under Major Beyerköhler received the word five minutes later. He had three companies and would attack from the Stuff Redoubt (*Feste Staufen*), north of 52 Brigade's old headquarters, shelled out the day before. Gruppe 3 under Major Roesch had the 2nd Battalion from Infantry Regiment 8, and received its order at 10.02 am. It had taken roughly an hour, from the receipt of the message that the Schwaben had fallen, to organise a three-pronged regimental size counter-attack to take it back. Von Auwärter also appointed Oberstleutnant von Bram to form a headquarters group to co-ordinate the three attack groups, none of whom were in contact with each other. He received the order to move by car at 10.25 to liaise personally with the brigade commander, who briefed him at 11.15 am.

The staff process was quickly accomplished. The actual conduct of the counter-attack now became subject to what the military philosopher Clausewitz termed the 'Friction of War': how to make this neat tactical solution work amid the chaos of events, changing by the hour, at the front. All that von Soden could do now at the Biefvillers château, and von Auwärter at Courcelette, was wait by the telephone. Leutnant Matthäus Gerster described the tension:

> *Brigade sat helplessly in the midst of nerve-wracking, feverish tension for the start of the counter-attacks. Nothing happened. Division and corps pressed and demanded situation reports. In vain: midday came, Thiepval Wood disgorged new masses against Hill 141 and the village. Ammunition, especially hand grenades, began to run low. Reserve Infantry Regiment 99 sent appeal after appeal for help.*

The 36th Ulster Division penetration was a blade stuck in the vitals of the German XIV Corps defence on the Thiepval plateau. Its fall would compromise the whole sector of the German first line, which had so spectacularly repelled the British attacks to its left and right. For now, all division could do was ensure that the gap torn in its defences was at least sealed off with artillery fire. 'Black smoke clouds rose from the tangled trunks and branches' of Thiepval Wood, now furiously burning 'as the divisional artillery brought down concentrated fire,' recalled Gerster, 'which decimated the massed enemy assault troops.' There was nothing more to be done, except hold the shoulders of the breach until it could be sealed by the gathering counter-attack. 'The situation was very serious,' Gerster remembered.[21]

The soldiers in the three counter-attack groups from Bavarian Regiment 8, steadily plodding forward through a wasteland of levelled communication trenches, were exhausted even before the start. They had been marching considerable distances to work at nights on the second and third line positions since arriving at Bapaume two weeks before. Latrine rumours since February had suggested they were heading for the maelstrom of Verdun, so they felt themselves lucky when they arrived at the Somme, a quiet area. But within a week of arrival they were working under constant artillery fire. Frequent accommodation changes had resulted in their being kept in the open in bivouacs under canvas, as villages were menaced by artillery fire. They were tired of constant digging in wet chalk under the rain. Clothes could not be dried under canvas, neither were there washing facilities. Seven men had been killed and three wounded simply labouring in the support trenches. The 4th Company had already been overwhelmed in the Schwaben Redoubt. Battalion and company commanders had been up all night conducting recces for the 99th Regiment relief in line due the following night and had barely returned to the rear before the final British bombardment was upon them. The II Battalion had been on stand-by since 4.30 am and was moved forward by von Soden 20 minutes after the British attacks had begun. Key commanders had been denied sleep for 36 hours.[22]

One of those company commanders was Hauptmann Herbert von Wurmb. At 4 am that morning he had been speaking with his friend Hauptmann Schorer, who was commanding the 4th Company and, unknown to von Wurmb, had since been killed in the Schwaben Redoubt. Von Wurmb's 3rd Company was due to take over the very sector the Ulsters had stormed through that morning. Schorer had advised not to go forward and look because there was insufficient time. Once it was light 'the English pilots could even pick out a mouse crawling around'. Von Wurmb had chosen to set off anyway, with other commanders, and found that the communication trenches to the rear of the Schwaben were so badly battered that he elected to move back in the open on his return. He got back exhausted, just as the British artillery barrage intensified at 7 am. Now, advancing again, he knew his sector of the front had been lost and Schorer in all probability was dead. Von Wurmb's 3rd Company was laboriously wending its way forward with Major Beyerköhler's Gruppe 2.

Von Wurmb recalled the confusion and delays that impeded the start of the three-pronged counter-attack. First of all they heard a report that a German attack was already going in against Authuille, the base of the British penetration, but this proved to be a 'false report, always the case in a tense situation'. It was German prisoners being pushed back across towards the British line. Artillery support could not be guaranteed, because the conflicting reports and the inability of any of the three counter-attacking groups to speak with each other meant an H-Hour time could not yet be fixed. Accurate reporting was proving a problem. 'Just imagine the impact of thousand upon thousand shell bursts on the wasted landscape ... the difficulty of being able to accurately observe from any number of trenches,' von Wurmb pointed out. 'How do you get a clear picture of the situation,' he asked, 'when nobody wanted to lose half his head waving it above the parapet?'

It took four hours for Gruppe 1, the right flank counterattack group under Prager, to even receive the attack order. A bogus report stating the redoubt had already been retaken caused much of the delay. All forward movement and preparations for the attack were conducted under heavy artillery fire and constant strafing runs by British aircraft. Newly laid telephone wires were cut and many runners did not make it through. The 8th Company Bavarian Regiment 8 lost all contact during the advance and drifted right, ending up in 51 Brigade's area, where it was dispatched alongside 40 engineers to reinforce St Pierre Divion, on the northern shoulder of the Ulster break-in. Oberstleutnant von Bram, the attack co-ordinator, arrived in the midst of all this confusion at 1 pm and established his headquarters at Stuff Redoubt, on the steps of a dugout overflowing with wounded.

It was two and a half hours since von Soden ordered this vital counter-attack. Von Bram was able to personally confer with Hauptmann Graf Preysing from Artillery Regiment 26, to co-ordinate fire support from 'Berta'. Preysing had burned all his security documents having spotted the advancing Irish at the very forward edge of the artillery positions. Major Beyerköhler also arrived and was directly briefed by Bram. Regiment 99 was visibly teetering forward under the impact of fresh British attacks while, unknown to von Bram, Gruppe Prager to their right had already started the attack.

Von Wurmb's company marching in single file was worn out 'moving through unbelievable mud' of the second position trench network. The day was heating up, and in the absence of direct orders from Beyerköhler, he began to shake out his company into assault formation. They were distracted by 'the enemy, strafing us heavily from observation aircraft'. At 2.45 he saw several infantry sections 'probably from the 2nd Recruit Company with Regiment 180' and they were 'closing with fixed bayonets against the English!' That was enough for him, 'a sign that we should be off'. After 'a last hand shake with Engelhardt', his lead platoon commander, the three platoons moved into the attack in echelon order, one after the other. 'A few words of encouragement', von Wurmb remembered, 'then forward against the enemy, to the death!'[23]

The attack was not the decisive trident thrust envisaged by the staff solution to von Soden's urgent attack directive. Rather the attack was gradually trickling forward. Oberstleutnant von Bram, co-ordinating the assault, sensed that with the Gruppe Prager obviously under way to his right and no sign of Roesch's Gruppe 3, he must press on. A swift counter-attack with the force available probably stood more chance of success than a later H-Hour with all three earmarked groups. So at 3 pm Bram instructed Beyerköhler to proceed. This was *Auftragstaktik* in action. Bram was reading von Soden's intention, even now on its way to him by runner. Junior commanders were already exercising initiative and were in the attack.

Generalmajor von Soden had been waiting anxiously by his telephone in the château at Biefvillers since ordering the recapture of the Schwaben Redoubt at 9.45 am. The group set up with preliminary orders within an hour had taken nearly five hours to get its units somewhere near its start line, and only about two thirds of it was going into the attack in a co-ordinated fashion. The 60-year-old veteran commander was taking a calculated risk, like a free climber swinging from three to two pressure points to gain greater egress on a sheer rock face. He was denuding his second line to restore the situation in his first. Von Soden was aware by now of the growing crisis on his left flank with the 28th Division and in particular that of the 12th Division bordering the River Somme, attacked by both the French and British. He knew he would attract no more reserves from corps.

Generalleutnant von Stein, the XIV Corps commander, could also see the risk. XVII Corps under Generalleutnant Pannewitz to his left was under pressure from the French. The French XX Corps had made spectacular progress on the Allied front, in parallel to the achievements of Congreve's XIII Corps at Montauban and the 7th Division at Mametz. The French had attacked south of the Somme at 9.30 am, completely surprising the Germans, and the Sixth Army was to take 4,000 prisoners. As serious as the French advance was, it would be constrained by the course of the marshy Somme and then blocked by its change of direction at Péronne. This would buy time to bring forward German reserves. There was not the luxury of time to deal with the threatening development in the centre of von Stein's line at Thiepval north of the Somme. It could unhinge the very cohesion of the first line in this sector.

Von Stein later recalled the pressure to the left of his line beginning on 1 July. 'Here I experienced,' he admitted, 'difficult decisions and the meaning of venturing into the unknown':

In order to block a breakthrough on the left wing, I had to take battalion after battalion from the right wing, that had just defeated the attack. They had to be taken out, put on lorries and thrown against the left wing.

His oldest General Staff officer Major von Löwenfeld pointed out, after the final available battalion was ordered out, 'Excellency, that is the last one!'

'Never forget this moment in your entire life,' von Stein responded. 'One has to find the right decision and commit the last, because the enemy can also be at the end of his tether.' Prevarication was not an option in a crisis.[24]

On the right flank, the 2nd Recruit Company with the Gruppe Prager attacked the furthest point of the 36th Ulster Division penetration, where it had reached the abandoned gun positions in the Grandcourt artillery hollow. The two-wave infantry assault got into the Hanseatic position, but at the cost of 23 men killed and 100 wounded. Sixty per cent of the unit was gone. Many of the Ulstermen streaming back to the Schwaben Redoubt were caught in the open and eliminated.

To their left the Gruppe Beyerköhler fought its way along the Staufen Trench, approaching the redoubt from the north-east. Both the 11th and 12th Company commanders were soon down and English hand grenades had to be substituted for German when they ran out. By the time von Wurmb's 3rd Company reached the junction of the Lachweg and Staufen trenches casualties were mounting as they came under fire from three machine-guns from three sides. At 4 pm Major Beyerköhler commanding Gruppe 2, the main impetus for the attacks, was struck down.

Beyerköhler had been with von Wurmb during the exhausting night-time reconnaissance of the Schwaben, for the intended relief in place. 'When the war is over,' he confided to him, 'I am going to take my pension. You young men must carry on the work.' A prophetic statement; he was surprised by a British soldier alongside his staff in the Staufen Trench, and shot dead after calling for a rifle to deal with him. 'That man was a second quicker than he,' von Wurmb recalled. It was a considerable blow to the impetus of the attack. 'I took over command of the assaulting group,' von Wurmb remembered. Then 'my faithful servant Adam Kneibert from Sippersfeld near Kaiserslautern was hit in the chest by a British bullet not half a pace behind me'. The attack was petering out with heavy casualties. Kneibert was picked up and taken away, 'his breath coming in gasps'.[25]

Majorgeneral von Soden telephoned von Auwärter at 52 Brigade headquarters at 3.35 pm to personally repeat and labour the same command given over six hours before. He insisted von Auwärter dispatch two patrols to Oberstleutnant von Bram at the Stuff Redoubt with a personal written order. It was totally uncompromising:

> *The Division expects and expressly orders Bavarian Reserve Regiment 8 to recapture the entirety of the Schwaben Redoubt, to occupy it and bring relief to the hard pressed parts of Infantry Regiment 99.*

There were to be no excuses. 'This is a direct order.'[26]

CHAPTER 9

The Lull —•

Midday to 9.30 pm

Midday to 9 pm

The Sun over No Man's Land

'Now the sun began to get up, and I was parched with thirst,' remembered Tommy Higgins, still snagged on the wire facing Gommecourt Wood. He no longer had his water bottle, 'knocked off somehow going over'. His situation, enmeshed in the wire in front of the German positions, like a trapped fly on a web, seemed to indicate his days were numbered. 'I mentally said goodbye to those I loved, as I did not seem to have the ghost of a chance of living through that day.'

A lull had descended along much of the Somme front, apart from brief flickering periods of violence between midday and 2.30 pm. The sun blazed down from a cloudless sky with hardly a whisper of wind. An occasional Royal Flying Corps aircraft wheeled overhead looking for signs of life, like vultures, adding to the desolation of the scene. The occasional crack of rifle fire rang out. German soldiers, furious at being sniped at by wounded British in no man's land, were trying to finish them off. A body that moved or involuntarily twitched attracted attention, followed by another crack, and he never moved again. 'From my shell hole I could see a dead man propped up against the German wire in a sitting position,' recalled Lieutenant Robert Heptonstall, with the 13th Yorks and Lancs at Serre. 'He was sniped at during the day until his head was completely shot away.' Buzzing flies were already beginning to cluster over bodies starting to swell in the hot sun.

'I thought at the time I should never get the peculiar smell of the vapour of warm human blood heated by the sun out of my nostrils,' remembered Captain Reginald Leetham, with the 2nd Rifle Brigade. 'I would rather have smelt gas a hundred times. I can never describe that faint sickening horrible smell which several times almost knocked me up altogether.'

Tommy Higgins, overcome by exhaustion and the heat, concurred. 'The smell of blood and dead bodies was sickening.' He dared not move and the sticky heat sent him off to sleep until late afternoon, when he was jerked awake by a sudden artillery bombardment:

> I glanced behind me as the ground seemed to shake under me. Oh God what a sight I saw. I'm sure my hair stood straight. The ground seemed a mass of fire. Shells were dropping in hundreds and seemed to be leaping towards where I lay. I now gave up all hopes of life and hoped for a quick death. With my teeth tightly clenched I awaited the worst.[1]

The line of fire abruptly lifted, passed over 'and was pounding on Fritz's line'. Higgins was lucky. 'I heard after they kidded him up we were going to attack here again.' Fortunately for him, they did not, 'instead they went over at Hébuterne on our right'. Higgins meanwhile hung on the wire, which stuck in his clothes and flesh.

Sergeant Richard Tawney, with the 22nd Manchesters, had fallen in front of Mametz and was still lying in the heat of the early afternoon sun, waiting and waiting. 'It was very hot,' he remembered, and acid drop sweets issued with his rations simply made him feel sick. He had no water. 'How

I longed for the evening!' he recalled. Lacking a watch, 'I tried to tell the time by the sun,' squinting from beneath his helmet.

> *It stood straight overhead in an enormous arch of blue. After an age I looked again. It stood in the same place, as though performing a miracle to plague me.*

He began to feebly call for stretcher-bearers, but none came. Calling was 'imbecile and cowardly', he admitted, 'it was asking them to commit suicide'. His situation was bleak and he had despaired. 'I'd lost my self respect … I hoped I should faint, but couldn't.'[2]

General Morland's hesitation to commit the 49th (West Riding) X Corps reserve to back up the Ulster Division penetration on the Thiepval plateau placed the reserve in a desperate position. By 9 am elements were crossing the marshy Ancre valley, having left the shelter of Aveluy Wood. 'We crossed the river on a very rickety bridge,' remembered Private JG Dooley, with the 1/6th West Yorks:

> *German prisoners were wading through the water, holding onto the sides of the bridge. Some of our fellows were hitting them on the hands and head, knocking them back into the water. I was horrified at the sights – dead men floating in the water, and wounded shouting for help.*

There appeared little urgency to support the 36th Division break-in. They stayed in the shelter of Thiepval Wood, loitering in the Ulster Division departure trenches until the middle of the afternoon.

Morland continued his fruitless frontal assaults against Thiepval village, 'masked with a wall of corpses' according to

Lieutenant-Colonel Frank Crozier, with the 9th Royal Irish. There seemed little point. Private ET Radband remembered escorting an officer to a hastily arranged conference 'where the brigadier (I think) told them we had to be at the row of apple trees in Thiepval Village at 4 o'clock'. When their colonel pointed out this was not practical in the time, the answer was 'Those are the orders'.

The moment the Yorkshire battalions emerged from the cover of the wood, they were lashed by the same German machine-guns in Thiepval that had impeded the passage of reinforcements all day. 'We went forward in single file, through a gap in what had once been a hedge,' remembered Private J Wilson, with the 1/6th West Yorks. 'Only one man could get through at a time':

> *The Germans had a machine-gun trained on the gap and when it came to my turn I paused. The machine-gun stopped and, thinking his belt had run out, or had jammed, I moved through, but what I saw when I got to the other side shook me to pieces. There was a trench running parallel to the hedge, which was full to the top with the men who had gone before me. They were all either dead or dying.[3]*

Clearly, whatever the command decisions, nobody could cross no man's land and the West Yorks were told to stop trying. The Ulsters would have to hang on until dark.

Wagon driver Otto Maute, with the German 180 Regiment on the Bapaume road, remembered, 'During the lull it was absolutely quiet, only the ammunition columns were driving like the possessed.' The ammunition was picked up in Bapaume and went forward, 'hauling everything with our nags from midday'. The wounded came back on the return journey. 'I had to drive like never before,' he wrote to his mother, 'the English shot over our heads, even as far as Bapaume.' It was hazardous:

> *We had a number of heavy strikes, which sent fist size pieces flying over from explosions from about two to three metres off the road. What would a direct hit from these 30 cm naval guns be like?*

The wagons were driven right up onto the positions where the infantry came back to unload the ammunition. 'The wounded say that our own regiment also had heavy casualties, but the majority were with the 99th, 50 per cent they say.' Maute told his mother that the enemy had broken through the 99th Regiment and came right up to their artillery positions.[4]

South of the Gommecourt park and village, the 56th London Division was pinned down inside the three German trench lines they had stormed. Lieutenant Richard Cary, enduring bombing and shelling, may well have dwelled at some stage on his pending engagement to Doris Mummery of Leytonstone, a thousand miles away now. 'If we could have only got bombs over to them,' recalled his commanding officer Lieutenant-Colonel VWF Dickins, 'I think they might have managed to hold on until dark … I made the reserve company "D" try and get parties across, they made three attempts, but each time all who started became casualties.' Sixty of them set out and three came back. The Londoners were under pressure from equally audacious German attacks, running through British shell fire across the top of the trenches to throw their bombs down. Trench mortars were now directly shelling the beleaguered men.

Major Cedric Dickens, with the 13th (Kensingtons) Battalion right of Cary, sent back a number of desperate messages during the early afternoon, charting their demise:

'1.10 pm.   Shelling fearful. Mackenzie killed. Trench practi-
            cally untenable, full of dead and wounded. Very
            few men indeed left ...'

1.48 pm.   Sap absolutely impassable owing to shell fire.
            Every party that enters it knocked out at once ...
            Our front line in an awful state ...'

2.40 pm.   I have as far as I can find only 13 men left besides
            myself. Trenches unrecognisable. Quite impossi-
            ble to hold. Bombardment fearful for two hours.'

'I am the only officer left,' he appealed, 'please send
instructions.'⁵

Richard Cary's friend Lieutenant W Goodinge wrote later
to his brother Jack that 'after taking the third Hun trench
we had no more ammunition and were bombed out'. Then
'together we were climbing out of the trench when he was
hit by a machine-gun bullet'. After the burst 'he said, "I am
done for, Goody. Goodbye"'. Goodinge wrote sparingly and
poignantly about what must have been a grim and traumatic
experience. 'I held his hand for some time, but he did not
speak nor move again.' Cary had been an inspirational platoon commander, encouraging his men 'in the face of awful
firing' during the attack. He died 'instantly and painlessly'
according to his companion, in a muddy trench amid a hideous cacophony of cracking machine-gun bullets, shell fire,
and the ominous approaching crumps of German hand grenades. 'Goody' was pinned down next to the dead Cary for
a further four hours, during which time his back was laced
with 'so much shrapnel' according to his father's correspondence, that 'he never imagined that he would get away alive'.
Neither was it possible to extract all the splinters when he
got back. 'My son is better,' he wrote, 'but I fear he will suffer for some time.' Goodinge was too injured to write; the

letter to Jack Cary was likely written by his wife Mary or his mother.

Throughout the remainder of the day and into evening the German counter-attacks bombed out the Londoners, back to the second line and then the first. 'From want of support on both flanks, and the supply of bombs etc. giving out, they were obliged to withdraw slowly,' Lieutenant-Colonel Dickins explained, 'holding each line as long as possible.' Signaller William Smith, attached to the Londons, remembered coming across a very young 12th Battalion private, whose arm was hanging limp, 'I should think broken in two or three places'. He was cut and bleeding about the face 'and was altogether in a sorry plight'. 'Is there a dressing station down there, mate?' the private asked, pointing the way Smith had come. Smith gave him directions and offered to bring back a stretcher-bearer. 'Oh, I don't want him for *me*,' he insisted, 'I want someone to come back with me to get my mate. *He's hurt!*'[6]

The regimental aid post was the first point at which rudimentary aid was given along the medical evacuation chain. It was the same for the Germans. 'My first-aid post was in a hollow dell,' explained German surgeon Stephan Westman, south of Beaumont Hamel, 'and the sappers had taken the precaution to provide it with two exits.' This was a factor of experience. 'One of these received a direct hit, but we had the other left and got busy clearing the first one – you never know!' Regimental aid posts were often located in the reserve trench or in an abandoned building or bunker. Not much could be done there, as Westman explained:

> *The medical officer in the trenches, or even at his advanced first aid post, could hardly do more than put, as often as not, improvised splints on fractured limbs and place field dressings over the wounds.*

German stretcher-bearers were not specifically medically trained. Westman described them as 'simple folk – dock workers, peasants or wood cutters, who often knew little more than the rudiments of first aid'. They were ordinary unarmed infantrymen carrying field dressings in their ammunition pouches. 'They had rarely volunteered for this kind of work; they were just prepared to do it, and so they were not filled with the innate urge to help others as doctors are, or should be.' Even so:

> *Often I saw stretcher-bearers, perspiring and exhausted, after having delivered their load, go out again, through the artillery barrage, to a place where they knew that more wounded were lying and waiting to be picked up, and frequently enemy soldiers were among those they brought back.*

Veteran German soldier Alfons Beil viewed the whole process in brutally pragmatic terms. 'We were not allowed to tackle the English prisoners' who were brought in injured. 'It was up to the medics to get the wounded, sick and the English out of the way.' Around the hotly contested Heidenkopf Redoubt, north of Beaumont Hamel, the Germans ignored British truce overtures to recover their wounded. This was the 51 Reserve Brigade area, and their front had not been penetrated; the few metres lost were fought back within hours. The German defenders felt vulnerable here, and regarded waving white handkerchiefs as suspicious. Not unlike Alfons Beil's attitude. 'If we had time, at the most we were allowed to bandage up [the English], but not using our field dressings, we had to take stuff from theirs.'[7]

The dilemma regarding the vulnerable British wounded, marooned in no man's land and exposed to the hot sun, was how to get them back for treatment. There was nothing the

British medics could do after the first failed attacks except look at them. Many of the wounded had fallen so far out that any attempt to reach them with stretcher-bearers would be suicide. There were some brave individual attempts. Cinematographer Geoffrey Malins had remained in the vicinity of White City after filming the awesome explosion of the Hawthorne mine that morning, and continued to film in the Marlborough Trench. 'Scenes crowded in upon me,' he recalled, 'wounded and more wounded; men who a few hours before had leaped over the parapet full of life and vigour, were now dribbling back.' Many of them were 'shattered and broken for life'. One young lad cheerfully announced, gesticulating from his stretcher: 'I shan't be able to play footer any more, look!' Malins saw from the rough bandage at the end of his leg 'that his foot had been taken completely off'. He was moved by their questions: 'Was I in the picture, sir?' The film would be shown across the country in about six weeks' time. Malins said 'Yes' to them all, 'which pleased them immensely'.

Geoffrey Malins like everyone else was acutely aware of the wounded lying out in the open. 'They were calling for assistance' but it was dangerous to help. A number of medics had already been cut down trying to approach them. 'The cries of one poor fellow' eventually attracted so much attention that a trench mortar man went out with a volunteer to bring him in. They threaded their way through the barbed wire, one dressed in a cardigan, the other in his shirtsleeves and braces. Malins watched, his camera ready: 'Nearer and nearer they crept. We stood watching with bated breath. Would they reach him? Yes. At last!'

The man's wounds were hastily bound up, they picked him up together and made a run for the parapet under machine-gun fire. Malins filmed the episode from start to finish. The rescue was to involve five men and lasted 30 seconds on the subsequent edited film *The Battle of the Somme*. In no man's land the exhausted soldier wearing a cardigan is seen to transfer the casualty from his back to that of Private George Raine, a tunneller with the Durham Light Infantry, in his shirtsleeves. They managed to reach the Marlborough Trench near the old Beaumont road, and came towards Malins, who filmed them passing by in the crowded trench, heading for the Tenderloin dressing station. Malins captured the iconic image of the clearly fatigued Raine glancing coldly upward at the camera, with the slumped casualty flopped across his shoulder. This scene, repeated in countless Great War film portrayals since, documented the hopeless pity of it all. 'They passed me in the trench,' Malins remembered, 'a mass of perspiration':

Upon the back of one was the unconscious man he had rescued, but 20 minutes after these two had gone through hell to rescue him, the poor fellow died.[8]

Malins was still there late morning when the Royal Fusiliers and Middlesex soldiers abandoned the fight for the smoky Hawthorne crater and fled for home. On film, clearly taken at trench level with sandbags and wire in the foreground, a dozen or so figures can be seen scurrying back in the middle distance. George Ashurst, pinned down in front of the German wire nearby, saw the figures break cover. 'Suddenly I noticed a few of them running for their lives back to their front line.' It was the spark to act. 'This made me think that Fritz was counter-attacking and I fully expected to hear him coming at the double for my shell hole.' He 'dashed madly' for the sunken road and threw himself into it 'as Fritz's bullets whistled all about me'. He was back and alive. His officer was very glad to see the return of an NCO and put him in charge of defending the bottom of the road. They all seemed to be in a state of shock. 'I recognised some of the boys lying there awfully quiet and still,' he recalled.

In a climate of confusion the 29th Division attacks were called off in this sector at 1.45 pm; the 4th Division to its left likewise 70 minutes later. Intermittent outbursts of gunfire ruled out recovering any wounded from the sun-drenched no man's land. They were left to their own devices. 'The wounded came creeping in,' recalled Harry Hall, with the 13th Yorks and Lancs further north. 'The least opportunity they had when they'd recovered their senses, they came creeping back.'[9]

The apparent calm in front of Fricourt was broken at 2.33 pm when, in blazing sunlight and with hardly any artillery preparation, trench whistles signalled another Green Howards assault over the top. The 21st Division committed the 50th Brigade to its pre-planned frontal attack, programmed to go in after the salient had been pinched off at either side. But it had not been. The 7th Green Howards had already lost a company that had mistakenly attacked in isolation that morning. The commanding officer withheld details of the afternoon attack until the last minute, to prevent a similar error. Private AW Askew remembered their officer had promised them a tot of rum before H-Hour. This expectation was dashed when in all the confusion of timings at 2.30 pm 'a runner came along shouting "Zero. Over the top!" "What about our rum issue, sir?" was the immediate response, but their officer said, "No time for that now, I'm taking it with me. We'll drink our health in Jerry's front line."' Very few got even beyond the trench. 'Some of us got out, some of us didn't,' recalled Askew, 'we were falling like ninepins.' The attack was shot to pieces.

Lieutenant Phillip Howe had barely survived 21st Division's early morning H-Hour attack seven hours before. Only a few of his men had got back to the British lines. He was a personal friend of the CO of the 7th East Yorks, who was committed to this fresh attack and invited Howe to join them. Much against Howe's better judgement and with considerable foreboding, he went over the top again. Before they had gone 20 yards a sustained machine-gun burst traversed along the thin line of his men, shooting through Howe's rifle sling at both ends and grazing his face. Within three minutes the East Yorks lost 123 men killed or wounded, another debacle. Back in the trenches the disappointed Green Howards CO invited Howe and his even fewer men to join them for yet another attack. Howe was absolutely appalled. Surely he could not be expected to face this murderous fire three times in one day? He showed the CO his wounded hand and, with his gashed cheek demonstrating proven resolve, pointed to the exhausted state of his men. They were excused. Two attacks by both battalions had cost 400 men and achieved little more than a momentary distraction along this sector of front.[10]

Unteroffizier Otto Lais, with the 2nd Machine Company Regiment 169 at Serre, looked out at the British 'hanging, fatally wounded, whimpering draped over the remnants of the barbed wire entanglements'. He picked out some survivors sheltering in the slight dead ground beyond the wire shooting 'at us as if possessed, without taking much aim'. Ever the consummate professional, he redirected bursts of fire into the tangled mass of metal stakes and wire, counting on unpredictable ricochets to silence them. The British momentum was spent. 'New waves appear over there; they half emerge above their cover,' he recalled, 'and then sink down again behind the parapets.' Officers were directly exposing themselves on the opposing parapets, exhorting their men to advance. 'Numerous flat helmets appear again,' he observed, 'only to disappear again immediately.' The opposing parapet was being flayed by a crossfire of several intersecting German machine-guns. 'English officers no longer leave the trenches', they appeared shocked into inactivity, and 'the view across the attack terrain took their breaths away.' There would be no more attacks, nothing could move in no man's land.[11]

Somewhere ahead of him was a disorientated and pinned-down Private Frank Lindley with the 14th Yorks and Lancs. 'I didn't know anybody in the shell holes I got into,' he remembered. 'We were all mixed up. There was no conversation, it was self-preservation; dive in and risk what you got.'

He was crammed into a hole with three others when a 'whizz bang' came over 'that put paid to the lot'. The shrapnel burst 'came over us and split' with a resounding crack – 'I never heard it coming.'

> *A piece of shell went right through my thigh and took all my trousers in with it. I looked down and I had no trousers and there was blood all running out and the piece of shell stuck in my thigh.*

Lindley knew there would be no help – 'the orders were: no coming back' – and he had passed wounded on the way. Once he regained his composure he knew he needed treatment. He began to roll along the ground towards the British trenches. This was the start of an odyssey all the wounded went through on entering the casualty chain. The Regimental Aid Post would be in the reserve line some way back and there were no stretcher-bearers. If Lindley was in any dilemma what to do, he was spurred on when a shrapnel burst took down one of his companions nearby, 'and a piece of the hot shell burnt a little hole in my leg'. He set off pulling himself along the ground towards the rear.

All the wounded, who were able, had to do it, 'dragging at the side of the trenches' and 'sliding over different people that had been done in the other trenches'. Lindley was traversing the follow-on waves that had been hit by German artillery. 'There were no reserves left,' he recalled, 'they were in pulp':

> *One bloke must have been climbing out of the trench and it had done him across the middle. It left his feet and bottom half in the trench and all his insides were hanging down the side of the trench. I remember thinking, 'So that's what a liver and kidney look like.'*

Once past the dugout where he had seen the 'heads and tails', he found 'the Boss', his company commander. He and the sergeant-major were 'marching up and down outside this dugout, with white faces, looking over towards the front'. If they had asked him, 'How are things going over there?' he would have responded, 'Bloody well go and find out for yourself,' but they didn't.

Charley Swales in Lindley's unit remembered, 'We couldn't see any officers to co-ordinate us into any kind of order, so we just dropped into a trench and that was it.' A sergeant rounded up a few of them. 'I think they were talking about making another attack but they hadn't enough men,' much to their relief. 'If we had tried to make another attack, that would have been it.' By late morning it was all over at Serre.[12]

Frank Lindley was one of the lucky ones; he reached the start of the chain, 'a bit of an aid post' where 'there was a bloke patching you up':

He had a go at me and gave me a shot of tetanus and then they picked us up and slotted us in a little ambulance feet first, on little shelves, and away we went.

He would be transported to the next leg in the medical chain, an Advanced Dressing Station. His wound would be inspected and he would likely be given a hot drink and some pain-killers. The next stop was the Casualty Clearing Station, with 200 beds manned by a staff of 110 officers and men, commanded by a lieutenant-colonel. Lindley had some sympathy for the stretcher-bearers who 'must have thought all Hell was let loose', he recalled. 'With a disaster on the scale as it was, you wondered how the hell they'd shifted 'em.' It was a very relevant question. 'There's a lot still there, there must be.'

'It was the wounded that made the place such a hell,' explained Captain Reginald Leetham, with the Rifle Brigade. He had watched the attacks with his heart in his mouth, before his was cancelled. 'I did not mind the dead,' he admitted, 'I could do nothing for them, but one felt so incapable of doing much for the wounded.' They had to help recover some of them from a trench. 'One was actually climbing over corpses in every position and when one trod on human flesh it sent a shudder down one's spine.' There was hardly a stretcher-bearer in sight. 'What was the use,' he complained, they were completely swamped and did not see a doctor before 2 pm. By then he had given out two tubes of morphia alongside two large flasks of brandy.[13]

The Director of Fourth Army Medical Services, General M O'Keeffe, had provided for an estimated 6,000 casualties on the first day. For that, he would need seven ambulance trains and three so-called more primitive trains, used in a crisis to move up to 1,000 minor wounded cases. By day's end there were actually 30,000 men wounded, for which the maximum total capacity in the Casualty Clearing Stations was 10,000. General Rawlinson, the army commander, had taken a personal interest in this, having experienced the disaster that had occurred at Loos in 1915. As early as 14 June, he had asked O'Keefe for 18 trains. Despite apparent inconsistencies he was assured by his own quartermaster-general that 'the number required will be brought into use as and when necessary'. Only five trains, sufficient to carry 2,000 men, actually turned up on 1 July. 'What I thought mainly, the very first thing I thought,' recalled Private Frank Lindley, having entered the medical chain, 'was how the bloody hell are they going to clear this mess up?'[14]

Lieutenant Edward Liveing, wounded in front of the German wire at Gommecourt, faced the same problem: how to get back? 'For God's sake stop firing,' he had called out to soldiers coming up in subsequent waves, but had been ignored. The personal odyssey often began with the motivating thought, 'I must get home now for the sake of my people' in England. Orientation was the first issue; Liveing was weak from his wounds. 'My notions in general were becoming somewhat hazy,' he recalled, and 'the trenches themselves were entirely unrecognisable.' They had been filled with debris and earth up to about half their original depth. By the time he reached the Regimental Aid Post 'hardly a shell was falling and the immediate din of battle had subsided'. The sun was beating down but the aid post was in the shade of trees, offering both physical and psychological relief. He was unrecognisable as an officer:

I was an indistinguishable mass of filth and gore. My helmet was covered with mud, my tunic was cut about with shrapnel and bullets and saturated with blood; my breeches had changed from khaki to a purple hue; my puttees were in tatters; my boots looked like a pair of very muddy clogs.

He had to wait for the more serious cases to be attended to. A total of 863 officers and 22,826 men were in the medical chain between the Advanced and Main Dressing Stations; 14,400 men, including 304 wounded Germans, were on their way to the Casualty Clearing Stations, where there was room for just 10,000. Rawlinson at this point thought the casualty level was about 16,000; it was actually twice that. With insufficient trains to maintain the flow beyond the bottlenecks at the Casualty Clearing Stations, many who had arrived that far were left out in the open, with untreated wounds. Some would needlessly die. Even the padres were giving out anaesthetics. 'I had no right to be doing this, of course,' one admitted, 'but we were simply so rushed.' Waiting their turn 'would have been too late for many of them; as it was, many died'.

'It was one continuous stream of wounded and dead and dying,' remembered Private HD Jackson, with the 75th Field Ambulance. 'You had to forget all sentiment,' he maintained, 'it was a case of getting on with the job.' The morphine ampules carried by the stretcher-bearers were too big for a single dose. They often went along the lines and administered fatal doses to the hopeless cases, to alleviate their suffering.

Liveing described his bloody progress along the chain. The Advanced Dressing Station was a well sandbagged house with a courtyard, where he got 'a blood-stained mug with a little tea at the bottom of it'. Despite its grisly appearance, 'I can honestly say that I never enjoyed a drink so much as that one.' Soldiers peering inside the packed ambulances were envious. 'Our fate was decided, theirs still hung in the balance.' At the Casualty Clearing Station in the grounds of a château Liveing's wound was pronounced 'a Blighty', which meant transportation to one of the huge base hospitals in France by rail or a hospital ship to England. Liveing described numerous incidents of shell shock along the way. 'It took four or five of us to get him back into the ambulance and hold him down,' remembered Private Jackson of one such case. 'He thought we were taking him back into the trenches again, instead of taking him to hospital.'

It was going to take a further three days to clear the backlog of casualties from that first awful day. Casualty Clearing Stations had twice as many men as they could accommodate, and the five ambulance trains that appeared could only move 2,317, even carrying double their capacity. Bald figures do little to convey the reality of such shortfalls. One wounded man gave Jackson a letter. 'See this goes,' he implored him, 'it's to my wife, bless her heart.' Jackson pocketed the letter. Later that night, in order to sleep, he had to share a dugout with the dead. There was an arm protruding from a blanket, and when he covered it, he saw 'it was the chap who'd given me the letter … When things happened like that,' he admitted, 'it really brought it home to you. Life seemed so cheap.'[15]

Albert Andrews, with the 19th Manchesters, had been caring for his wounded mate outside Montauban but did not see a doctor until 7 pm, when one came up with some stretcher-bearers. He had shaded his friend's face all afternoon. His CO came across him and asked how long he had lain there. 'About five hours,' Andrews replied. When the doctor finally looked at the boy, he 'shook his head and the lad was carried away,' Andrews remembered; he died on the stretcher on the way back.[16]

The Germans north of the Albert–Bapaume road appreciated the mid-afternoon lull. The British attacks here had been largely repulsed. They posed no threat to the German defenders. 'Well, that's got the dust out of the weapons,' remarked one of Leutnant Matthäus Gerster's Tübingen soldiers, with 119 Regiment, wiping the sweat from his brow. It was typical veteran black humour. The men had fired rifles at the rapid rate so long that morning that barrels blackened with scorching heat had nearly 'cooked off' and burned their hands. The scene around the Hawthorne crater resembled an alien moonscape. Chlorine gas had bleached and corroded the long grass. The huge hole resembled a chalk-white star burst, littered with khaki-brown British dead, with a field-grey rim of fallen German defenders on the east side. Dugout entrances in flattened trenches were heaped with piles of brilliant sunlit white chalk.

At about 1 pm a small hole appeared in one pile, dislodging soil that trickled down the chalk spill. After some urgent scrabbling and burrowing a hand appeared, followed by a chalk-encrusted head. Leutnant Renz, who had been buried all morning with several men from the 9th Company 119 Regiment, suddenly emerged from their tomb entrance at the edge of the Hawthorne crater. While the storm of battle raged overhead, these men had fought their own intensely physical, emotional and personal battle to survive within. They held back the black dog of claustrophobia and madness in complete darkness, scraping their way out, utilising bare hands and whatever tool was available. At the very moment their air was giving out they had finally punched through. They were born again and the entire battalion realised it. Their appearance was an enormous fillip to the morale of the decimated 9th Company. Death might be cheated after all.

Landsturmmann Schneider at the crater spoke good English. He had noticed some of the 'dead' British soldiers raising their heads from time to time. Inspired by the good fortune of their own entombed men, Schneider coaxed 36 of the wounded English in, including five officers. The German defenders held their fire throughout, observing with irritation that their adjacent 10th Company alongside was fired at constantly by British artillery the whole time. The survival of prisoners was, as ever, a matter of human whim.[17]

1 to 9.30 pm

'Stop the Rot'. The Schwaben Penetration

Unteroffizier Friedrich Hinkel, on the southern shoulder of the Ulster Division break-in point south of the River Ancre, was not enjoying a lull. Well aware their flank had been turned 'we subsequently endured an awful time of it', he recalled. Lost trenches to their right were incessantly shelled and the 'largely uneventful waiting time got on our nerves'. Brief periods of activity punctuated the waiting. 'Wherever a [British] steel helmet showed itself, it was dealt with, just as in a hare shoot.' It was obvious 'these lads did not seem to know where they were in our trenches'. Disorientated British groups were allowed to approach closely before being dispatched with hand grenades. Hinkel and his men were, however, vulnerable to British air superiority. 'British aviators circled above,' he observed, 'seeking out the exact positions where the men in field grey were still holding out and firing at our little group.'

It was the white steam escaping from the cooling jacket of Vizefeldwebel Laasch's machine-gun at La Boisselle that gave his position away. 'Rifle shots went past our head and kicked up the dirt in front of us,' he remembered. Circling RFC aircraft had picked out the signature and brought down artillery fire. 'I was cowering behind a turn in the trench with a comrade when a large splinter hit him in the head, covering my uniform with his brains.' Laasch was shocked and 'thought I too was done for', but the aircraft flew on, seeking fresh new targets for the artillery. Allied aircraft flew constant lazy circles over the German front and rear.[18]

The conundrum for the strategic thinkers on the Western Front was that it was quicker to mass defensive force from railheads than it was for attackers to exploit their gains on foot and overcome the defence build-up. The German rail network was already busy. 'Western Front, we knew,' remembered one German soldier who made the journey there by troop train, and recalled the atmospheric tension of such moves; 'nothing more was said.' They passed through Osnabrück, then the Ruhr. The pervading memory 'was that every few metres we passed a set of points' as they went through the marshalling yards, 'and we heard "click, click", and then came the Rhine.' At 3.30 pm the 1st Battalion of the 71st Reserve Regiment, along with the 11th Reserve Jaeger Battalion, were waiting on railway platforms at St Quentin, east of the Somme, to entrain for the French part of the line. Arms were piled as they lingered waiting for the regimental transport to be loaded.

'At this moment,' a witness recalled, 'English aeroplanes appeared overhead and dropped bombs.' The raid, by three British BE2cs, achieved a lucky strike on one of the ammunition sheds, which went up with a huge explosion. 'There were 200 wagons of ammunition in the station at the time; sixty of them caught fire and exploded,' the onlooker remembered, and 'the remainder were saved with difficulty.' The troop train blazed furiously by the platform, consuming all the heavy equipment and stacked arms. 'The men were panic-stricken and fled in every direction, and

180 men were either killed or wounded.' It took several hours before it was possible to reassemble the survivors from the 71st Regiment, who were sent back to billets. A regiment's worth of equipment and supplies was destroyed and the division move delayed by 18 hours, when time was of the essence.[19]

When the Gruppe Prager atttacked into the Grandcourt artillery hollow with fixed bayonets shortly before 3 pm, it opened up the first cracks in the vulnerable 36th Ulster Division penetration of the German line. Courage is a finite commodity, and after seven desperate hours of trench clearing in the teeth of 99 Regiment local counter-attacks, the Ulstermen were running short. Under fire from three sides all day with no support, the Ulster Division's situation, pinned down and besieged in the German trenches, was precarious. 'We should call it a draw and I'll give our garden in with it,' remarked one joker to Private FG Gardner, with the 109th Trench Mortar Battery. Lieutenant William Montgomery, with the 9th Royal Irish Rifles, could see large numbers of Germans steadily moving up through the communication trenches from the fourth line. The trident-shaped counter-attack by the 8th Bavarian Regiment was on its way. Tommy Russell from Newcastle, County Down, was lying wounded at the Schwaben Redoubt. He could see out to Grandcourt, where hundreds of German helmets were glinting in the sun. The Ulstermen were desperate and burned by the summer afternoon sun. One man nearby tried to drink his own urine. It was obvious to all that the Germans were moving up in strength.[20]

Prager's group suffered horrific casualties getting into the artillery hollow but set off the first panic among the Irish, many of whom had been stretched beyond emotional and physical limits. At 3 pm 'a lot of men from the 8th and 9th Royal Irish Rifles have broken under Bosch counter-attack from the direction of Grandcourt,' remembered Lieutenant-Colonel FO Bowen, with the Belfast Young Citizens Battalion. Leutnant Gerster, with the German 52nd Brigade, remembered 'the British were blasted out of the battery position in Grandcourt by the combined fire of the artillery and small arms fire from Recruit Company Infantry Regiment 180 and MG company Mehl ... As they streamed back towards the Schwaben Redoubt they were destroyed.' Bowen recalled this panic-stricken flight:

We had to stop them at revolver point and turn them back, a desperate show, the air stiff with shrapnel, and terror stricken men rushing blindly. These men did magnificently earlier in the day, but they had reached the limit of their endurance.

An hour later Major Beyerköhler's second attack group began its advance to the left of Prager. They approached the redoubt from the northeast along the Staufen Trench. At about this time, Bowen remembered, 'I received a message from Captain Willis of our D Company that he was hanging on but hard pressed. He was never heard from again.'[21]

Bombing trenches clear of enemy opposition was considered a vital German tactical infantry skill. They trained very methodically and regularly, often every two weeks, to develop a competence considered as fundamental as firing a rifle. Bombing squads consisted of two groups of four men. Each of these had a number one, or 'thrower', who worked closely with his number two 'carrier'. Carriers fed their throwers ready prepared hand grenades, from sandbags with six in each. The first group of four was armed with pistols, bayonets and grenades; the follow-up group had rifles and grenades. The latter included a man who had 25 additional sandbags fastened to a haversack strap, on stand-by to be filled. The first four men cleared each trench traverse and fought back any serious counter-attacks, while the second group erected a sandbag barrier, to block off the trench behind. Care was taken to stay spread out, to avoid any well-aimed grenade counter-throws.

The attack drill was that forward throwers counted 22 to 24 seconds before lobbing their bomb, to ensure they exploded virtually on impact and could not be thrown back. After a traverse was taken, the number two called '*Geräumt!*' meaning Clear! The squad leader would then shout '*Vor!*' or Advance! The theory was to mark progress with white markers, stuck on trench sides; practice was different. Reverses up front were countered by '*Sandsäcke Vor!*' or 'Bring up the sandbags!' to erect a barricade. The disciplined combination of precise throwing and speedy aggressive rushes in the confusion of trench fighting could be highly effective. Private Jim Maultsaid, a prolific sketch artist with the 14th Royal Irish Rifles, had an enduring memory of 'a big black-bearded German bomber [who] caused havoc in our ranks'. A proficient German bomber could accurately throw a stick grenade out to 40 metres and there were regular enthusiastic inter-company competitions to nurture the skill.[22]

As the 8th Bavarian Regiment counter-attack groups, spearheaded by bombers, re-entered their trenches, bitter fighting broke out in the depth of the German line as they closed in on the Schwaben Redoubt during the late afternoon. 'A carpet of dead and dying Ulstermen and Germans' coated the B line trenches near the River Ancre, remembered a soldier with the 14th Royal Irish Rifles. 'Blood lay like a layer of mud and, do you know, you couldn't tell one blood from the other.' Several Inniskilling soldiers lay in ambush, hiding in shell holes, awaiting the German counter-attacks:

> *The Germans re-entered their own trench. The sound of the first hand grenade exploding was the signal to start bombing the two or three hundred yards of the trench where the German soldiers were collecting.*

They immediately went in with the bayonet after the last grenade exploded. 'There was not one German soldier left alive,' a soldier recalled. 'They collected all the grenades, ammunition, even rifles, water and food the Germans were carrying – a bloody messy job.' Every effort was made to improvise to stem the German flow, but ten hours of non-stop fighting exacted a steady toll. Mercy was in short supply, both sides reluctant to take prisoners in the hurly-burly of trench fighting. By the time the Germans were back in the third line, verging on the Schwaben Redoubt, Young Citizen Volunteers were resorting to 'Bangelore tubes'. These were a form of phosphorous device intended to melt through barbed wire entanglements. One soldier remembered how, after a squad of German soldiers were driven inside a dug-out, they managed to get the tubes burning and thrust them inside to incinerate the occupants. 'We were a right distance away,' he remembered, 'but we could smell the burning flesh as the Germans inside the dugout were burnt to death.'[23]

Twenty-year-old German soldier Hermann Baass described what it was like to be part of such counter-attacks, in effect a series of drills. 'As a simple soldier you appreciated, "That is a long way, that is where the enemy is, where the shooting is coming from."' Once they got moving, 'the aim was basically to get to a safe place,' which meant, 'throw yourself behind a rise or fall into a hole,' and there were craters everywhere:

Then you had to find the enemy. When you rubbed one out you thought 'one less that can do anything'. That was roughly the feeling.

Nobody, he remembered, wanted to be viewed a coward and this resulted in differing approaches by mature married men and the younger unattached. 'There were those we always said were afflicted by a form of "Iron Cross pain",' or were after medals and wanted to be promoted. Veteran soldiers kept moving forward because they knew enemy artillery fire would blanket the launch point. 'Therefore run forward for your own safety,' he ironically recalled, 'because the shell splinters will be heading behind you.' His reasoning was: 'Whoever ran to the rear copped it, everyone knew it, so you ran forwards.'[24]

With the 36th Ulster attack teetering, 'I hear a rumour about riflemen retiring on the left and go out to stop the rot,' recalled Lieutenant-Colonel Frank Crozier, with the 9th Royal Irish Rifles. Soon he sees 'a strong rabble of tired, hungry and thirsty stragglers approach me from the east'. He asks them where they are going. 'One says one thing, one another.' All this is clearly unsatisfactory. They are marched to the water reserve, given a drink and 'hunted back to the fight'. He sees an even larger group cutting across to the south, which obviously 'mean business'. He watches as a young subaltern sprints up and heads them off:

They push by him. He draws his revolver and threatens them. They take no notice. He fires. Down drops a British soldier at their feet. The effect is instantaneous. They turn back to the assistance of their comrades in distress.

Crozier was dispassionate but understood the cumulative corrosive effect the disastrous day was having. 'The moral appeal is generally stronger than the armed threat,' he acknowledged, 'if there is time. But there seldom is time.' Crozier's battalion was down to 70 men from 700.[25]

At 6 pm the 1st Recruit Company of 180 Regiment conducted a three-wave infantry assault against the Schwaben Redoubt, the right prong of the counter-attacking groups. Leutnant Arnold was in the second wave, a hundred metres behind the first. As his company crested the high ground beyond the artillery hollow 'it received such a hail of machine-gun and rifle fire, that further advances were out of the question for the time being'. His company commander, Leutnant Schnürlen, coming on behind with the third wave, was swept away as the company was engulfed and decimated by a sudden British artillery barrage, that came crashing down. The company was reduced to a non-effective state.

Coincidental with this debacle was a sudden penetration of the British right flank by a 99 Regiment fighting patrol, in the area of the former German intermediate position. Led by Offizierstellvertreter Luneau, it emerged unexpectedly from the eastern shoulder of the Ulster penetration. Luneau had been directed by the 14th Company 99 Regiment to establish how far forward the British had penetrated. Without further orders Luneau exploited an apparent gap, after capturing an enemy machine-gun and clearing a section of British-occupied trench. He pressed on, fighting through 1,000 metres of trench and capturing three more machine-guns, one of which had been checking the advance of Bavarian Gruppe 2, now commanded by von Wurmb. In effect a possible attack route to the Schwaben Redoubt had been opened up, although von Wurmb's group, which until now had been bearing almost the entire weight of the counter-attack, was down to about 40 men left standing.

The crisis echoed what Generalleutnant von Stein was experiencing at corps level. Committing the final reserve might just be the straw to break the camel's back. Oberstleutnant von Bram at the Stuff Redoubt suspected the Gruppe 2 momentum was petering out. He was unaware of the parlous situation of the British defence, or the mixed results being achieved both right and left of the counter-attack sector; and he was still not in contact with many of the groups engaged in the attack. But he did instinctively realise more men were needed. Additional forces from the 1st Company 185 Regiment previously held back in the area of the Stuff Redoubt were made available to him by 52 Brigade. As more and more exhausted troops from the scattered companies of Major Roesch's Gruppe 3 straggled up, von Bram fed them into the battle.

Further north across the River Ancre 'the fighting was beginning to die down', recalled cinematographer Geoffrey Malins. He was still filming in the 29th Division area around White City, west of Beaumont Hamel. It was late afternoon and the light was beginning to soften as the evening wore on. He watched the remnants of four regiments come in and start to muster. 'I realised,' he recalled, 'that the roll-call was about to take place,' and decided to focus on the remnants of the Seaforth Highlanders. 'I filmed them as they staggered forward and dropped down utterly worn out, body and soul.' Such poignant scenes were being played out all along the front as survivors came in. They were assembled, counted, reorganised and marched back to their billets in the rear.

The men he saw were certainly tired enough, but 'by an almost superhuman effort many of them staggered to their feet again, and formed themselves into an irregular line'. Unknown to Malins, they were the battalion carrying parties and had not gone over the top. Many of their comrades were pinned down in the German lines around the Quadrilateral or Heidenkopf Redoubt. They would not be able to crawl back until after it got dark. For audiences back home, who had never seen anything so real, it would look grippingly authentic. Malins filmed as:

The sergeant stood there with notebook resting on the end of his rifle, repeatedly putting his pencil through the names that were missing.

The scene atmospherically encapsulated the losses and missing of that desolate day. It was noticeable that the soldiers regarded the camera with very little interest. A powerful contrast to the smiling enthusiasm and energetic waves he had attracted while filming over the past few days. The front grumbled ominously in the background, unheard on the silent reels. It was becoming progressively louder south of the Ancre, where the gathering momentum of the German counter-attacks pushed back the Ulstermen to the Schwaben Redoubt.[26]

As the evening light began to dim, the tenuous line held by the London Regiment in the German trenches on the south side of the Gommecourt salient became unhinged. Increasing numbers of small groups were forced out of their captured positions, and made to run the gauntlet back to their own line. It was virtually impossible to get across unscathed in daylight. 'Everybody hung on as long as possible,' recalled Sergeant Gilbert Telfer, with the 1/9th Battalion. 'Then small parties began to evacuate, but none got far before they were bowled over by machine-gun fire.' He sprinted for home and 'I got one from the left through my thigh and, in getting up, one across my back from the right, just taking the skin off my spine and ripping a nice lump out of my left side in the small of the back.' He got up again and rushed into a shell hole, where he would have to wait until dark.

Lieutenant Richard Cary's commanding officer with the 1st Queen Victoria's Rifles remembers that only 64 of the battalion made it back. They did not include Richard. One of his company commanders, Major Samuel Sampson, wrote at the time, 'The trying thing is that many of them are left wounded or killed in the German trenches, and whether they are alive or dead we do not know.' The correspondence following the Territorial Record Office notification of Cary's death on 6 July ran to six letters and telegrams before the family definitively heard he was dead. On 18 August his friend 'Goody', badly wounded himself, wrote with assistance to say that he was with him when he died. It had taken six weeks. Richard Cary's body was never recovered. Sampson summed up the feelings of the few survivors:

> *We are filled with pride for all that has been done, bitterness for the little there is to show for it, and sorrow for those we shall never see again.*[27]

At 8 pm, with barely two hours of daylight left, Major Hans von Fabeck commanding 99 Regiment, which was hanging on either side of the Ulster Division breach, desperately sought support from 52 Brigade. 'Own casualties are very severe,' his battle log reveals, '1st, 3rd and 4th companies completely finished.' He needed help now. 'All the platoon commanders of the 3rd Company are dead,' he reported. 'Hand grenades, signal cartridges, water and rations are urgently required.' Thirty minutes later the response from Oberstleutnant von Bram was:

> *Further reinforcements cannot be made available at present. This is because instead of there being a complete regiment available for the attack on Schwaben Redoubt, only four companies are.*

Two 8th Regiment companies had left the old 52 Brigade headquarters at the Zollern Redoubt three hours before, and were still heading for Thiepval, with two kilometres to go, led by 99 Regiment guides. The first company did not straggle in until 9.04 pm. It was too exhausted to be committed to battle.

Unteroffizier Friedrich Hinkel's 7th Company group, with 99 Regiment, still held its barricade, blocking off the south side of the Ulster penetration. Sandbags and wire blocked the trench known as the *Marktgasse*, or Market Way, where it intersected the road to the Thiepval churchyard and cemetery. Much of the day following the traumatic breakthrough had been uneventful. They broiled in the sun, thirsty, hungry and listless. As it began to grow dark, the tempo of battle activity increased. They detected furtive movement in the lengthening shadows downhill towards the British line and took aimed shots at the scurrying activity. Hinkel and his men never doubted they would eventually be relieved. 'I knew our counter-attacks would be deployed for sure and I was also certain of their success.'

'At last! One could hear rifle fire from time to time and the constant detonations of hand grenades coming nearer.' The noise appeared to be coming from the Hanseatic position or the Schlüter Trench, from the north and east. The movement on their right flank and below was probably the British 'moving back in fear of our counter-attack'. He moved along to the battalion dugout with two NCOs and 'eliminated a few groups of Englishmen with our hand grenades and drove others off'. They decided to move back to their barricade, so as not 'to end up in the hand grenade fire of the Bavarians, who were mopping up the trench'.

They knew now they would survive. Leading elements of Hauptmann von Wurmb's Gruppe 2 were in the bottom of the Lachweg Trench, 800 metres away.[28]

CHAPTER 10

Blood-Red Sunset —•

9.30 pm to midnight

9.30 to 10.05 pm

Merciful Dusk

A blood-red sunset reflected what looked like Hell's fire across the crater-pocked desolation of no man's land, strewn with black skeletal wire. 'The sun went down that first evening back over our old trenches,' remembered Private HL Wide, with the 9th Devons. At first it reflected a hue 'in gold which turned to blood, and it seemed symbolic', he recalled. One hundred and fifty of Wide's battalion had perished in minutes that morning but they had reached their objectives. 'We had kept our nerve and at the end of the day were where we were supposed to be, and that seemed triumph enough to be going on with.' The cost to the right of the line was not dissimilar to the catastrophe experienced along the entire 16-mile front. By sunset it was becoming apparent that less than a quarter of the attacks had achieved anything at all. Now, as gold transitioned to blood-red and then black in the last half-hour before 10 pm, the battlefield, like an African veldt, began to come to life. Spectre-like forms stirred amid the shadowy mounds of dead in a bizarre rebirth as the wounded crawled unsteadily like migrating crabs back to the British line.[1]

'It was a lovely evening, and a man stood beside me,' Sergeant Richard Tawney of the 22nd Manchesters remembered. He had been lying out in no man's land in front of Mametz since the middle of the morning. 'I caught him by the ankle in terror lest he should vanish.' It was an RAMC corporal, who shouted to a doctor to come and look. They promised they would come back, but first he had to attend to another more seriously wounded man. 'That was the worst moment I had,' Tawney recalled, 'I thought they were deceiving me – that they were leaving me for good.' Wounded men all over the battlefield prayed and willed for a merciful dusk. They felt helpless and abandoned. 'I did so want to be spoken kindly to,' Tawney remembered, 'and I began to whimper, partly to myself, partly aloud.' Under the cover of darkness, the medics were going about their business. Tawney viewed the doctor 'like an angel'; he was 'one of the best men I had ever met'. He personified the tantalising possibility of survival. There were still no stretcher-bearers available. Tawney was ultra-sensitive to the tone in the doctor's voice, when he told him he had been shot in the abdomen and chest; it suggested something was amiss. 'I real-ised he thought I was done for.' He was tightly bandaged and given morphine. Whatever the outcome:

I had felt that divine compassion flow over me. I didn't care. I was like a dog kicked and bullied by everyone, that's at last found a kind master, and in a grovelling kind of way I worshipped him.

Tawney's battalion had gone over the top with 820 men; two days later only 54 would be left. The doctor directed the orderly into a trench when Tawney told him snipers were active, 'but he wouldn't keep down or go away himself'. Tawney was happy he had human contact.[2]

Tommy Higgins, with the North Staffs further north at Gommecourt, remembered the same wraith-like battlefield at dusk, where the dead seemed to come to life. After being caught up in barbed wire and feigning death, he made his move when darkness descended. When 'I saw the Germans crawling out and turning the bodies of our chaps over,' he recalled, 'I thought it time to get a move on.' Meanwhile 'Jerry made it almost like day' by sending up scores of signal flares. He did not anticipate mercy. 'I wriggled backwards for a good way, dragging yards of broken wire with me that was stuck in my clothes', impelled, like all the other spectres crawling that night, to get back. 'I ripped my flesh but I took no heed of that' and after a struggle 'I got it off me, then I got up and started to run, or rather stagger,' he remembered, because 'I was so done up'. All around 'other forms rose from the ground' – they were the wounded and others pinned down all day, heading back.

He was joined in a stumbling run by Jack Heywood, 'who had been lying close to me all day'. Their movement was detected by German machine-gunners, who began firing predictive bursts across no man's land to interdict the general rearward movement they sensed was happening. 'What a rush for the advance trench,' Higgins recalled, and both he and Heywood 'tumbled in, a nice pair of broken down nervous wrecks'. They were totally spent. 'We simply lay on our backs in the bottom of the trench, too beat to move for a while.' Then their odyssey continued, moving through the communication trenches, helping each other over the piled dead bodies. 'Some of them lay under water,' he remembered; 'in places it was so deep I think some of the poor chaps must have been drowned.' They were directed through Foncquevillers onwards to Souastre in the rear, which meant walking another three miles.[3]

The 'last ditchers' from the London Division got out at about 9.30 pm, sprinting for the British line in the gathering dusk. 'Everyone for himself!' Private Arthur Schuman, with the 1/5th Battalion, was told. 'By now I was just petrified,' he admitted. 'I knew that if I stayed in the trench I would most certainly be killed. I hardly waited for the order.' It was a nightmare experience. He went over the top 'like greased lightning', falling flat to survive a hail of bullets:

Then trying to imagine I was part of the earth, I wriggled along on my belly. Dead, dying, feigning death – who knows? The ground was covered in them. I sped from shell hole to shell hole. Never had I run faster.

In one hole he threw himself on top of a badly wounded German, who was piteously moaning *Schlecht! Schlecht!* Bad! Bad! 'I don't know what made me do it, but I gripped his hand and sped on,' he remembered. The next handshake was a more solemn affair with his adjutant and regimental sergeant-major, who were waiting to redirect survivors along the communication trenches. 'I was told that only 20 had returned so far.'

'The battle had considerably died down by now,' remembered George Ashurst, with the Lancashire Fusiliers opposite the Hawthorne crater. 'It was like the calm after the storm.' The crater had glowed gold then red, picking out the prone shadowy forms lying like so much debris around the lip of the crater. Ashurst could see that 'Fritz had held us and also wiped us out'. Stretcher-bearers were at last on the move in the gloom, 'totally untroubled by the sniping that Fritz kept up in the darkness'.

The position in the sunken lane forward of Jacob's Ladder, where Geoffrey Malins had filmed that morning, was precarious. All the survivors bar one officer, an NCO and 20 men had been withdrawn. Both ends of the lane were barricaded, a process that had cost the engineers an officer and nine men wounded. 'Fritz had played havoc with the poor fellows', which had made the task 'almost impossible'. Ashurst was left as the NCO in charge of the lower end, facing the crater, with seven of the men. They would be the trip-wire in the event of a German counter-attack.[4]

Unlike much of the rest of the battlefield, the artillery fire around the Schwaben Redoubt had been increasing rather than decreasing in intensity since 9 pm. With an hour to go before darkness, Oberstleutnant von Bram had been guaranteed an hour-long preparatory bombardment by Generalleutnant von Auwärter, the commander of 52 Brigade. At nine o'clock all the German batteries within range of 'Berta', 'Zollern' and 'Cäser' artillery concentration areas began to bring down effective fire onto the redoubt.

Promised reinforcements for the besieged Ulstermen were clearly not coming. Only about eight companies of Yorkshire men from 146 Brigade had survived the ordeal of crossing no man's land. Men who had been fighting non-stop for well over 12 hours had reached the point where spirit alone was insufficient. Some did try and settle for the night in the German lines, but the intensification of the artillery bombardment and the onset of dusk persuaded them otherwise. The nocturnal exfiltration back to their home trenches began.

Lieutenant William Montgomery, in Crozier's 9th Royal Irish Rifles, detected a major thinning of the ranks between 9.30 and 9.40 pm, in the fading light. The withdrawal appeared to have been initiated by men from a Stokes mortar battery. Montgomery ran after 150 soldiers he saw retiring towards Thiepval Wood and remonstrated with them. About 40 were persuaded to pause in the first German line and even fired their rifles, but within 20 minutes, with total darkness, they headed for home. Seven Ulster battalions had fragmented elements in and around the Schwaben Redoubt, but over 5,000 casualties that day meant these fragments taken together numbered perhaps a few hundred men. Only a few score men were still standing in scattered companies and decimated platoons. The gradual melting away meant there was no coherent defence around the redoubt as the German artillery fire grew heavier and heavier.

Many survivors were like Private John Kennedy Hope, a Young Citizen Volunteer wandering lost and alone in the German front line, looking up into an empty summer sky with 'that clearness associated with a July night'. He came across Major John Peacoke, from the Royal Inniskilling Fusiliers, sent up by his CO, Colonel Ricardo, to see what was going on and tie up defence measures. 'We were told reinforcements were at hand,' Ricardo recalled, 'and to hold on', but 'at any rate, help did not come'. Soldiers were beginning to realise their position was hopeless. 'Retirement is never a pleasant task,' recalled one, 'especially after you have fought your corner as we fought ours … We felt that the ground won was part of ourselves.' They had earned it. 'It brought a lump to our throats,' remarked another, 'when we thought of all the friends that were dead or wounded.' John Hope, attracted by voices in the dark, found a British group sheltering in a large crater. He stayed a while before moving off with a smaller group heading back. Many were 'so exhausted that most of them could not speak', Ricardo remembered, 'the Germans I suppose being as exhausted as we were'. Hope was not challenged when he jumped into a British trench at the head of Elgin Avenue. The Germans were still shelling.

The defence of the Schwaben Redoubt was dependent upon a few parties of men who had elected to stay after dark. 'We collected all the ammunition we could from our own dead,' recalled one soldier:

A terrible task, but it was necessary, for we knew we would need every bullet we could get. In the big trench we set up sentries and

some of us tried to get some rest. It was hard, for we kept seeing
the bits and pieces of the dead bodies and the terrible bleeding of
the wounded, and the smell of sweat and the hunger kept us
from sleeping.

This was hardly a cohesive defence, more about small bands of determined men hanging on. 'Funny thing was,' the soldier remembered, 'we found ourselves taking orders from other privates and giving them ourselves.'

Private Albert Bruce was hard at work, clearing the sunken or 'bloody road', from which they had attacked. About 40 corpses had been stacked outside a dugout in Thiepval Wood. Bruce was aghast to realise that one of the broken bodies inside the pile was faintly calling out that he was alive. He managed to extract the living corpse and placed him on a stretcher. A soldier standing nearby came forward and looked hard and long at the pallid face and saw it was his brother. After a few minutes the stretcher-bearers came up and carried him off into the depths of the wood, still under artillery fire. They were never seen again. The miracle of his recovery had not sufficed. Several times after the war Albert Bruce saw the dead man's brother, who always asked him hauntingly, 'Whatever happened to that brother of mine? Whatever happened to that brother of mine?'[5]

'At long last, evening came and the light began to fade,' recalled Private WJ Senescall, who was across the River Ancre in Mash Valley with the 11th Suffolks. He had been pinned down all day. 'I ventured a look forward and there was Jerry out of his trench, moving among the fallen.' Senescall had no intention of 'going to Berlin too soon' and the sight of the Germans moving about 'decided me; I jumped up and ran as best I could, for I was stiff. I kept treading on wounded and they called out to me for help.'

Eric Haylock in the same battalion nearby had been sitting there all day, his tin hat held across his face, forlornly trying to keep out the sun and bullets.

When it got dusk I began to see some of our boys what had been lying around – I suppose they were hit in their arms or got a good pair of legs – they were getting up and running like hell back to our line.

He joined the rush in the dark. No man's land was about 800 yards wide at this point, so it was a considerable challenge. Senescall won his race: 'Jerry let me have a few more shots as I ran, but the light had now gone … Anyway,' he rationalised, 'he couldn't hit me that day in daylight, could he?'[6]

It was just as well both men had run back. Major Henry Hance, a Royal Engineer Tunnelling Company officer, retraced their steps two weeks later, when Ovillers was finally captured. 'The old no man's land, Mash Valley was a fearful sight,' he remembered, especially the final stretch, 400 yards in front of the German trenches:

We noted that all the dead had been bayoneted, and always thro' the neck. All the dead hanging on the wire, where it was still intact, had had the backs of their heads bashed in. Now you can't bayonet a man 400 yards away, and you can't bash the back of a man's head in from in front and across a belt of wire. No!

Hance concluded that German patrols had come out at night and finished off the wounded 'or mutilated our dead'. He was outraged; it was 'the worst sight I saw in the whole war'. The Germans, embittered after seven days of non-stop artillery fire, were doubtless at the end of their tether and felt vulnerable. They were incensed at being shot at all day by the

British wounded, who needed to be eradicated. They were hardened and cynical veterans, having survived thus far; they had no intention of taking chances and besides had scores to settle. It was unlikely they could contain another assault on this scale and took the opportunity to level the odds. 'For sheer brutality,' Hance concluded, 'it exceeded anything I could have believed, even of a Hun.' Kitchener's New Army had been christened by Total War.[7]

Lieutenant Alfred Bundy, with the 2nd Middlesex, was also pinned down in a Mash Valley shell hole all day. 'An impenetrable barrier' of bullets prevented movement right or left and 'exposure of the head meant certain death,' he recalled. 'None of our men was visible but in all directions came pitiful groans and cries of pain.' After hours of waiting he was tempted to try and crawl out in daylight. 'I was dreading the dark,' he admitted, 'for I thought I should lose my sense of direction in my distraught condition.' When the dying rays of the sun bathed the desolate landscape blood-red 'I started to crawl flat on my stomach … At times I made short wild dashes and finally came to our wire.' As he gathered strength for the final sprint, he was dismayed to observe sparks continuously flying off the wire as the Germans traversed the parapet with fire. There was a pause, and then, tearing clothing and skin, Bundy tumbled himself into a front-line trench filled with dead and wounded. He came across 'my company commander, Hunt, who was almost insane'. Bundy took over C Company, reduced to 'about 30 men!'

Lieutenant-Colonel Edwin Sandys, his commanding officer, was distraught. He had lost 23 of his officers and 517 men; his fine regular command had been massacred. One of the few surviving officers, Captain Lloyd Jones, recalled of him that 'he wished he had been killed with his men'. Hit five times, Sandys was awarded the DSO but never got over the loss of his battalion; he blamed himself. Only one officer and 28 men were left to be relieved that night.[8]

Unteroffizier Otto Lais, with 169 Regiment, observed the blood-red dusk in front of Serre to the north. 'Evening falls,' he later wrote, 'the attack is dead.' He summed up the situation before the German wire north of the Roman road from Albert to Bapaume:

> In front of our division sector lie the British in companies, in battalions; mowed down in rows and swept away. From no man's land, the space between the positions, comes one great groan. The battle dies away; it seems to be paralysed at so much utter misery and despair.

The day had been hard fought, German casualties had been 'severe', but 'enemy casualties are unimaginable'. Medics and stretcher-bearers picked their way around the shadowy mounds of dead and writhing wounded. 'Where to begin?' Lais asked. 'Whimpering and moaning confronts them from almost every square metre.' German first-aiders not required on their own side participated in spontaneous truces and went forward to assist the British wounded back to their own front line. 'It is a rare and deeply moving sight,' he acknowledged, 'in trench warfare.'[9]

Only to the south, along the line of the Willow Stream, flowing north of Mametz and Montauban, was the situation different. This was the 20 per cent of the British attack line where objectives had been taken. Oberleutnant Franz Gerhardinger's 2nd Battalion 16 Regiment was tentatively advancing south at nightfall, towards the Mametz–Montauban ridge line, thought to be occupied by the British. Part of his platoon was the vanguard for the 7th and 8th Companies following on. They had no precise idea where the British were as they probed southward. This war of movement was unsettling for German soldiers, who had been locked into static positional warfare on the Western Front since late 1914. According to a German group they met falling back from the forward line, there were British at the northern edge of Montauban, across the Willow Stream. They picked out their objective silhouetted against the glare from flares, and flashes of machine-gun fire. The advance was losing coherence in the darkness. They suddenly and unexpectedly blundered into the 1st Company, which had shifted too far left. Fortunately fire was not exchanged. When Gerhardinger tried to orientate his 7th Company commander, who came up in the night shortly after midnight, there was a sudden outbreak of shooting, 'when about 250 metres left of us, the 8th Company went into the English positions on the northern edge of Montauban with a *Hurrah!*' His own company immediately went into the attack.

'There was no time to lose, as the sky was already beginning to lighten.' In the glare of the flares Gerhardinger saw a British trench 'packed head to head'. If the company got inside the position they would be surrounded and 'rubbed out'. It was too strong to take, 'so we dug in about 25 to 30 metres away'.

Private Pat Kennedy, with the 18th Manchester Regiment, was dug in nearby. For much of the afternoon the terrain before them had been empty. When the counter-attacks began to come in he was concerned. 'I couldn't get my ammunition out of my pouches quick enough.' An old sergeant with a Boer War ribbon showed him what to do. 'Eh, lad, put your clips on the top of the parapet, it's easier!' he said. 'That was a good tip,' Kennedy acknowledged, 'because I had to load very quick and fire.' During the next attack, the Germans started to close with fixed bayonets:

The old sergeant said, 'By God, if we get any in here, we'll have to go and meet them with the bayonet!' I had a round in my breech, to shoot in case I missed with the bayonet. They got very near on top of us – a few feet away – and they were coming full pelt, yelling at the top of their voices. It was a nasty feeling. But they were beaten off.[10]

At about 10 pm, after an hour-long artillery preparation, Hauptmann von Wurmb put in the final desperate assault on the Schwaben Redoubt. His Gruppe 2 had been reduced to a few score men, all that was left to conquer the division commander's *Schwerpunkt*, the vital ground lost that morning. Generalmajor von Soden had ordered it to be retaken at any cost. If they delayed to the following day, the British would have reinforced. They pressed into the Schwaben Redoubt from the Lachweg Trench shouting and firing wildly, in an effort to deceive the defenders into believing they were a larger force. Leutnant Zimmerman peeled off to the right to encircle the redoubt, as von Wurmb's main force stormed in from the northeast, joining Offizierstellvertreter Luneau's group that had come in from the east. The combined force bombed its way inside the redoubt along the Auwärter Trench. All the time their numbers were being steadily whittled away as they lost men to casualties and the need to secure prisoners.

Even as the attack went in at 10.30 pm, von Wurmb saw 'dense lines of troops withdrawing on a broad front'. The British were already falling back, convinced they would have no chance against this final attack. 'We could hardly believe our eyes,' he remembered. 'Could they possibly be advancing lines of German troops?' In the pitch darkness it was hard to make out the close-quarter fighting in the network of trenches inside the redoubt. It was only when signal flares went up from German-occupied Thiepval that 'we recognised the steel helmets: British soldiers!' They were running. 'Rapid fire!' von Wurmb barked to his machine-gun crews. They sang *Die Wacht am Rhein*, a stirring patriotic soldier's song, to identify themselves to Zimmerman's group fighting their way into the redoubt from the other side. Shortly after 10.30 pm it was all over. 'The Schwaben Redoubt was ours!' von Wurmb announced. 'A tiny band had succeeded in ejecting a much stronger force.' There was only some truth in the claim, as the British were withdrawing as the attack came in.

Hauptmann Herbert von Wurmb was to receive the Knight's Cross of the Bavarian Military Max Joseph Order for this exploit, alongside the masterful co-ordinator of the recovery operation, Oberstleutnant Alfons von Bram. 'Only the will to win gains victories,' von Wurmb later claimed. There were some 700 corpses of Ulstermen littering the trenches and parapets of the Schwaben Redoubt. Numerous machine-guns and about 100 prisoners were taken. Generalmajor von Soden's vital *Schwerpunkt* had been taken back, and by midnight a hasty defence had been erected around the shambles of the fortification.

Many of the Ulstermen fleeing the Schwaben Redoubt in the inky darkness fell victim to Unteroffizier Hinkel's isolated 99 Regiment group, which had held firm in the area of the Thiepval churchyard and cemetery. 'Once again our machine-guns rattled and our rifles glowed red hot,' he recalled, as the departing shadows were swept by fire. His men became as reckless and animated as they had been in repelling assaults that morning. 'Many an Irish mother's son lay down to the eternal sleep from which there is no awakening,' he later wrote melodramatically. They were critically short of hand grenades, 'otherwise I have no doubt that we should have cleared the enemy that same night out of our entire position as far as the Ancre.'[11]

'Dear Mother,' one of the survivors, Fusilier Beattie with the 2nd Royal Inniskilling Fusiliers, subsequently wrote home:

> Just a few lines to let you know I am safe and thank God for it, for we had a rough time in the charge we made. Mother, don't tell V. Quinn's mother or Archer's [mother] that they must be killed [or] wounded for they are missing from roll call, and tell Hugh that the fellow who used to chum about with E. Ferguson, called Eddie Mallon (he used to kill pigeons – if Hugh does not know him) has been killed. Tell them that there is not another Grosvenor Road fellow left but myself. Mother, we were tramping over the dead; I think there is only about 4 hundred left out of 13 hundred. Mother, you can let Alfred know something about all this. Mother, I have some German helmets and sausages, and I am sorry that I could not send them home. Mother, if God spares me to get home safely, I will have something awful to tell you. If hell is any worse I would not like to get to it. Mother, let me hear from you as soon as possible, as I have no word from you this fortnight. Don't forget to let me hear from you soon.
> From your loving son Herbie

Herbie's whole local community had disappeared.[12]

10.05 pm to midnight

'A Good Day'

Lieutenant John Stewart-Moore, serving with a trench mortar battery, was dozing in his dugout in Thiepval Wood at about midnight when an infantry officer barged inside, in a state of utter exhaustion. 'We have been fighting all day,' he cried out, 'and we have got nowhere.' All that remained of the epic 36th Ulster Division penetration was a scattering of survivors hanging on in pockets in the German front line. More than 5,000 men had fallen. Thirty minutes before, General Nugent, the division commander, was told he would be given the 148th Brigade from the X Corps reserve to get the Schwaben Redoubt back. But the troops were unfamiliar with the terrain and could not realistically attempt such an operation in the dark. Thiepval was still in German hands, which meant any attempt by day would be massacred. During the night the proposed operation was cancelled.[13]

War correspondent Phillip Gibbs was preparing his dispatch for the next day's edition of the *Daily Chronicle* and *Daily Telegraph*. Gibbs was hardly an apologist for British generals on the Western Front, but what little he had seen from the Grandstand view above Albert suggested 'the attack which was launched today against the German lines on a 20-mile front began well'. He acknowledged 'they are fighting their way forward not easily but doggedly'. He could see Fricourt and the Mametz sector off to his right. It was not a victory, he judged, because 'this is only a beginning', but from his vantage point 'our troops, fighting with very splendid valour, have swept across the enemy's front trenches along a great part of the line'. Gibbs, coincidentally, was facing that part of the 16- to 18-mile front that had achieved 20 per cent success. Like all his contemporaries, having viewed the shock and awe of the bombardment, he assumed the Germans had been cowed. The very size and scale of the huge logistic build-up for the 'Big Push' suggested it would change the course of the war. 'His dead lie thick in the track of our regiments,' Gibbs reported. He had seen hundreds of German prisoners. There was no clue at this stage that it had all gone so catastrophically wrong along the rest of the front.

Rawlinson, the army commander, thought he had lost perhaps 16,000 men by late evening; in fact Fourth Army had lost more than 50,000. Gibbs, nevertheless, felt able to write:

With the British Armies in the field, July 1st, 1916.

After the first day of battle, we may say: it is on balance, a good day for England and France.

This view was echoed by General Sir Walter Congreve, commanding XII Corps next to the French. 'Reports kept coming in of satisfactory progress all day,' he wrote to Billy, his serving son, that night. 'We were in full possession of our objectives before the time laid down, i.e. two hours and fifty minutes after the zero hour.' Major-General Maxse, commanding his 18th Division, was also upbeat. 'The best thing that can be said about the Division is that it captured all its objectives and held them.' Congreve wrote, 'My wire was splendidly cut everywhere … I believe we dumped 80,000 tons of ammo before the attack began.' They had captured a German regimental and battalion commander, and 'the 30th Division did particularly well and took Montauban at first rush'. He was less complimentary about the 'huge quantity' of walking wounded, which he attributed 'to the dark class of my troops who think a scratch a serious wound'. He had lost over 6,000 men but declared, 'I am proud of my splendid fighting troops.' All in all, it had been 'a perfect day'.[14]

Lieutenant Billy Lipscomb of the 1st Dorsets wrote to his free-spirited actress sweetheart Vera within two days: 'Don't mention the word "staff" to me or I shall be ill,' he wrote. 'Somebody ought to be hung for this show.' His battalion had lost its commanding officer and his company was down to 70 from the customary '250 or so'. Private Herbert Hall, with the 12th Yorks and Lancs, had survived the debacle at Serre. Once they were back in their own line 'a general came to see us. I know his name and I won't mention it.' He surprised the survivors by asking: 'Did any of you people see anything meritorious?'

> *There wasn't a single sound. There was only about seventy of us, and that included the first line reinforcements. Not a sound. We thought it was a very unnecessary question. And of course, to insult us, they awarded the medals to the colonel's runner and the senior stretcher-bearer.*[15]

British château decision-makers were feeling uncomfortable at midnight. Walter Congreve's XIII Corps had taken its objectives and Henry Horne's XV Corps had taken Mametz and precipitated the German withdrawal under way at Fricourt, although he was not yet aware of it. Further north the results were grievously disappointing, an 80 per cent debacle along the line. The III, X and VIII Corps had achieved nothing of substance. Staff officer Major Charles Ward-Jackson with VII Corps had seen the army commander Rawlinson alongside the Chief of Imperial General Staff Robertson speak to General Snow at Pas. 'They have been very nice to the Corps Commander,' he observed, 'who took the disappointment of not attaining his objective very pluckily and did not fuss.' Snow was already looking for a scapegoat. If he did not find one, the Third Army commander Allenby would. The only brief glimmer of hope had been the Ulster dash up onto the Thiepval plateau, finally snuffed out just before midnight.

The casualty differential between success and failure was minimal. Failure came where it mattered, whereas success occurred where it was not needed, in tactically irrelevant areas. Indeed, Rawlinson proposed to renew the attack against the centre and left, where it had failed, rather than exploit the gains on his right. Haig was not responsive to this view; he was looking for the next day, for collaboration with the French to the right. 'The chief fault,' Lieutenant Billy Lipscomb wrote to Vera, 'is that the General Staff sit behind and look at maps of trenches and say "If that is taken so and so will happen", but it doesn't ... trenches are impossible things to judge from maps.'

At midnight, the gulf between front and château had never been so great. Private S Megaw, with the Belfast Young Citizens Battalion, remembered General Nugent's post-action address. 'Men, you've done very well,' he said, 'but you might have done better.' This was not particularly well received. 'There was a lot of murmuring in the ranks,' remembered Megaw, 'and some thought he was anything but a gentleman.'[16]

The biggest attack by the largest British army so far in this war had collapsed, and senior commanders were feeling vulnerable. Brigadier-General Charteris, Haig's intelligence chief, remained eternally optimistic. They 'have done well on the main part of the attack (Fourth Army)', he sanguinely wrote in his diary that night, 'where we have penetrated to the depth of one mile'. This, however, represented less than a quarter of the frontage; 'on the left', in other words the rest, 'we have not done well'. He blamed the troops, who 'failed to take advantage of situations offered to them, because they had not been ordered to carry out the particular operation'. Soldiers in Kitchener's New Army did what they were told to do. They had sacrificed themselves in impossible conditions, reflecting poorly on a leadership unable to effectively communicate with them, once they had gone over the top. Charteris in his diary entry for that day accepted the lack of initiative 'must happen with a new army' and noted, 'we improve daily'.

Haig and Rawlinson were in effect protected by the immensity of the disaster. The Somme developed into a battle of attrition that would last until 18 November. Each passing day would serve to balance somewhat the degree of tragedy that occurred on day one. Political opportunities for swift recalls back to England were superseded by the battle becoming immersed in ever more pressing phases. Within 24 hours Haig would learn the casualty estimate had passed 40,000. 'This cannot be considered severe,' he wrote in his diary, 'in view of the numbers engaged, and the length of front attacked.' The British Army had in fact lost 21,000 soldiers killed and over 35,000 wounded, with nearly 600 taken prisoner. At midnight, Haig and Rawlinson's senior commanders were becoming acutely aware of the true figures and feeling vulnerable. They had already been unsettled by the command changes that had been enacted five hours before, when it was clear the attack was not succeeding.[17]

General Rawlinson's Fourth Army was a big one, with five corps, three of which were obviously in trouble. Haig placed the VIII and X Corps under the command of Lieutenant-General Gough, who had commanded the cavalry divisions during the day, ready to exploit the anticipated breakthrough. The newly appointed head of the Fifth Army, as it was called, was uncomfortable news for Hunter-Weston, whose VIII Corps had fared badly north of the Ancre. General Morland's only X Corps success had been the capture of the Schwaben Redoubt by the Ulster Division. Perched in his tree-top command post he had watched it given up again. 'Goughy' had a reputation as a thrusting general, not known to be sympathetic, who could be expected to drive these failing corps to greater efforts and hopefully success. The change cut across the former well-established and obsequious chain of command. Both commanders had now to prove themselves all over again with a new and unpredictable chief. 'The VIII Corps seems to want looking after' was Haig's disdainful view of Hunter-Weston. Gough visited him first and lost no time in making his mark. Rawlinson had ordered him to make a fresh attack in a few hours' time. Gough quickly read the situation and concluded such an attack would be pointless. Although he was not due to take over until 7 am on 2 July, he immediately cancelled the attack. Unlike some of his peers Gough did not lack moral fibre and undoubtedly saved hundreds of lives. Morland was next, and Gough arrived in time to learn the Schwaben Redoubt had been lost and the Ulster Division ejected. Morland appreciated that Gough's arrival would not be a career enhancing change.

The château generals and staffs spent a dispiriting night reviewing what had gone so catastrophically wrong on a day so beautifully preceded by singing larks and royal blue skies. Hunter-Weston and his corps staff were to be moved to a quiet sector far from the Somme by the end of the month. Gough tried to get rid of Morland, whose insistence on supporting fruitless attacks on Thiepval, in preference to exploiting the Ulster's success, had not impressed. Haig turned down the request. General Allenby, the Third Army commander, knew he was not popular at Haig's GHQ, and was apprehensive lest he be blamed for the failure to capture Gommecourt. It was ironically a deception, but cost two of his divisions nearly 7,000 men. Lieutenant-General Snow, the corps commander on the spot, had been away on ten days' leave prior to the battle and was blamed by Allenby for not paying sufficient attention to preparations. As Allenby suspected that Haig would never agree to sending Snow home, another scapegoat was found. Major General Stuart-Wortley's North Midland Division had failed to link with and provide support for the embattled London Division, which had penetrated three German trench lines to the south of the salient. Allenby convened a Court of Inquiry three days later, but had Stuart-Wortley sent home even before the investigation reported.

General Horne's III Corps was brought to a standstill in Mash Valley, despite his ruthless style of leadership. Horne removed Major-General Pilcher, the commander of 17th Division. Pilcher had to stand idly by and watch the destruction of his 50th Brigade in front of Fricourt, only to be dismissed for not driving his division hard enough. 'It is very easy to sit a few miles in the rear and get credit for allowing men to be killed in an undertaking foredoomed to failure,' Pilcher later explained. 'The part did not appeal to me and my protests against these useless attacks were not well received.' He was cashiered. Stuart-Wortley was posted to Ireland while Pilcher remained in England, both never again to receive an operational command. Their soldiers were convinced they were sacked for losing too many men; ironically, they were dismissed for refusing to sacrifice more. Like their apparently under-trained men, one of the early lessons evident in the châteaux behind the Western Front was that soft-hearted generals need not apply for tenure. The hard-driving Horne was promoted in the autumn to command the First Army. He had won his spurs on the Somme, having been a corps commander for just five months.

The day had taken a toll of nerves, confidence and appointments at British command châteaux. At trench level it took lives, bodies and minds. 'Every now and then a wounded man crawled in,' recalled Reginald Leetham, with the Rifle Brigade:

I shall never forget the agony in their faces, especially towards midnight, when some had been out for 16 hours. Quite a number, for the time I hope, had gone stark staring mad.[18]

General von Below, in command of the Second German Army, had spent a trying day at his St Quentin headquarters. There had been three British air raids on the marshalling yards, and his subordinate XIV Reserve Corps commander General von Stein – covering his key sector – had been shelled out of his Bapaume headquarters. By early afternoon it was clear the enemy was breaking into parts of this sector. Much of von Stein's corps reserve had already been committed. Shortly before midnight he was preparing orders for the 12th Reserve Division to attack Montauban by night. A series of hesitant, company size advances had already been committed. General von Stein decided to abandon Fricourt, already outflanked. The 111 Regiment elements inside had to be clear by daylight or risk being surrounded. Generalmajor von Soden's proud report at midnight, to the King of Württemberg, that his entire line was now back in his hands, must have come as some relief. Only small 'English nests' of resistance remained. Von Stein could now turn his attention to the 28th Division, left of von Soden, where a break-in, but not breakthrough, had occurred. It was clear the coming British offensive, of which von Below's repeated predictions to the Supreme Commander von Falkenhayn had fallen on deaf ears, was under way. Inside ten days some 15 fresh German divisions were either committed to this opening battle or heading towards it.

At the château at Biefvillers, before midnight, von Soden received the news that his *Schwerpunkt* at the Schwaben Redoubt had been restored. He was proud and relieved. He knew his division had stemmed a massive onslaught and inflicted crippling casualties on the British at the outset of the new offensive. The 26th Division had fought two and a half British corps to a standstill, odds of six to one. It was a remarkable achievement. The château remained a hotbed of urgent staffing activity at midnight as the remainder of the night was spent identifying and consolidating the line, sorting out reliefs and reorganising.

It was a resounding defensive victory, but the coming of the huge British offensive had been a chastening experience. Its wide extent came as a surprise. 'Today has been a great day,' 16-year-old artilleryman Walther Kleinfeldt wrote to his mother, 'and a real hellfire.' Kleinfeldt's battery had lost guns and men near Pozières. The young Kleinfeldt had taken some dramatic pictures with the small Contessa camera that his mother had sent him. His pictures would become increasingly bleak as the war progressed. 'Please do not worry about me and don't get upset,' he assured his mother. 'The English offensive has been brought to a halt on all sides.' Ammunition wagon driver Otto Maute of 180 Regiment likely resupplied Kleinfeldt's battery off the Bapaume–Pozières road that day. 'You at home have simply no idea what it's like in war,' he wrote to his mother the following day.[19]

Von Soden's division had held its own, but this was only the first of 142 days of battle to come. The 99th Regiment swept aside by the 36th Ulster Division lost two companies at the penetration point. It was already earmarked for relief that day, having lost 472 casualties during the seven-day artillery bombardment. 180 Regiment next to it lost 293 over the same period and 273 on the day. The figures are imprecise but 99 Regiment according to anecdotal claims lost half its strength. 109 Regiment in 28th Division's area opposite Mametz and Montauban lost 556 officers and men killed or fatally wounded on 1 July and 943 prisoners. The regiment, normally numbering about 2,800 men with its three battalions, lost one man less than for the entire period from September 1914 to this day on the Somme. German losses are difficult to reconcile because their units generally submitted ten-day casualty returns. On this heavy day, many did submit returns and rough calculations point to 8,000 casualties between Gommecourt in the north to the French boundary in the south. This was seven to one in favour of the German defence, the exact reversal of the British and German numbers involved.[20]

At midnight, from Serre to Fricourt, there was quiet satisfaction that the English had been bloodily repulsed. Machine-gunner Otto Lais reflectively regarded the medics and stretcher-bearers at Serre picking up the grim harvest from his guns. An awful undercurrent of whimpering and moaning rose up from virtually every square metre of ground to their front.

On the Schwaben Redoubt, south of the Ancre, the body of its dead commander Oberleutnant Fassbender was sprawled alongside those of a machine-gun crew, which according to the heaped empty cases must have fired off 20,000 rounds. Hauptmann von Wurmb was moving about, consolidating and preparing the location for all-round defence. Patrols were sent forward to identify if any of the overrun 99 Regiment trenches still contained any groups of British soldiers. Unteroffizier Friedrich Hinkel also looked at 'great piles of dead and wounded, a product of the violent success achieved with our machine-guns'. They had held on to the southern shoulder of the penetration. The Schwaben counter-attack had come from their rear, and it was still not apparent whether the trenches to their right held British survivors or not. Friendly fire contacts in the dark were a huge risk at such a vulnerable moment, and '1st July had long slipped into the past before we regained our old positions at the front'. The situation was precarious, but they still held the village of Thiepval to their left. One of the machine-guns had fired 18,000 rounds across his front from there that day, at a time when 4,500 rounds was considered the normal combat requirement. German infantry in Thiepval had fired an average of 350 rounds apiece, with two to three re-supplies, as normally between 100 to 150 was carried on the man.[21]

Vizefeldwebel Laasch, with 110 Regiment at La Boisselle, was still observing the heaped mounds of dead in no man's land in the light of the flares, searching for signs of movement. There appeared to be a general exodus back to the British lines. His men were wary and vengeful. They had been sniped at all afternoon by British wounded, and patrols were now out in the darkness bayoneting and bashing in heads of those that could be found. Wagon driver Otto Maute was sleeping fitfully with his horses at midnight inside a farmhouse with shattered windows. British artillery fire was still intermittently coming down on registered targets alongside the Albert to Bapaume road.

There was a different atmosphere in the line beyond the road from Fricourt south of the Willow Stream between Mametz and Montauban. 111 Regiment was pulling back from Fricourt. Rudolf Stadelbacher's machine-gun had fired off 22,000 rounds that day. He and his companion Otto Schüsele were withdrawing around midnight, 'despite the fact the British were so close that we could hear them talking'. They pulled back to the area of Contalmaison. All this was of concern to Feldwebel Karl Eisler, with Artillery Regiment 29, who was supposed to be covering them. The news was bad. Height 110 at Fricourt was soon to be relinquished, and the right flank between them and La Boisselle 'is already lost and in English hands', Eisler reported. 'No worthwhile reinforcements and no orders from above,' he complained. The forward observation post on the high ground at Fricourt had only depressing information:

Leutnant Mayer fallen in a crater field, Musketier Baumann fatally wounded and Unteroffizier Hittler and Musketier Viehoft with telephone operator Enderle taken prisoner by the British.

Eisler was aware there was hardly any German infantry ahead of them. 'With a shudder,' he recalled, 'one could think of only one phrase: No reinforcements!' Morale was at a tipping point. 'A profound bitterness gripped us – why have we been left alone, without any reinforcements or reliefs?' The English rifle fire was fading. 'Is that a sign of exhaustion,' he asked himself, 'or will a fresh attack come?'

Just before midnight a company from Landwehrbattalion 55 came into Contalmaison, near where the battery was located. This did not inspire much confidence because 'the officer did not have a map and couldn't decide what was going on'. When their remaining three artillery pieces hidden behind the castle opened up, they immediately attracted counter-battery fire. Midnight came with a steady trickle of wounded from 110 and 111 Regiments passing by them through the village, heading for the rear.[22]

About three and a half miles east, Franz Gerhardinger's faltering advance with 16 Regiment had come up against strong resistance in the Montauban Alley. The British were not budging. Gerhardinger stumbled back to get further orders from his battalion. The British were packed head to head in the trenches before them. Without appreciating it, the battle of attrition had already begun for the Germans. It had started with the inability to conduct reliefs during the seven-day bombardment. There was an increasing sense of desperation in the way the defence was conducted, reflected in Eisler's sense of developments being out of control. Battalions such as Franz Gerhardinger's 16 Regiment were being broken up and rushed forward to plug gaps, regardless of the consequences for these small units on the ground. It was the overture to the 'meat grinder' that would follow over the next five months.

A British machine-gun picked up the tell-tale signs of Gerhardinger's movement from shell hole to shell hole and hit him in the back with a burst. He was lucky, the rounds glanced off his pack and merely grazed his back. 'Only the fact that I had a tin of conserved meat in the pack deflected the shot from a severe chest wound,' he recalled. He was next blown off his feet and knocked unconscious by the air pressure from a nearby shell burst. It dropped him into a shell hole and this saved him from the machine-gun.[23]

The last recorded action of the first day on the Somme flared up at Gommecourt at midnight. Two platoons of the 1/5th Lincolns were ordered to conduct a fighting patrol to locate and relieve men, allegedly trapped and still holding out in captured German trenches. The patrol was caught in the light of flares and lashed by German machine-gun fire. There were no cut-off British soldiers. The Lincolns pulled back under heavy fire after losing 48 men killed and wounded.

Peace descended on the line between Gommecourt and Montauban, interrupted occasionally by flickering episodes of violence. There was time to reflect, for those not engaged in digging, repairing or recovering wounded, on what had been an awful day. Tommy Higgins struggled along the road west of Gommecourt between Foncquevillers and Souastre, looking for his battalion with his mate Jack Heywood. 'We crawled rather than walked' the three miles, he remembered, and found them 'or what was left of them lying in some old trenches'. The quartermaster was still up and serving rum. 'Hello,' he said, shaking his hand, 'I heard you were killed, old man.' Others like Private Frank Lindley, wounded at

Serre, had been rattling along in an ambulance for much of the afternoon on a circuitous route to Etaples via Amiens. Every time the vehicle jolted to a halt civilians had surged forward to offer the parched wounded a sip of cooling water. On arrival, there was little chance of putting the 16-year-old to sleep for his operation; the order of the day was simply 'do it'. When the doctor yanked the shrapnel from his thigh, Lindley was convinced his innards would follow. As he lapsed into unconsciousness, he was also sure he heard the sound of sawing.

Surviving Tommies in the line at Serre were still emerging from the trauma of the day. 'Everybody had the same opinion, they'd had enough and seen enough,' remembered Harry Hall in the 13th Yorks and Lancs. 'It was more what you saw than what you experienced,' he reflected. 'To see fellows coming in maimed, oh it was terrible.' Corporal Bill Partridge, with the 7th Middlesex Regiment, had been in reserve. 'Well,' he recalled, 'if I said the morale was high I'd be telling a lie.' The day had been a sobering experience:

> *The thoughts of most of us, after the maiden attack, was that we wanted either a Blighty one or ones that were a top storey. We didn't want to be mutilated – that was our main thought. That, and smoking a cigarette, and wondering if it was going to be the last one.*[24]

Opposite Beaumont Hamel further south, Lancashire Fusilier George Ashurst manned his barricade on the German side of the sunken lane in the dark. His close-knit regular battalion which had fought at Ypres and Gallipoli had been decimated. Only one of 22 officers was still on his feet, and 486 of the 697 men who went over the top that morning were gone. 'I'd lost most of my friends,' Ashurst remembered.

'These were my platoon lads, they'd been boozing with us in the villages … But it was no use bothering,' the phlegmatic corporal reflected, 'we knew they'd gone.'

Cinematographer Geoffrey Malins was resting in the trenches not far away. He instinctively knew he had exposed some remarkable footage that day and hoped the reels were unspoiled. There had been some dreadful sights. Sympathetic aversion and the absence of a telephoto lens had precluded the graphic reality that was to characterise the work of more recent combat cameramen. Some of his material was to be stage managed later as part of the editing process, primarily to tell a story. Distance was a subtle censor. Only recently has it been established that Malins did actually capture scenes of men falling in battle, in the middle or far distance, on several reels. Little did he realise, as he thought about what to film tomorrow, that he had already captured some of the most iconic images of the Great War.[25]

Lieutenant-Colonel Frank Crozier's command post in the still smouldering Thiepval Wood saw a succession of wounded officers and men, returning from the shambles of the withdrawal from the Schwaben Redoubt. 'My dugout door that night is like the entrance to a mad house,' he recalled. Acting Captain William Montgomery came in 'torn, tattered, filthy and worn out, with a wound on head and dent in helmet'. At midnight Montgomery was numbed, exhausted and totally desolate. His state of mind is reflected in a letter sent shortly after. 'Mother would have cried and quite possibly you also when I called the remnant of my company to attention,' he wrote to his father. They had gone over the top with four officers and 115 soldiers; at the day's end he dismissed 34 men. 'Not a few of the men cried and I cried,' he remembered. 'A hell of a hysterical exhibition it was.' A day later he wrote:

I am still funking writing to Mr Gaffkin about his son George. He got his death wound when fighting desperately side by side with me in the wildest hand grenade and machine-gun fight man could live or die in.

Like so many others, William Montgomery discovered things about himself he never knew before. Fortified by wine, he wrote that he was nerveless. 'I have seen and done since 30th June some truly awful things and they never even fizzed on me and I have had absolutely no reaction.' During all these awful events 'I never even stopped smoking'. He was now a husk of his former self. He tried to rationalise these feelings: 'excitement or exhaustion – finest sensation in life', but he was alive. 'Please tell Bertha I ate her lovely bread last thing before going into action and wore her white heather,' he wrote in conclusion. 'It certainly did bring me luck.'

Crozier's Dantesque dugout continued to receive its bleak visitors.

McKee, a bright lad, is practically delirious, shot through the lung he still walks and talks. He has lain out in the broiling sun all day. I give him a brandy and soda for which he gives me abuse … Robbins, a smart youngster, is carried in by two soldiers who are themselves badly wounded, his shrieks can be heard hundreds of yards away, for the firing has now ceased, both sides being exhausted. His leg is fractured below the knee, and he will probably lose it.

The recapture of the Schwaben Redoubt after such an epic advance was a bitter blow for the Ulster Division. 'At 10 pm the curtain rings down on hell,' was Crozier's epilogue. 'The cost? Enormous.' His battalion had lost all but 70 men out of 700. The Division in its first major action of the war had lost 5,104 men.[26]

Sergeant-Major Ernest Shepherd, with the 1st Dorsets, was relieved near Authuille Wood further south at midnight, by the 15th Highland Light Infantry. They had been shelled on and off all afternoon. 'Literally we were blown from place to place,' he recalled. The men prior to the relief were 'very badly shaken', having cleared their trenches of dead and debris prior to the Highlanders coming in. The dead 'we piled in heaps', he remembered. 'Enemy shells pitching on them made matters worse.' Shepherd was lightly wounded himself, but still took the remnants of B and C Companies to the rear, which was 'only 10 NCOs and men'.

'We'd lost so many people, and taken so little ground,' recalled Lieutenant Ulick Burke with the 2nd Devons, just southeast of Shepherd's group. 'Men began to wonder, *Why?* There was no feeling of giving up; they were just wondering "why?"' Grimly watching 'endless lines of walking wounded, and ambulances' they began to wonder 'how long we could exist' – and this was just the first day.[27]

Around the corner of the Fricourt salient and moving east toward Montauban, the mood in the line was lighter. Albert Andrews, with the 19th Manchesters, came across a Yorks captain outside Montauban who said:

Pleased to see you here, boys. I have been in this war since it began but that was the prettiest sight I have seen, you boys set off to the Germans smoking and walking and keeping line.

Sergeant Richard Tawney was still lying out in no man's land at midnight. 'It was out of the question to get me in that night,' he was told by the medical orderlies. The advance had been up to a mile deep, and the over-worked stretcher-bearers had yet to come up. Having spent the entire afternoon bereft of human contact, Tawney was content with having someone around him.

All the wounded craved this personal contact. German soldier Günther Becker was asked after the war what it was like to lie in no man's land waiting for help. His first thoughts were, 'Now you are out of this dog's breakfast, now you'll never be back at the front.' Being wounded was a solution, an end-state of sorts. 'I was as happy as anything,' he admitted, 'although I was severely wounded.' Was it all about being rescued in himself? he was asked. 'No,' he responded. 'I thought, now you can die in peace.'

For every yard of the 16-mile 'L' shaped front between Gommecourt and Montauban, two British soldiers had fallen, and one man in three of those was at peace.[28]

Beyond 24 Hours

Katie Morter's husband Percy never came back. 'He was a very steady young man, very big and fair,' she recalled, 'and he was all that a young woman would wish to see.' Percy Morter was a car painter, and he had been stolen from her by Vesta Tilly at the Palace Theatre Manchester to the refrain of the popular song 'We don't want to lose you, but we think you ought to go'. Now she had lost him. 'He was a lovely man, really good and was a member of the St Cross Church at Clayton.' She had last seen him over six months before. 'Open the door,' he had called, 'the Jerries are here!' and he came in 'all mucky and what have you, right from France'. Soldiers came directly from the front, dirty and louse-ridden.

Katie was seven months pregnant and had just given up her job at a leather factory the previous Friday when she received the letter on Monday morning. It was from his sergeant. 'Dear Mrs Morter, I'm very sorry to tell you of the death of your husband,' it read. 'That was as far as I could read, you see,' she remembered. 'I couldn't read anything else, and I felt I didn't want to live.' The pregnancy had been difficult. Unable to read the death notification, the normally reclusive Katie took it next door. 'I thought perhaps it was just an error, I wasn't sure exactly what happened.' For a while she was too shocked to respond to the sergeant's letter. When she did, she discovered he had been killed too. The baby arrived 'but my world had come to an end', she admitted.[1]

Over 21,000 such letters were dispatched with the same bleak news: 35, 493 letters told of wounds and mutilation in bureaucratically bland terms. Nearly 60,000 casualty notices were sent out. Each one impacted on the lives of at least ten relatives and friends, so that six million people from a population of 43 million received the same terrible news in the first weeks of July. Over one in ten inhabitants of the United Kingdom knew someone intimately, who had been lost. Many more were depressed by the grievous impact the losses had upon the fabric of close-knit local communities across the British Isles.

Little thought had been given to the effect on a local community of the complete annihilation of its own specially raised fighting force. 'We were two years in the making and ten minutes in the destroying,' said Private AV Pearson of the Leeds Pals. 'The companionship was marvellous, absolutely marvellous,' declared Private George Morgan, with the 1st Bradford Pals. 'Everyone seemed to help one another and agree with one another. It was lovely.' Nobody thought, in the midst of the frenetic recruiting process in the autumn of 1914, that the amazing concept of the Pals battalions, of friends from civil life serving together in the companionship of war, could go wrong. They served together, but they died together as well.

Certain parts of the country were denuded of a large number of their menfolk overnight. Yorkshire lost 9,000 men, Ulster and Lancashire 6,000 each. In Ulster, for the first time ever, Orange Day was not celebrated on 12 July. Instead, all work and movement in Belfast was suspended for five minutes after noon. Business and household activity stopped; machinery was silent; shop and business premises, rail and street traffic, all ground to a halt. Blinds were down, flags were at half-mast and citizens stood bare-headed in the pouring rain as church bells tolled mournfully for the dead. There were no Orange parades. 'In 1916 crying could be heard in the streets of Belfast and in the provincial towns and villages of Ulster,' remembered Mr James Page. 'The sight of a uniformed telegram boy sufficed to cause fear, so dread were the tidings of the Division's fate.' An Orangeman in Lurgan wrote to a friend explaining, 'There is hardly a house in Hill Street in which at least one member of the family has not been killed or wounded.' The impact on the future development of communities would be incalculable:

> It is terrible, terrible hard news to bear with equanimity, for however just and right a cause it may be, the death of so many young men leaves our land that much the poorer.

'Dear Friend Mary,' wrote Mrs M Johnston on her postcard from Portadown, after learning she had lost her brother in France.

> I am sorry that one so dear to you is dead and I want you to know how I feel about it. I said Mass on Sunday. You may think it will do him no good but it eased the burden I have in my heart for you. Love Lizzie.[2]

Some cities suffered especially badly, the effect magnified in terraced back-to-back communities. London lost over 5,000 casualties, Manchester 3,500, Belfast 1,800 and Edinburgh, Newcastle, Bradford, Leeds and Birmingham – all over 1,000.

Lieutenant Richard Cary's great-great-nieces have perpetuated his memory long after his death at Gommecourt; some are still Londoners. He never fulfilled his engagement promise to Doris Mummery of Leytonstone. His name is inscribed as one of the missing on the majestic Thiepval monument, which his mother Ellen visited twice in 1932 and 1934 before her death. He is also remembered at the Cary grave in Norwood cemetery, London, alongside his mother and others.[3]

Of the 1st Pals Battalion, only three officers of 24, which was every officer that actually went over the top, and 201 men from 650, emerged from the first day of the battle. Two thirds of them were missing without trace. This battalion had enlisted almost to a man in Salford just outside Manchester, or were resident nearby. The 2nd and 3rd Pals lost 60 per cent of their officers and 55 per cent of their men from Pendlebury, Swinton, Eccles and Patricroft, all districts nearby. Captain EB Lord remembered the appearance of the 1st Pals survivors making their way to the rear, with 'weary, haggard and drawn faces, bodies exhausted and legs that almost could not carry their burden, but their thoughts were too tragic for words'. He walked with them awhile trying to cheer them up, knowing they had lost so many friends, but 'I felt like a warder escorting a condemned prisoner'. The battalion band joined them, poignantly playing 'Keep the home fires burning till the boys come home'. But very few would. 'I nearly wept with the impotence and sadness,' he admitted.[4]

It was to take eight days for the press at home to comprehend what had happened, and three days for the full extent of the casualties to be officially learned. 'Victory for our Brave Boys,' trumpeted the *Salford City Reporter*, seven days after, fancifully describing how they had 'swept through the little town of Thiepval'. An ambiguous passage reported 'the losses of some units are very heavy' amid flowery phrases like 'an ecstasy of sacrifice, an exhilaration of mind' that had 'transcended human effort'. This was at a time when 4,000 Salford dockers were on strike for an additional penny an hour. Normally the strike would have dominated local interest, but the actual focus in newspapers and pubs was on 'what had happened?' The *Barnsley Chronicle* had even commented in its editorial on 1 July that 'no doubt good and solid reasons explain why there has been no great spring "push" all along the Western Front'. Explanations were still a long way off, and when the story of the 'Big Push' finally broke on Saturday 8 July, there were only contradictory official, semi-official and anecdotal journalist accounts to report on. 'The progress of our gallant troops is being watched with the keenest interest,' the *Chronicle* wrote. 'Serre and Montauban, two important tactical points, were soon captured.' The journalists felt sufficiently informed to announce:

> *The initial success of defeating the enemy on a 16 mile front has naturally elated the whole British Army and nation, and aroused the utmost confidence of further triumphs.*

Then the memorial notices started to pour in, and stories told by some of the casualties did not match what their relatives were reading in the newspapers. The *Chronicle* did admit that 'all sorts of wild rumours were yesterday current locally concerning the Barnsley Battalions'. The Scout Movement boys in Pendleton outside Salford were devastated to learn that their Scoutmaster, 25-year-old Second Lieutenant Cyril Crossly, had been killed in action on 2 July. The *Barnsley Chronicle* then announced the death of Captain George de Ville Smith, the former curate of St Thomas's church at Worsbrough Dale. The congregation was in tears when it was announced from the pulpit.[5]

Disaster on the scale of 1 July 1916 was unprecedented in the annals of the British Army. The release of information was insensitively handled, compassion overwhelmed by the enormity of the figures. The imperative was to dispense the awful news quickly, which was a bureaucratic challenge. 'What was wrong about it was that even though it was a complete failure,' Lieutenant WJ Brockman with the Lancashire Fusiliers complained, 'it was reported as being a success in the newspapers.' This was compounded by the general ignorance of the true nature of the war at home. Norman Demuth, with the London Regiment, found his parents 'didn't seem in the least interested in what had happened'. They 'had no idea of what kind of danger we were in'. Private Demuth was exasperated by the lack of 'any conception of what it was like, and on occasions when I did talk about it, my father would argue points of fact that he couldn't possibly have known about because he wasn't there'. 'What was worse' with the inaccurate newspaper reports, Lieutenant Brockman argued, 'was that they still persisted, knowing perfectly well that they were getting nowhere. It went on, and on, and on.' The first day of the Somme came as a shock to a populace in whose minds, Demuth maintained, there was 'of course the general idea that England could not possibly lose'.[6]

The debacle of the first day resulted in a loss of innocence, a puncturing of unrealistic expectations that the war would be over by the next Christmas. The Germans had brushed aside the best the British could set against them in about two hours. 'You've done a good job, chaps, you've done a very good job!' Private Clifford Hollingsworth heard his brigadier saying. 'We've hell as like!' retorted one soldier. 'I beg your pardon?' the brigadier asked. Hollingsworth described the irreverent conversation:

'We've hell as like, we've lost!'
He said, 'Don't talk like that, lost, you musn't speak like that, man!'

'Have we won then? Cos if we've won, God help us if we lose! If we'd won that battle [where] we'd lost 600 men, I don't know how we should have got on if we'd lost.'

Three days later Captain Lionel Ferguson of the 13th Cheshire Regiment encapsulated the essence of this exchange in his description of the survivors of a Highland Division moving back, after a mauling on the Somme:

It was a sight to me to see really tired men, they were just walking along in twos and threes, holding each other for support, unshaven, covered with mud, and war worn, in fact never have I seen troops in worse condition.

They 'had an awful time' and 'they were a smashed division'.[7]

It took until mid November for the British to finally push the Germans back to Bapaume, due to be captured in the first week of July. Thiepval and most of the plateau did not fall into Allied hands until 30 September. After very hard fighting the final small strip of the Schwaben Redoubt still in German hands, its northwest corner, was taken on 14 October. By 19 November the British had gained a strip of land about 20 miles long and six miles deep. None of it was of strategic importance. The British lost 400,000 killed, wounded and missing, the French 200,000. Included among them was a large part of Kitchener's New Army. Conscript soldiers were now replacing them. Revisionary accounts that point to the beneficial enhancement of British veteran fighting power as a result of these brutal battles of attrition miss the point. That the British Army learned to defeat their German enemy on the Somme is broadly correct, but this was a consequence of the losses; it was why they fought the battle.[8]

The German Army was subjected to bludgeoning frontal attacks for 142 days and was to suffer between 600,000 and 680,000 casualties, probably more on balance than the Allies. The meat-grinder of Verdun at the beginning of 1916 transitioned on the Somme, by the end of the year, to a degree of attrition the German Army was unable to sustain. The traditional German Army lost a huge proportion of its junior officers and especially experienced NCOs, who were irreplaceable. Hauptmann von Hertig, a staff officer with the Guards Reserve Division, claimed 'the Somme was the muddy grave of the German Field Army and of the faith in the infallibility of the German leadership'.

The average German infantryman of 1916 would not disagree. The Somme was a killing field. German soldier Gerhard Bahrmann arrived as a summer reinforcement and asked about the big ditches they passed as they entered the forward positions. 'They are the graves for those that will fall today,' he was informed. Another soldier with an aviation unit used to watch the reinforcements go past, heading for the front on roads 'black with troops'. It was a haunting spectacle 'he would never forget' as he watched replacements pass by 'four or five ranks deep in column and sometimes in completely unordered crowds'.

> *They passed shambling by, the faces of the condemned, sentenced to death, led off to the havoc. I stood hours long and thought, 'You were blessed by the Lord God to be on the verge side on a motorbike with an aviation unit, while these people, who have done no wrong to their fellow man, are off to become cripples or die.'*

Artillery soldier Willi Marquardt thought 'the attacks on the Somme were worse than Verdun'. As the autumn rains descended, the last remnants of Infantry Regiment 180 pulled out of Thiepval, which was lost on 27 September. Leutnant Matthäus Gerster, who had also experienced the first day, watched them pass by in thick fog and pouring rain:

> *They came past one by one or in squads; walking lumps of clay, with torn clothing, hollow cheeks and sunken eyes. Stubble, days old, covered their faces and their helmets were pushed back on their heads. There was a dreadful weariness, but a wildness burning in their fevered eyes, showing what this appalling hand to hand fighting had cost them. Utterly unforgettable for me ...*

They were the ghosts of the first day of the Somme. The village of Thiepval, Gerster explained, was 'written in blood and iron in the history of the 26th Reserve Division'. When a later reconstituted 1st Battalion Infantry Regiment 180 reformed in new barracks in 1938, prior to the next World War, there was little debate over what these should be called – Thiepval Barracks.[9]

Generalmajor Franz von Soden's 26th Reserve Division remained in the Somme battle until October, wintered in Artois, fought at Arras in 1917 and was part of the Ludendorff Spring Offensive in 1918. This offensive momentarily recaptured all that had been lost by the Germans during the long drawn-out battle of attrition in 1916. Von Soden's achievements on the first day of the Somme battle and after were rewarded with Corps command. He commanded both the VII and V German Corps before leading his troops back to the homeland and demobilisation in November 1918. After the war he headed up the 125th Division's retired officers association, living long enough to see Germany defeated a second time before he died in November 1945.

The two heroes of the retaking of the Schwaben Redoubt – lost in 15 minutes and regained in 14 hours – Hauptmann Herbert Ritter von Wurmb and commander Oberstleutnant Alfons Ritter von Bram, were awarded the 'Blue Max'. This was the Knight's Cross of the Military Max Joseph Order, and on par with the British Victoria Cross. Von Wurmb was wounded at Ypres the following year and left the army as a major in June 1920. He went on to study economics and art at the University of Munich and was recalled as a lieutenant-colonel, this time for the Third Reich and appointed colonel in early 1942. Von Bram retired as a major-general in November 1921; he was too old to be recalled during the Second World War but lived long enough to witness the catastrophic demise of Hitler's Reich before dying in 1951 aged 86.

Many of the German survivors of the first day were not to survive the war. Most have disappeared into historical obscurity because of the loss of many Great War unit histories and accounts, destroyed by Allied bombing and the maelstrom of fighting that ended the next war. Machine-gunner Otto Lais from 169 Regiment was seduced, like many others, by Adolf Hitler's National Socialist rhetoric. *'Führer, befiehl! Wir folgen dir!'* he trumpeted in the introduction to his personal memoir of his experiences as a machine-gunner in the Great War. The Nazi slogan – 'Leader, command! We will follow you!' – summed up the blind acquiescence of many of his contemporaries during the inter-war years. Lais became an artist of some erotic and moralist note and lived until 1988.

1916 was the year of peak effort for Germany, before a resigned spirit of dogged acceptance of their situation took over. The realisation that the war would indeed be long and terrible was also starkly apparent to the British after 1 July. Second Lieutenant Kenneth Macardle, with the 17th

Manchesters, reflected on the loss of his friends six days after their *successful* attack on Montauban:

> *All the world was forever dead to Vaudrey, Kenworthy, Chesham, Sproat, Ford, and the 'other ranks' we did not know how many. Vaudrey used to love rousing parades; Chesham had loved to hunt the buck in Africa when the heat was shimmering with the birth of a day … Young Victor was killed – his problem of marriage to a woman six years senior to him finally settled. Towers Clark too was dead and Captain Law of County Down …*[10]

They had gone over the top with 800, but by nightfall were down to 400.

The fact that it was always the other chap that would be killed is what sustained them. Macardle was killed three days later. Many alive at midnight on 1 July would not see out the end of the war. Sergeant-Major Ernest Shepherd, with the 1st Dorsets, was commissioned in November, but killed in action at Beaucourt near Beaumont Hamel on 11 January 1917. When he knew his position was hopeless, he characteristically warned the supporting company to fall back, so that it was not overwhelmed as well. He is buried on the Somme at Flers. His vivid diary, recorded in 18 small pocket books, complete with sketch maps of trench systems, covers his service from Hill 60 in early 1915 to death on the Somme. The books lay undisturbed for over 60 years in a chocolate box left in a bedroom wardrobe.

Sergeant Richard Tawney, with the 22nd Manchesters, had to lie out in the open in no man's land for 30 hours before he was recovered and evacuated back to England. His radical socialist beliefs led him to turn down a commission. The war heightened his sense of urgency about the need for meaningful social, economic and political change. He became an eminent economic and social historian and active contributor to the Labour Party, before passing away in 1962, aged 81. Private Tommy Higgins, with the North Staffs, survived Gommecourt only to be captured at Loos in July 1917. He endured 16 traumatic months as a prisoner before being demobilised in 1919.

George Ashurst, with the Lancashire Fusiliers, finished up a sergeant, awaiting a commission, but was demobbed in January 1919. He was a locomotive driver with the Lancs and Yorks Railway Company and ran the railway depot Home Guard unit in the Second World War. Even after retiring, aged 65, in 1960, he continued to do part-time insurance and office work until he was 80.

On 3 July, two days after the attack, Albert Andrews, with the 19th Manchesters, was burying their dead. 'Burying your own lads is not a job that I want again,' he recalled, 'some seemingly by their looks to have died very easy, others very hard.' Some of the half buried had first to be dug out again. 'The game wanted sticking!' he complained. 'You could hardly stand the stench as you got hold of them, often having to put them down, go out of the way and have a smoke.'

Five days later he was blown up when a 'coal box [shell] dropped right in front of four of us', wounding and killing three and sending him 'skating' with concussion. Just over two weeks later he was wounded again. What he did not appreciate was that he was already suffering shell shock from the first blast. Mental treatment continued after his discharge in February 1918, when he worked in a railway carriage works and then for the *Daily Herald*. During the Second World War he tried unsuccessfully to join the Tank Corps in his late forties, still suffering shell shock, which was to dog him for the rest of his days until his death in 1952, aged 61.[11]

Newfoundland soldier Leo O'Neil was visibly surprised when he woke up several days later, after being struck down at Beaumont Hamel, to learn that he was not in heaven. A woman in white was bent over him and 'even her head was covered by a white veil'. She spoke in a foreign language and he realised he was wounded and in hospital. After losing his leg he would lie there for a year. His regiment had virtually ceased to exist, with 710 killed, wounded or missing.

When he was evacuated back to Newfoundland, O'Neil was met by the Governer's wife Lady Walwyn, as he hobbled down the ship's ramp on one leg. To each of the wounded a packet of cigarettes was handed and she said 'thank you'. Only 68 of O'Neil's regiment got back to their own line that day. Nearly 10 per cent of the total male population of Newfoundland, or 35.6 per cent of the cream of its youth aged between 19 and 35, had volunteered. The Newfoundland Regiment distinguished itself at Beaumont Hamel, Gueudecourt, Manchy and Cambrai, twice being very nearly destroyed. A quarter died, with 72 per cent casualties or 58 per cent of the total nominal roll of those who went. This devastating outcome left Newfoundlanders feeling bereft and confused, with a sense of loss that was to scar an entire generation.

Leo O'Neil was given some crown land for his war service and spent his working life as a Newfoundland Railway caretaker. He mopped and swept floors until he retired in the 1960s, limited by an artificial leg and part of his hand being missing. His grand-daughter Elizabeth Clarke remembered being fascinated watching him take off his wooden leg at the end of each day. 'It felt good to get it off,' she recalled, because the woollen sock he wore over the stump caused chafing. 'He spent the remaining years of his life quietly and never went away again.' Till the day he died in 1977 'we never heard him speak about the war' and 'he never expressed a desire to be laid to rest in the Soldier's Field of Honor in St John's'.[12]

General Sir Douglas Haig kept the Somme battle going until November. His generalship has attracted opprobrium for his attrition tactics and disregard for human life. Huge further casualties were incurred at Arras and Passchendaele in the spring and autumn of 1917. Prime Minister Lloyd George mistrusted him and his acceptance of colossal casualties. Haig, however, was coming to grips with commanding five individual armies, each three times larger than the original BEF of 1914. He had to assimilate and deal with new, modern methods of waging war with new weapons, as well as having to confer daily with his political masters. It would have taxed a lesser man. Lloyd George lacked the courage to replace him and probably nobody else could. Despite the collapse of his front in March 1918, Haig came back to deliver the victories of Amiens, during his final months of command. After the war, he retired completely into private life, devoting himself to the affairs of ex-servicemen through the British Legion.

His equestrian statue appropriately faces the nation's memorial to its dead at the Cenotaph in Whitehall. His soldiers were aware of his immense resilience and endurance. Ted Rimmer, with the King's Liverpool Rifles, summed him up:

I thought he was a good commander. If he hadn't sent them over, what would have happened? The war would have gone on and on. It was a war of attrition, who could stand it the longest?[13]

Corporal Harry Fellows, with the 12th Northumberland Fusiliers, thought differently. 'Haig was a man who never cared for men's lives,' he claimed, 'and he became known to us as "The Butcher".' The truth lies at some point between these opposing views, which were not shared by the majority at war's end. As many as a million people, including 100,000 soldiers, lined Haig's funeral procession in 1928. The 'Lions led by Donkeys' epithet applied to the First World War generals in the 1960s by Alan Clark's *The Donkeys* was actually a phrase coined from a senior German officer's view of French performance during the Franco-Prussian War of 1870. In fact 58 British generals were to be killed in the Great War; they too were both human and vulnerable. General Walter Congreve, responsible for the success to the right of the line, lost his son Billy on the Somme. Major William Congreve was killed in action at Longueval on 20 July. He had been married just one month before and left a young pregnant wife. General Congreve was at a conference when the bleak news arrived. He declared his son 'a good soldier' (he had won the VC, DSO and MC), and felt impelled by duty to carry on.[14]

Sir Henry Rawlinson's reputation was also tainted by a determination and apparent willingness to accept seemingly unbelievable sacrifices in the pursuit of objectives set by Haig. In 1918, he still commanded the Fourth Army to victory at the battle of Amiens, 'the Black Day of the German Army' as Ludendorff called it. Rawlinson's daring crossing of the Canal du Nord broke the Hindenburg Line during the final campaign and was a far more competently planned operation than that of 1 July 1916. After the war he was appointed Commander-in-Chief India in 1920, a post he held until his death in 1925, aged 61, characteristically following a cricket match and polo.

Until the late 1920s, senior officers such as Haig and Rawlinson were accorded respect verging on homage. During the Great Depression, however, there was a change in the public mood, reflected by a series of classic anti-war books, poems and films like *All Quiet on the Western Front*, based on Remarque's book. In 1934 Madame Tussaud's exhibition of waxworks decided to reduce the prominence of its gallery of *The Men Who Won the War*. The real cause of the British debacle on 1 July 1916 was the inability to feed timely information to senior decision-makers, conducting operations with inexperienced troops on an unprecedented scale for the first time. Future planning and in particular British artillery management was to become far more sophisticated. Wellington in 1815 won an iconic victory at Waterloo that cost him a quarter of his force, not dissimilar to the casualty ratio on the Somme, but that achieved total rather than 20 per cent success.

The Home Front misunderstood the Western Front in much the same way as disillusioned anti-war authors, who achieved a moral ascendency in the wave of anti-war literature that emerged in the late 1920s and early 1930s. 'I've read the poems of Owen and Sassoon. I thought they were nonsense,' claimed Major Murray Hill, with the 5th Battalion Royal Fusiliers:

> *No point. It goes without saying. No need to write it up. Sassoon was off his head. He threw his medals into the sea. But he wrote a very good book about fox hunting.*

Charles Carrington, with the Royal Warkwickshire Regiment, regretted that the 1930s view prevailed. It did scant justice to 'the silent millions who did not want the war, did not cause the war, did not shirk the war, and did not lose the war'. The duty, sacrifice and guts of men who advanced into a hail of machine-gun fire cannot be explained in terms of being simply victims. He wrote:

I saw far more fighting than Siegfried Sassoon, or Edmund Blunden or Robert Graves, far more than Liddell Hart, four or five times as much as Wilfred Owen, and I didn't go home with a nervous breakdown.[15]

Carrington followed an academic career after being demobbed in 1919 and died in 1990.

'The people at home did not understand the conditions under which we were fighting,' explained Second Lieutenant WJ Brockman. 'I don't think they wanted to.' It was simply 'not fashionable', he claimed, to talk about the war. Cinematographer Geoffrey Malins did more than any other during the months during and after the Somme battle to educate the public about what their menfolk were doing at the front. His film *The Battle of the Somme* was mass released in August and was probably seen by almost half the population of the country. Twenty million out of 43 million watched it, a record not since exceeded even by successful Hollywood extravaganzas such as *Star Wars.* 'The real thing at last,' enthused the *Manchester Guardian.* It gave audiences the opportunity to identify with the reality on the Western Front for the first time. 'For sheer realism,' claimed the *Daily Express,* 'there has perhaps never been anything to excel this wonderful film.'[16]

It was uncomfortable viewing for some. 'Oh my God, they're dead!' cried out a woman in one audience. Some scenes were in fact staged, but many were not. The author H Rider Haggard saw it, and commented, 'There is something appalling about the instantaneous change from fierce activity to supine death.' Audiences had never been confronted with such stark reality. 'War has always been dreadful,' Rider Haggard observed, 'but never, I suppose, more dreadful than today.' In October, Mrs Wilson leaped to her feet in the Droylsden Electric Theatre, near Manchester, crying, 'It's Jim, my husband!' He was seen being carried off on a stretcher, *Screen* magazine reported. She had been notified on 6 July that her husband had been killed in action and, knowing he had been on the Somme, she had attended the theatre matinee. Other people in the audience confirmed her recognition of her husband. She was left a widow with nine children.[17]

Private Rowland Fielding watched the film in an openair screening at the front. He had turned up to see Charlie Chaplin, but arrived too late, 'and saw only the more harrowing part of the entertainment'. Although he thought it 'really a wonderful and most realistic production', it had an 'unpleasant part'. 'The machine-gun and rifle fire is entirely eliminated,' he pointed out, and the proximity of the screen to the front line made for uncomfortable viewing:

> *I have said that the battle is fought in silence; but no, on this occasion the roar of the real battle was loudly audible in the distance. I must say that at first the wisdom of showing such a film to soldiers on the brink of battle in which they are to play the part of the attackers struck me as questionable.*

Malins's film provided that link between front and home that until now had never been authentically crossed. 'As to reality,' one of Fielding's companions remarked, 'now you knows what you've got to face.' Frances Stevenson, who was Prime Minister Lloyd George's secretary and mistress, accompanied him to a viewing on 2 August 1916. It helped her to deal with the loss of her brother. 'I'm so glad I have seen the sort of thing our men had to go through,' she later admitted:

> *There were pictures which reminded me of what Paul's last hours were. I have often tried to imagine to myself what he went through, but now I know I shall never forget.*[18]

As Rowland Fielding was told by a recruit companion, 'If it was left to the imagination you might think all sorts of silly bloody things.' Malins also unwittingly provided an authentic link between past and present audiences, ageless onlookers. The celebration of this quality came in 2005, when the film was accorded global recognition by being inscribed in the UNESCO Memory of the World Register.

Malins and his companion 'Mac' McDowell were awarded the MC and OBE respectively for their wartime film contributions. After the war Malins continued as a film director, scriptwriter and even actor in a number of short and feature-length movies. In 1932 he settled in South Africa, where he died of cancer in 1940. McDowell survived him until 1954.

For many these traumatic 24 hours were to remain an enduring memory for the rest of their lives. Tommy Ervine, who assaulted the Schwaben Redoubt, confessed to an interviewer in 1986 that every time he tried to remember the face of 'Old Fritz', a POW with whom he became friendly, he could only see the bleeding face of the German soldier he had shot dead on the Somme. Hugh Adams, another veteran of the Ulster Division, admitted in the 1980s, 'I still hear the guns firin'!' Anything vaguely resembling a trench smell or sound was sufficient to trigger off bleak reactions.

Some tortured souls did not even endure that long. Lieutenant-Colonel Edwin Sandys, with the 2nd Middlesex Regiment, continually blamed himself for the death of the 540 men he had left lying in Mash Valley. He wished he had been killed with them. 'I have come to London to take my life,' he wrote to a friend on 6 September 1916, 'I have never had a moment's peace since 1 July.' He was found in a bed at the Cavendish Hotel with a revolver in his hand and a bullet in his head. He died at St George's Hospital nearby.[19]

Survivors never forgot. 'I first went back to the Somme on a motor bike in 1935,' remembered Private HC Bloor in the late 1960s. He had gone over the top with the Accrington Pals at Serre.

I have been going back twelve times since then and I intend going as long as I can. I try to be there on 1ˢᵗ July. I go out and, at 7.30 am, I stand at the exact spot where we went over the top in 1916.

Former Corporal Sidney Appleyard, who was with the Queen Victoria Rifles at Gommecourt, was back for the 50th anniversary in 1966. He was always awed by the huge Somme memorial to the missing at Thiepval, and admired its immaculate maintenance. 'This is the only place for miles,' he recalled, 'where the flower beds don't have signs telling the public not to walk on them.' One of his veteran friends remarked: 'They would be irrelevant here.' Appleyard agreed:

I think everyone understands what this earth cost. The only people who really know about it are underneath.[20]

Bibliography

General Published Sources

Barton, P., and Barning, J., *The Somme: The Unseen Panoramas* (Constable, 2011)

Bird, A. & N., *Eyewitness to War* (Summersdale, 2006)

Brown, M., *Tommy Goes to War* (Dent, 1978)

—— *The Imperial War Museum Book of The Somme* (Pan, 1997)

Creveld, M. van, *Command in War* (Harvard University Press, 1985)

Emden, R. van, *The Trench* (Bantam Press, 2002)

—— *Britain's Last Tommies* (Abacus, 2005)

Farrar-Hockley, A., *The Somme* (Batsford, 1964)

Fraser, A.H., Robertshaw, A., and Roberts, S., *Ghosts on the Somme* (Pen & Sword, 2009)

Gliddon, G., *Somme 1916. A Battlefield Companion* (Sutton, 2006)

Grant Grieve, W., and Newman, B., *Tunnellers* (Herbert Jenkins, 1936)

Gilbert, M., *Somme* (John Murray, 2007)

Hart, P., *The Somme* (Weidenfeld & Nicolson, 2005)

Holden, W., *Shell Shock* (Channel 4 Books, 1998)

—— *The Western Front* (BBC Books, 1999)

Holmes, R., *Tommy* (Harper Perennial, 2005)

Jones, S., *Underground Warfare 1914–18* (Pen & Sword, 2010)

Keegan, J., *The Face of Battle* (Barrie & Jenkins, 1988)

Laparra, J-C., and Hesse, P., *The German Infantryman 1914–1918* (Histoire et Collections, 2008)

Lewis-Stempel, J., *Six Weeks* (Orion, 2010)

Liddle, P., *The 1916 Battle of the Somme: A Reappraisal* (Leo Cooper, 1992)

—— *The British Soldier on the Somme 1916* (Strategic and Combat Studies Institute, Paper No. 23, 1996)

MacDonald, L., *The Somme* (Penguin, 1993)

Martin, C., *Battle of the Somme* (Wayland, 1973)

Middlebrook, M., *The First Day on the Somme* (Penguin, 1971)

Passingham, I., *All the Kaiser's Men* (History Press, 2003)

Philpott, W., *Bloody Victory: The Sacrifice on the Somme* (Abacus, 2009)

Price, S., *If You're Reading This...* (Frontline Books, 2011)

Prior, R., and Wilson, T., *Command on the Western Front* (Blackwell, 1992)

Sheldon, J., *The German Army on the Somme 1914–1916* (Pen & Sword, 2005)

—— *The Germans at Thiepval* (Pen & Sword, 2006)

—— *The Germans at Beaumont Hamel* (Pen & Sword, 2006)

Sheffield, G., and Todman, D., *Command and Control on the Western Front* (Spellmount, 2004)

Smith, R., *The Utility of Force* (Penguin, 2006)

Whitehead, R.J., *The Other Side of the Wire*, Vols 1 and 2 (Helion & Co., 2013)

Williams, J., *The Home Fronts* (Constable & Co., 1972)

British Personal Accounts

Andrews, A.W., *Orders Are Orders* (private publication, Manchester, 1987)

Arthur, M., *Forgotten Voices of the Great War* (Ebury, 2003)

Ashurst, G. (Holmes, R., ed.), *My Bit, a Lancashire Fusilier at War* (Crowood, 1987)

Charteris, J., *At GHQ* (Cassell, 1931)

Chapman, G., ed., *Vain Glory* (Cassell, 1937)

Foley, R.T., and McCartney, H., *The Somme: An Eyewitness History* (Folio, 2006)

Gibbs, P., *The Battles of the Somme* (Heinemann, 1917)

—— *The Realities of War* (Heinemann, 1920)

'GSO' [Frank Fox], *GHQ, Montreuil-sur-Mer* (Philip & Allan, 1920)

Haig, Douglas (Sheffield, G., and Bourne, J., eds.), *War Diaries and Letters 1914–1918* (Weidenfeld & Nicolson, 2005)

Higgins, T.J., *Tommy at Gommecourt* (Churnet Valley Books, 2005)

Jünger, E., *Storm of Steel* (Penguin, 2004)

Levine, J., *Forgotten Voices of the Somme* (Ebury, 2008)

Liveing, E.G.D., *Attack on the Somme* (SPA Books Ltd, 1986)

Malins, G., *How I Filmed the Great War* (Legacy Books, 2011)

Masefield, J., *The Battle of the Somme* (Heinemann, 1917)

—— *The Old Front Line* (Heinemann, 1917)

Moynihan, M., ed., *Greater Love: Letters Home, 1914–18* (W.H. Allen, 1980)

Remarque, E.M., *All Quiet on the Western Front* (Berlin, 1929)

Shepherd, E., *A Sergeant-Major's War* (Crowood Press, 1987)

Tawney, R.H., 'The Attack', *Westminster Gazette* (Aug. 1916)

German Personal Accounts

Eisler K., taken from Hirschfeld, G., Krumeich, G., and Renz, I., *Die Deutschen an der Somme 1914–1918. Krieg, Besatzung, Verbrannte Erde* (Klartext, Essen, 2006)

Gerhardinger, F., *Inf. Regt 16* (Bayeriches Hauptarchiv Abt. IV, HS 2105)

Hinkel, F., taken from Müller, Fabeck and Riessel, *Geschichte des Reserve-Infanterie Regiments Nr 99* (Verlag Bernhard Sporn, 1936)

Laasch, Greiner & Vulpius, *Res. Inf. Regt Nr 110 im Weltkrieg 1914–1918* (Karlsruhe, 1934)

Lais, O., *Die Schlacht an der Somme 1916* (Karlsruhe, 1935)

Maute, O., taken from Hirschfeld, G., Krumeich, G., and Renz, I., *Die Deutschen an der Somme 1914–1918. Krieg, Besatzung, Verbrannte Erde* (Klartext, Essen, 2006)

Osburg, W-R., *Hineingeworfen* (Aufbau Tachenbuch, 2014)

Riebike, O., *Unsere Pioniere im Weltkriege* (Kyffhäuser Verlag, Berlin, 1925)

Soden, F.L. von, *Die 26. (Württembergische) Reserve-Division im Weltkrieg 1914–1918* (Stuttgart, 1939)

Westman, S., *Surgeon with the Kaiser's Army* (William Kimber, 1968)

Regimental Accounts

Alexander, J., *McCrae's Battalion* (Mainstream, 2003)

Cooksey, J., *Barnsley Pals* (Pen & Sword, 2006)

Haigh, R.H., and Turner, P.W., *The Battle of the Somme 1916* (Pavic, 1986)

MacDonagh, M., *The Irish on the Somme* (Hodder & Stoughton, 1917)

Müller, Fabeck and Riessel, *Geschichte des Reserve-Infanterie Regiments Nr 99* (Verlag Bernhard Sporn, 1936)

Orr, P., *The Road to the Somme* (Blackstaff Press, 2008)

Stedman, M., *Salford Pals* (Leo Cooper, 2007)

Wilkinson, R., *Pals on the Somme 1916* (Pen & Sword, 2006)

Archive Sources

Published

Mace, M., and Grehan, J., *Slaughter on the Somme 1 July 1916*, Official accounts Corps to battalion level (Pen & Sword, 2013)

Unpublished

Fabeck, H. von, *Gefechtsbericht fur die Zeit vom 24.6–30.6.16. Res. Inf. Regt Nr 99 den 17.8.1916*

—— *Gefechtsbericht RIR Nr 99. Schlacht bei Thiepval 1 Jul. 1916*

Gerster, M. (Sheldon, trans.), *History of the 52nd Res. Inf. Bde, Part II: The Battle of the Somme*

Wurmb, H. von, *Erinnerungen an die Eroberung der 'Feste Schwaben' an der Somme 1.7.16. Zur 10. Wiederkehr des Ehrentages des K.B. Res. Inf. Regts No. 8, 1926* (Kriegsarchiv München HS, 1984)

Bavarian Regt 8

—— *Anteil des Bayer. Res. Inf. Regts. No. 8 an der Somme Schlacht* (Kriegsarchiv München HS 2205)

Regt 119

—— *Gefechtsbericht des Res. Inf. Regts Nr 119 über die Zeit vom 24.6.–14.7.1916* (15 Jul. 1916. Hauptstaatsarchiv Stuttgart M107, Bü 42)

—— *2nd MG Kp R 119 Battle Reports* (Stuttgart M107, Bü 48)

—— *Bericht über die Gefechtstätigkeit der 7.Komp RJR 119 vom 24 Juni bis 2 Juli 1916* (8 Jul. 1916, Stuttgart, M107, Bü 42)

52 Bde

— *Einleitung zum Gefechtsbericht des stabes der 52. (Württ) Res. Inf. Brigade über die schweren Kämpfe südlich der Ancre in der Zeit vom 24.6. bis 9.7.1916* (Hauptstatsarchiv Stuttgart M410, Bü 239)

Various unpublished single-page German documents are referred to in the notes.

Periodicals

Broadhead, J., 'Diary of a Bradford Pal.' *Stand To! Journal of the Western Front Association* No. 70 (Apr. 2004)

Cherry, N., 'The RAMC on the Somme 1916.' *Stand To!* No. 64 (Apr. 2002)

Whitmarsh, A, 'Preparing for War: Tactics in European Armies before 1914.' *Stand To!* No. 59 (Sep. 2000)

Zabecki, D.T., 'Colonel George Bruchmueller and the Birth of Modern Artillery Tactics.' *Stand To!* No. 53 (Sep. 1998)

Film and TV

Barton, P., *The Somme: Secret Tunnel Wars* (BBC, 2013)

Bettinson, H., and Rees, L., *Timewatch – Haig: The Unknown Soldier* (BBC, 1996)

ten Cate, H., *The Battle of the Somme: The True Story* (Channel 5, 2006)

Connolly, M., *I Was There: The Great War Interviews* (BBC NI, 2014)

Holmes, R., *War Walks: The Somme* (BBC, 1996)

—— *The Western Front* (BBC series, 1999)

Humphries, S., *Hidden Histories: World War I's Forgotten Photographs* (BBC 4, 2014)

Malins, G., *The Battle of the Somme* (DVD, Imperial War Museum, 2008)

Robinson, T., *The Somme's Secret Weapon* (Channel 4, 2011)

Siebert, D., *The Somme: From Defeat to Victory* (BBC, 2006)

Twaddle, A., *The Machine Gun and Skye's Band of Brothers* (BBC Scotland, 2014)

Notes

Prologue

The Grandstand. 30 June 1916. 11 pm

1. Gibbs, *The Battles of the Somme*, pp. 22–4.
2. Ashurst, *My Bit*, pp. 97–8.
3. Lewis, interview, *I Was There. The Great War Interviews*, BBC TV 2014. Shepherd: Diary, 25 Jun. 1916, *A Sergeant-Major's War*, p. 105.
4. Haig: Gibbs, *The Realities of War*, pp. 23–4.
5. Gibbs, *Battles*, pp. 25–6.

Chapter 1. *Materialschlacht*: Inside the German Bunkers

Fritz. 00.10 am

1. Lehnert: Osburg, *Hineingeworfen*, p. 182.
2. Lais, *Die Schlacht an der Somme 1916*, p. 4.
3. Laasch, Greiner and Vulpius, *Res. Inf. Regt Nr 110 im Weltkrieg 1914–18*, p. 132.
4. Cassel: IWM Doc. 76/208/1. Baass: *Hineingeworfen*, p. 451.
5. Braungart: Report by 2nd MG Coy of 119(R) Regt 28 Jun. and 30 Jun. 1916, Sheldon Collection. Siebe, *Hineingeworfen*, p. 370.
6. Rupp: *Bericht über die Gefechtstätigkeit der 7.Kp von 24.Juni bis 2.Juli 1916*. Dated 8 Jul. 16. Schulze: Gropp, H., *Hanseaten im Kampf, Erlebnisse bei dem Res. Inf. Regt 76 im Weltkriege 1914/18*, pp. 158–60.
7. Cassel: IWM Doc. 76/208/1.

8. Eversmann: MacDonald, *The Somme*, pp. 42, 49. Westman, *A Surgeon with the Kaiser's Army*, p. 94. Gerster: Sheldon, *The German Army on the Somme 1914–1916*, p. 121.

9. Data concerning 109 Relief: Whitehead, *The Other Side of the Wire*, Vol. 1, p. 473, and Vol. 2, pp. 381–2.

10. Westman, pp. 95–6. Rehder: *Hineingeworfen*, p. 373.

11. Von Wurmb: Sheldon, p. 111.

12. Stahlhofer: Wurmb, *Das KB Reserve Inf. Regt Nr 8*, pp. 149–50.

The Trench Pigs. 2 to 4 pm

13. Final Hurrah! *Das Kleine Buch vom Deutschen Heer*, 1901.

14. Kottmeier, Siemers and Thiel: *Hineingeworfen*, pp. 76, 79, 86.

15. Benecke and Griesmann: ibid, pp. 137, 165.

16. Jünger, *Storm of Steel*, pp. 72, 80–1. Remarque, *All Quiet on the Western Front*, p. 72. Marquardt: *Hineingeworfen*, p. 177.

17. Measures: *Massnahmen zur Aufrechterhaltung des guten Geistes und der Spannkraft der Truppen während einer Tages unterbrochenen Beschiessung*, dated 5 Oct. 1915, Kriegsarchiv (KA) München 8RJR Bd 3.

18. Heinz: I Passingham, *All the Kaiser's Men*, p. 99.

19. Kirchner: Whitehead, Vol. 1, p. 476.

20. Owen, poem 'Mental Cases'. Rehder: *Hineingeworfen*, p. 320.

21. Cassel, IWM Doc. 76/208/1. Lange: Middlebrook, *The First Day on the Somme*, p. 100. Soldier: P. Gibbs, *Daily Chronicle* 1917.

22. Gerster: Sheldon, p. 133. Soldier, Anon 'MD': *Hineingeworfen*, p. 378. Ratschky: ibid, p.176.

23. Gerster: Sheldon, pp. 133–4. Götzmann: *Hineingeworfen*, p. 378.

24. Westman, p. 91. Letters: Middlebrook, pp. 59–60.

25. Griesbaum: Sheldon, p. 120. Schumacher: ibid, p. 134. Baass: ibid, p. 352.

26. Artillery data: Keegan, *The Face of Battle*, pp. 209, 213.

27. Stöckle: Sheldon, p. 125.

28. Combating gas: *Merkblatt für den Schützengraben*. KA München, 6 RJR Bd 8.

29. Jünger, *Storm of Steel*, pp. 82–3. Remarque, *All Quiet on the Western Front*, p. 48. Gaup and Kaufman: Holden, *Shell Shock*, pp. 30–1. Weiher: *Hineingeworfen*, p. 379.

'Lord God! Just Let Them Come!' In the Line. 4 pm

30. Maute, Letter 25 June, from Hirschfeld etc, *Die Deutschen an der Somme 1914–18*, p. 92. Gerhardinger, *16 Inf. Regt II Bn Oblt d. Res. F. Hardinger*, KA München HS 2105. Lais, *Die Schlacht an der Somme 1916.*
31. Eisler: from Hirschfeld etc, *Die Deutschen an der Somme 1914–18*, pp. 100–1. Kleinfeldt, *Hidden Histories: World War One's Forgotten Photographs*, BBC 4 TV, 2014.
32. Relief operation: *Anteil des Bayer. Res. Inf. Regts Nr 8 an der Somme Schlacht*, KA München HS 2205.
33. Hinkel: from Müller, Fabeck and Riessel, *Geschichte des Reserve Infanterie Regts Nr 99*, p. 107. Kircher: Whitehead, Vol. 1, p. 477. Diary accounts: ibid, pp. 468, 478.
34. Lais, p. 11.
35. Spies, 10. Bayer. Inf. Div. Communique 'In Confidence'. Div. HQ St Quentin 4 May 1916, KA Munchen 8 RJR Bd 21. Bahrmann, *Hineingeworfen*, p. 256. Kury: Whitehead, Vol. 2, p. 384.
36. Moritz message: Mace and Grehan, *Slaughter on the Somme 1 July 1916*, pp. 298, 302.

Chapter 2. Boulevard Street to Culver Street: The British Trenches

'Lord I shall be very busy this day …' The March-Out. Midnight to 1 am

1. Hodgson poem extract, quoted in Hart, *The Somme*, pp. 106–7.
2. Ellenberger and Carrington: Brown, *The IWM Book of The Somme*, p. 2.
3. Carrington, interview, *I Was There. The Great War Interviews*, BBC TV 2014.

4. Liveing, *Attack on the Somme*, pp. 26–8

5. Ward-Jackson: Moynihan, ed., *Greater Love: Letters Home, 1914–18*, pp. 98–9. May: extracts from May's diary, *The Times*, 21 Jun. 2014. Liveing, p. 29.

6. Lindley and Hall: Cooksey, *Barnsley Pals*, p. 198.

7. Weights, Bryan: Arthur, *Forgotten Voices of the Great War*, pp. 148–9. Veitch: *McCrae's Battalion*, p. 154. Swales: Cooksey, p. 198.

8. Masefield, *The Old Front Line*, p. 26. Liveing, pp. 29–32.

9. Figures: Holmes, *Tommy*, p. 103.

10. Shepherd, Diary 16 and 17 Jun. and 1 Jul. 1916. *A Sergeant-Major's War*, pp. 100–1, 108.

11. Lethbridge, interview, BBC TV.

12. Neame: Hart, *The Somme*, p. 56.

13. Cary letters, Susan Bishop and Helen Kemp, dated: 6 Jun., 15 Jun., 18 Jun., 22 Jun., 27 Jun., 28 Jun. 1916.

14. Agricultural labourer: MacDonagh, *The Irish on the Somme*, pp. 114–15.

15. Katie Morter, interview, *I Was There. The Great War Interviews*, BBC TV Mar. 2014.

16. Andrews, *Orders Are Orders*, pp. 44–5.

17. McCrae: Alexander, *McCrae's Battalion*, Introduction. McCartney, *Hearts in World War I,* website.

18. 'The Beck': MacDonagh, pp. 11–12. Stewart: Orr, *The Road to the Somme*, p. 96.

19. 16 Rifles soldier: Orr, p. 96. Shooting results: Farrar-Hockley, *The Somme*, p. 69.

20. Holding: Cooksey, p. 85.

21. Lindley: Cooksey, p. 188. German Aircraft: Mace and Grehan, ed., *Slaughter on the Somme 1 July 1916*, p. 2. Murray and Bracey: Levine, *Forgotten Voices of the Somme*, pp. 86, 87. Ward-Jackson: Moynihan, p. 99.

22. Plan: Stedman, *Salford Pals*, pp. 114, 108–9.

23. Howard, Coombs and Morey: *The Battle of the Somme: The True Story*. Channel 5 TV Documentary. O'Neil: E Clarke (his daughter), Beaumont Hamel Newfoundland Memorial Park

Museum account. Steele, *Newfoundland Regiment, Somme 1 July 1916*, pp. 339–40.

24. Andrews, p. 44. Adlam and Goodman: Levine, p. 63.
25. Malins, *How I Filmed the Great War*, p. 111. Laing, WO 95/2300 IWM letter, Fraser, Robertshaw, Roberts, *Ghosts on the Somme*, p. 57. Ashurst, *My Bit*, pp. 95–6

'Stumbling in the Dark'. The Trenches. 1 to 4.30 am

26. Ogle: Foley and McCartney, ed., *The Somme*, pp. 63–4. Gun figures: Hart, p. 68. Ward-Jackson: Moynihan, ed., *Greater Love*, p. 103. Higgins, *Tommy at Gommecourt*, p. 35. May: Hart, pp. 84–5.
27. Jones: Brown, *The IWM Book of The Somme*, pp. 50–1.
28. Masefield, *The Old Front Line*, p. 112. Tawney, 'The Attack', *Westminster Gazette*. Brockman and Quinnell: Levine, pp. 48, 33–4.
29. Masefield, p. 28. Ulster Soldier: MacDonagh, p. 13. Day: Levine, p. 32. Carrington, interview, BBC TV.
30. Liveing, pp. 34, 38. Higgins, *Tommy at Gommecourt*, pp. 31–2, 35–6. Ulster Soldier 'GHM': Orr, p. 191.
31. Fellows: Levine, p. 38.
32. Potter: Wilkinson, *Pals on the Somme 1916*, pp. 134–5.
33. Heaton: Price, *If You're Reading This…*, pp. 134–6. Jarman: R van Emden, *Britain's Last Tommies*, p. 172.
34. Jones: Brown, pp. 58–9. Hunt, Fellows and Brockman: Levine, pp. 62, 59, 60. Liveing, pp. 39–40.

Chapter 3. Château Generals

'With God's Help'. The British. Midnight to 4.30 am

1. Fox, F., *GHQ, Montreuil-sur-Mer* 'by GSO', p. 29. Charteris, *At GHQ*, Diary 28 Jun. 1916, p. 149, and Holmes, *The Western Front*, p. 117.
2. Charteris, 30 Jun, p. 151.

3. Fox, p. 60. Charteris, 28 Jun., pp. 149–50.

4. Haig, Letter 30 Jun., *War Diaries and Letters 1914–18*, p. 195

5. Rimmer, interview, *Haig: The Unknown Soldier. Timewatch* BBC TV.

6. Kiggell: Whitmarsh, 'Preparing for War: Tactics in European Armies before 1914', *Stand To!*, No. 59, Sep. 2000, p. 6.

7. Fox, pp. 51, 53. Gibbs and Hanbury-Sparrow: Holmes, *The Western Front*, p. 117.

8. Gibbs, *Realities of War*, p. 35. 'Loaf' joke: R Holmes, *Tommy*, p. 224.

9. Ward-Jackson, letter to wife 27 Jun.: Moynihan, ed., *Greater Love*, pp. 104–5.

10. Nicholson, Holmes, p. 188. Paperwork: Creveld, *Command in War*, pp. 158–9. Rees: Brown, *The IWM Book of The Somme*, pp. 37–9.

11. Carrington: Holmes, *Tommy*, p. 234. Haig, *War Diaries*, 30 Jun. 1916, pp. 194–5.

German Châteaux. Midnight to 4.30 am

12. Von Stein, *Gefechtsbericht des Stabes der 52. (Württ) Res. Inf. Bde über die schweren Kämpfe südlich der Ancre 24.6. bis 9.7.1916.* Hauptstaatsarchiv Stuttgart M410 Bu 239.

13. Von Soden, speech 26 Jun. Whitehead, *The Other Side of the Wire*, Vol. 1, p. 461.

14. British gun figures: *British Official History Military Operations France and Flanders*, Vol. 1, and extracts from War Diary CRA VIII Corps.

15. Jünger, *Storm of Steel*, p. 67. Kottmeier, *Hineingeworfen*, p. 418.

16. Von Kuhl and directive: Creveld, *Command in War*, pp. 171–2. Von Soden: Whitehead, p. 461.

17. Geiger: Sheldon, *The German Army on the Somme*, p. 127.

18. Wheat: XIV Corps PW Report. 24.6.16, KA München, 8RJR Bd 21. Coones, Barrow and Lipmann: PW Report St Quentin, 5.7.1916, KA München, 8RJR, Bd 4. 2nd MG Company report dated 1 Jul. 1916. Sheldon Archive.

19. Von Auwärter, *Einleitung zum Gefechtsbericht des Stabes der 52. (Württ.) Res. Inf. Bde über die schweren Kämpfe südlich der Ancre in der Zeit von 24.6 bis 9.7.1916.* Hauptstaatsarchiv Stuttgart. M410, Bü 239. Gerster: *52 Bde War Diary*, Sheldon Archive 30 Jun. 1916, pp. 7–8.

Chapter 4. Over the Top

'The Larks Were Singing' ... Hours to go. 4.45 to 6.30 am

1. Gibbs, *The Battles of the Somme*, p. 26.
2. Lt G Lewis: P. Hart, Pen & Sword article, *Somme Success*, p.106. Cecil Lewis, interview, *I Was There. The Great War Interviews*, BBC TV 2014. Wyllie and Balfour: Hart, ibid, pp. 105 and 108.
3. Gibbs, ibid, p. 26. Andrews, *Orders Are Orders*, p. 48. Liveing, *Attack on the Somme*, p. 43. Tawney, 'The Attack'. Conn: Hart, *The Somme*, p. 63.
4. Quinnell: Levine, *Forgotten Voices of the Somme*, pp. 45–6.
5. Stewart: Orr, *The Road to the Somme*, pp. 193–4.
6. Lewis, interview, BBC TV.
7. May and Bland: Brown, *The IWM Book of The Somme*, pp. 54, 59.
8. Rees was awarded the VC for this action. J. Miller, *DH2 Vs Albatros DI / DII Western Front 1916*, Osprey, pp. 51–2.

Minutes to Go. 6.30 to 7.30 am

9. McKay, McParlane, McEvoy and Anderson: Alexander, *McCrae's Battalion*, pp. 155–6, 157–8.
10. Malins, *How I Filmed the Great War*, p. 123.
11. Dawson, interview, *The Battle of the Somme: The True Story*. History TV documentary, 2006. Malins, p. 128.
12. Tweed: Stedman, *Salford Pals*, pp. 15–16, 33–4. Additional material from D. Siebert, director, *The Somme: From Defeat to Victory*, BBC TV.
13. Malins, p. 127. Lip-reader: *The Battle of the Somme. The True Story*, Channel 5 TV, 2006.

14. Carrington, interview, BBC TV.
15. Liveing, p. 44. Frankau: Martin, *The Battle of the Somme*, p. 26. Holdstock: Levine, p. 94. Tawney, 'The Attack'. Ashurst: Levine, p. 96.
16. McFadzean: Orr, pp. 195–6.
17. Liveing, pp. 27–8, 46–7.
18. Quinnel: Levine, p. 58. Masefield, *The Old Front Line*, 1917.
19. Tawney, 'The Attack'. Andrews, *Orders Are Orders*, p. 48. Masefield, *The Battle of the Somme*, 1917. Stewart: Foley and McCartney, eds., *The Somme: An Eyewitness History*, p. 57. Soldier: Holmes, original IWM recording, *War Walks*, BBC Bristol TV, 1996. Cousins: Middlebrook, *The First Day on the Somme*, p. 121.
20. Ashurst, *My Bit*, p. 99. Malins, pp. 131–3. McMillan: Middlebrook, p.120.
21. Lindley: Cooksey, *Barnsley Pals*, pp. 204, 208, and Levine, p. 32.
22. Ricardo: Orr, p. 198. Gaffkin and veteran accounts: MacDonagh, p. 36.
23. Lewis, interview, BBC TV.
24. Burke and Coldridge: Levine, p. 108. Andrews, p. 48. Jose: personal account.
25. Figures: Philpott, *Bloody Victory*, p. 175. Soldier quotes: Masefield, *The Battle of the Somme*.
26. Kerridge, interview, Holmes, *The Western Front*, BBC TV 1999. Ashurst, *My Bit*, p. 99.
27. Gibbs, *The Battles of the Somme*, pp. 29–30 and *The Realities of War*, p. 41. Intelligence figures: Gilbert, *Somme*, p. 36.

Chapter 5. The Race to the Parapet

Raus! Raus! Out! Out! 7.15 to 7.45 am

1. Gerster, *History of the 52nd (Royal Württemberg) Res. Inf. Bde. Part II. The Battle of the Somme*, Sheldon Archive.
2. Hinkel: from Müller, Fabeck & Riessel, *Geschichte des Res. Inf. Regts 99*, p. 107. Trench routine, *Merkblatt für den Schützengraben*, Oct. 1915, KA München, 6RJR, Bd.8.

3. Anon. German officer: Farrar-Hockley, *The Somme*, p. 99. Crawford: Fraser, Robertshaw & Roberts, *Ghosts on the Somme*, pp. 88–9.

4. Hinkel, pp. 107–8. Westman, *Surgeon with the Kaiser's Army*, p. 95.

5. Machine-gun numbers 1 to 4, *Battle Activity of the MGs of the 2nd MG coy R119 during the British attack on 1 Jul. 1916*, dated 7 Jul. 1916, Sheldon Archive.

6. Grünig: *Hineingeworfen*, p. 170. MG figures: *Zusätze der Brigade zu Ziffer 3 umstehenden Div-Befehle*, dated 6.6.1916. Hauptsarchiv Stuttgart, M410, Bü 254.

7. Foulkes: Barton and Barning, *The Somme*, p. 167.

8. Siemens: *Hineingeworfen*, p. 202.

9. Livens flame projector, background material from D. Brady: *The Somme's Secret Weapon*, Channel 4 TV 2011. Foulkes: Barton and Barning, pp. 167–8. Cude: Brown, p. 88. German instructions against flame-throwers: *Merkblatt für den Verhalten der Truppen bei einem Flammenangriff des Feindes*, KA München, 8 RJR Bd 3.

10. Gerster, 52nd Bde History. Masefield, *The Old Front Line*, pp. 113–14.

The 'Kaiser's Oak'. Gommecourt. 7.30 to 9 am

11. Liveing, *Attack on the Somme*, p. 45. Snow: Mace & Grehan, eds., *Slaughter on the Somme*, British Army War Diaries, p. 6.

12. Liveing, pp. 49–50.

13. Kerridge, interview, Holmes, *The Western Front*, BBC TV 1999. Russell: Barton, *Somme*, p. 79. Masefield, p. 127. George: Chapman, ed., *Vain Glory*, pp. 315–17.

14. Liveing, pp. 52–3.

15. 1/9th Battalion London Regiment after action report, *Slaughter on the Somme 1 July 1916*, p. 41.

16. Kerridge, interview, BBC TV. Schuman and Hawkings: Hart, *The Somme*, p. 119. Koch: Sheldon, *The German Army on the Somme 1914–16*, pp. 139, 141.

17. Hubbard: Brown, *Tommy Goes to War*, pp. 166–7.

18. Liveing, pp. 53–6. Russell: Barton and Barning, p. 79.
19. Higgins, *Tommy at Gommecourt*, pp. 37–9.

The 'Danger Tree'. North of the Ancre. 7.30 to 9.30 am

20. Beck: Sheldon, *The Germans at Beaumont Hamel*, p. 86.
21. Höpfner: *Hineingeworfen*, p. 248. Lais, *Der Schlacht an der Somme* 1916, p. 13.
22. Blenk: Middlebrook, *The First Day on the Somme*, p. 157.
23. Rees: Brown, *Tommy Goes to War*, p. 163. Raine and Glen: Hart, *The Somme*, pp. 137–8. Swales: Cooksey, *Barnsley Pals*, p. 210.
24. Lindley and Burgess: Cooksey, p. 210.
25. Lais, p. 16.
26. Pearson: Hart, p. 136. Lais, pp. 16–19, Lindley: Cooksey, pp. 211–12.
27. Beck: Sheldon, *The Germans at Beaumont Hamel*, pp. 86–7. Colyer: Hart, pp. 141–3.
28. Fusilier officer: Jones, *Underground Warfare 1914–18*, pp. 117–18. Aicheler: Sheldon, 2nd MG Coy 119 account.
29. Malins, *How I Filmed the Great War*, pp. 133–4.
30. Ashurst, *My Bit*, pp. 98–100.
31. Mauss: Whitehead, *The Other Side of the Wire*, Vol. 2.
32. Ashurst, pp. 98–101.
33. Anon. 1st Border Soldier and casualty figures: Barton and Barning, p. 107.
34. O'Neil: Letter E. Clarke, Newfoundland Park Museum. Observer: Raley 37–40, *Newfoundland Regiment Somme, Website account*. Witness, Official Newfoundland History: Gilbert, *Somme*, p. 63. Coombs, interview, *The Battle of the Somme. The True Story*. Channel 5 TV, 2006.

Chapter 6. *Schwerpunkt:* Thiepval Plateau

The 'Devil's Dwelling Place'. The Schwaben Redoubt. 7.40 to 10 am

1. Stewart and Bruce: Orr, *The Road to the Somme*, pp. 198–9.

2. Stewart: ibid, p. 200.

3. Hope, soldier and Stewart: ibid, pp. 201–3.

4. Kottmeier: *Hineingeworfen*, p. 348.

5. Von Wurmb, *Erinnerungen an die Eroberung der 'Feste Schwaben' an der Somme am 1.7.16.*

6. Stewart: Orr, p. 204. Irish soldiers: MacDonagh, *The Irish on the Somme*, p. 38.

7. 9th Fusilier soldiers: Orr, p. 215. Mainz: 2nd MG Coy 119 Regt report 7 Jul. 1916, Sheldon archive.

8. Lange: Whitehead, *The Other Side of the Wire*, p. 191. Hinkel: from Müller, Fabeck and Riesel, *Geschichte des Res. Inf. Regts Nr 99*, pp. 108–9. Maultsaid, Orr, p. 201.

9. Crozier: Chapman, ed., *Vain Glory*, pp. 326–8.

10. Ervine: Orr, p. 209. Crozier: ibid, pp. 328–9.

11. Adams and stretcher-bearer: Orr, pp. 212–13, 211.

12. Dutton and Marriot: Stedman, *Salford Pals*, pp. 120, 122.

13. Tweed: Stedman, p. 126. Additional material from D. Siebert, director, *The Somme: From Defeat to Victory*, BBC TV, 2006.

14. Shepherd, *A Sergeant Major's War*, pp. 108–10.

15. R.H. Stewart and Pte Hugh Stewart: Orr, p. 205.

16. Soldier accounts: MacDonagh, p. 43.

17. Stewart: Orr, p. 210.

18. Von Soden, *Einleitung zum Gefechtsbericht des Stabes der 52 (Württ) Res. Inf. Bde über die schweren Kämpfe südlich der Ancre in der Zeit vom 24.6 bis 9.7.1916*, Hauptstaatsarchiv Stuttgart M410, Bü 239.

19. Soldier: MacDonagh, p. 44.

Sausage and Mash. 7.28 to 11 am

20. Baumber: Hart, *The Somme*, pp. 167–8.

21. Tansley: Hart, ibid, pp. 164–5. Officer: Gilbert, *Somme,* p. 56. Deighton: MacDonald, *The Somme,* p. 72.

22. Kienitz: Sheldon, *The German Army on the Somme 1914–16*, p. 159. Eisler, *Die Deutschen an der Somme 1914–18*, p. 102. Artillery figures: Foley and McCartney, *The Somme*, p. 76.

23. Laasch, etc, *Res. Inf. Regt Nr 110 im Weltkrieg 1914–18*, pp. 132–3.

24. Hanbury-Sparrow: Hart, p. 166.

25. J. Harris, novel, *Covenant With Death*, p. 96.

26. Haylock: Barton, *Somme*, p. 143.

27. Campbell, Ross and Mowatt: Alexander, *McCrae's Battalion*, pp. 161–2.

28. Hill: Barton, p.140.

29. Newspaper reports and sergeant eyewitness: Brown, *Tommy Goes to War*, pp. 170–1. Irwin: Levine, *Forgotten Voices of the Somme*, p. 135.

30. Crozier: Chapman, p. 327. Russell: Barton, p. 79.

31. Liverpool soldier: Foley and McCartney, *The Somme*, pp. 189–90. Tawney, 'The Attack'.

32. Clinical trials, Dr H. Witchel (Brighton and Sussex Medical School) and P. Wilson, audio trial (Glasgow School of Art) and M. Stedman: *Pipers of the Trenches*, BBC Scotland TV, 2014.

33. Deighton: MacDonald, *Somme*, pp. 72–3.

34. Miller and Stewart: Alexander, *McCrae's Battalion*, pp. 164–5.

35. Frick: Sheldon, p. 159.

36. Hearts football team background material: Alexander, *McCrae's Battalion*.

37. Murray: Levine, p. 123.

Chapter 7. Break-In

The Shrine. Fricourt to Mametz. 7.30 am to 1 pm

1. Masefield, *The Old Front Line*, p. 100.

2. Mortimer: Barton and Barning, *The Somme*, p. 155.

3. Gee: Hart, *The Somme*, pp. 177–8.

4. MG Coy Report, Sheldon, *The German Army on the Somme, 1914–1916*, p. 161. Fife: Brown, *The IWM Book of The Somme*, p. 85.

5. Martin: Middlebrook, *The First Day on the Somme*, pp. 86, 125–6. Soldier: Gliddon, *Somme 1916*, pp. 310, 231.

6. Tawney, 'The Attack'.

7. Eisler, *Die Deutschen an der Somme 1914–1918*, pp. 102, 105.

8. Scheytt and Kury: Whitehead, *The Other Side of the Wire*, Vol. 2, pp. 386, 393. Eisler, p. 104.

9. Jünger: Foley and McCartney, eds., *The Somme*, p. 165. Burke, Probert and Conn: Hart, pp. 182–3, 181.

10. Bahrmann: *Hineingeworfen*, p. 463. McCauley: Barton and Barning, p. 157.

Break-In. Mametz to Montauban. 7.30 am to 1 pm

11. Bastable: Coates, *The Somme*, p. 28. Cousins and Payne: Levine, *Forgotten Voices of the Somme*, pp. 134–5.

12. Preuss: Whitehead, Vol. 2, p. 389.

13. Busl: Sheldon, pp. 163–4. Lüttgens: Whithead, p. 405.

14. Andrews, *Orders Are Orders*, pp. 49–50. Maxwell and soldier witness: Foley and McCartney, *The Somme*, pp. 164–5.

15. Cousins, Bell and Hurst: Levine, pp. 136, 138, 136–7.

16. Macardle: Foley and McCartney, p. 105–6. Bell: Levine, p. 138.

17. Payne: Levine, p. 134, 140. Bastable: Coates, p. 28.

18. Andrews, pp. 50–1. Kennedy: Levine, p. 138.

19. Hurst: Levine, p. 137. Macardle: Foley and McCartney, pp. 105–6. Holdstock: Levine, p. 140. Bahrmann: *Hineingeworfen*, p. 463.

20. Hurst: Levine, p. 137.

21. Gerhardinger, *16 Inf. Regt II Bn, Somme-Schlacht 1916*, KA München, HS 2105. Goebelbecker: Whitehead, p. 410.

22. Kennedy: Levine, pp. 142–3.

Chapter 8. 'Silly Old Devils': Château Decisions

'The Invisible Battle'. British Headquarters. 8.30 am to 3 pm

1. Carrington, interview, BBC TV.

2. Cleeve: Arthur, *Forgotten Voices of the Great War*, pp. 140–1.

3. Gibbs, *Realities of War*, p. 298. Lewis, interview, BBC TV, and Gilbert, *Somme*, p. 76.

4. Cardon-Roe: Barton, *Somme*, pp. 96–7.

5. Rees: Brown, *Tommy Goes to War*, p. 75–6.

6. Stephen: Chapman, ed., *Vain Glory*, pp. 314–15.

7. Rees: Hart, *Somme*, p. 139. Gibbs, p. 312. Reports: Cooksey, *Barnsley Pals*, p. 224.

8. Wilson: Middlebrook, *The First Day on the Somme*, pp. 150, 201.

9. 36th Division witness: Orr, *The Road to the Somme*, p. 213.

10. Young: Middlebrook, p. 208.

11. Ward-Jackson: Moynihan, ed., *Greater Love*, pp. 106, 108. Ounsworth: Levine, pp. 260–1.

12. Leetham: Brown, *Tommy Goes to War*, p. 173.

13. Reports: Prior and Wilson, *Command on the Western Front*, p. 183. Middlebrook, p. 201.

14. Haig, *War Diaries and Letters*, 29 Jun. 1916, p. 194, and 1 Jul., p. 196.

15. Rawlinson: Middlebrook, p. 226.

The Direct Order. German Headquarters. 7.30 am to 5 pm

16. Bainier: *Hineingeworfen*, pp. 370–1.

17. Gerster and 26th Div report, *Einleitung zum Gefechtsbericht des Stabes der 52 (Württ.) Res. Inf. Bde über die schweren Kämpfe südlich der Ancre in der Zeit vom 24.6 bis 9.7.1916* (Hereafter 52 Bde reports.)

18. Battle Log 99 Regiment, *Bericht RIR Nr 99. Schlacht bei Theipval. 1 Jul 1916. Dated 2.9.1916.*

19. Von Soden, *Die 26 (Württembergische) Res. Div. im Weltkrieg 1914–1918*, p. 103.

20. 9.45 message, 52 Bde reports.

21. Gerster, *Das Württembergische Res. Inf. Regt 119 im Weltkrieg 1914–1918.*

22. Bavarian Regt 8, *Anteil des Bayer. Res. Inf. Regts Nr 8 an der Somme-Schlacht*, pp. 1–5.

23. Von Wurmb, *Erinnerungen an die Eroberung der 'Feste Schwaben' an der Somme am 1.7.16.* Document 1926.

24. Von Stein, *Erlebnisse und Betrachtungen aus der Zeit des Weltkrieges*, p. 80.

25. Von Wurmb, *Erinnerungen*, ibid.

26. Order: *Brig. Befehl an Feste Zollern*. 52 Bde Reports, 5.02 pm. (One hour ahead of British time.)

Chapter 9. The Lull

The Sun over No Man's Land. Midday to 9 pm

1. Higgins, *Tommy at Gommecourt*, pp. 39–40. Heptonstall: Cooksey, *Barnsley Pals*, p. 223. Leetham: Brown, *Tommy Goes to War*, p. 204.

2. Tawney, 'The Attack', *Westminster Gazette*, August 1916.

3. Dooley: Middlebrook, *The First Day on the Somme*, p. 209. Crozier: Chapman, ed., *Vain Glory*, p. 329. Radband and Wilson: Middlebrook, pp. 209–10.

4. Maute, letter, 2 Jul. 1916 Warlencourt, from *Die Deutschen an der Somme 1914–1918*, p. 92.

5. Dickins, private letter to Lt-Col. Shipley, undated, courtesy Sue Bishop. Major Dickens: Hart, *The Somme*, p. 125.

6. Cary, letters, 11 Aug. and 18 Aug. 1916, Dickins undated private letter, Bishop family correspondence. Smith: Hart, p. 126.

7. Westman, *Surgeon with the Kaiser's Army*, p. 94. Beil: *Hineingeworfen*, p. 227.

8. Malins, *How I Filmed the Great War*, p. 136. Fraser, Robertshaw and Roberts, *The Ghosts on the Somme*, pp. 96–8. The Imperial War Museum has correspondence relating to over 50 individuals who claim to be the unidentified rescuer in the film. Raine was identified from family photos analysed by a Metropolitan Police face recognition expert. He may not be the last claim. K. Burgess, *Times* newspaper article, 3 and 16 Apr. 2014.

9. Ashurst, *My Bit*, p. 102. Hall: Cooksey, *Barnsley Pals*, p. 222.

10. Askew and Howe: Middlebrook, p. 206–7.

11. Lais, *Der Schlacht an der Somme 1916*, pp. 20–1.

12. Lindley: Cooksey, pp. 220–1. Swales: ibid, p. 223.

13. Leetham: Brown, *Tommy Goes to War*, pp. 204, 207.

14. O'Keefe and medical figures: Cherry, 'The RAMC on the Somme, 1916', *Stand To!* No. 64, Apr. 2002, pp. 37–9. Lindley: Cooksey, p. 222.

15. Liveing, *Attack on the Somme*, pp. 57, 59, 66–7. Medical figures: Cherry, p. 39. Jackson: Levine, *Forgotten Voices of the Somme*, pp. 124, 126.

16. Andrews, *Orders Are Orders*, pp. 51–2.

17. Renz and Schneider: Sheldon, *The German Army on the Somme*, p. 176, and Whitehead, *The Other Side of the Wire*, p. 56.

'Stop the Rot'. The Schwaben Penetration. 1 to 9.30 pm

18. Hinkel, from Müller, Fabeck and Riesel, *Geschichte des Res. Inf. Regts Nr 99*, p. 107. Laasch: McCartney and Foley, *The Somme*, p. 144.

19. Railway soldier: *Hineingeworfen*, p. 167. St Quentin witness: Hart, p. 203 and Farrar-Hockley, *The Somme*, p. 134.

20. Soldier: Middlebrook, p. 208. Montgomery and Russell: Orr, *The Road to the Somme*, p. 220.

21. Gerster, 52 Bde History, p. 13. Bowen: Middlebrook, p. 209.

22. Training in the use of hand grenades: 180th Regiment document, No. 729 dated 2 Jun. 1916, Sheldon Archive. Maultsaid: Orr, p. 235.

23. Inniskilling soldier: Orr, p. 223.

24. Baass: *Hineingeworfen*, p. 393.

25. Cozier: Chapman, p. 330, and Orr, p. 224.

26. Malins, p. 139 and Fraser, etc, *Ghosts on the Somme*, pp. 104–5.

27. Telfer: Hart, p. 132. Cary: Bishop family correspondence.

28. Von Fabeck, Battle Log 9 pm and 9.38 pm, *Gefechtsbericht RIR Nr 99. Schlacht bei Thiepval 1 Jul 1916*. Hinkel: from Müller etc, *Geschichte des Res. Inf. Regts Nr 99*, p. 109.

Chapter 10. Blood-Red Sunset

Merciful Dusk. 9.30 to 10.05 pm

1. Wide: Middlebrook, *The First Day on the Somme*, p. 225.

2. Tawney, 'The Attack'.

3. Higgins, *Tommy at Gommecourt*, pp. 40–1.

4. Schuman: Hart, *The Somme*, p. 130. Ashurst, *My Bit*, pp. 102–3.

5. Hope, Bruce and soldier: Orr, *The Road to the Somme*, pp. 225–6. Ricardo and other soldier witnesses: MacDonagh, *The Irish on the Somme*, p. 42

6. Senescal: Middlebrook, p. 225. Haylock: Barton and Barning, *The Somme*, p. 143.

7. Hance: Barton and Barning, p. 141.

8. Bundy: Brown, *The IWM Book of The Somme*, pp. 68–9. Sandys: Foley and McCartney, *The Somme*, pp. 223–4.

9. Lais, *Der Schlacht an der Somme 1916*, pp. 24–5.

10. Gerhardinger, *16 Inf Regt II Btl 1.2 und 3. Juli*, KA München, 2105. Kennedy: Levine, *Forgotten Voices of the Somme*, p. 138.

11. Von Wurmb, *Erinnerungen an die Eroberung der 'Feste Schwaben' an der Somme am 1.7.16*, KA München, HS 1984. Hinkel, from Müller etc, *Geschichte des Res. Inf. Regts Nr 99*, p. 109.

12. Beattie: Brown, *Tommy Goes to War*, pp. 197–8.

'A Good Day'. 10.05 pm to midnight

13. Stewart-Moore: Orr, p. 228.

14. Gibbs, *The Battles of the Somme*, p. 21. Congreve: Foley and McCartney, p. 103.

15. Lipscomb: Brown, *The IWM Book of The Somme*, p. 70. Hall: Levine, p. 115.

16. Ward-Jackson: Moynihan, ed.,*Greater Love*, p. 109. Lipscomb, ibid. Megaw: Middlebrook, pp. 255–6.

17. Charteris, Diary 1 Jul., *At GHQ*, pp. 151–2. Haig, *War Diaries and Letters*, p. 197. Casualty figures: Middlebrook, p. 243.

18. Pilcher: Middlebrook, p. 259. Leetham: Brown, *Tommy Goes to War*, p. 207.

19. Kleinfeldt, Producer S. Humphries, *Hidden Histories. World War I's Forgotten Photographs*, BBC 4 TV, 2014. Maute, from *Die Deutschen an der Somme 1914–1918*, p. 93.

20. 99 Regt casualties, 52 Bde report 30 Jun. 180 Regt casualties, Sheldon p. 158. Regiment 109 Casualties: Whitehead, *The*

Other Side of the Wire, Vol. 2, p. 411. German casualties overall: Middlebrook, p. 264.

21. Fassbender, Patrol Report, 1/RJR 119. 2.7.16. M43/Bu 7 ser 800, KA Stüttgart. Hinkel, p. 109. Ammo expenditures: Sheldon, pp. 155–6.

22. Maute, p. 93. Stadelbacher: Sheldon, p. 162. Eisler, *Die Deutschen an der Somme 1914–1918*, p. 105.

23. Gerhardinger, *Inf. Regt. 16* II Btln. Somme Schlacht 1916. 1, 2 und 3 Juli. KA München, HS 2105.

24. Higgins, p. 41. Lindley and Hall: Cooksey, *Barnsley Pals*, p. 226. Partridge: Levine, p. 144.

25. Ashurst, pp. 103–4 and Levine, p. 144. Malins, IWM film *The Battle of the Somme*, and *How I Filmed the Great War*, p. 139.

26. Montgomery: Orr, pp. 232, 234. Crozier: Chapman, ed., *Vain Glory*, p. 330.

27. Shepherd, Diary 1 Jul. 1916, *A Sergeant Major's War*, pp. 110–11. Burke: Levine, p. 144.

28. Andrews: Tawney, 'The Attack'. Becker: *Hineingeworfen*, p. 436. Morgan: Brown, *The IWM Book of The Somme*, p. 102.

Beyond 24 Hours

1. Morter, *I Was There. The Great War Interviews*, BBC TV NI, 20 Mar. 2014.

2. Page: Brown, p. 195. Orangeman and Johnston: Orr, pp. 241, 243. City figures: Middlebrook, p. 269.

3. Cary: Bishop family correspondence.

4. Lord: Stedman, *Salford Pals*, p. 136.

5. *Barnsley Chronicle*, 8 Jul. 1916, Cooksey, *Barnsley Pals*, pp. 229–30, 231.

6. Brockman: Levine, p. 144. Demuth: Arthur, *Forgotten Voices of the Great War*, p. 169.

7. Hollingsworth: Foley and McCartney, *The Somme*, p. 232. Ferguson: Brown, p. 196.

8. Detlef Siebert, *The Somme: From Defeat to Victory*, BBC TV Production.

9. Hertig: Holmes, *Tommy*, p. 47. Bahrmann, aviation soldier and Marquardt: *Hineingeworfen*, pp. 448–9, 346–7.

10. Macardle: Brown, *Tommy Goes to War*, p. 196.

11. Andrews, *Orders Are Orders*, pp. 52–3 and Preface.

12. Account by Elizabeth Clarke of her grandfather Leo O'Neil. Beaumont Hamel Newfoundland Memorial Museum.

13. Rimmer, interview, *Haig: The Unknown Soldier*, BBC TV documentary.

14. Clark, *The Donkeys*, 1961. Congreve background and generals' fatalities: Holmes, *Tommy*, pp. 58, 214.

15. Hill: Levine, p. 257. Carrington, 1975 letter to friend, quoted M Hastings, *Times* newspaper article, 12 May 2014.

16. Roger Smither interview, IWM documentary *The Battle of the Somme* viewing notes.

17. Mrs Wilson: Fraser etc, *Ghosts on the Somme*, pp. 128–9.

18. Fielding: Foley and McCartney, pp. 46–7. Stevenson: Smither interview, IWM *Somme* viewing notes.

19. Ervine and Adams: Orr, p. 274. Sandys: *Times* newspaper report on inquest, 15 Sep. 1916, Foley and McCartney, pp. 223–4.

20. Ibid, pp. 243–4.

Acknowledgements

My friend from German Staff College days, Dr Jack Sheldon, gave unstinting support, ground orientation and advice as well as unselfish access to his extensive archive of German unit and post action accounts. I am grateful for the generous hospitality of his wife Laurie, looking after and accommodating me as I harvested Jack's material during a rewarding week-long stay in Vercours, France. Andrew Orgill and the staff of the Royal Military Academy Sandhurst library provided access to many rare books. My friend, former Royal Artillery Colonel Richard Williams, provided excellent technical gunnery advice and orientation of the artillery battle from the perspective of both sides as we drove the entire Somme line from north to south during a brilliant summer. Sue Bishop and her family provided copies of Lieutenant Richard Cary's personal correspondence before the battle and after his death. I hope I have done them justice. The O'Neil correspondence was from the Beaumont Hamel Newfoundland Park Museum, an essential venue for any serious Somme battlefield tour. Teddy Colligen gave a vivid orientation of the Ulster Division battles around Thiepval and the Schwaben Redoubt, which made huge sense and was vital in terms of ground orientation. My thanks to them all.

Index

Entries in *italics* indicate illustrations.